More Praise for HATRED'S KINGDOM

"Dore Gold is best known as an Israeli foreign policy analyst and diplomat, but he has also long been, since writing his Ph.D. dissertation at Columbia University on this subject, a specialist on the Kingdom of Saudi Arabia. With Saudi support for militant Islam and for terrorist operations making front-page news, Gold adds a historical dimension to the debate, explaining in this important book where the hatred comes from and its full implications, as well as offering helpful suggestions on how to counter it."

—DANIEL PIPES, director of the Middle East Forum

"Some senior officials, most notably in the Pentagon, echo the views of Dore Gold, a former Israeli ambassador to the United Nations, whose recent book, *Hatred's Kingdom*, cites the Wahhabi extremism of Saudi Arabian clerics as a root cause of terrorism."

—TOBY HARNDEN, *London Daily Telegraph*

"Gold argues persuasively that contributions from some of Saudi Arabia's wealthiest families, and from charitable arms of the Saudi government, were important for al-Qaeda's evolution."

—HUME HORAN, former U.S. ambassador to Saudi Arabia

"For the general reader interested in the origins of Middle Eastern terrorism, *Hatred's Kingdom* will shed a great deal of light; for policy-makers in Washington, it ought to be required reading."

—ALEX ALEXIEV, *Commentary Magazine*

"Indispensable reading"

—JEFFREY GEDMIN, *Die Welt*

"[a] thoroughly researched study"

—JOSEPH A. KECHICHIAN, *The Middle East Journal*

"... certain for many years to remain the standard work on the political and terrorist effects of Wahhabism in Saudi Arabia, the Islamic world, and the West."

—DR. JOSHUA TEITELBAUM, Moshe Dayan Center for Middle Eastern and African Studies, Tel Aviv University, in the *Jerusalem Report*

"*Hatred's Kingdom* author Dore Gold, former Israeli ambassador to the UN, explores in great detail the connection of Saudia Arabia and Wahhabi preachers to 9/11 and global terrorism. Gold pulls together shocking evidence of how Saudi Arabia, our ally, have used their billions in oil revenues to finance worldwide terrorism."

—JAMES TARANTO, *Wall Street Journal*

HATRED'S
KINGDOM

HATRED'S KINGDOM

How Saudi Arabia Supports the New Global Terrorism

Dore Gold

Since 1947
REGNERY
PUBLISHING, INC.
An Eagle Publishing Company • Washington, DC

Copyright © 2003 by Dore Gold

First paperback edition published 2004

ISBN 0-89526-061-1

Library of Congress Cataloging-in-Publication Data on file with the Library of Congress

Published in the United States by
Regnery Publishing, Inc.
An Eagle Publishing Company
One Massachusetts Avenue, NW
Washington, DC 20001

Visit us at www.regnery.com

Distributed to the trade by
National Book Network
4720-A Boston Way
Lanham, MD 20706

Printed on acid-free paper

Manufactured in the United States of America

10 9 8 7 6 5 4 3 2 1

Books are available in quantity for promotional or premium use. Write to Director of Special Sales, Regnery Publishing, Inc., One Massachusetts Avenue, NW, Washington, DC 20001, for information on discounts and terms, or call (202) 216-0600.

To Ofra, my wife and partner, with deepest love,
and to our treasured children, Yael and Ariel

Contents

List of Maps .... *xi*

Introduction   The Roots of Terror *1*

Chapter 1   Violent Origins
Reviving Jihad and the War Against the Polytheists *17*

Chapter 2   Countering the Wahhabi Menace *31*

Chapter 3   "White Terror"
The Ikhwan and the Rise of the Modern Saudi Kingdom *41*

Chapter 4   Building the Modern Saudi State
Oil, the Palestine Question, and the Americans *57*

Chapter 5   Reactivating Wahhabism *73*

Chapter 6   The Hothouse for Militant Islamic Radicalism *89*

Chapter 7   Wahhabism Reasserts Itself *105*

Chapter 8   Wahhabism's Global Reach *125*

Chapter 9   Countdown to September 11
*The Gulf War and Wahhabism's
New Outburst in the 1990s* *157*

Chapter 10   The Hatred Continues *185*

Chapter 11   Was Saudi Arabia Finally Changing? *213*

Conclusion   Ending the Hatred *233*

Appendix   Saudi Support for Terrorism: The Evidence *249*
Notes *273*
Glossary *307*
Acknowledgments *311*
Index *315*
About the Author *333*
Other Works *335*

Maps

The Arabian Peninsula and the Greater Middle East ....*xii*

The First Wahhabi-Saudi Emirate: 1744–1818 ....*21*

Afghanistan and Its Neighbors *128*

Islamic Resurgence in Chechnya and Dagestan........................*140*

The Arabian Peninsula and the Greater Middle East

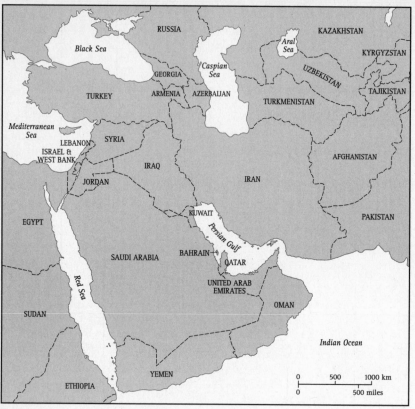

Introduction

The Roots of Terror

S ince the September 11, 2001, terrorist attacks on the World Trade
Center and the Pentagon, a great deal of mystery remains about the
precise source of the hatred that impelled nineteen Middle Eastern
terrorists to take their own lives in an act of mass murder. Why would the
masterminds of these attacks set out to kill thousands of innocent people?
Though more is now known about the terrorists—their coconspirators,
their stated objectives, their organizational affiliations, even some of their
financial backing—the key question remains unanswered: What larger
forces drove the perpetrators to undertake the most lethal terrorist attack
in America's history? In other words, can the source of their hatred be
identified, beyond the hijackers themselves and their commanders, so that
it, too, can be addressed as part of the larger effort to understand and prevent terrorism?

In studying the September 11 attacks, some American investigators
have looked at the possible supporting role of Saudi Arabia. After all, fifteen of the nineteen terrorists, as well as their ultimate commander,
Osama bin Laden, were born and raised in Saudi Arabia. A third of the
prisoners the United States held from the war against bin Laden's al-
Qaeda organization were Saudi nationals, as of the summer of 2002.[1] The

1

Saudi state, moreover, was one of only three countries that recognized and backed Afghanistan's Taliban government, which harbored al-Qaeda in the late 1990s. And there are hints of even wider Saudi support for bin Laden. High-level U.S. intelligence sources have identified two Saudi princes who have made regular payments to bin Laden since 1995.[2] Furthermore, in August 2002, the families of six hundred Americans killed in the September 11 attacks filed a lawsuit in a U.S. district court in Washington, D.C., contending that three Saudi princes—including Saudi Arabia's minister of defense, Prince Sultan bin Abdul Aziz—gave money to charitable foundations and other groups that funded al-Qaeda.[3]

One might protest that the Kingdom of Saudi Arabia is supposed to be an American ally, not a sponsor of international terrorism like Libya or Syria. Indeed, since it was established in 1932 by King Abdul Aziz (known in the West as Ibn Saud), Saudi Arabia has been economically aligned with U.S. oil interests; witness, for instance, the Arabian-American Oil Company (ARAMCO) consortium. Moreover, Saudi Arabia backed the United States in the Cold War, procured billions of dollars of advanced American weaponry for decades, and opened its air bases to the U.S. Air Force in the 1991 Gulf War against Iraq.

But September 11 has forced America to reassess Saudi Arabia's reliability as an ally. In fact, in July 2002, a RAND Corporation analyst told the Pentagon's Defense Policy Board that Saudi Arabia was an *enemy* of the United States. The analyst concluded that the Saudis were active "at every level of the terror chain."[4] Suspicions over Saudi state involvement in the September 11 attacks have only deepened. In late November 2002, it was disclosed that U.S. authorities were investigating how checks written by Princess Haifa bint Faisal—the wife of Prince Bandar, the Saudi ambassador to Washington—ended up with Omar al-Bayoumi, a Saudi who hosted two of the September 11 hijackers when they reached America.[5]

Commentators in the Islamic and Arab worlds have also examined the Saudi role in the September 11 attacks, but unlike their American counterparts, they have looked beyond the tactical elements of terrorism—the recruiting of operatives, the training, the financing, the planning, the acquisition and transfer of weapons and explosives, and so forth. Specifically, they have investigated the root *causes* of terrorism, zeroing in on the main creed or version of Islam practiced in Saudi Arabia, known as Wahhabism.

Wahhabi Islam, which was established in mid-eighteenth-century Arabia by Muhammad ibn Abdul Wahhab, remains the dominant religious creed in Saudi Arabia. Many regard Wahhabism as a radical and violent departure from the mainstream Islamic tradition. For example, in a Bangladesh newspaper column, the London-based Pakistani Tariq Ali concluded that after the fall of the Taliban in Afghanistan, "the deployments in Pakistan to cut off the tentacles of the Wahhabi octopus may or may not succeed, but its head is safe and sound in Saudi Arabia, guarding the oil-wells and growing new arms, and protected by American soldiers and the USAF base in Dhahran."[6] More recently, the brother of Zacarias Moussaoui, the captured twentieth hijacker in al-Qaeda's September 11 plot, denounced Wahhabism for inspiring Moussaoui's extremist actions.[7]

Former *New York Times* Arab affairs commentator Youssef M. Ibrahim stated, "The money that brought Wahhabis power throughout the Arab world...financed networks of fundamentalist schools from Sudan to northern Pakistan."[8] Taliban leaders, in fact, were a product of these Saudi-funded Islamic academies, which are known as *madrasas*, in Pakistan. Mohamed Charfi, a former minister of education in Tunisia, wrote in the *New York Times*:

> Osama bin Laden, like the 15 Saudis who participated in the criminal operations of September 11, seems to have been the pure product of his schooling. While Saudi Arabia is officially a moderate state allied with America, it also has been one of the main supporters of Islamic fundamentalism because of its financing of schools following the intransigent Wahhabi doctrine. Saudi-backed madrasas in Pakistan and Afghanistan have played a significant role in the strengthening of radical Islam in those countries.[9]

Some Saudis have openly acknowledged the ideology of hatred fostered in their country. In December 2001, Sahr Muhammad Hatem, a doctor in Riyadh, bravely wrote a letter to a London-based Arabic newspaper; in the letter, which was headlined "Our Culture of Demagogy Has Engendered bin Laden, al-Zawahiri, and Their Ilk," she explained:

The mentality of each one of us was programmed upon entering school as a child [to believe] that...anyone who is not a
Muslim is our enemy, and that the West means enfeeblement,
licentiousness, lack of values, and even Jahiliya [a term used to
describe the backward, pre-Islamic era] itself. Anyone who
escapes this programming in school encounters it at the
mosque, or through the media or from the preachers lurking
in every corner....

We all focus on bin Laden and his ilk...but we have yet to
focus on the more dangerous people, and I mean those who
fill our heads with this rhetoric in the schools, the mosques,
and the media, who disseminate words without hesitation,
without considering the consequences or even understanding
that in this era, the entire world hears what is said.[10]

The clear target of Hatem's critique was the government-backed version
of Islam in Saudi Arabia—Wahhabism—for she declared that the "solution"
was "the Islam that was taught by the Prophet of this nation—an Islam of
tolerance—and not the Islam of those who control our media." Hatem was
defending mainstream Islam from its radical offshoot, renewing the call for
an Islam that draws from authentic sources, for coexistence with and tolerance of non-Muslims, which prevailed for much of Islamic history.

Muslim scholars outside of the Middle East have also focused on Wahhabism. Khaled Abou El Fadl of the UCLA School of Law has argued that
al-Qaeda was "anchored" in a theology that was "the byproduct of the
emergence and eventual dominance of Wahhabism" and other recent
militant Islamic trends.[11] Sheikh Hisham Kabbani, the Lebanese-born
chairman of the Islamic Supreme Council of America, characterized Wahhabism as "the modern outgrowth of a two-century-old heresy."[12] Kabbani reflects a whole line of anti-Wahhabi Islamic thinking dating back to
the Ottoman Empire. In addition, the Chechen government's special
envoy to Europe, Hajj Salih Brandt, noting with alarm the spread of Wahhabism in the Northern Caucasus, stated:

The whole political agenda of Wahhabi Fundamentalism (what
the West now calls Islamism)...[is] a deviation of Islam taught

in Madinah University in Saudi Arabia, sponsored by the Saudi government and exported from there....Out of it have come Hamas, the Taliban, Osama bin Laden, the FIS [Islamic Salvation Front], Sudan, and now the gangs roaming Chechnya and Daghestan.[13]

In October 2002, after the devastating bombing that left more than 180 dead in Bali, Indonesia, Indonesian commentator Jusuf Wanandi targeted the ideological threat of Saudi Wahhabism in outlining the upcoming challenges for the Jakarta government:

> Perhaps the most important thing is the ideological struggle against radicalism and terrorism in the name of Islam. Although Muslims in Indonesia are mainly moderate, they need help and assistance in expanding their educational systems...which have so far been able to withstand the extremist influences of Wahhabism from Saudi Arabia.[14]

In fact, Indonesian police found that the prime suspect in the bombing came from a violent Wahhabi cell in East Java that had previously clashed with other Muslims and even torched the tomb of a local Muslim saint.[15]

Thus, to these Muslim commentators, Wahhabism is nothing less than the religious and ideological source of the new wave of global Islamic terrorism—from Indonesia to Algeria, from Russia to Yemen, and finally to the United States. Their critique is not confined just to Wahhabism as a doctrine, but rather it extends to Wahhabi institutions—educational networks and channels of funding, the actual mechanisms that the Saudi state erected to give it worldwide outreach. What they are saying to the West is that unless the influence of Saudi Wahhabism is understood, it is impossible to explain how September 11 occurred—or to prevent a future attack.

These commentators are right. The United States and its allies can win the most spectacular military victories in Afghanistan; they can freeze terrorists' bank accounts and cut off their supplies of weaponry; they can eliminate terrorist masterminds. But even taken together, such triumphs are not enough to remove the terrorist threat, for they do not get at the source of the problem. Terrorism, on the scale of the September 11 attacks, does not occur in a vacuum. People do not just decide spontaneously that they are going to hijack an aircraft, crash it into a building, and commit mass murder (and take their own lives) because of some political grievance or sense of economic deprivation. No, there is another critical component of terrorism that has generally been overlooked in the West: the ideological motivation to slaughter thousands of innocent people. The ideological sources for terrorist attacks are no less important than the questions of where terrorists received their training and which bank accounts they used.

All terrorists must be indoctrinated—indeed, brainwashed. Terrorists must totally dehumanize their victims and thus deny them the basic right to live. Terrorists must even be taught to show no mercy to children. Since suicide goes against the human instinct for self-preservation, special efforts need to be made to prepare individuals for suicide attacks. Without an unshakable conviction in the merits of martyrdom and in its rewards in the afterlife, terrorists would never have undertaken the suicidal attacks of the past decade.

In short, unless the ideological roots of the hatred that led to September 11 are addressed, the war on terrorism will not be won. It will be only a matter of time before the next Osama bin Laden emerges.

The Real Problem

The tendency in the West is to not deal fully with the ideological basis of terrorism, but one need look no further than the terrorist organizations themselves to understand the centrality of ideology. An al-Qaeda training manual found in Great Britain outlines the necessary qualifications for any new member: the first qualification is a commitment to Islam, the second a "Commitment to the Organization's Ideology."[16] But what is that ideology? What do bin Laden and his operatives take to be Islam? According to at least one militant religious leader in Saudi Arabia, it is Wahhabi Islam that has provided the foundation for bin Laden's vast terrorist network. Sheikh Abdul Aziz bin Salih al-Jarbu asserted in a book written after September 11 that "Osama bin Laden is a natural continuation from Muhammad ibn Abdul Wahhab."[17]

This is a crucial point, for even when Americans have considered the source of the hatred that impelled the terrorists, many have not known where to look. In the days and weeks after September 11, many wondered whether Islam was the enemy. But Islam is not the problem. Rather, the problem is the extremists in the Middle East who have manipulated Friday sermons in the mosques, textbooks in the schools, and state-controlled television to one end: to systematically prepare young people to condone the cold-blooded murder of innocent civilians.

That is why Wahhabism as it has developed in Saudi Arabia is so dangerous, why it demands the attention of America and its allies. This radically intolerant form of Islam has shaped public opinion toward the West in Saudi Arabia and in key parts of the Islamic world; it has influenced Osama bin Laden from his earliest years.

How, then, has Saudi Wahhabism fostered the ideology of hatred that spawned suicidal terrorism? This question is inevitably linked to the question of how Wahhabism has treated the Islamic concept of jihad (literally, "struggle," but commonly translated as "holy war").

According to Islamic tradition, a warrior who gives his life in a true jihad, a holy war, becomes a *shahid*, or martyr (literally, "witness"), and is guaranteed entry into Paradise. But beginning in the ninth century, as two centuries of Muslim holy wars and territorial expansion ended, Muslim theologians broadened the meaning of jihad, deemphasizing armed struggle and, under the influence of Sufism (Islamic mysticism), adopting more spiritual definitions. True, some sectarians who broke off from Islam continued to stress the older, militant meaning of jihad. For example, the Kharajites ("seceders"), who left the Islamic mainstream in the seventh century, even made jihad into a sixth pillar of the Islamic faith (the five pillars of Islam accepted throughout the Muslim world are: affirming God and his messenger; prayer; charity, or *zakat;* the Ramadan fast; and the pilgrimage to Mecca, known as the hajj).[18] But the Islamic mainstream had shifted away from this focus on the religious requirement of a universal campaign of jihad. Consequently, the meaning of *shahid* changed as well. Whereas the term had originally applied to one who gave his life in battle, a scholar or someone who led Muslim prayers could now be compared to a *shahid* when his day of judgment arrived.

The Wahhabis, however, restored the idea of jihad as armed struggle, and they spread their new doctrine across the Arabian peninsula and beyond in the latter part of the eighteenth century. Even today the revival of jihad, and its prioritization as a religious value, is found in the works of high-level Saudi religious officials like former chief justice Sheikh Abdullah bin Muhammad bin Humaid: "Jihad is a great deed indeed [and] there is no deed whose reward and blessing is as that of it, and for this reason, it is the best thing one can volunteer for."[19] And in October 2001, during a Friday sermon delivered in a Mecca mosque, a Saudi cleric went so far as to describe jihad as "the peak of Islam."[20]

If, as has been seen, Wahhabism has drawn such pointed criticism in the Islamic and Arab worlds, why has it eluded the conceptual radar screen of most analysts in the West, especially in the United States? The name seems innocuous enough: Wahhabis, who prefer to see themselves as theological advocates of the oneness of the Divine, call themselves in Arabic *muwahhidun*, or advocates of oneness. In part because of that, Wahhabism has been greatly misunderstood. During the 1950s, analysts for ARAMCO in Saudi Arabia described the Wahhabis as "Muslim Unitarians"—a term meant to increase the comfort level between Protestant America and Saudi Arabia at a time when the Saudi-U.S. relationship was in an embryonic stage.[21] Yet the Unitarian Church is one of the most liberal and inclusive churches in Protestant Christianity; Wahhabism certainly could not be called liberal or inclusive. In a 1980 book commemorating the rule of King Faisal, Professor George Rentz of Johns Hopkins University, who had previously headed the intelligence and analysis section of ARAMCO's Arabian Affairs Division, described Muhammad ibn Abdul Wahhab's activities as "the [Islamic] Reformation,"[22] echoing language used by other historians.

Perhaps "outsiders" are uncomfortable even investigating Wahhabism as a particularly radical form of Islam, especially given the American tradition of freedom of religion. It is difficult for American scholars of Islam to take a critical approach to a particular offshoot of Islam, even a radical minority sect, because it might be misconstrued as an attack on an entire religious tradition. In general, religious viewpoints are considered sacrosanct and hence beyond scrutiny. Yet Western analysts *must* delve into the distinction between particular forms of Muslim militancy and the rest of mainstream Islam, so as not to make Islam, as a whole, into a new enemy.

The Saudi national Nawaf E. Obaid, in a 1998 master's thesis for Harvard University's Kennedy School of Government, charges that the U.S. intelligence community "misunderstood the nature of Wahhabism."[23] Obaid believes that U.S. experts underestimated the power of religion, and specifically the Wahhabi religious establishment, in decision making in Saudi Arabia. In part this could be because American analysts have not wished to look at the religious roots of political behavior; one could argue that they have preferred explanations based on economic or strategic interests or tribal and dynastic political factors. In fact, a former U.S. intelligence officer made this very point: "Throughout much of the 1990s, when I was part of the intelligence community in Washington, we were not quite forbidden to consider religion as a strategic factor, but the issue was considered soft and nebulous—as well as potentially embarrassing in those years of epidemic political correctness."[24]

Finally, there is the factor of the Arab-Israeli conflict. Often, policymakers suffer from a kind of myopia when looking at the underlying reasons for problems in the Mideast; they focus exclusively on this conflict, and have become riveted to the Palestinian issue in particular. Consequently, disproportionate diplomatic energy is invested in Israeli-Palestinian diplomacy at the expense of addressing larger regional issues, such as the 1979 Iranian revolution or Saddam Hussein's threats to Kuwait in 1990. Indeed, these major Middle Eastern developments came as complete surprises to the Carter administration and the first Bush administration, which were so mired in the details of Arab-Israeli diplomacy.

The almost singular Western focus on the Palestinian issue is based on the assumption that resolving this conflict would solve many other Western problems in the Middle East—from obtaining basing rights for the U.S. Air Force in the Arabian peninsula, to forming an effective coalition against Iraq, to achieving oil price stability.

This mistaken tendency has influenced the debate over the sources of contemporary terrorism. For example, British foreign secretary Jack Straw told an Iranian newspaper, "One of the factors that helps breed terror is the anger which many people in this region feel at events over the years in Palestine."[25] Caryle Murphy of the *Washington Post* put it even more directly: "If we want to avoid creating more terrorists, we must end the Israeli-Palestinian conflict quickly."[26] After September 11 came a whole spate of articles on the same theme.[27]

Of course, achieving a peace settlement between Israel and the Palestinians is a highly desirable goal. But resolving that conflict would not be a panacea. To focus solely on this conflict is to ignore the real motivating forces behind terrorism against the West. It also serves as a diplomatic diversion that prevents the United States and other nations from dealing with the more fundamental factors that have destabilized the Middle East.

Arab analysts have been more intellectually honest on this point; they tend to be among the first to point out that Osama bin Laden was not motivated by the Palestinian issue. For example, Hisham Melhem, the Washington bureau chief of the Lebanese daily *as-Safir*, stated on CNN, "He never served the Palestinian cause. He never did anything to help the Palestinian people. His focus was on Afghanistan and on Chechnya."[28] In fact, the Arab press criticized bin Laden for his indifference to the Palestinian question.[29] Even when, in 1998, bin Laden spoke about a "crusader-Zionist alliance," his declared priorities were first Arabia, second Iraq, and only third Jerusalem.[30] Clearly, something else was motivating bin Laden and his supporters—something more fundamental than antipathy to Israel.

For many Arab radicals, hatred of Israel stems from its being perceived as a Western outpost. They resent the many European incursions into the Middle East, from Napoleon's 1798 invasion of Egypt to the British and French colonial regimes throughout the Mideast. Al-Qaeda's training manual introduces its members to its historical grievances by starting with the fall of the Ottoman Empire to the allied powers after the First World War, the dissolution of the office of caliph (successor to the Prophet and spiritual head of Sunni Islam), and the rise of secular regimes in the Arab and Muslim world: "After the fall of our *orthodox* caliphates on March 3, 1924 and after expelling the colonialists, our Islamic nation was afflicted with apostate rulers who took over in the Moslem nation. These rulers turned out to be more infidel and criminal than the colonialists themselves."[31]

In any case, Israel, which is not mentioned in the al-Qaeda manual, is a small thread in a much larger historical tapestry. The West and pro-Western regimes in general are more significant. Reflecting that proportionality, Iranians refer to America as "The Great Satan" and Israel as "The Little Satan." Bin Laden himself began to talk more extensively about the Israeli factor only *after* his September 11, 2001, attacks on the United States, in a transparent effort to prevent the emergence of a Middle Eastern coalition against him.

In short, the Arab world has a problem with Israel because of its deeper anger toward the West.

The Religious-Ideological Underpinnings of Violence

Fortunately, some analysts in the West have started to look at the possible impact of religious factors, including the Wahhabi ideology, in motivating the new international terrorism. Their conclusions are similar to those that have been emerging from the Arab and Islamic worlds for years. A Council on Foreign Relations collection of analytical essays on the reasons for the September 11 attacks and America's counterstrategy includes an analysis by F. Gregory Gause III, a leading U.S. expert on the Persian Gulf, that is provocatively titled "The Kingdom in the Middle: Saudi Arabia's Double Game." Gause concludes that the Saudis have some "soul-searching to do," adding, "Official Wahhabism may not encourage antistate violence, but it is a particularly severe and intolerant interpretation of Islam. . . . The Saudi elites should consider just what role such a severe doctrine and the vast religious infrastructure they have built around it played in bin Laden's rise."[32]

In a subsequent essay, Gause reaches a more clear-cut conclusion: "It is undoubtedly true that the extremely strict, intolerant version of Islam that is taught and practiced in Saudi Arabia created the milieu from which Osama bin Laden and his recruits emerged."[33]

In addition, a Lebanese-born French analyst, Roland Jacquard, has concluded, "Bin Laden may be the CEO of [al-Qaeda], but there's a whole board of directors in Saudi Arabia and other countries around the Gulf." He adds that ignoring al-Qaeda's religious underpinnings is a deep flaw in the campaign against terrorism.[34] Rohan Gunaratna, who has written a detailed analysis of al-Qaeda, concurs: "The Saudi export of Wahabiism [*sic*] has helped bring about the current Islamist milieu. Saudis must reform their educational system and they must create a modern education system."[35] A particularly strong attack on Wahhabism, written from a perspective sympathetic to Sufi Islam as practiced in the Balkans, came from author and journalist Stephen Schwartz in October 2002.[36]

To understand how and why terrorism has come to afflict the West, we must delve deeper into the Saudi system and examine Wahhabism. We will look at both the religious ideology of Wahhabism and its translation into action—the global impact of Saudi Arabia's Wahhabi clerics and their international Islamic organizations.

By examining the history of Wahhabism, this work will trace the development of the ideological fervor that has spawned the new global terrorism. From the beginning, Wahhabism has been a movement of total intolerance toward those who did not adopt its principles, including other Muslims. Such extreme religious intolerance has demanded, first of all, that Wahhabis eradicate symbols of non-Wahhabi civilization. This had not been the universal practice of Islam in the past. Even when Muslim rulers appropriated holy sites for the Islamic faith, pre-Islamic holy structures were frequently spared. When the Muslim armies invaded Egypt in the seventh century, they did not smash the symbols of ancient Egyptian civilization; they did not dismantle the Sphinx. But when Wahhabi armies attacked the holy cities of Shiite Islam in southern Iraq in the early nineteenth century, they destroyed tombs and ransacked other religious shrines.

For Wahhabis, such actions are part of their war against idolatry. It is not a tremendous leap from the Wahhabi sacking of the Shiite holy city of Kerbala in 1802 to the Taliban's destruction of Buddhist statues in the Bamiyan Valley in Afghanistan in March 2001. Indeed, Osama bin Laden and other al-Qaeda spokesmen adopt Wahhabi terminology when they call America "the Hubal of the age"—the Hubal being a seventh-century stone idol.[37] By implication, just as the Hubal had to be destroyed, so too does American civilization have to be eradicated.[38] One person influenced by this worldview was the Egyptian El-Sayyid Nosair, a key underling of hard-line Egyptian cleric Sheikh Omar Abdul Rahman who, along with Rahman, was involved in the 1993 World Trade Center bombing. Police found documents in which Nosair called for smashing the idols of American civilization, "destroying the structure of their civilized pillars...and their high world buildings which they are proud of and their statues."[39]

Wahhabism's religious intolerance has also led to repeated massacres of non-Wahhabis. This, too, was a distortion of basic Islamic tenets, for although Islam traditionally mandated an inferior position for Jews and Christians under its rule, it protected "people of the book," prohibiting the slaughter of adherents of other monotheistic faiths. Although Wahhabis in the eighteenth century did not generally encounter Christians and Jews—there were virtually none on the Arabian peninsula at that time—they defined even Shiite Muslims as polytheists *(mushrikun)*. Wahhabi forces thus slaughtered thousands of Shiites in what is today southern Iraq in 1802. Sunni Muslims who did not subscribe to Wahhabism frequently did not fare much better.

Wahhabism, according to the Berlin-based Islamic expert Aziz al-Azmeh, attributed to its immediate neighbors a status of being *kufar*, or infidels, "which makes conquest and subjugation incumbent, under the banner of jihad, both as the political act of an expanding polity and as a legal-religious obligation."[40] In the 1920s, Ibn Saud's Ikhwan armies were just as brutal as had been the Wahhabi forces who slaughtered Shiites in 1802. Other Islamic extremist groups, influenced by Wahhabism, attacked secular Arabs as apostates, and sometimes even attempted to assassinate their leaders.

The brutality of Wahhabi organizations has only continued. As one Egyptian columnist in the Cairo newspaper *al-Ahram* put it, "Mass murder is regarded by these groups as an act of faith that can bring them closer to God, especially during Ramadan, as evidenced by the blood baths they created in Algeria."[41] Indeed, veterans of Osama bin Laden's Afghanistan units provided one of the building blocks of the brutal Groupe Islamique Armé (GIA), which massacred civilians during an Algerian civil war that claimed 100,000 lives between 1992 and 1997.[42]

In fact, for al-Qaeda, the ideological readiness to commit mass murder has reached an entirely new scale. One al-Qaeda spokesman, Sulaiman Abu Ghaith, asserted, "We have a right to kill 4 million Americans—2 million of them children—and to exile twice as many and wound and cripple hundreds of thousands."[43]

This is how Osama bin Laden's mass terrorism works—and it has sprung from the Wahhabi tradition of delegitimizing other religious groups, labeling their adherents as infidels or polytheists, and sanctioning their murder.

In the late 1990s, Saudi mosques were serving as centers for vicious religious incitement, according to which Christianity was a "distorted and twisted religion."[44] Interfaith dialogue was called "sinful," and it was "forbidden for man to bring together Islam and blasphemy, monotheism and polytheism ... Allah's straight path of righteousness and the satanic path of heresy."[45] Since Christians and Jews were infidels, it was permissible, according to Saudi religious textbooks, "to demolish, burn, or destroy [their] bastions."[46]

Apologists for the Saudis will argue that every society has its fringe elements. But as will be demonstrated, those who are voicing extreme religious intolerance—verging on incitement to murder—are not simply a Saudi version of an extreme, intolerant, but minuscule group such as the Ku Klux Klan. Rather, they are a product of mainstream Saudi society and culture, and maintained by the government.

It can also be argued that some fire-and-brimstone sermons in Mecca mosques against Americans or Christians prove nothing much. After all, some might assert, nobody pays attention to the rhetoric of the clergy. Visiting reporters noting the familiar symbols of Western consumer society in Saudi shopping malls might mistakenly assume that Saudi Arabia is no different from Western societies. Certainly, in many other traditional societies, a great deal of intolerant, antimodern rhetoric emanates from religious leaders and other highly conservative forces; simultaneously, a highly modernized, Western-educated component of the population has little patience for such rhetoric. Usually, it is this cosmopolitan element that conducts diplomacy with foreign policy elites in Washington or London.

But in fact, only a tiny minority in Saudi Arabia actually has graduated from Western universities. Underneath Saudi society's thin veneer of modernity, a far larger, traditionally educated population listens very carefully to what is preached in the mosques. It is useful to remember that Muhammad Atta, the Egyptian leader of the al-Qaeda attacks on America, attended a Hamburg mosque whose imam, or religious leader, was known to preach, "Christians and Jews should have their throats slit."[47] Whether this imam was under any kind of Saudi Wahhabi influence has not been determined. Nonetheless, the Atta case makes clear how religious incitement can become an integral part of terrorism.

A Saudi professor of Islamic law in Riyadh told a *New York Times* reporter, "Well, of course I hate you because you are Christian, but that doesn't mean I want to kill you."[48] He basically challenged his Western listener to prove the nexus between hatred and violence. But the recent history of al-Qaeda demonstrates how deadly extreme religious incitement can be.

Still, this analysis does not mean to brand a whole branch of Islam as terrorists. The adherents of Wahhabism can have their own internal religious debates about such matters as the role of saints and intermediaries in prayer; they can have legitimate debates with other Muslims about whether it is fitting to celebrate the birthday of the Prophet Muhammad. These are matters for Islamic religious leaders to decide among themselves. The problem begins when certain religious beliefs lead to claims that entire groups of people have no right to live and deserve to be slaughtered.

This is no longer an issue of religious intolerance but rather a question of global security, for such claims have spawned the modern scourge of global terrorism. To put an end to the sorts of horrors that have been perpetrated by Osama bin Laden, it is absolutely necessary to understand the unique environment whence the hatred sprang. A cold eye must be cast, therefore, on the internal dynamics of America's purported ally Saudi Arabia.

Chapter 1

Violent Origins

Reviving Jihad and the War Against the Polytheists

Islam spread across the Middle East from the Arabian peninsula in the middle of the seventh century with the military conquests of the Prophet Muhammad and his successors. Within one hundred years, the armies of the Islamic faith had extended their control from southern France to India. A thousand years later, in the eighteenth century, this extraordinarily successful military campaign would serve as a model for a new militant religious movement in the Arabian peninsula, Wahhabism. The Wahhabis resurrected jihad (holy war) as central to their cause, motivating their followers with the rewards of martyrdom, including the promise that those killed on the battlefield—fulfilling their duty of spreading the faith—would go directly to Paradise.

The Saudi-Wahhabi Covenant

The founder of Wahhabism, Muhammad ibn Abdul Wahhab, was born sometime between 1699 and 1703 in the village of Uyaina, which was situated on the Najd plateau in east-central Arabia. This relatively isolated, inland region of Arabia differed from the Hijaz, where the holy cities of Mecca and Medina and the cosmopolitan Red Sea port of Jeddah were located, and from al-Hasa, along the Persian Gulf coast.

Muhammad ibn Abdul Wahhab did not remain confined to the Najd. After studying with his father, the *qadi* (religious judge) of Uyaina,[1] he moved to Medina, where he came under the influence of Hanbali Islamic scholars, admirers of the writings of the fourteenth-century scholar Ibn Taymiyya (died 1328). Ibn Taymiyya argued that insidious foreign influences had seeped into Islam after the Mongol invasions of the Middle East. He denounced Muslims who had adopted Christian practices and objected to the excessive veneration of Jerusalem, since such practice was borrowed from Judaism.[2] According to one account, ibn Abdul Wahhab found his works so gripping that he actually copied them in his own hand.[3]

Ibn Abdul Wahhab traveled outside of Arabia to what is today Iraq and Syria. The evidence indicates that he studied in the Persian cities of Isfahan and Qum during the reign of Nadir Shah (1736–47), who tried forcibly to return Persia to the mainstream branch of Islam, Sunni ("orthodox path"), after it had adopted Shiite (literally, "partisan") Islam as a state religion in the early sixteenth century.[4] For a while, ibn Abdul Wahhab became an exponent of Sufism, the mystical movement of Islam, but he would eventually repudiate it.[5] He also visited Basra, in southern Iraq, but was expelled, probably for his strong religious views.[6] In short, having traveled throughout the main centers of the Muslim world, he was fully acquainted with the major schools of Islamic practice.

The Islamic world during this period was changing because the military expansion of Islam had stagnated after the armies of the Ottoman Empire were blocked at the gates of Vienna in 1683. By 1771, the Ottomans would be ceding land to the Russian Empire for the first time. British and Dutch ships were regularly sailing into the Persian Gulf, establishing a commercial presence, as the Portuguese had a century earlier. These developments might have been beyond the horizons of many of the residents of the Najd but were probably discussed in the larger urban centers of the Middle East that ibn Abdul Wahhab visited.

Returning to Arabia, ibn Abdul Wahhab concluded that the Islam practiced throughout the Ottoman and Persian cities he had visited had been corrupted by foreign influences. The armies of Islam had vanquished many earlier civilizations but in the process had absorbed many of their practices. The veneration of saints, for example, including pilgrimage and prayer rites at their tombs, had become widespread.

Ibn Abdul Wahhab may have been trying to explain the rising power of the Christian West, which he tied to the degeneracy in Islam under the Ottoman Empire. As a result, he developed his own unique approach to Islam, one that stressed the need to expunge any departures from traditional Islamic doctrine, especially practices that seemed to indicate polytheism. He sought to restore the puritanical Islam of the Prophet Muhammad and the early caliphs *(al-salaf al-salihin)*. Years later, his followers would, in fact, call themselves *salafis*. But in general, his movement was better defined by what it opposed than by what it advocated.

Ibn Abdul Wahhab also found certain bedouin practices in his native Najd highly objectionable, including the sanctification of the dead, which involved supplications and sacrifices at their shrines. At a shrine in Jubaila, people sought success in business. Infertile women used to rub themselves against an idol in order to conceive. Some Muslims even worshiped at sacred trees. Imputing sacred powers to inanimate objects did not comport with ibn Abdul Wahhab's conception of true Islam.[7]

In his *Book of Tawhid*, ibn Abdul Wahhab wrote, "We must find out what true Islam is: it is above all a rejection of all gods except God, a refusal to allow others to share in that worship which is due to God alone *(shirk)*. *Shirk* is evil, no matter what the object, whether it be 'king or prophet, or saint or tree or tomb.'"[8]

The war against *shirk* (polytheism) became his central preoccupation. In this, ibn Abdul Wahhab was following what he understood to be pure Islam, for the Koran states, "Kill those who ascribe partners to God, wheresoever ye find them."[9] Polytheists *(mushrikun)* were his declared enemy—but his definition of polytheism was far different from that of the rest of the Islamic world.

In the name of his new strict monotheism, ibn Abdul Wahhab destroyed the tombs of the companions, or first disciples, of the Prophet Muhammad, which had become objects of veneration. He demolished the tomb of Zayd bin al-Khattab, the brother of the second caliph of Islam, Umar bin al-Khattab.[10] Praying at tombs, he averred, imitated Christian saint veneration. But Christian influences were not his only concern. Just after its birth, Islam became divided between the mainstream Sunni branch and the Shiite branch. Initially, the two branches fought about who should be the Prophet Muhammad's successor *(khalifah*, or caliph). Sunni Islam soon won out; by modern times, only 16 percent of Muslims belonged to one of the various Shiite groups.[11] During ibn Abdul Wahhab's time, however, large concentrations of Shiites were in what is today Iran, Iraq, and Bahrain, and along the eastern coast of the Arabian peninsula.

The Shiites, who were the "partisans of Ali," Muhammad's son-in-law, added a theological dimension to the succession debate. They attributed special religious qualities to Ali and his sons, Hasan and Hussein, as well as to their descendants. Ali and his successors established an imamate, a hereditary dynasty, of spiritual leaders who possessed secret knowledge and miraculous powers; the twelfth imam is expected to return as a *mahdi*, or messianic savior, an intermediary between man and God. According to some Shiites, Ali even shared the power of prophecy with Muhammad. Because of Shiite Islam's veneration of Ali and his successors, the Shiites drew the wrath of ibn Abdul Wahhab and his followers.

Ibn Abdul Wahhab even enforced the old Islamic punishment for an adulteress, stoning her to death, which other Muslim leaders of his time considered outmoded.[12] His zealotry was fed by a desire to re-create the true Islam, based on what he understood to be Islamic practice in seventh-century Arabia at the time of the Prophet Muhammad. But because many of ibn Abdul Wahhab's activities antagonized the local *ulama*, or religious leadership, he was expelled from Uyaina and sought a new protector—all the more necessary because he quarreled with both the emir (prince or commander) of his tribe and his own father.

In the end, Muhammad ibn Saud, the ruler of Diriyah, near modern-day Riyadh, gave him shelter. The Najd, at this time, may have been under the nominal rule of the Ottoman Empire, but it was essentially divided among many tribal families, like the Saudis of Diriyah. The two men struck an alliance in 1744. Ibn Saud, according to one source, assured his new ally, "This oasis is yours, do not fear your enemies. By the name of God, if all Najd was summoned to throw you out, we will never agree to expel you." Ibn Abdul Wahhab responded, "You are the settlement's chief and wise man. I want you to grant me an oath that you will perform jihad against the unbelievers."[13]

Muhammad ibn Saud and Muhammad ibn Abdul Wahhab thus established a *mithaq*, or covenant, under which ibn Saud established the first Saudi state and ibn Abdul Wahhab determined its official creed. It was,

The First Wahhabi-Saudi Emirate: 1744–1818

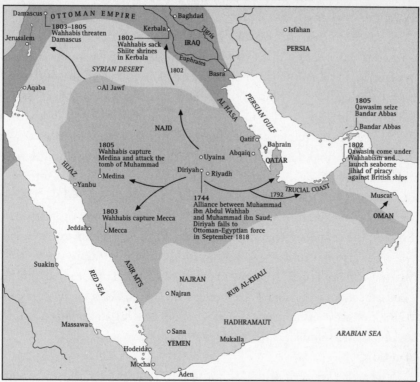

in short, a political bargain: ibn Saud would protect ibn Abdul Wahhab and spread his new creed, while ibn Abdul Wahhab would legitimize Saudi rule over an expanding circle of bedouin tribes, which were subdued through a new jihad. Ibn Saud also became the imam of ibn Abdul Wahhab's new religious community. (He apparently used only the title *emir*, however; subsequent generations of Saudi leaders actually adopted the term *imam*.)[14]

Their covenant even involved a dynastic marriage: ibn Saud married ibn Abdul Wahhab's daughter.[15] The descendants of these two families— the Al Saud and the Al al-Sheikh (the sheikh's family)—would serve as the leaders of the original Saudi state for generations.

The new community called its movement *al-da'wa ila al-tawhid* ("the call to the doctrine of the Oneness of God"). But in the West the new puritanical doctrine was named Wahhabism after its founder, and its adherents were called Wahhabis.

Radicalism and Brutality

With this political-religious alliance, tribal raiding could now be carried on as a religious cause. What had been once taken as tribal booty was now demanded as *zakat* (the charitable payments required as one of the five pillars of Islam). Significantly, ibn Abdul Wahhab legitimized jihad against fellow Muslims for the first time. And thanks to his military alliance with ibn Saud, he could duplicate the Muslim conquests of the seventh century.

Since that time, four different legal interpretations or orthodox *madhahib* (schools of law) had emerged within mainstream Sunni Islam alone: the Shafii school, the Hanbali school, the Hanafi school, and the Malaki school. The Hanafi school was largely followed within the Ottoman Empire; the schools varied most with respect to the conduct of religious rites, but also with regard to political philosophy. Although ibn Abdul Wahhab did not establish a new school, his *da'wa* (call or creed) within the Hanbali school marked a sharp break with mainstream Islam. For centuries, followers of one Sunni Islamic school of law had regarded followers of another school as true Muslims; ibn Abdul Wahhab broke with this tradition.

The radical nature of ibn Abdul Wahhab's dispute with mainstream Islam was captured by Sheikh Jamil al-Zahawi (1863–1936), a late-nineteenth-century cleric in Baghdad whose father had been the mufti of Ottoman Iraq. In an anti-Wahhabi history of the movement, al-Zahawi wrote, "His practice was to declare a group of famous scholars of the past unbelievers ... [and to maintain that] the Muslim community has existed for almost six hundred years in a state of unbelief *(kufr)*, and he said the same of whoever did not follow him."[16]

Al-Zahawi related how ibn Abdul Wahhab—who established that prayers must not allude to any sort of human intervention, even through the Prophet Muhammad—went so far as to burn books containing prayers to the Prophet and to destroy tomes on Islamic law, commentaries on the Koran, and scientific analyses of *hadith*, Islam's oral tradition.

Ayyub Sabri Pasha (died 1890), a rear admiral in the Ottoman navy during the reign of Sultan Abdul Hamit Khan II (1876–1909), coauthored a history on the origins of Wahhabism. According to this account, ibn Abdul Wahhab and ibn Saud declared that those who would not accept

Wahhabism were "disbelievers and polytheists," and so it was permissible "to kill them and confiscate their possessions."[17] Wahhabism could thus be spread by force, militarily.

One of the central doctrines of Wahhabism was *takfir*, a charge that Muslims could become infidels, or worse, by engaging in improper religious activities. Even a person who uttered the proclamation of Islamic faith, the *shahada*, but still practiced polytheism should be "denounced as an infidel and killed."[18] In a letter to a critic, ibn Abdul Wahhab identified an infidel as one "who has known the religion of the Prophet and yet stands against it, prevents others from accepting it, and shows hostility to those who follow it."[19] This definition opened the door to religious war against fellow Muslims who defined Islam differently from the Wahhabi creed.

Domingo Badía y Leblich, a Napoleonic agent who visited Arabia in 1807 under the name Ali Bey, described how the Wahhabi-Saudi alliance treated those who did not adhere to Wahhabism:

> The reform of Abdoulwehhab being admitted by Ibn Saaoud, was embraced by all the tribes subject to his command. This was a pretext for attacking the neighboring tribes, who were successively reduced to the alternative of embracing the reform or of perishing under the sword of the reformer.[20]

The Wahhabis were brutal to their enemies. To captured "polytheists" the Wahhabis offered a choice: embracing Wahhabism or death.

This spread of religion by the sword was actually a departure from, not a continuation of, classical Islam. True, the Prophet Muhammad had commanded Muslims to "strive in the path of God," which is understood as the source for jihad. And in the seventh century, Muslim armies had extended the geographic dominion of Islam—the "House of Islam"—by expanding into the outside world, the adversarial "House of War," which included the Byzantine and Persian Empires.

But the victorious Muslim armies did not *forcibly* convert the peoples of these vanquished areas; Christians and Jews were protected as monotheists, "people of the book." Throughout the centuries, many did convert to Islam, but not because their lives were at risk. Rather, they hoped to get out from under the discriminatory taxes that successive Muslim empires subjected them to, such as the *jizya* (poll tax) and the *kharaj*, a discriminatory land tax.

In short, the popular image that Islam was spread by the sword held to the throat of potential converts is simply untrue. According to Bernard Lewis, the eminent historian of the Middle East, "The application of jihad wasn't always rigorous or violent."[21] Lewis explains that 150 years after Islam's founding, the Islamic conquest—which had extended as far as France, India, and China—lost most of its steam: "While the universal Caliphate broke up into smaller states, the irresistible and permanent jihad came to an end, and a relationship of mutual tolerance was established between the Muslim world and the rest." Even when, as late as the seventeenth century, the Ottomans carried on a new holy war of expansion, the war was not universally pursued. They fought in the Balkans, right to the gates of Vienna, and in (Orthodox) Russia as well, but they made no effort to recover Islamic Spain and Sicily. In many cases, new Muslim conquests into the "House of War" were simply unfeasible, so that, as Lewis explains, jihad was "postponed from historic to messianic time." When the Ottomans issued a call for jihad against the Allied powers during World War I, their appeal was no longer able to unite the Muslim world.

Sir Hamilton Gibb, the great British expert on Islam, observed that "in the historic Community the concept of jihad had gradually weakened and at length been largely reinterpreted in terms of Sufi ethics."[22] Another analyst noted, "Jihad petered out."[23] With the stagnation of Islamic expansionism, the concept of jihad became internalized as a moral or spiritual struggle.[24] Thus, unsurprisingly, fundamentalist groups in the 1990s, like Egyptian Islamic Jihad, called jihad "the neglected duty."[25] The fundamentalists were clearly nostalgic for the militant jihad of the seventh century.

In purely religious terms, the traditional military concept of jihad was not easy to carry out even when politically feasible. Under strict Sunni Islamic law, a jihad can be declared only when it has a reasonable prospect of success. The Koran advises, "Fight in the way of God against those who fight against you, but do not commit aggression."[26] Jihad, it is important to remember, is *not* one of the five pillars required by the Islamic faith.

As recently as March 2002, the grand imam of Egypt's al-Azhar mosque, Mohammed Sayed Tantawi, explained that only a head of state or leader of all Arab peoples can proclaim jihad, and only when Arab lands have been invaded and occupied.[27] This implies that a central political-religious authority of Sunni Islam, like a caliph, is needed to declare jihad and thus guarantee that its martyrs enter Paradise.

Sunni Muslim theologians attempted to downplay jihad in several ways during the late Middle Ages. They proposed that the merits of those who die in a jihad could be earned through other types of religious devotion, such as traveling to Medina to learn or teach Islamic wisdom. In order to quell fanatical religious movements against the central authority of the state, theologians even ruled that "jihad waged out of opposition to authority had no claim to God's reward." They were concerned with the outbreak of *fitna*, or armed sedition, against a legitimate ruler.[28]

Under Shiite Islam, an offensive military jihad against nonbelievers could be undertaken only with the return of the twelfth, or hidden, imam; jihad was suspended until "the Imam reappeared as the messianic restorer of pristine Islam."[29] Only the Kharajites, a violent minority movement that seceded from mainstream Islam and revolted against the caliphate in the seventh century, actually defined jihad as a sixth pillar of their faith.

Wahhabi writings, however, elevated jihad to a central obligation of Islam by attributing to the Prophet Muhammad such sayings as: "Jihad is the ultimate manifestation of Islam, as the Messenger said.... It is a furnace in which Muslims are melted out and which allows the separation of the bad [Muslim] from the good one. It is also a pass to the Eden [Paradise] and the Eden is in the shade of swords." This jihad is, again, nothing less than an "armed struggle," rather than an inner struggle of the soul.[30]

In his *Book of Tawhid*, ibn Abdul Wahhab advanced an extremely anti-Christian and anti-Jewish agenda, describing the followers of both religions as sorcerers who believed in devil worship (*al-shaitan*). He cited a *hadith*, or oral tradition, that the punishment for the sorcerer is "that he be struck with the sword."[31] He wrote that both groups had improperly made the graves of their Prophets into places of worship, and warned Muslims not to replicate their historical errors.[32] Ibn Abdul Wahhab concluded, "The ways of the people of the book are condemned as those of polytheists."[33] This analysis made Wahhabism far more intolerant of Christianity and Judaism than classical Islam had been.

Embracing jihad allowed Wahhabism to grant its warriors the full advantages of martyrdom—that is, immediate entry into Paradise. This was a huge enticement, for according to Islamic tradition, upon their death all Muslims face a "day of judgment" that determines whether they enter Paradise or are banished to Hell. The Koran describes Paradise as "Gardens of Delight" with rivers of water, milk, and honey, and filled with dark-eyed virgins who serve as "loving companions."[34] By reviving jihad and condemning enemies as polytheists who have no right to live, Wahhabism set the stage for the swift success and infamous cruelty of its eighteenth- and early-nineteenth-century military campaigns.

The Saudi-Wahhabi Military Campaigns

Although Muhammad ibn Saud died in 1765, his son, Abdul Aziz, continued the Wahhabi wars, reaching the Persian Gulf coast in 1780, when he took al-Hasa. The Wahhabis advanced toward Kuwait in 1788. Bahrain recognized their sovereignty by paying *zakat* to the Saudi leader. But the Wahhabis soon came under attack. In 1790, Sharif Ghalib ibn Musaid, the Ottoman-appointed ruler of Mecca, sent an army from the Hijaz against them but was defeated. Seven years later, the Ottoman governor of Baghdad sent seven thousand Turks and fourteen thousand Arabs against a Wahhabi army headed by Saud, the son of Abdul Aziz. The Ottoman army lost this battle as well.

Muhammad ibn Abdul Wahhab died in 1791, but the Wahhabi campaign of expansion continued. Abdul Aziz sent a copy of ibn Abdul Wahhab's writings to the rulers of Oman, demanding that they and their people adopt the Wahhabi creed, a proposal the Omanis rejected. An Omani chronicler, Ibn Razik, wrote about the work, "It is a small book. . . . It legalizes the murder of all Muslims who dissent from them [the Wahhabis], the appropriation of their property, the enslavement of their offspring, the marriage of their wives without first being divorced from their husbands."[35]

In the spring of 1802, twelve thousand Wahhabis under the command of Saud invaded the southern part of Ottoman Iraq. That April, the army entered Kerbala, massacred some four thousand Shiites, and sacked holy Shiite shrines, including the tomb of Hussein, the martyred grandson of the Prophet Muhammad.[36] Looting the city, the Wahhabis made off with precious spoils, including jeweled sabers, handguns, gold ornaments, and Persian carpets, all carried on the backs of four thousand camels.[37]

Ali Bey recorded the nature of the Kerbala attack: "The inhabitants made but a feeble resistance; and the conqueror put to the sword all the men and male children of every age. Whilst they executed this horrible butchery, a Wahhabite doctor cried from the top of a tower, 'Kill, strangle all the infidels who give companions to God [that is, who engage in polytheism].'"[38] Indeed, the conviction that their opponents were "polytheists" gave the Wahhabis all the justification they needed for the slaughter.[39]

Another Western source, J. Rousseau, who lived in Iraq in this period, detailed the horrors of the Wahhabi attacks in Kerbala: "Old people, women and children—everybody died at the barbarians' sword. Besides, it is said whenever they saw a pregnant woman, they disemboweled her and left the foetus on the mother's bleeding corpse. Their cruelty could not be satisfied, they did not cease their murders and blood flowed like water."[40]

In 1805, Wahhabi forces besieged Najaf, the other Shiite holy city in Iraq, which was the burial place of Muhammad's son-in-law, the revered Ali. In response, a leading Shiite cleric, as the deputy of the hidden imam, who is to return as a messianic savior, called for a defensive jihad, which was justified against "enemies of Islam."[41] Unlike Kerbala, Najaf was not vanquished.

But Najaf was an exception during this period. In 1803, the holy city of Mecca fell to a Wahhabi army led by Saud, and the Wahhabis continued their practice of smashing shrines. Ali Bey relates that "Saaoud ordered all the mosques and chapels consecrated to the memory of the Prophet and his family to be razed to the ground." They destroyed "sepulchers of the saints and heroes which were held in veneration."[42] The army demolished the chapel on Jebel Nur, the mountain on which, according to Muslim tradition, the Angel Gabriel had brought the first chapter of the Koran to Muhammad. The Wahhabis then posted a guard on the mountain to prevent pilgrims from praying at its summit.[43]

But on November 4, 1803, a Shiite assassin, taking revenge for the sacking of Kerbala, murdered Abdul Aziz in the mosque of Diriyah. Undeterred, the Wahhabis continued their campaigns under Saud, and Medina fell a year later.

The 1802 Wahhabi assault on the fortress of Taif, in particular, became known as an act of unmitigated barbarism. The Taifians had raised a flag of truce on their fortress. The Wahhabis' envoy demanded, as the terms of surrender, all the possessions of Taif's residents. In return, he would guarantee the lives of the men only; women and children were to be put in chains.

The envoy's mission failed. One historian wrote that the Wahhabis, in their ensuing attack on Taif, "killed every woman, man, and child they saw, cutting even the babies in cradles." Those who survived surrendered after twelve days, but these "three hundred and sixty-seven men, together with women and children, were put to the sword."[44]

In Medina, the Wahhabis applied their religious doctrine of destroying shrines and of banning anything that resembled the veneration of saints. Going beyond their actions in Kerbala, the Wahhabis tried to destroy the magnificent domed structures over the tomb of the Prophet Muhammad himself.[45] The Wahhabi conquerors also removed all precious objects from the tomb and plundered the treasury of the Prophet's mosque.[46] In an act that clearly antagonized the Ottoman Empire, they expelled Medina's large Turkish population.[47]

By 1802, the Wahhabis had subdued the entire coastline of the Persian Gulf, from Basra in the north to the Gulf of Oman. Under Wahhabi influence, pirates from the Qawasim tribe in the lower Gulf targeted British shipping. One British assessment claimed that the Qawasim had been "urged by the Wahhabis" to extend their activities to the coasts of India.[48] The Qawasim Wahhabis even crossed the Persian Gulf and, in 1805, seized Bandar Abbas (today the main base for Iran's navy). In the late 1950s, Donald Hawley, the former British political agent in the Trucial States (today the United Arab Emirates), summarized the history of these Wahhabi pirates: "Wahhabi religious fervour affected the Qawasim, who were driven by the zeal of the converted to a degree of aggressiveness at sea which they might otherwise not have attained."[49]

According to this account, Wahhabi militancy and expansionism extended to the sea, to such an extent that European sailors called the shoreline of Sharja and Ras al-Khaimah the "Pirate Coast." One commentator referred to the Wahhabi piracy as a "seaborne *jihad*."[50] The British eventually pacified the Arabian shoreline and reached separate truces with each tribal sheikh to suppress piracy. Because of these truces, these sheikhdoms of the Pirate Coast became known as the Trucial States.

The Wahhabi incursions into Iraq resumed in 1805 and extended to Syria as well. In 1808, Saud demanded that the sheikhs of Damascus and Aleppo adopt Wahhabism. His allies from the subdued tribes of Jabal Shammar raided the Syrian desert on his behalf and, in 1810, challenged Damascus.[51] In 1808, 1810, and 1812, Wahhabi raids threatened Baghdad. The Wahhabi sphere of influence soon reached from Palmyra in the north, deep in the interior of Syria, to Oman in the south. The resulting Saudi state became the largest single political entity to have emerged on the Arabian peninsula since the time of the Prophet Muhammad.

The magnitude of these military successes threatened the political order in the Middle East. Much of this region was still nominally controlled by the Ottoman Empire, but Ottoman subjects could interpret the Wahhabi victories as an expression of God's displeasure with the innovations introduced by the Ottoman sultan, Selim III (1789–1807).[52] His political authority challenged, Selim III in 1803 appointed a new governor of Damascus to handle the Wahhabi menace.[53]

But the Wahhabi threat was not only political. With Sultan Selim III also serving as the caliph (and thus protector) of Sunni Islam, each Wahhabi victory against his Ottoman subjects undermined his religious authority as well. An Ottoman backlash against Wahhabism, and in the defense of Sunni Islam, was inevitable.

Chapter 2

Countering
the Wahhabi Menace

In the nineteenth century, the Ottoman Empire stood as the last in a series of great Muslim powers that began with the seventh-century military conquests under the Prophet Muhammad. After the Prophet's death, Muslim expansion continued under Muhammad's successors—the Rashidun (based in Medina from 632 to 661), Umayyad (based in Damascus from 651 to 750), and Abbasid (based in Baghdad from 750 to 1258) caliphates. The Ottoman Empire, at its height, stretched from Algiers in the west, across North Africa and the Middle East, into western Persia, and up to the Caspian Sea; in the north it covered Greece, the Balkans, Hungary, and the southern Ukraine; and in the south it controlled the Arabian peninsula down to Yemen.

In 1453, the Ottomans conquered Constantinople—the capital of Eastern Christendom, which had resisted the assaults of all previous Muslim powers—and changed the city's name to Istanbul. With this victory, the Ottoman sultan could claim an uncontestable position of superiority vis-à-vis other Muslim leaders as the "Commander of the Faithful," for in the centuries of Muslim expansionism, spiritual authority had always accompanied political authority. This was reinforced when the sultan seized the Muslim holy cities of the Hijaz in 1517.

The Ottomans claimed that the last Abbasid caliph, whose family had lived in exile in Egypt ever since the Mongols had destroyed Baghdad in 1258, ceded his title to Sultan Selim I when the Ottomans conquered Cairo in 1517. Thereafter, Ottoman sultans based in Istanbul were also caliphs, the highest religious authority in orthodox (Sunni) Islam. It was a tough claim to make, since according to Sunni Islamic doctrine, the caliph must come out of the Arabian tribe of Quraish.[1] The Ottomans were ethnically Turks, not Arabs. Moreover, many scholars consider the story of the transfer of the caliphate from the Abbasids to the Ottomans to be apocryphal. Nevertheless, Ottoman sultans described themselves as "the supreme religious leader of Islam" from at least 1774.[2]

Although Ottoman sultans had become the spiritual leaders of Sunni Islam, they did not use their authority to attack other Islamic groups or branches. Initially, Ottoman rulers did brand Shiites as heretics, but in later years, they demonstrated considerable tolerance toward their Shiite population. In Ottoman Iraq, local Ottoman officials sometimes even attended Shiite religious events, such as *ashura* processions commemorating the martyrdom of Hussein, rather than oppressing Shiites, as the Wahhabis did.[3] With the exception of its Persian Gulf coastline from Kuwait down to al-Hasa and Oman, as well as the area of Yemen, the heart of Arabia—where Wahhabism developed—was solidly Sunni Muslim. But the Ottoman territories to the north were hardly as homogeneous, so the rulers had to be more accommodating to minority religious groups.

The Wahhabi raids on the Arab provinces of the Ottoman Empire were more than a challenge to the sultan's political rule. Since the Wahhabis regarded those who did not adopt their creed as less than true Muslims— and since the religious prestige of the Ottoman sultan-caliph grew out of the Ottoman Empire's military reputation as the protector of Muslims[4]— Wahhabist military expansion was a direct challenge to the sultan-caliph's religious authority. With Mecca and Medina now in Wahhabi hands, the sultan could no longer call himself "Custodian of the Two Holy Cities" or guarantee the security of his subjects during the pilgrimage to Mecca (hajj). As a result, Sheikh Jamil al-Zahawi, a late-nineteenth-century religious authority in Iraq, described the founder of the Saudi-Wahhabi alliance, Muhammad ibn Saud, as "the Rebel who turned his face in disobedience to the greater Islamic Caliphate."[5]

Counterattack

The Ottomans would gain the opportunity to challenge Wahhabi power, however.

In 1798, after conquering most of continental Europe, Napoleon invaded Ottoman Egypt. By gaining control of the main route from the eastern Mediterranean to the Indian Ocean, he would cut off the British from their empire in India. The French assumed that this indirect strategy would be easier than a direct assault on the British Isles.

But French forces were forced to withdraw from the Middle East a few years later, after suffering defeat at the hands of Admiral Horatio Nelson and the British navy.[6] When the French left Egypt, the Ottoman Empire appointed Muhammad Ali, an Albanian-born officer, as governor of Cairo and charged him with countering the Wahhabi menace. In response to the sultan's request, he organized an expeditionary force, initially under his young son, Tusun, to recover the holy cities of Islam from the Wahhabis.

The initial Egyptian force, which arrived by sea, occupied the Arabian coastal town of Yanbu in October 1811. A detachment of cavalry came by land. Together, the two forces numbered eight thousand troops. The Egyptian religious leadership, the Cairo-based *ulama*, accompanied the expeditionary force.

But the Saudi leader, Saud, was prepared for the Egyptian attack, deploying a Wahhabi army of eighteen thousand men between Yanbu and Medina. Under the command of Saud's son Abdullah, the Wahhabis crushed the Egyptian forces, which fled for the seacoast.[7]

The Egyptians nonetheless persisted. Their campaign against the Wahhabis lasted another six years, until 1818. Medina fell to Egypt in November 1812, Jeddah capitulated in January 1813, and Mecca and Taif came into Egyptian hands shortly thereafter. Egypt's conquest of Mecca and Medina was celebrated in Cairo, and Muhammad Ali sent the keys of the cities to the sultan in Istanbul, where a weeklong festival was held.

When Saud died on April 27, 1814, in the Saudi capital of Diriyah, Abdullah took power as the new leader of the Saudi state. According to Jean Louis Burckhardt, a Swiss explorer who traveled in Arabia during this time, Saud's last words of advice for Abdullah were "Never engage the Turk in open plains."[8] Understanding the superiority of the Ottoman-Egyptian forces, Saud preferred that Wahhabi forces harass them from positions in the mountains. But this advice was not always followed.

Not satisfied with his conquest of the Hijaz and the holy cities of Islam, Muhammad Ali decided to penetrate the Arabian interior and destroy what remained of the Saudi state. He designated his eldest son, Ibrahim, to lead this expedition. This new Egyptian force enjoyed special advantages: it employed European doctors, used Napoleonic techniques in warfare, could depend on resupply from the Ottoman governor in Baghdad, and, most important, had European artillery pieces. The Egyptians had learned from their crushing defeat at the hands of the French fifteen years earlier; despite the warriors' intense religious convictions, their scimitars, which were engraved with Koranic verses, had been no match for French military technology and firepower.

Ibrahim's army swept through the Najd. On September 11, 1818, Abdullah surrendered to Ibrahim and was taken prisoner. After Diriyah fell to the Egyptians and was leveled, the first Saudi state was terminated—the fall of the Wahhabis being celebrated in Cairo with a festival complete with fireworks. The prisoner Abdullah was brought to Istanbul, where he was presented to the Ottoman sultan, Mahmud II (1808–39), in heavy chains. After being forced to march through the Ottoman capital for three days, he was beheaded in front of the main gate of Haghia Sophia (St. Sophia), not far from the sultan's Topkapi Palace, along with one of his ministers and his imam. As heretics, they were denied a Muslim funeral, and so their bodies were simply thrown into the sea after being displayed for several days. According to another account, the bodies were abandoned to stray dogs.[9]

The Ottomans celebrated their victory over the Wahhabis as "the defeat of the adversaries of the Muslim religion." Even the rival Persian shah, who was the protector of Shiite Muslims, acknowledged the Ottoman victory over the Wahhabis in a letter to Muhammad Ali. The sultan-caliph ordered that prayers be offered throughout the Ottoman Empire to thank heaven for "the annihilation of the sect that had devastated Mecca and Medina."[10]

Wahhabism Survives—and Spreads

But Wahhabism did not die with the execution of Abdullah. In fact, after the original Saudi state fell, Wahhabism acquired a surprising degree of influence elsewhere in the Islamic world. Farther east, Said Ahmad Barelwi, who became familiar with the teachings of Muhammad ibn Abdul Wahhab while visiting Mecca in the 1820s, declared a jihad against the infidels, fighting against the Sikhs in the Punjab (in what is now India) and establishing a Wahhabi state in Peshawar (in what is today Pakistan). He was killed in 1830, but his followers declared a jihad against the British to resist colonialism. Wahhabi preachers promised Indian Muslims "deliverance or paradise...in every sermon."[11]

In addition, Indonesians making pilgrimages to Mecca in 1803 had come under Wahhabi influences and brought the Wahhabi creed to Sumatra, where they directed their energies against non-Muslims. In the 1830s, the Sumatran Wahhabis, known as the Padri movement, would take on Dutch colonial authorities. The Dutch, in fact, waged war against the Wahhabis of Sumatra for nearly fifteen years.

Nor did the fall of the Saudi state mean the end of Wahhabism in Arabia, where it had originally developed. In 1825, Abdul Rahman ibn Hasan Al al-Sheikh, grandson of ibn Abdul Wahhab, returned from exile and called on the tribes to return to "genuine Islam" and reject the polytheistic practices of the "so-called Muslims." This was classic Wahhabi terminology.

Meanwhile, a direct descendant of Muhammad ibn Saud, the founder of the Saudi-Wahhabi alliance, returned to reestablish his family's claim to leadership. Turki, a cousin of Abdullah who had escaped the Egyptian onslaught, in 1823 led new raids into the heart of Arabia and seized Riyadh from the Egyptians. He ruled a new, second Saudi state until he was assassinated in 1832. His brother, Faisal, then became ruler in Riyadh, but was taken prisoner by an Egyptian force in 1838 and brought to Cairo.

At the same time, Muhammad Ali's growing power faced a challenge. The Egyptian leader had advanced northward into Syria, threatening the authority of the Ottoman sultan. British policy since the time of Lord Palmerston, the foreign secretary in the 1830s, had been to protect the territorial integrity of the Ottoman Empire in order to preserve the delicate balance of power in Europe. Thus, the European powers soon intervened to save the Ottoman Empire, forcing Muhammad Ali back to Egypt.

As a result, in 1841 the Egyptians were compelled to withdraw most of their forces from the Arabian peninsula. Faisal escaped from his Cairo prison soon thereafter, in 1843, returned to Riyadh, and resumed power as the Saudi imam. Abdul Rahman, who continued to spread his grandfather's Wahhabi teachings, became a judge in Riyadh in 1845 and, from the early 1860s until his death in 1869, was viewed as the "chaplain of the palace." Wahhabism was firmly seated at the center of power in the second Saudi state.

Wahhabis continued to abuse Shiites and subjugate them to inferior status, as the British traveler William Palgrave attested after visiting Riyadh in 1862 and witnessing what happened to Persian pilgrims making the hajj to Mecca through Saudi territory:

> Here Feysul, after exacting the exorbitant sum which Wahhabee orthodoxy claims from Shiya'ee heretics as the price of permission to visit the sacred city and the tomb of the Prophet, had assigned for [their] guide and leader one Abd-el-Azeez-Aboo-Boteyn, a Nejdean of the Nejdeans, who was to conduct and plunder them in the name of God and the true faith all the rest of the way to Mecca and back again.[12]

According to Palgrave, the Wahhabis still viewed everyone but themselves as "enemies of God." Each Shiite pilgrim, he estimated, had to provide the Wahhabis with a special tax of about sixty pounds sterling. Even residents of the Najd were afflicted with "excessive Wahhabee taxes," Palgrave noted. Extraordinary levies were imposed when a jihad was undertaken; refusal to pay meant being treated as a heretic or infidel.

Faisal's subjects adhered to Wahhabism, and he even formally proclaimed a jihad in the early 1860s in order to subdue his tribal adversaries. These Wahhabi attacks were brutal, surpassing the Arabian bedouin raids, whose objective was to obtain booty. According to Palgrave, "The Nejdeans distinguish themselves from the rest of their Arab countrymen by preferring slaughter to booty; they neither take nor ask for quarter, and so long as there are men to kill, pay no attention to plunder."[13]

But despite the harshness of religious life under this militant and intolerant branch of Islam, and the fierceness of Wahhabism's conduct of war in the Arabian interior, the rise of the second Saudi state did not translate into the religious expansionism that drove the policies of Muhammad ibn Saud. Power politics somewhat offset Wahhabist ideology in this period. Saudi leaders had learned to appreciate the limitations of their strength after their armed encounters with the Egyptians and Ottomans. Although Faisal did, in 1850, occupy Qatar, which subsequently was converted to Wahhabism, in general his campaigns were limited. Forces loyal to Faisal prepared to invade Bahrain in 1859 but were dissuaded from doing so by the British. There were no invasions of Syria and Iraq. And unlike his predecessors, Faisal did not challenge the Ottoman Empire's control over the holy cities of Islam; he even paid an annual tribute to the sultan in Istanbul.

That does not mean, however, that the Wahhabis had abandoned their ambitions of recovering Mecca and Medina. Indeed, Sir Richard Burton, who visited the Hijaz in the early 1850s, wrote, "And I have heard from authentic sources that the Wahhabis look forward to the day when a fresh crusade will enable them to purge the land of its abominations in the shape of silver and gold."[14] But realistically, the Wahhabis could do little to realize their aspirations at this time.

With the opening of the Suez Canal in 1869, the Ottoman Empire effectively projected its power to the Red Sea. In 1871, an Ottoman force of 3,000 men, backed by 1,500 Arabs, landed at al-Hasa, along the eastern coast of the Arabian peninsula, in an attempt to reestablish Ottoman authority. Rather than using their Egyptian governor to intervene in Arabia, as they had earlier in the century, the Ottomans turned to Midhat Pasha, the Ottoman governor of the province of Baghdad, just north of the Najd. The Ottomans still perceived the Wahhabis as a threat; as one knowledgeable student of Wahhabism wrote in this period, it remained "a politico-religious confederacy, which legalizes the indiscriminate plunder and thraldom of all people beyond its own pale."[15] The Ottoman sultan also reasserted his religious authority over the Hijaz, intervening in the appointment of the sharif of Mecca, who by tradition was a descendant of the Prophet Muhammad and came from one of three Hashemite clans.[16] Although a Wahhabi campaign in western Arabia under these conditions almost certainly would have proven fruitless, there were lingering anti-Ottoman sentiments in the Hijaz. For example, in 1855, reports reached Mecca that the Ottoman Empire was initiating new reforms, including the abolition of black slavery, the granting of equal

rights to Christians, and women's emancipation.[17] Sheikh Jamal, chief of
the Mecca *ulama*, issued a fatwa (legal ruling) denouncing these innovations and stating that if they were implemented, the Ottomans should be
considered infidels; a proclamation of jihad against the Ottomans followed. The Ottomans could not take their position in the Hijaz entirely
for granted.

Ottoman officials' apprehension about a possible revival of Wahhabism was understandable. In his *Fitnatu-l-Wahhabiyyah* ("The Wahhabi
Insurrections"), Sheikh Ahmad bin Zayani Dahlan, the chief mufti of
Mecca, attacked the record of Wahhabism: "As their territories expanded,
their evil and harm increased. They killed countless numbers of Muslims,
legitimated confiscating their money and possessions, and captured their
women."[18] Leaving little doubt as to how he viewed the movement, he
described the Wahhabi creed as a "wicked doctrine," and elsewhere he
wrote, "The founder of this vile sect, Muhammad b. 'Abd al-Wahhab,
originated in the eastern part of the Arabian peninsula among the tribe of
the Bani Tamim. He lived for almost a hundred years, which enabled him
to spread his misguidance."[19]

But the second Saudi state ultimately collapsed because of internal dis-
sension following Faisal's death in 1865, as his sons—Abdullah, Saud,
Muhammad, and Abdul Rahman—fought over the succession. Their
rivalry brought about increasing external intervention. When Saud ousted
Abdullah, the latter appealed to the Ottoman sultan to intervene on his
behalf.[20] Besides fighting for control of the Arabian peninsula, the brothers
reportedly differed over the application of Wahhabi doctrine, particularly
regarding "the killing of non-Wahhabis."[21]

The Ottoman forces demonstrated their continuing technological
superiority over Arabian tribesmen when, in the early 1870s, 1,600 Ottoman riflemen defeated as many as 8,000 tribal warriors loyal to Saud.

The Ottomans had created strong strategic positions to contain any
future Wahhabi revival—along the Red Sea in the Hijaz, along the Persian Gulf in al-Hasa, and in northern Arabia through the Rashidis of Jabal
Shammar, the Saudis' rivals. Thus, the Saudi homeland of the Najd was
surrounded on three sides by the newly reasserted power of the Ottoman
Empire on the Arabian peninsula.

Yet the Ottomans would not remain unchallenged in Arabia forever.

Wahhabism's Lingering Influence

In the late 1870s, the British explorer Charles M. Doughty visited Arabia and detailed the declining fortunes of what remained of the Saudi state: "The town of er Riath with her suburbs, and the next village country about, is all that remains of the Wahaby dominion; which is become a small and weak principality—such as Boreyda.... Ibn Saud's [the Saudi ruling family's] servants abandon his unfortunate stars and go hire themselves to Mohammed ibn Rashid. No beduins now obey the Wahaby."[22] According to Doughty, neighboring towns recalled the days of the "Wahaby tyranny," which they were happy to have overcome.[23]

But, he added, while the political power of the Wahhabis might have declined, the appeal of their religious doctrine was still strong, so that many people in the area refused to cooperate with local authorities. Saudi tax gatherers were sent back empty-handed by many villages. And the bedouin "cleave inseparably to the reformed religion," Doughty noted, using a common term for Wahhabism.

Doughty wrote that the lingering commitment to Wahhabism also meant that Christians, whom the bedouin called Nasrany, risked their lives traveling in the Arabian peninsula: "A Nasrany they think to be a son of the Evil One, and [therefore] deserving of death: and half of this townspeople are Wahabies."[24] Although the Wahhabis were barely in contact with any Christians, they still regarded them as the sons of the devil.

Even the Saudis' Arabian rivals, the Rashidis, retained an interest in Wahhabism. When the Rashidis captured Riyadh in 1891, the Rashidi emir asked Abdullah bin Abdul Latif—a Wahhabi scholar who was a descendant of Muhammad ibn Abdul Wahhab—to move to Hail, the Rashidi capital. He returned a year later to Rashidi-controlled Riyadh and continued to preach and teach the Wahhabi creed. (Later, in 1902, Ibn Saud, the founder of the modern Saudi state, would forgive him for his links to the Rashidis. Indeed, Ibn Saud would marry Abdullah bin Abdul Latif's daughter, Tarfa Al al-Sheikh; their son, Faisal, would later become king of Saudi Arabia.)[25]

Indeed, Wahhabism had spread in the early nineteenth century. Because Wahhabism had once ruled Mecca and clearly had left a major impact there, Muslims making the pilgrimage were exposed to the creed, and as a result, Wahhabism reached other Muslim societies. Sayyid Muhammad Ali al-Sanusi (1791–1859), an Algerian, first studied in Fez and later went to Mecca, where he came under Wahhabi influence. In the holy city, he established the Sanusiyyah, an organization that advanced a new puritanical fundamentalism. In the 1840s, he took his ideas to Cyrenaica (today's Libya), where they became the country's dominant religious force. One of his descendants, King Idris, would in the twentieth century become Libya's first monarch. (In 1969, Colonel Muammar Qaddafi, who was raised under Sanusi traditions, would overthrow Idris.)

As Wahhabism spread, the British came to regard the Wahhabis as a permanent danger to their Indian empire. After considerable bloodshed, in 1870 and 1871, the heads of the older Muslim communities of India, both Sunni and Shiite, issued official declarations dissociating themselves from the Wahhabi doctrine of jihad.

Wahhabism would reach as far as Russian Central Asia by the early twentieth century, for in 1912 a native of Medina, Sayed Shari Muhammad, established Wahhabi cells in the Fergana Valley (an area located in what is today eastern Uzbekistan).[26] And it would continue to spread. As the century went on, and Wahhabis witnessed political decay and weakness around them, Wahhabi-dominated organizations would ultimately adopt a strategy of militant Islamic activism—that is, outright violence.

As will be seen, many of those who started such militant Islamic movements traced their intellectual and ideological roots to nineteenth-century Wahhabism. In short, radical Islamic thought as it developed in Arabia in the nineteenth century significantly contributed to the campaigns of anti-Western violence and militant Islamic terrorism that came to be known in the twentieth century.

Chapter 3

"White Terror"

The Ikhwan and the Rise of the Modern Saudi Kingdom

Modern Saudi Arabia, like most other states of the Middle East, emerged from the ruins of the Ottoman Empire after World War I. The demise of the Ottoman state, which had long been known as the "sick man of Europe," had been gradual and also had immediate implications for Wahhabism. For Ottoman power had held the expansion of the second Wahhabi state in check during the latter part of the nineteenth century, particularly by protecting the holy cities of Mecca and Medina.

By keeping the Wahhabis in check, however, the Ottoman Empire also enabled them to consolidate their power in Arabia. Wahhabi leaders, recognizing the Ottomans' military superiority, prudently did not embark on a militant expansionist campaign, but they also recognized that tribal warfare in the interior of Arabia was not always a paramount concern for Istanbul. Nor had the Wahhabis aroused the concerns of the great powers of Europe, except when they briefly threatened British commerce in the Persian Gulf. Wahhabism had, therefore, developed deep roots by the beginning of the twentieth century.

Nevertheless, a revived Wahhabi campaign in the twentieth century would not go unchecked, for the Wahhabis would have to cross newly established international borders fixed and policed by the British Empire, the rising world power.

Britain asserted its hegemony in the Middle East well before the collapse of the Ottoman Empire. After Napoleon invaded Egypt in 1798 in an attempt to cut England off from its imperial jewel, India, London set out to control the gateways to the Indian Ocean: the Red Sea and Persian Gulf; Cape Town, South Africa; and Singapore in the Far East. By the 1880s, Britain's army had occupied Egypt and the Sudan, and taken control of the newly dug (primarily by the French) Suez Canal, which connected the Mediterranean Sea with the Indian Ocean. British India signed a series of protectorate agreements with the the Persian Gulf's Arabian rulers, beginning with Bahrain in 1880. In 1899, Lord Curzon, the viceroy of India, extended the protectorate system to Kuwait. Under these agreements, each Arabian sheikh (local ruler) received British recognition and, in exchange, agreed to surrender his sovereign powers to conduct foreign affairs.

These agreements also limited the freedom of the sheikhdoms to engage in foreign commerce with non-British companies, for mineral or railroad concessions often led to coaling stations and to naval or commercial fleets that could challenge Britain's imperial hegemony. As early as 1893, the British foreign secretary, Lord Lansdowne, described "the establishment of a naval base, or a fortified port in the Persian Gulf by any other power as a very grave menace to British interests."[1]

One who witnessed the importance of this growing British power was a young man named Abdul Aziz bin Abdul Rahman Al Saud, who became known in the West as Ibn Saud. Born in 1880, Ibn Saud was the son of Abdul Rahman, one of the four sons of Faisal who fought over the Saudi succession. As a boy, Ibn Saud had been taken into exile in Kuwait; his father fled because the Ottomans were backing the Saudis' eastern Arabian rivals, the Rashidis of Jabal Shammar, who captured Riyadh in 1891. Now, from Kuwait, which had become a British quasi-protectorate in 1899, Ibn Saud watched as the British scrambled to keep other European imperial powers out of the Persian Gulf.

Ibn Saud Breaks with the Ottomans

At that time, the Germans posed the greatest threat to British control of the Middle East. Germany was staking out its position in the collapsing

Ottoman Empire with its proposed Berlin-Baghdad railway. Britain's interest in the Persian Gulf region by this point had to do with more than just strategic waterways. Oil had recently been discovered there, and with the Royal Navy converting its warships from coal- to oil-burning engines at the turn of the century, the British Admiralty needed to keep the region in British hands.[2]

Arabian leaders exploited the ensuing competition among European powers. In 1900, for example, Kuwait's ruler, Sheikh Mubarak, and his Saudi guests came under attack from the Ottoman-backed Rashidis (the Saudis' Arabian rivals) and were saved by calling for a British warship in the Persian Gulf. The British gunboat opened fire on the Rashidis, forcing them to withdraw. British naval units also prevented a Turkish assault on Kuwait in 1901.

One year later, at the age of twenty-two, Ibn Saud retook his ancestral capital of Riyadh from the Rashidis and began a campaign to recover Saudi territories lost in the nineteenth century. The campaign was to last twelve years. Recognizing Britain's growing power in the region—in 1903, Lord Curzon led into the Persian Gulf the largest British naval flotilla ever assembled up to that time—Ibn Saud elicited British help against the Ottomans. He met with London's political agent in Kuwait, Captain William Shakespeare, explaining, "We Wahhabis hate the Turks only less than the Persians for the infidel practices which they imported into the true and pure faith revealed to us in the Koran."[3] Unlike many Wahhabi clerics who voiced strongly anti-Christian sentiments, Ibn Saud was known actually to prefer Christians over non-Wahhabi Muslims; Christians, he once explained, at least act in accordance with their religion, whereas non-Wahhabi Muslims who fail to understand the importance of not diverting from *tawhid* (belief in the oneness of God) are guilty of *shirk* (polytheism).[4]

His overtures to the British were also based on an appreciation of the declining power of the Ottomans. In 1911, the Ottomans sought Ibn Saud's assistance in putting down a revolt in Asir, just north of Yemen. Unable to reinforce their military strength in the Arabian peninsula, they sought his assistance one year later to defend their positions in al-Hasa, along the Persian Gulf coast. Moreover, while the Ottomans were preoccupied with the Balkans at the time, Ibn Saud exploited their vulnerability to evict their garrison from al-Hasa in May 1913. In pursuing these military campaigns, he knew he had the backing of British political agents—that is, as long as he did not invade the territories of sheikhs under British political protection.[5] He had to be careful about asserting old Wahhabi claims to Bahrain, Qatar, and parts of Oman. Having reached the shoreline of the Persian Gulf with his conquest of al-Hasa, Ibn Saud agreed to British requests and formally joined the protectorate system on December 26, 1915.

There is little evidence that Wahhabism played a major role in these initial stages of Ibn Saud's consolidation of territories. But while these campaigns were under way, an independent revival of Wahhabism emerged in the Saudi-controlled Najd. This revival would prove vital to the new Saudi military drive.

The Ikhwan Movement

A descendant of Muhammad ibn Abdul Wahhab, Abdullah bin Abdul Latif, who was the *qadi* (religious judge) of Riyadh, promoted a new religious movement that settled the area of al-Artawiya, a village in the Najd north of Riyadh. There, Najdi settlers established the Ikhwan—a Wahhabi organization that insisted its "brethren" live according to strict Wahhabi tenets, avoid contact with Europeans, and reside in communal agricultural settlements known as *hujar* (*hijra*, in the singular).

The *hijra* movement spread through Arabia; some 52 settlements had been erected by 1920, and 120 by 1929. The bedouin residents of the *hujar* continued to engage in military raids—but not just to plunder caravans, as they had in the past. Raiding in the Wahhabi tradition had a religious dimension; it entailed wars against the "polytheists."[6]

Harold R. P. Dickson, who worked for the British political agent in the Persian Gulf, Sir Percy Cox, analyzed Ibn Saud's attitude toward the growing power of the Ikhwan movement:

> In late 1915 or early 1916 Ibn Sa'ud found that Ikhwanism was definitely gaining control of affairs in Najd. He saw that he had to make one of two decisions: either to be a temporal ruler and crush Ikhwanism, or to become the spiritual head of this new Wahabism. Probably in the first place he had thought to make use of it to strengthen his position, but in the end he was

compelled to accept its doctrines and become its leader, lest he should go under himself.[7]

Essentially, Ibn Saud sought to co-opt the Ikhwan by providing them with funds and religious instructors. He appointed the *qadi*s, who provided religious and legal guidance to the *hujar*, from among the descendants of Muhammad ibn Abdul Wahhab. He hoped to draw the Ikhwan members away from their primary political allegiance—their tribal leaders—and thereby weaken the strength of his potential rivals.

Tribalism was a serious problem for any Arab leader seeking to unify the Arabian peninsula. In his book on Arabian tribes, Fuad Hamza, who would serve as Ibn Saud's deputy minister for foreign affairs, identified ninety-seven separate major tribes in the peninsula.[8] Ibn Saud needed a means to unite these highly independent tribes. Wahhabi Islam would be the glue for holding together the emerging Saudi state, and the Ikhwan would be the instrument for molding the new Wahhabi society.

Since the Ikhwan often came from bedouin backgrounds and usually had not had extensive training in Islam, they tended to exhibit zealotry, if not fanaticism, in applying their newly found religion to their everyday lives. They beat fellow Ikhwan who did not pray five times a day, and regarded other Muslims as polytheists. The Ikhwan also wore distinctive clothing, including white turbans, instead of the traditional Arab *kufiya* (roped headcloth). They covered their faces when they encountered Europeans or Arabs from outside Saudi Arabia, rather than allow themselves to be "defiled."

They brought this religious extremism to warfare, much as eighteenth-century Wahhabis had done. In 1916, Ibn Saud issued an order by which all bedouin tribes of Arabia had to join the Ikhwan and pay him *zakat*, the charitable donations required in Islam, because he was to be recognized as their imam. If they failed to make this payment, they faced conquest.[9] The Ikhwan viewed those who did not join them as polytheists—to whom they were utterly brutal. One Soviet historian called the Ikhwan the "white terror" of Arabia.[10] They became instrumental in Ibn Saud's subsequent conquests, inspiring Arabian tribes to join the cause.

The First World War revolutionized the position of the British Empire in the Middle East in general, and around the territories of Ibn Saud in particular. Britain took control of most of the Arab territories that had been part of the Ottoman Empire. Also, the British established a special relationship with Sharif Hussein, who had been the Ottoman-appointed Hashemite ruler of Mecca since 1908. They promised him an independent Arab state stretching from Arabia to what is today the Syrian-Turkish border in exchange for his backing the British war effort against the Ottomans. Accordingly, on October 29, 1916, Sharif Hussein proclaimed himself "King of the Arab Countries."

The new title implied that his rule extended to territories that were already under the jurisdiction of other Arab leaders. New borders needed to be drawn to separate the former Ottoman territories from the rest of Arabia, and in particular to establish where King Hussein's Hijazi territories ended and Ibn Saud's Najdi territories began. Between them were the oasis towns of Khurma and Turaba. The tribes living in these areas owed their allegiance to King Hussein, though Ikhwan missionaries had been actively converting them to Wahhabism.

In the spring of 1919, King Hussein sent his son Abdullah, who would later become the king of Jordan, to occupy Turaba. But the Ikhwan utterly destroyed Abdullah's army; only three of his five hundred infantrymen survived, and Abdullah himself barely escaped in his nightshirt.[11] Ibn Saud retreated from the disputed oases only after the British insisted that these areas remain neutral zones until a border could be drawn.

But informed that Abdullah's brother Faisal was about to be made king of Iraq by the British, Ibn Saud hurried to vanquish what was left of the Rashidi-controlled Jabal Shammar, in north-central Arabia, before Iraq could take possession of it. He led a ten-thousand-man Ikhwan army to Hail, the Rashidi capital, in August 1921.

With the fall of Hail, the Saudis' Rashidi rivals forfeited their independence. Yet all was not lost for the Rashidis. Although Ibn Saud took the Rashidi emir, Muhammad ibn Talal, prisoner, he married his defeated adversary's daughter. Abdullah bin Abdul Aziz, Ibn Saud's son from this marriage with the daughter of his Rashidi rival, would many years later become the crown prince of Saudi Arabia, in 1982.

Demarcating clear boundaries for the new states emerging in the Middle East had now become a matter of urgency, given the success of Wahhabi expansionism. Ibn Saud and his Ikhwan forces needed to be contained.

On November 21, 1922, negotiations began at Uqair to determine the border between Ibn Saud's territories and those of the new Iraq. Heading the negotiations was Sir Percy Cox, who had been promoted to British high commissioner for Mesopotamia. Cox first asked Ibn Saud the extent of his territories in the Najd. But the Saudi leader had never heard of international boundaries, a Western concept; the jurisdiction of Arabian rulers had always been determined by tribal loyalties.

Ibn Saud's map was ambitious. Noting the migration patterns of the Najdi bedouin, he felt that his domain should extend northward to the Euphrates River. The large Shammar tribe, in fact, had regularly migrated from Arabia into the Syrian desert. (In the mid–twentieth century the Shammar could still be found near the Syrian-Iraqi border.) Cox essentially ended the discussion by imposing on Ibn Saud his northern boundary; he simply took out a red pencil and carefully drew the Saudi-Iraqi boundary. Ibn Saud was clearly distressed by the territory he was being forced to sacrifice, so, holding the Saudi leader's hand, Cox said, "My friend, I know exactly how you feel, and for this reason, I give you two-thirds of Kuwait's territory."[12]

Nonetheless, the Ikhwan continued to terrorize the Middle East. They followed the recently completed Hijaz railway (1909), which linked Mecca and Damascus and stretched deeply into Transjordan, reaching the vicinity of Amman. Ikhwan warriors raided a village near Ziza, outside of Amman, killing its entire population. In response, British armored cars and Royal Air Force (RAF) squadrons pursued the Ikhwan, decimating most of the camel-mounted forces in the desert.

But the Ikhwan attacks into Transjordan and village massacres did not let up, even in the face of further RAF retaliation. In 1927, the Ikhwan raided southern Iraq with the apparent goal of sacking the Shiite shrines of Kerbala, as the Wahhabi armies had done more than a century earlier.[13] In this case, however, British airpower contained the Wahhabis.

More Wahhabi Brutality:
The Saudi-Hashemite War

As it turned out, there had been no need to draw a boundary between the territories of King Hussein in the Hijaz and those of Ibn Saud in the Najd.

In March 1924, when the new Turkish Republic (which had replaced the defeated Ottoman Empire) abolished the Ottoman caliphate in Istanbul, King Hussein decided to proclaim himself caliph. Five months later, Ibn Saud convened the Ikhwan in Riyadh and declared a jihad against King Hussein. The war was enthusiastically received by the Ikhwan, who wanted to "purify" the holy cities of Mecca and Medina. On August 24, Ibn Saud's Ikhwan armies entered the Hijazi city of Taif and murdered some four hundred men, women, and children. The British diplomatic record of the Ikhwan assault on Taif establishes the connection between Ikhwan brutality and the Wahhabis' ferocious religious intolerance: "There is evidence that the invaders showed religious fanaticism. They constantly addressed their victims as 'kuffar' (infidels)... and 'mushrikin' (polytheists)."[14] And indeed, Ibn Saud's religious leaders, the *ulama*, had provided the religious justification for the zealous Ikhwan's Saudi invasion.[15]

On October 3, 1924, King Hussein abdicated and was succeeded by his eldest son, Ali. In December, Ibn Saud's forces renewed their offensive in Jeddah and repeated the kind of actions taken by Wahhabi armies one hundred years earlier: destroying religious shrines that were not, in the Wahhabist view, part of the true Islam. Thus, they destroyed the dome of the shrine that supposedly contained the remains of Eve, and banned popular devotions at the site.[16] King Ali abdicated in December 1925, seeking refuge in Iraq.

When the British understood that the balance of power in Arabia had changed, they evacuated King Hussein to Cyprus. They quickly transferred the cities of Maan and Aqaba from the Hijaz to Hashemite Transjordan, where the British had placed King Hussein's son Abdullah in power. (This area, and Maan in particular, would retain ties to Arabia. Many residents practiced Wahhabi Islam, and decades later, during riots in 1989, a good number of these Jordanians actually raised the Saudi flag.)

On December 5, 1924, Ibn Saud entered Mecca, recovering the holy city that his ancestors had ruled more than a century earlier. The remains of the Hashemite regime in the Hijaz crumbled shortly thereafter. A year later, Ibn Saud acquired a new title: King of the Hijaz and the Sultan of Najd and Her Dependencies. It is noteworthy that he adopted the Hashemite title of *king* rather than *emir* or *sultan;* Ibn Saud probably could not have allowed himself to have a title that was inferior to that of his ousted Hashemite rival. He did not, however, use the title *imam*, for he did not want to give the impression that he had any pretensions to make himself caliph.

The Saudi military campaign in Arabia was costly in terms of civilian lives. Said Aburish, a Palestinian journalist, has written an anti-Saudi account describing the brutality of the Ikhwan conquests: "No fewer than 400,000 people were killed or wounded, for the Ikhwan did not take prisoners, but mostly killed the vanquished. Well over a million inhabitants of the territories conquered by Ibn Saud fled to other countries: Iraq, Syria, Egypt, Jordan and Kuwait."[17] For example, non-Wahhabi sections of the Shammar tribe sought asylum in British-administered Iraq after the fall of the Rashidis in their capital of Hail.[18]

Collision Course

Eldon Rutter, an English convert to Islam, recorded his impressions of the first hajj under Wahhabi rule in 1925. He visited the Prophet Muhammad's birthplace in Mecca *(mawlid al-nabi)*, which traditionally had been one of "the objects of pious visitation. [It consisted of] a small square mosque surmounted by a dome and flanked by a short minaret." Rutter noted the changes that the Wahhabis, who fiercely objected to the cult of dead saints, had introduced:

> The Wahhabis, true to their principles, demolished the dome and the minaret of this building and removed the draperies and other ornaments from it. They also prohibited the hereditary custodians from sitting at its doorway to receive alms. Before their occupation of the Holy City, this placid occupation had furnished the principal source of income for a family of sharifs. Now, whenever the *mulid al-nabi* was mentioned in a gathering of Meccans, faces grew grave and here and there among the company a bitter curse would be uttered against the Najdis.[19]

The Ikhwan constituted the "cutting edge" of Wahhabism in the 1920s even more than the nascent Saudi state itself, which still had to recognize the dictates of British power. They were driven by a deep religious conviction, with no sense of the political constraints faced by Ibn Saud. This put the Ikhwan and Ibn Saud on a collision course, for the latter had to practice realpolitik. The emir of nearby Kuwait observed, "When Bin Saud started his religious crusade, the Ikhwan were inflamed with the idea that the days of the Prophet had returned.... When the expansion of Bin Saud's power was checked [by Britain], he was compelled to check his Ikhwan and to renounce his jihad."[20]

Angry that they were not given positions of power in the Hijaz, Ikhwan leaders confronted Ibn Saud with a list of complaints. Negotiations with the British, they argued, involved collaboration with an infidel power. In areas like al-Hasa, where Ibn Saud had annexed large Shiite populations, the Ikhwan claimed that he should "either convert them to Islam [meaning Wahhabism] or massacre them."[21] Of course, these terms were completely unacceptable to Ibn Saud.

The Ikhwan armies clashed with Ibn Saud's other forces in 1929 at the battle of Sibila and were finally defeated. Had the British not repeatedly held the Ikhwan in check by using RAF airpower based in Iraq and Transjordan, it is possible that the Ikhwan would have gained sufficient strength to overwhelm Ibn Saud. In that sense, the British were his secret ally.

But the Ikhwan did not disappear. Ibn Saud subsequently made sure not to rely on one military force, and instead set up competitive military frameworks that held one another in check. He realized, also, that he had to protect the Saudi position as the custodian of Mecca, for at the time of the Saudi campaign in the Hijaz, Ibn Saud was viewed by many in the Islamic world as an "intolerant sectarian."[22] Reflecting Shiite reservations about Wahhabism, Iran's prime minister stated, "The Persian government is unable to stand by and view unconcernedly the actions of a small band of bigots who are engaged in endeavoring to force their opinions on the Mohammedan world."[23]

This distrust of Saudi rule over Islam's holy cities could have been politically devastating for the Saudis. In British India, which at the time was the home of the largest Muslim population in the world, there was talk of internationalizing the Hijaz and its holy cities. Sheikh Muhammad al-Ahmad al-Zawahiri, who would later become the rector of Cairo's al-Azhar mosque, visited Mecca in 1926 as the head of an Egyptian delegation to a

Congress of the Islamic World, convened by Ibn Saud. (Interestingly, al-Zawahiri's grandson, Ayman Muhammad Rabi al-Zawahiri, would rise in the world of militant Egyptian fundamentalism, eventually becoming Osama bin Laden's deputy within the al-Qaeda organization.) Al-Zawahiri, in 1926, described the attitude of the delegates to the Mecca congress: "They were collectively opposed to the government of Ibn Saud and the Wahhabis in the Hijaz, although an unheeded minority among them sided with the Wahhabis. . . . When Ibn Saud's movement had arisen, they turned their hopes toward him, but when they came to Mecca and saw what they saw, he let them down also."[24]

What did al-Zawahiri and the other delegates see in Mecca? Under strict Wahhabi doctrine, it is forbidden to open prayers with "Oh, Prophet of God," for this is viewed as a polytheist tendency. Only God himself is to be addressed in prayer. In Mecca's Grand Mosque, al-Zawahiri witnessed Wahhabis surround an Egyptian and castigate him, saying, "You prayed 'Oh, Prophet of God.'" Terrified, the Egyptian denied having used that formulation. Al-Zawahiri tried to calm down the frightened Egyptian, but then admitted, "I will not deny to you that I concealed in my heart that I, too, open my prayers with 'Oh, Prophet of God.'"[25] In other words, the man who would become one of the most important religious figures in Egypt, and then in the entire Sunni Muslim world, felt too intimidated in Wahhabi-ruled Mecca of 1926 to pray freely as a religious Muslim. Wahhabi excesses clearly could have jeopardized the Saudi position in Mecca by increasing the demand for the internationalization of the holy cities.

For Ibn Saud, more than Saudi sovereignty was at stake. During the Saudi expansion of the previous two decades, the money derived from the Ikhwan and the *zakat* that the tribes paid to Ibn Saud was a major source of the kingdom's revenue. After having occupied Mecca, Ibn Saud also gained the fees from the annual pilgrimages. These substantial resources were not worth risking.

Thus it was imperative for Ibn Saud to clarify just what Wahhabism meant. He was not establishing a new branch of Islam or a new school of Islamic law. If Wahhabism were so perceived, he would undercut his new position as protector of Mecca and Medina. On May 11, 1929, he delivered a speech at his royal palace in Mecca clarifying this point:

They called us the "Wahhabis" and they call our creed a "Wahhabi" one as if it were a special one ... and this is an extremely erroneous allegation that has arisen from the false propaganda launched by those who had ill feelings as well as ill intentions towards the movement. . . . This is the creed which Sheikh al-Islam Muhammad ibn Abdul Wahhab is calling for, and it is our creed. It is a creed built on the oneness of the Almighty God, totally for His sake, and it is divorced from any ills or false innovation.[26]

Ibn Saud succeeded in calming the Islamic world's fears about Wahhabism. This required a careful balancing act between his own Wahhabi clerics and other Muslim states.

Also, to protect the Saudi position, he had to balance Saudi interests with the interests of the major power controlling the foreign policies of most Muslim states at the time: the British Empire.

Wahhabism Contained—Partly

The shape of the modern Middle East finally emerged in the aftermath of the Saudi-Hashemite conflict of the mid-1920s. Before its dissolution, the Ottoman Empire conceded sovereignty over its Asiatic territories, beyond Anatolia, which it had held since 1517. By 1932, Ibn Saud had unified the Hijaz, the Najd, and other Arabian regions, such as the formerly Rashidi areas of Jabal Shammar. Together they became the Kingdom of Saudi Arabia.

Had the Hashemites defeated Ibn Saud, what would have emerged might have been called Hashemite Arabia. Wahhabism would have become a peripheral Islamic movement and not the dominant religious force controlling Mecca and Medina. But the Hashemites lost most of their Hijazi ancestral homeland to the new Wahhabi kingdom. Their remaining footholds were in Maan and Aqaba, which the British tore away from the Hijaz and granted to Transjordan just before the completion of the Saudi conquests. The British were, indeed, key players in the Hashemite-Saudi rivalry. British relations with Ibn Saud had grown out of British India's protectorate system in the Persian Gulf in the late nineteenth century, and the India Office protected these interests in London. At the same time, however, the War Office and the Colonial Office protected the British-Hashemite connection. Each British department, therefore, had its own Arab client.[27]

But even after losing Arabia, the Hashemites did not come up completely empty-handed. Sharif Hussein's son Faisal first took power in Syria, but was driven away by the French. The French had been empowered by the League of Nations to administer the mandate for Syria and Lebanon, which Paris had regarded as part of its sphere of influence since the secret 1916 Sykes-Picot Agreement. After Faisal lost Syria, the British installed him in Baghdad, where he became king of Iraq. (The Hashemites would rule Iraq until 1958, when they were violently overthrown in a military coup.)

The British needed to find another square on the Middle Eastern chessboard for Sharif Hussein's other son, Abdullah. The British imperial planners decided to put him into power in Transjordan. His territory had been part of the British mandate of Palestine and thus had been committed to the Jewish people and the Zionist movement, in accordance with the 1917 Balfour Declaration. But in 1922, the British effectively separated Transjordan from the rest of the Palestine mandate, creating an emirate for Abdullah. Under the Ottomans, this area had been part of the *vilayet* (administrative division) of Damascus, which meant that Abdullah hoped eventually to rule Syria, once French objections to another Hashemite regime could be addressed. (After Transjordan annexed the West Bank following the first Arab-Israeli War, of 1948–49, Abdullah would change his country's name to the Hashemite Kingdom of Jordan. Later Syrian governments would try to reacquire the territory granted to Abdullah, seeing the area as *bilad al-sham*, or part of the original Greater Syria.)

Britain carefully drew the map of its two Hashemite states, in Transjordan and Iraq, so that they would be contiguous through two narrow panhandles. Besides assuring British imperial communications—including oil pipelines—from the Persian Gulf to the Mediterranean, the panhandles were a buffer between Saudi Arabia and Syria. Britain wanted to prevent a recurrence of Wahhabi expansion toward the Syrian desert, such as their eighteenth-century raids on Aleppo and Damascus, or the northward migrations of the Shammar tribe, which had lived in the area near where Transjordan, Iraq, and Syria met.

The new map, therefore, contained the militant spread of Wahhabism. British military power restricted Wahhabism to Arabia, while London established new borders within the former Ottoman territories of the Middle East. One seasoned British diplomat, Laurence Grafftey-Smith, noted that had it not been for the British presence in the Middle East, Wahhabism would have overtaken Transjordan and Iraq.[28]

But even with Arabia's northern borders determined, Wahhabi ideas would proliferate inside of Saudi Arabia and eventually beyond. As much as the Ikhwan had aroused fears in some parts of the Middle East, in the late 1920s the Saudi Wahhabis were admired and imitated in other circles in the Middle East. In Syria, for example, Ibn Saud and his armies were respected because they were untainted by foreign control, having prevented Arabia from falling under direct European rule.[29] They were authentic Muslim warriors.

One enthusiastic backer of Wahhabism at this time was Muhammad Rashid Rida (1865–1935), who along with his mentor, Muhammad Abduh, began the Islamic reform movement in Cairo. Indeed, Rida was perhaps the most important individual to be deeply influenced by Wahhabi doctrines. Like the Wahhabis, he followed the Hanbali school of Islamic law. He felt that the Muslim world had declined because it had veered away from the true Islam of the Salaf (those who accompanied the Prophet Muhammad); thus, only a return to the true Islam could rejuvenate the Islamic world and rid it of political decay and weakness. And also like the Wahhabis, he called for Islamic unity but was critical of Sufism and Shiism, writing that the latter was full of "fairy tales and illegitimate innovations."

True enough, Rida's writings differed in certain important ways from the doctrines of Wahhabism. He carefully limited the applicability of the concept of jihad, stating that offensive wars to spread Islam were lawful only in areas where the peaceful preaching of Islam was prohibited. Rida also stipulated that it was wrong to compel the "people of the book"—Jews and Christians—to become Muslims.[30] Rida regularly published many of these ideas in his journal, al-Manar ("The Beacon"). And even if he did not adopt all of Wahhabism's harsh positions, he familiarized many others with its doctrines.

In any case, his close affinity with Wahhabism was undeniable. In 1908, Rida had been denounced by a mob in Damascus for supporting

Wahhabism.[31] He later wrote a pro-Wahhabi book called *al-Wahhabiyyun*, and in the 1920s he defended the Wahhabi reconquest of the Hijaz, rejecting charges that Wahhabism was heresy. Rida was so outspoken in his pro-Wahhabi positions, in fact, that he aroused his contemporaries' suspicion that he was on the Saudi payroll—a suspicion confirmed when an advisor to Ibn Saud, Sheikh Hafiz Wahba, confessed, "There is money in the affair."[32] According to one source, the Saudi king had paid Rida as much as six thousand pounds sterling. Of course, this would not be the last time that the Saudis supported a major Arab intellectual; as will be seen, Ibn Saud's successors often extended their influence by means of their financial support.

Rida's espousal of Wahhabi doctrines, and his admiration of the Saudis' Muslim warriors, would have profound consequences. For it was Rida's student Hasan al-Banna (1905–49), following his mentor's calls for radical reform, who would emerge as the main figure behind the revival of Islamic fundamentalism in Egypt.[33] (Al-Banna would even take over Rida's journal, *al-Manar*, after the latter's death in 1935.) Despite the collapse of the main Islamic institutions of the defunct Ottoman Empire—the Ottoman caliphate had been abolished in 1924, and European powers governed the main Islamic centers of Cairo, Damascus, and Baghdad—al-Banna did not want Egypt to adopt a secular constitution, but rather he sought to restore Islam as the primary guide for political action. Thus, as his first major step toward reform, in 1928 he founded an organization devoted to reestablishing a political agenda for Islam.

It is no wonder that this student of Muhammad Rashid Rida called his new Islamic organization Ikhwan al-Muslimun ("The Muslim Brotherhood"), since it sought to emulate the pure Islamic society created by the Wahhabi Ikhwan. Nor was it surprising, given those authentic Muslim warriors' record of brutality and intolerance, that the Muslim Brotherhood's credo was a strong message of Islamic militancy: "God is our objective; the Quran is our constitution; the Prophet is our leader; struggle is our way; *and death for the sake of God is the highest of our aspirations* [emphasis added]."[34]

Ultimately, after several decades, the Muslim Brotherhood would form paramilitary units and adopt a strategy of outright violence—terrorist acts, including bombing secular movie theaters, attacking Egypt's non-Muslim minorities (Jews and Christian Copts), and assassinating Egyptian leaders. Branches of the Muslim Brotherhood would emerge in other parts of the Arab world, including Syria, Sudan, and Jordan.

The militant force of Wahhabism, in other words, could not be contained forever, even by British military power. It would spread far, throughout the entire Muslim world.

Chapter 4

Building the
Modern Saudi State

Oil, the Palestine Question, and the Americans

D uring the struggle between Ibn Saud and the Ikhwan, one allegation made against the Saudi leader was that he was collabo-
rating with an "infidel power," meaning Britain. Indeed, in
1915, Ibn Saud had agreed to make the Najd a British quasi-protectorate
and to take a monthly subsidy from the British Indian government. In his
agreement with British India, he undertook "to refrain from entering into
any correspondence, agreement or treaty, with any Foreign Nation or
Power." He even forfeited his right "to grant concessions...to the subjects of any Foreign Power, without the consent of the British government."[1] But he had tried to hide his financial dependence on London,
explaining to his followers that he was only collecting *jizya* from the
British—the taxes that vanquished non-Muslims who lived in Islamic
states traditionally paid.[2]

Ibn Saud had good reason for denying his relationship with Britain,
since Wahhabi doctrine forbade such ties. Sheikh Sulaiman bin Abdillah,
Muhammad ibn Abdul Wahhab's grandson, banned *all* connections with
the *kufar* (infidels)—one could not employ them, consult with them, seek
their advice, or be friends with them.[3] The British understood the sensitivities in Saudi Arabia. Once Ibn Saud took over the Hijaz, where the

holy cities of Islam were situated, London knew that Saudi Arabia could not be a British colonial protectorate like Kuwait, Bahrain, or the Trucial States (which would become the United Arab Emirates). To make the Islamic holy land part of the British Empire would alienate Muslims worldwide. As a result, in 1927, the British dropped the Saudi state's protectorate status and recognized its independence, and a new Anglo-Saudi treaty replaced the earlier 1915 agreement.

But surrounding countries that were once part of the Ottoman Empire were still dependent on the British Empire. Egypt was occupied, while Transjordan and Iraq were British-administered League of Nations mandates. Meanwhile, the Trucial States were reduced to quasi-protectorates of British India.

Essentially free of imperial control, Ibn Saud could concentrate on building the Saudi state—and he never overlooked the centrality of Islam, and Wahhabism in particular, to his cause. Years later, in a meeting with the British minister in Jeddah, F. H. W. Stonehewer-Bird, Ibn Saud explained why he still stressed Islam as the glue of Saudi society:

> The Arabs have two characteristics, Islam and "Arabiyah" [Arabism]. . . . But to be an Arab is not enough. There are still too many primitive and ignorant people among the Arabs for them to form themselves into a great united nation. There remains their Islam: that is something capable of a basis on which to found a nation. That is if it be true Islam uncorrupted by ignorance and innovation.[4]

In speaking of Islam corrupted by "innovation," he was using classic Wahhabi language for many practices found in Sunni Islam. Ibn Saud's words indicated that he still valued Islam (or at least Wahhabism) because it provided the foundations for the Saudi state.

Nevertheless, Ibn Saud had to balance his followers' religious sensitivities against his need to form alliances in order to build up the Saudi kingdom. It became clear, in fact, that the need for international contacts had overtaken his commitment to maintaining a society based on a strict interpretation of Islam.

Money and Oil: Keys to Saudi Power

Once Ibn Saud's Ikhwan were no longer a factor, he could not rely on Wahhabism alone to unify the Arabian tribes. Thus, his payments to the bedouin tribes became more important. The British government had given Ibn Saud about 60,000 pounds sterling per year for this purpose; in the early 1920s, the British subsidy was raised to 100,000 pounds sterling per year.

But holding his enlarged kingdom together became an increasingly expensive proposition. Through his system of grants to the tribes, Ibn Saud had accumulated a sizable entourage of Arabian sheikhs, whom he supported not only with food and lodging but also with automobiles, houses, wives, and money.[5] And he faced continuing military expenses, particularly because of a revolt against Saudi rule in Asir in 1933 and a three-month war against Yemen in 1934.

At the same time, Ibn Saud's revenues were declining sharply because of the Great Depression. By virtue of his control of Mecca, he benefited from the hajj. But the number of pilgrims to Mecca decreased from 130,000 in 1926 to 40,000 in 1931, and accordingly, hajj revenue fell by two-thirds. British officials told their American counterparts in Baghdad that Ibn Saud was "practically bankrupt."[6] A strained national budget meant fewer subsidies for the bedouin—and fewer subsidies meant more difficulty holding the desert kingdom together.

American diplomats stationed in Aden questioned whether Ibn Saud would stay in power. One cable written in August 1933 predicted, "Neither he [Ibn Saud] nor his government can be expected to last much longer without money." Seven months earlier, another cable had stated, "Undoubtedly the Wahhabi family, as it has done twice before, will abandon the Hijaz and retire to Najd, soon after Ibn Saud's death or possibly even earlier."[7]

Only by quickly improving Saudi Arabia's cash flow could these trends be offset. In 1933, therefore, Ibn Saud granted Standard Oil of California (SOCAL) a huge oil concession covering 360,000 square miles in the eastern portion of the Saudi kingdom. SOCAL paid an annual fee of $35,000 and provided loans of $210,000 and $140,000 for the first two years of the concession. It also created a special subsidiary for its Saudi operations: the California-Arabian Standard Oil Company (CASOC). CASOC took on Texaco as a partner in its Saudi concession in 1936. When oil was struck in 1938, Saudi Arabia earned $3.2 million in royalties that year alone.

Saudi oil royalties reached $10 million in 1946, $53 million in 1948, and $212 million in 1952.[8] After the Second World War, CASOC took on two additional partners: Standard Oil of New Jersey and Standard Oil of New York. The expanded subsidiary changed its name to the Arabian-American Oil Company (ARAMCO).

Why did Ibn Saud let American oil companies into his kingdom and not British companies? In the first decade of the century, he had played the British off against the Ottoman Empire, so he had learned how to deal with the great powers. And the United States was clearly competing with Great Britain as an industrial and commercial force. But there were political considerations as well.

Under Ibn Saud's old 1915 quasi-protectorate agreement with the British, he was supposed to favor only British companies. That agreement was, as noted, no longer in force, so legally he was not violating any commitment to London. Still, Ibn Saud knew the British wanted to protect their economic interests within their spheres of political influence—"imperial preference," they called it. In contrast, the Americans spoke only about an "open door" for their corporations, one that would give them an opportunity to compete economically without having to erect a supportive American empire. Allowing SOCAL into Arabia was like poking John Bull in the nose.

Arguably, Ibn Saud's most compelling motivation was economic. After all, SOCAL offered the Saudis five times what the British-dominated Iraq Petroleum Company (IPC) had. Although the IPC consortium included American companies, its largest component was the Anglo-Persian Oil Company, in which the British government was the majority stockholder. (Back in 1914, the first lord of the admiralty, Winston Churchill, had negotiated the British government's purchase of 51 percent of Anglo-Persian in order to safeguard the Royal Navy's access to oil.)[9] Ten years earlier, in 1923, Ibn Saud had granted an oil concession to another British company, Eastern and General Syndicate, but the syndicate defaulted on its payments when its Swiss geologists could not locate petroleum in eastern Arabia. SOCAL, which had struck oil in Bahrain in 1932, seemed a safer bet. Therefore, Ibn Saud overruled other members of the royal family—including his brother Abdullah bin Abdul Rahman, who preferred the IPC to SOCAL[10]—as well as the Wahhabi *ulama*, who had initially objected to the intrusion of non-Muslims into Saudi Arabia.

Of course, as the *ulama* position indicated, Ibn Saud faced domestic problems in making *any* foreign concession, whether to the Americans or the British. One who understood this was former British government official H. St. John Philby, who had become disgruntled with British policy, converted to Islam, and joined Ibn Saud's entourage. (His son, Kim Philby, would later emerge as one of the most notorious spies for the Soviet Union operating in Great Britain.) Philby wrote, "The King, in view of his recent troubles with the more fanatical leaders of the Wahhabi movement, was reluctant to open his country to the infidel."[11] But in the end, American corporate interests won out. (Philby won out as well: SOCAL put him on its payroll.)

Although money was clearly a key factor in Ibn Saud's decision, he never lost sight of geopolitical considerations. The British viewed his kingdom as the successor state of the Ottoman Empire within Arabia and had boxed him in with new borders in the north and east. Ibn Saud, meanwhile, saw Saudi Arabia as the successor state of the Wahhabi empire of the eighteenth century. And a British-dominated concession in Saudi Arabia would require him to accept British hegemony. Having Washington as a partner rather than London might provide him with greater flexibility to realize his ambitions.

Generally, the United States in the 1930s was not a country with long lists of political demands or regional Middle Eastern interests. It did not have an Indian empire with a huge number of Muslim subjects to consider.

In 1932 and 1933, the U.S. State Department and the Saudis negotiated exchanging diplomatic representatives. The Saudis hesitated, fearing that Washington would insist on the right to manumit Saudi slaves—something the British had demanded. But first President Herbert Hoover's acting secretary of state, W. R. Castle Jr., and then President Franklin D. Roosevelt's secretary of state, Cordell Hull, reassured the Saudis that U.S. law did not authorize American consular offices to liberate slaves.[12]

The United States, in short, was a far less intrusive power than Britain. It did not try to impose its values on the Wahhabi kingdom—even its opposition to slavery, which was not abolished in Saudi Arabia until 1962.

The U.S. success in obtaining Saudi Arabian oil rights led to a full-scale Anglo-American rivalry over oil. The British-dominated IPC now made a special effort to grab the remaining Arabian concessions in the smaller sheikhdoms of the Persian Gulf, including the Trucial States, to preempt American advances. In Qatar, for instance, Anglo-Persian tried to claim for the IPC its option on the oil concession there. With the option set to expire in August 1934, the British government concluded that the Qatari leaders were rebuffing IPC advances so they could grant the concession to SOCAL when Anglo-Persian's option lapsed. The British also suspected that Ibn Saud was advising Qatar to go with SOCAL; with the Americans, rather than the British, holding the oil concession, the Saudis would have an easier time annexing Qatar. Great Britain was ever concerned about Saudi efforts to expand.

Ultimately, in 1935, Qatar went with the IPC oil concession, but in exchange, the British had to guarantee Qatar military support in the event of land attack. The chief threat to the Qataris came from Saudi bedouin.

By 1939, the IPC had preempted SOCAL in Dubai, Sharja, Ras al-Khaimah, Abu Dhabi, and Ajman (the sheikhdoms that would form the United Arab Emirates during the 1970s). Another IPC subsidiary obtained oil rights in Oman. Having blocked the Americans in the rest of the Arabian peninsula, the British were now a significant deterrent to Ibn Saud and his dreams of reclaiming his ancestral Wahhabi empire.[13]

Wahhabism, Alive and Well

Although oil revenues were vital for Ibn Saud, he did not ignore the Wahhabi religious establishment, which had legitimized the rule of the Saudi royal family. After putting down the Ikhwan revolt in 1929, the king relied more than ever on the *ulama*. He regularly used this religious leadership for legal rulings—fatwas—on a host of political questions; he had, in fact, obtained a fatwa before suppressing the Ikhwan. And even though the *ulama* had originally objected to the foreign presence that the oil concession brought, he had been sure to approach the religious leaders about permitting American oil exploration.

Ibn Saud consulted the Wahhabi religious leaders on the oil issue well into the 1940s. In 1944, the head of the U.S. legation in Saudi Arabia, William A. Eddy, issued a report about "a venerable and unreconstructed Wahhabi leader and fanatic" named Sheikh Abu Bahz, who was from an area near the remote Empty Quarter (Rub al-Khali), the large, landlocked region south of the Najd. Abu Bahz was openly preaching that Ibn Saud had betrayed his trust "by selling the land to the *Agnabi* [foreigners]." He was referring, apparently, to Americans who were engaged in an agricultural development project. Ibn Saud thereupon summoned Abu Bahz to Riyadh, where they both appeared before the *ulama*. Abu Bahz rephrased his charge, stating that Ibn Saud had put land and people "into [the] bondage of unbelievers." The king turned to the *ulama*, asking whether the Prophet Muhammad had employed Christians and other "people of the book," and whether, on that basis, he could employ foreign experts "to increase the material resources of the land, and to extract for our benefit the metals, oil, and water placed by Allah beneath our land." The *ulama* ruled that Ibn Saud was right and Abu Bahz was wrong.[14]

Ibn Saud won in that instance—and he had probably been certain that the *ulama* would support him. Nevertheless, Eddy's report underscored the critical role that Wahhabi religious attitudes played in Saudi Arabia. A Saudi could openly challenge the king's authority when it appeared that he had failed to adhere to Wahhabi principles. No Saudi king could rule successfully without the backing of the *ulama*.

The *ulama* also exercised a monopoly over educational and religious policies, ensuring that Saudis learned, and followed, Wahhabi principles and values.[15] Thus, despite the American commercial "incursions" into Saudi Arabia, Wahhabism was alive and well. Eddy felt that his report illustrated "the reactionary xenophobia and religious fanaticism" of remote tribal leaders in Saudi Arabia.[16] But at least during the 1930s and 1940s, that fanaticism was not crossing state borders.

Saudi Arabia and the Struggle for Palestine

Unquestionably, as Ibn Saud's resources grew, he felt more confident about protecting Saudi Arabia's sovereignty. And since Saudi Arabia was looking more like a permanent state than a temporary tribal federation, it was increasingly expected to take a leading role in Middle Eastern affairs.

That meant that Ibn Saud would get drawn into the question of the establishment of a Jewish state in the British mandate of Palestine.

Until the 1930s, Palestine had been far more an issue for the Hashemites than for the Saudis. After all, toward the end of the First World War, the British had made seemingly conflicting commitments: to Sharif Hussein, to establish a great Arab state over the Asiatic territories of the Ottoman Empire (1915); to the French, to divide these same territories into British and French spheres of influence (1916); and to the Zionist movement, to establish a national home for the Jewish people in Palestine (1917). The onus to rectify these different British positions fell on the Hashemites, not on the Saudis.

Sharif Hussein's son Faisal engaged the Zionist movement directly, striking the Faisal-Weizmann Agreement (1919). Under this agreement, the Arab national movement would support a Jewish national home in Palestine, and in exchange, the Zionist movement would back a great Arab state stretching over the remaining Arab territories of Asiatic Turkey (Syria, Iraq, and Arabia). But when the Hashemites felt double-crossed by the contradictory British commitments, Sharif Hussein refused to sign a new British-Hijazi treaty, because it would have recognized the legality of former Ottoman territories—Syria, Iraq, and Palestine—as British- and French-administered League of Nations mandates.

During the 1930s, Ibn Saud was reluctantly drawn into the Palestine question. Palestinian Arabs launched their "Great Revolt" in 1936, trying to motivate the Arab states to intervene with Great Britain on their behalf. After receiving appeals from leading Palestinians like Hajj Amin al-Husseini, the Jerusalem mufti, Ibn Saud turned to the British—not to lobby on behalf of the Palestinian Arabs but to get advice on how to avoid interfering in an affair outside his political jurisdiction.

The mufti of Jerusalem sent out invitations in 1931 for an Islamic congress in Jerusalem. But because the Saudis were suspicious of the mufti, their delegation arrived after the congress was over.[17] In 1939, Saudi Arabia was invited to send a delegation to London, along with Egypt, Yemen, Iraq, and Transjordan, to discuss possible solutions to the Palestine issue. This time the Saudis attended, but clearly they were not taking a lead role.

A year earlier, in correspondence with President Roosevelt, Ibn Saud had begun to articulate his position against Jewish statehood. It particularly troubled him that the first proposals for the partition of the British mandate of Palestine, such as the 1937 Peel Commission Report, assigned Arab portions of Palestine to his old Hijazi rivals, the Hashemites.[18]

At one point, the British tried to make Ibn Saud part of the solution to the Palestine problem. In May 1941, Prime Minister Winston Churchill considered giving the Saudi king "general overlordship of Iraq and Transjordan." Churchill, who believed that Ibn Saud was "the greatest living Arab," envisioned the creation of "an independent Jewish unit in the Arab caliphate."[19] Less than two decades earlier, the Wahhabis had been seen as unfit to control the holy cities of Mecca and Medina, and now, remarkably, the British were pushing the head of that Islamic sect as the leading candidate to head a new "Arab caliphate." Ibn Saud was now the focal point in many of the initiatives for resolving the Palestine question that Britain and others proposed.

What was Ibn Saud's view of this issue? In 1943, meeting on a confidential basis with Britain's top representative to his kingdom, F. H. W. Stonehewer-Bird, he articulated his ambivalence toward Arab leaders who called for Arab solidarity on the Palestine issue:

> We have talked about Palestine. I, an Arab, tell you that the Arabs created the Palestine problem. Who but the Arabs called for their conferences, raised their clamor and preached and prated about Palestine? And who were these Arabs? There were three types: the man who sought to make a worldly reputation for himself and win fame in men's mouths; the adventurer who had no stake in Palestine and Syria; and the greedy man who sought to enrich himself. Let the Arabs of each country look to the improvement of their own country first.[20]

These candid thoughts did not mean that Ibn Saud had no strong ideological views on the Palestine question. In his correspondence with President Roosevelt, he had rejected Jewish historical claims to Palestine. He asserted many of these same positions in his February 1945 meeting with Roosevelt aboard the USS *Quincy* in Egypt's Great Bitter Lake. The Roosevelt administration was concerned that the Second World War had depleted America's oil resources in Texas and Oklahoma; anticipating that the Middle East would henceforth be the center of world oil, the administration decided that the United States had to increase its dealings with Ibn Saud, even on the sensitive issue of Palestine.

Privately, Ibn Saud harbored strong anti-Jewish sentiments and could not be helpful diplomatically. He told ARAMCO executives in early 1947 that while the Koran called on Muslims to respect Christians, according to his interpretation the same did not apply to Jews.[21] But Wahhabi ideological predispositions were one thing; national interests were another matter altogether.

The real test of Ibn Saud's policy on Palestine came in the aftermath of the United Nations Resolution 181 (II). On November 29, 1947, the UN General Assembly voted to recommend the partition of Palestine and the creation of a Jewish state. Though the resolution was not binding international law, it provided tremendous international backing for, and legitimacy to, the establishment of a Jewish state.

The United States supported the resolution; the British abstained. The U.S. State Department's professional assessment was that Saudi Arabia would retaliate against America for supporting the UN partition resolution, perhaps by revoking the great American oil concession.

At the time, U.S. companies were building the Trans-Arabian Pipeline (TAPLINE) to carry Saudi oil to the eastern Mediterranean, where it would be shipped to America's European allies. The United States felt that the availability of Saudi Arabian oil would be a key factor in their postwar recovery and ability to resist Soviet Communism.

The moment of truth for the United States regarding a Saudi oil cut-off came on December 3, 1947, four days after the UN vote. Ibn Saud called J. Rives Childs, the head of the U.S. diplomatic mission to Riyadh, for an audience. Dramatically, the king dismissed both the American and Saudi official interpreters, perhaps to emphasize the gravity of the situation, and one of his royal advisors was forced to translate.

Ibn Saud began by trying to reassure his American guest: "Although we differ enormously on the question of Palestine, . . . we still have our own mutual interests and friendship to safeguard." He did not attempt to get the United States to alter its position; instead he focused on whether he could rely on the Americans for his security, including the provision of weapons. He feared that there was an Anglo-American secret understanding by which Saudi Arabia was recognized as being within a British sphere of political influence.[22] Childs could not answer on the spot; he would have to cable Washington for instructions.

In a second meeting with Childs the next day, Ibn Saud explained the connection between the Palestine question and his probing about future American military assistance. He was facing new pressures from his old Hashemite rivals in Transjordan and Iraq. Baghdad's purpose, he said, was to break "economic relations between Saudi Arabia and the United States, particularly the oil concessions." The Saudi king added:

> I shall henceforth be subject to ever greater pressure in this respect extending to demands that I cancel the oil concessions. The crucial question for me is to know whether and to what extent I may count on United States aid in enabling me to resist any incursion from Iraq or Trans-Jordan which might be the consequence of my failure to yield to the pressure being put upon me to come into open economic conflict with the United States.[23]

America's acting secretary of state, Robert Lovett, cabled Childs to tell Ibn Saud that the United States would act through the UN to support the territorial integrity and political independence of Saudi Arabia.[24] The response must have disappointed Ibn Saud, for he had no patience for a UN role in his security; two years later he would complain to Childs that if he were invaded in the Hijaz, the U.S. government would refer the matter to the UN, which would do nothing.[25]

It is unclear whether Ibn Saud really feared a Hashemite invasion or simply was nurturing his own territorial ambitions. Certainly, he still harbored hopes of recovering the Transjordanian cities of Aqaba and Maan, which the British had taken away from the Hijaz just before the Saudis defeated the Hashemites in 1925. It was one thing to respect the border between Saudi Arabia and British-controlled Transjordan; it was quite another to respect an independent Transjordanian kingdom under the Hashemites.

Yet Ibn Saud's fears of Hashemite encirclement, or even invasion, could also have resulted from Hashemite doubts about whether a Wahhabi regime in the Hijaz would endure. Prince Talal of Transjordan had told British diplomats, "While it is unlikely that [the] Hashemite house, particularly King Abdullah, would ever attempt any armed action…it is clear that [the] Muslim world would not continue to sanction [the] Wahabis as guardian of [the] Holy places in [the] Hedjaz."[26]

The military struggle over Palestine that followed the UN vote probably made matters worse for Ibn Saud. The British withdrew from Palestine, and Israel declared independence on May 15, 1948, prompting the armies of seven Arab states to invade the new Jewish state. The Egyptian army, in a two-pronged attack, advanced along the coast to Ashdod in the west and to the southern outskirts of Jerusalem in the east. Meanwhile, Transjordan's Arab Legion aimed to cut off Jerusalem from the coastal plain at Latrun and occupied the eastern half of Jerusalem, including the Old City. Some units of the Arab Legion were still commanded by British officers. Egypt, Iraq, and Transjordan all benefited from British arms and training.

Meanwhile, Syrian and Lebanese forces pressed Israel from the north. One-third of the Iraqi army crossed Transjordan, occupied western Samaria (located in what is today called the "West Bank," on the Jordan River), and, driving toward Rosh Ha'ayin, nearly reached the Mediterranean Sea. The Iraqi force, which numbered about ten thousand soldiers, came close to cutting the nascent state of Israel in two.

The Arab states scrambled for what they expected to be the remains of the British mandate of Palestine. Iraq eyed Haifa, the Mediterranean outlet of the IPC pipeline. The Syrians claimed the waters of the Sea of Galilee. Egypt wanted a land bridge from Sinai to the Fertile Crescent through the southern Negev. And Transjordan sought the part of Palestine designed for the Palestinian Arabs as a first step in establishing its long-term goal of a Greater Syria.

Saudi Arabia's interests were less well defined, and its military contribution to the Arab war effort was negligible. The Ikhwan armies of thirty years earlier, which had terrorized the frontiers of Iraq and Transjordan, were nowhere to be found. Just two companies of Saudi troops took part in the war effort;[27] fighting under Egyptian command, they were concentrated along the coastal plain in the area of Gaza, Ashkelon, and Ashdod.[28] The Saudis' commander was an ex-Hijazi policeman who, upon receiving his mission to lead the Saudi troops, rushed "in a panic" to the commander of the British military mission in Saudi Arabia and asked for instructions in military strategy.[29]

If they did not take an active role in the war, the Saudis publicly articulated a stunning position on the Palestine question. In a speech in Mecca in early 1949, the Saudi minister of foreign affairs, Prince Faisal, unleashed his rage primarily against the West and the Soviets. Extracts of his speech were printed in the official Saudi gazette, *Umm al-Qura*. Faisal explained, "The Arab world appeared to be under the misapprehension that they were fighting the Jews. . . . We are now not fighting the Jews but the tyrannical imperialist states whose greedy aims are to captivate the nations of the world in order to enslave and exploit the weak."[30] British ambassador A. C. Trott was astounded by Faisal's remarks and prepared a high-level communication for Britain's foreign secretary, Ernest Bevin.[31] He called Faisal's speech "deplorable"; given the Western powers' past generosity to the Saudis, he was stunned that the prince had charged, "The true enemies of the Arabs in Palestine are not the Jews . . . but the imperialist states of Great Britain, the United States of America, and the Soviet Union."

By the end of 1949, the nascent Israel Defense Forces had beaten back most of the Arab armies, but the Hashemite armies of Transjordan, with the help of their allies from Hashemite Iraq, had made substantial territorial gains. In 1950, Transjordan annexed the territories of the West Bank that had come under its military control, as well as East Jerusalem, including the Old City. Subsequently, Transjordan changed its name to the Hashemite Kingdom of Jordan. The Arab states, including Saudi Arabia, refused to recognize the sovereignty of the Hashemites in these territories. Only Great Britain and Pakistan recognized the annexation, and even London stipulated that this recognition did not cover East Jerusalem.

Ibn Saud had to be concerned about the Hashemites. Both Hashemite states, which had received British arms and training, had unquestionably demonstrated their military power. If the Iraqis could project their power hundreds of miles westward in a war with Israel, they probably could move deeply into Saudi territory as well. Moreover, Jordan's King Abdullah made clear that he had not abandoned his claim to the Hijaz. In fact, in 1949, there had been talk of Syria's unifying with Hashemite Iraq, which would have increased the power and influence of the Hashemite states to Saudi Arabia's north. And the British continued to support the Hashemites,

particularly after the Saudis made new territorial claims in the coastal Trucial States, which threatened British oil companies' concessionary rights.
British officials proposed to send Arab Legion personnel from Jordan to
form the nucleus of a new military force for the Trucial States.

Ibn Saud sensed that with the British backing the Hashemites, he had
good reason to fear Hashemite encirclement.[32] When, in March 1950,
America's assistant secretary of state for Near Eastern affairs, George
McGhee, visited Riyadh, Ibn Saud revealed why he thought the British
were opposing him: the Saudi oil concession. "Although the British had
been given first refusal of the oil," he said, "they had always resented the
fact that the concession had been given to America." He stated that his
"difficulties with the British had begun from that time."[33]

For Ibn Saud, oil was tied to security. After all, those were the original rules of British India's protectorate agreements with the Arabian
sheikhs: they would receive British protection in exchange for not granting economic concessions to other European powers. But since 1927, Ibn
Saud had had no formal agreement with the British, and because he had
not granted them Saudi oil, he could not rely on them for protection.

In light of the Anglo-Hashemite threat, Ibn Saud wanted something
from the United States. Two of Ibn Saud's advisors privately approached
Assistant Secretary of State McGhee to state explicitly what the aging
Saudi king was seeking: a formal treaty of alliance with the United States.[34]

"The Hard Crust"

The Saudis had been schooled in the rules of the British Empire. Early in
the century, the British had tied access to oil to their military strength as an
imperial power. British oil companies like Anglo-Persian and the IPC were
even partly owned by the British government. The United States, in contrast, wanted a straight business arrangement with no imperial trappings—
it wanted American oil companies to be able to operate freely in Saudi
Arabia, not any new formal security commitments. The American oil companies that owned ARAMCO were private firms; the U.S. government was
not a shareholder.

Though Ibn Saud was looking for something that the United States
was not prepared to deliver—a formal defense treaty—Washington
agreed to step up its military presence in Saudi Arabia. President Harry

Truman sent a letter to Ibn Saud on October 31, 1950, reaffirming "U.S. interest in the preservation of the independence and territorial integrity of Saudi Arabia."[35] America also explored expanding its training missions for the Saudi armed forces. The growing American military and economic role in Saudi Arabia created new domestic problems for Ibn Saud, for Saudi Arabia was still a very traditional country. True, Ibn Saud had proven that he was a pragmatic state builder and not a fierce ideologue. But while Wahhabism's influence on Saudi policymaking had been contained, it was still very much a part of Saudi life. The British embassy's annual review for 1950 concluded, "The hard crust of the discipline of Wahabi morality was still almost entirely intact." The report stressed that beneath the veneer of modernity—"the incidentals of Western civilization," such as Cadillacs, Coca-Cola, and football—Western ideals had not replaced the earlier Saudi outlook.[36]

Any American military presence clearly had to take these sensibilities into account. Perhaps it was because of such sensibilities that as the Cold War began, the United States did not make full use of the U.S. Army airfield at Dhahran, which had been built after the Americans reached an agreement with Ibn Saud in August 1945. The United States kept Dhahran as a transport base rather than integrate it into the worldwide network of the Strategic Air Command, the intercontinental-range bombers used to encircle the Soviet Union.

For many Saudis, the increased presence of Americans meant a proliferation of infidels. Americans organized their own religious services, including at the Dhahran Air Base, which were attended by ARAMCO and U.S. Air Force personnel. The Saudis objected. They believed that one American officer was engaged in Christian missionary activity. Remarkably, their reservations applied not only to Christian services in the Islamic holy region—the Hijaz—but to Christianity publicly observed *anywhere* in the Saudi kingdom.[37]

Prince Faisal explained to Ambassador J. Rives Childs that Ibn Saud was already perceived as someone who had gone too far in accommodating the Americans. He was "under very great pressure" to maintain the prohibition against any public religious services, except for those of "the four Orthodox Sunni sects." Faisal believed that the United States simply did not understand the extent of Saudi feelings on this issue.[38] The pressure probably came from the Wahhabi religious establishment, for whom the public practice of Christianity was illegal. And the pressure, of course, was not new.

Wahhabism demonstrated its continuing impact on Saudi Arabia's internal policies.[39] Twenty years earlier, American diplomats had had to reassure the Saudis that U.S. diplomatic personnel would not free slaves. And now, equally embarrassing, American diplomats had to assuage the Saudis' concern about the practice of Christianity by U.S. citizens.

The Saudi king was not much interested, however, preferring to focus on consolidating his territorial gains and building a stable new Saudi kingdom.

A New Era

Ibn Saud died in 1953. He had fathered forty-five sons from twenty-two different wives. The new king was his second son, Saud; the firstborn son, Turki, had died from influenza in 1919. Ibn Saud's fourth son, Faisal, became the new crown prince. (Ibn Saud's third son had also died.)

King Saud struggled to hold together his father's legacy. He terminated the American air base at Dhahran in 1962, sought to placate Arab radicalism in the late 1950s, and plunged his country's finances into disarray. It would take until the 1960s, and the leadership of a new and more self-confident Saudi leader, for the influence of Wahhabism to be felt again on the international scene.

Chapter 5

Reactivating Wahhabism

Saudi Arabia returned to its Wahhabi roots in 1964 when the third Saudi king, Faisal bin Abdul Aziz, assumed the throne after King Saud, his older brother, was deposed. Faisal's mother, Tarfa Al al-Sheikh, was a direct descendant of Wahhabism's eighteenth-century founder, Muhammad ibn Abdul Wahhab. Tarfa died when Faisal was just six years old, in 1912, so the prince was raised in the home of his maternal grandfather—who, born in 1849, could recall the earlier Saudi-Wahhabi state and was himself a major Wahhabi scholar who had been Ibn Saud's childhood tutor.[1]

In Arabian society, there were no established rules or regulations regarding the succession of tribal leaders; rather, according to tradition, rule over the tribe passed "to the oldest and most accepted male relative."[2] Apparently, Ibn Saud had stipulated on his deathbed that the succession of Saudi kings should go to the "eldest able son."[3] His use of the word "able" injected a great deal of subjectivity into the process of picking kings. And King Saud's struggles as the successor to his father had made him vulnerable.

In fact, the Saudi religious leadership, the *ulama*, had been instrumental in deposing King Saud and making Faisal the monarch. The *ulama* had attacked Saud for "his habits of life which fell below the position of one

whose title included the appellation Imam al Muslimin." Faisal, in contrast, was very close to the *ulama*. True, in 1962, when he was still crown
prince, he had issued a ten-point reform program that could have placed
him at odds with the more conservative elements of Saudi society. But like
his father before him, Faisal was a shrewd maneuverer, and he knew how
to pursue his own programs without alienating the ruling Wahhabi elite.
As one British Foreign Office analyst later commented on the progress of
the reforms, Faisal would "occasionally outmaneuver the *ulama* but avoid
a head-on clash with them."[4]

And so, on March 30, 1964, after the *ulama* had challenged King Saud's
authority, Faisal received King Saud's powers of government and his privi-
leges of kingship.[5] On October 28, some sixty-five leading members of the
ulama met at the house of the grand mufti of Saudi Arabia, Muhammad
ibn Ibrahim Al al-Sheikh, and subsequently joined one hundred princes in
deciding that King Saud should abdicate. Saud was deposed on November 2, 1964, and Faisal became king. In 1965, the royal family decided that
Faisal's brother Khalid would become crown prince, with another brother,
Fahd, second in line to inherit the throne.[6]

One Arab correspondent at the time noted, "The two key elements in
the government of Saudi Arabia were firstly the King, his Crown Prince
and the administration, and secondly the Higher Council, composed of
the princes and the *Ulama*. When the first fails to operate properly, the
second automatically steps in to correct the situation."[7]

Faisal would never forget the role the *ulama* had played in his rise to
power. They were still very much part of the Saudi king's power base,[8] and
therefore he would have to provide the old Wahhabi establishment a major
role in Saudi affairs. But he would have to balance other considerations as
well. His first real test came with Saudi Arabia's struggle against the Arab
nationalist movement inspired by Egypt's Nasser, which forced King Faisal
to become more active abroad. In the end, however, this struggle would
only strengthen the relationship between Wahhabism and the Saudi state.

The Muslim World League:
Spreading Wahhabism Internationally

Gamal Abdel Nasser, the president of Egypt, first rose to power in 1952
as part of the "Free Officers" coup against King Farouk. He emerged from

his 1956 confrontation with England, France, and ultimately Israel over the Suez Canal as the unchallenged leader of Arab nationalism. Another Arab kingdom fell in 1958, when a military coup overthrew the Hashemite monarchy in Iraq. The forces supporting Nasser seemed ascendant as new Arab military regimes toppled the older Arab monarchies.

In the late 1950s, Nasser tried to expand his influence in the Arab world by unifying Egypt and Syria within a new entity, the United Arab Republic (UAR). After Syria seceded from the UAR in 1961, he turned his attention to the Arabian peninsula. Specifically, he focused on Yemen, where he dispatched an Egyptian expeditionary army to support the anti-monarchical forces in that country's civil war. Since the Saudis supported Yemen's royalists, an Egyptian-Saudi clash ensued. The Egyptian air force, using Soviet-supplied Ilyushin bombers, began striking Saudi border towns like Najran in December 1962.

But the Egyptian threat was not just external, for some Saudis rallied behind the cause of Nasserism. From 1958 to 1964, some Saudi princes, led by Prince Talal bin Abdul Aziz, voiced support for Nasser's ideology of a distinctively Arab socialism. This threatened the very foundations of the Saudi state. A Saudi pilot defected to Cairo in late 1962. Further signs of unrest and subversion came in 1965 and 1966, especially in the oil-producing areas. By 1969, the Saudi government had uncovered a pro-Nasserist plot within the Saudi armed forces involving twenty-eight army officers, thirty-four air force officers, nine other military personnel, and twenty-seven civilians.[9]

There was a global dimension to this struggle as well. Since the beginning of the Cold War, the United States had succeeded in ringing the Soviet Union with pro-American alliances: the North Atlantic Treaty Organization (NATO) in Europe, the Central Treaty Organization (CENTO) along the northern tier of the Middle East and South Asia, and the Southeast Asia Treaty Organization (SEATO) in Asia. Moscow backed the spread of Nasserism in order to skip over the Middle East's pro-American northern tier—Turkey, Iran, and Pakistan—and penetrate the Arab world.

Even before he became king, Faisal turned to Islam as a counterweight to Nasser's Arab socialism. The struggle between the two leaders became an Arab cold war, pitting the new Arab republics against the older Arab kingdoms. The Saudi government sponsored an international Islamic conference in Mecca in 1962 to devise a new Islamic strategy. On May 18, 1962, at the conference's close, 111 *ulama* and religious dignitaries established the Muslim World League, an international organization dedicated to the spread of Islam.[10] This new organization, dedicated to fostering pan-Islamic solidarity, would revive Saudi Wahhabism and spread it globally, for it sought not only to convert Christians to Islam but also to convince Muslims to adopt Wahhabism.

The Muslim World League, headquartered in Mecca, was under complete Saudi control. Senior Saudi religious leaders formed its Constituent Council, thus assuring a Wahhabi orientation for the organization's missionary activities. The grand mufti of Saudi Arabia, Sheikh Muhammad ibn Ibrahim Al al-Sheikh, served as president of the council. One of the Muslim World League's subsequent secretaries-general was Sheikh Muhammad Ali al-Harkan, a former Saudi minister of justice who, as will be seen, later would effectively fill the role of Saudi Arabia's grand mufti.

The Muslim World League was extremely effective in promoting Islam—and Wahhabism, in particular. The organization dispatched religious missionaries around the world, raised money to build mosques, and distributed the works of Ibn Taymiyya and Muhammad ibn Abdul Wahhab. This led one specialist on modern Islam to argue that the Muslim World League was an effort "to 'Wahhabize' Islam worldwide."[11]

And over the years, the Saudi leadership only consolidated its control of the Muslim World League. Some of the organization's secretaries-general became ministers in the Saudi government. Abdullah Umar Nasif, al-Harkan's successor as secretary-general, acknowledged in the early 1980s that "99 per cent of the [Muslim World League's] financing" came from the Saudi kingdom.[12] The league exerted a great deal of influence even beyond its own projects, as it often recommended to wealthy Saudis proposals that merited their support. That way, funds could move directly from Saudi contributors to Islamic groups without having to go through the Muslim World League's bank accounts.

It is no surprise, then, that the Muslim World League never stopped serving the interests of the Saudi state. The league was essentially a non-governmental mouthpiece for the Saudi kingdom, a means of protecting the Islamic world from radical alien ideologies. During the 1960s, that meant pan-Arabism and Nasserism. So, for example, in 1966 the

Muslim World League condemned Egypt's persecution of the Muslim Brotherhood.[13]

The Wahhabi Clerics Seize More Control

Under King Faisal, the Saudi government and the Wahhabi elite developed a close symbiotic relationship. When he ascended to the throne, he knew he had to maintain that relationship in order to remain in power. That meant giving the Wahhabi clerics their share of control over the expanding Saudi government.

Until 1951, the Saudi government under Ibn Saud had only three ministries: foreign affairs, finance, and defense. From 1951 to 1954, six new ministries were added. But then from 1960 through 1975, a further fourteen ministries were added. Faisal needed to find a formula to give the *ulama* a role in governance that would appease them but not undermine the supremacy of the Saudi royal family.[14]

Thus, the Wahhabi religious leaders were not given control over any of the three most important ministries—the original three under Ibn Saud—but several other ministries became their exclusive province. They naturally took control of the Ministry of Pilgrimage and Awqaf (religious endowments).[15] Then, in 1970, King Faisal created the Ministry of Justice and appointed Sheikh Muhammad Ali al-Harkan as its first minister. In effect, al-Harkan replaced the grand mufti; Sheikh Muhammad had died in 1969, and Faisal had never appointed a successor. In 1975, al-Harkan would be replaced by Sheikh Ibrahim bin Muhammad, a member of the Al al-Sheikh family and hence a descendant of ibn Abdul Wahhab.[16]

Most important, in 1963, Faisal gave the Wahhabi religious leaders control over Saudi education. Of all the moves to install the Wahhabis in the seat of power, this decision would have the most far-reaching consequences.

Prince Fahd, Faisal's close ally, had headed the Ministry of Education from its establishment in 1953 until 1960, when a member of the Al al-Sheikh family replaced him. When he assumed power, King Faisal left the Ministry of Education in the hands of the *ulama* and turned the Interior Ministry over to Fahd.[17] Even after further reorganization in the 1970s, the *ulama* retained control over Saudi universities and other places of higher education. And at least one university remained under the direct jurisdiction of the grand mufti and chief *qadi:* the Islamic University of Medina.

(The university's vice president during the early 1970s was Sheikh Abdul Aziz bin Baz, who would, during the 1990s, be appointed grand mufti.)

The entire generation that was born during the 1960s and came of age during the 1980s grew up on Wahhabi doctrines. Despite the *ulama*'s special responsibility for university education, the Education Ministry as a whole became a stronghold of religiously conservative bureaucrats. The Saudi government also installed backers of the Muslim Brotherhood at all levels of education.[18] The curriculum used in schools focused on Islamic and Arabic studies, helping to preserve the grip of Wahhabism on Saudi society.[19]

Under King Faisal, the *ulama* extended their influence over society through other institutions. The Directorate of Religious Research, Islamic Legal Rulings, Islamic Propagation, and Guidance supplied the contents of Friday sermons in Saudi mosques, and it published and distributed the books of Muhammad ibn Abdul Wahhab. Moreover, the *ulama*-controlled Committee for Commanding Good and Forbidding Evil, with its *mutawain*, or religious police, scrutinized behavior in public areas, ensuring that men and women did not mingle, that their attire was consistent with "public morality," and that public prayers were attended. Back in the 1930s, Ibn Saud had stripped the *mutawain* of its power to make arrests; it could only report to the police violations of religious practice. This had led to a surprising degree of laxity in the way Wahhabism was practiced in the Hijaz, particularly as radios, gramophones, and cigarettes proliferated.[20] Thus, beginning under Faisal, the Wahhabi elites aggressively countered the move away from traditional Wahhabi practices.[21]

Even when, during the 1970s, the *ulama* sacrificed some governmental powers to the state bureaucracy, the Wahhabi religious establishment still played a vital role in Saudi Arabia. In 1975, the Saudis named a new head of higher education, Hasan bin Abdullah Al al-Sheikh—another descendant of Muhammad ibn Abdul Wahhab.[22] Religious courses were made mandatory in even the more secularly oriented universities.[23] Three of Saudi Arabia's six main universities either were religious institutions or emphasized religious instruction.

The Saudi religious leadership's control of the education system gave Wahhabist doctrine incredible reach and influence. During the quarter cen-

tury from the mid-1960s through the end of the 1980s, the number of students in Saudi universities exploded. In 1965, there were 3,625 university
students throughout the Saudi kingdom; by 1986, the number had reached
113,529.[24] Yet relatively few Saudis went off to study at Western universities. In the mid-1980s, the number of foreign Saudi students reached a peak
of 12,500; the figure would taper off to 3,554 by 1990 and stay at that level
for the rest of the decade.[25] Thirty percent of Saudi students in Saudi universities majored in Islamic studies, while the other 70 percent devoted an
average of a third of their coursework to religious study.[26]

Consequently, the Wahhabi religious leaders exercised an enormous
degree of control over generations of young Saudis. Such control had
profound effects in Saudi Arabia. In 1992, one Saudi academic at Imam
Muhammad bin Saud University estimated that 65 percent of the Saudi
population wanted the country to be run along more traditional Islamic
lines.[27]

Also, because of its alliance with the Saudi government, the Wahhabi
establishment had a means of spreading its religious doctrine beyond Saudi
borders. In addition to the Muslim World League, there was the World
Assembly of Muslim Youth (WAMY), which was established under the
Ministry of Education in 1972 to propagate *tawhid*, the belief in the oneness of God, the central Islamic tenet that Wahhabism stressed.[28] WAMY
operated like a semigovernmental arm, protected by Saudi embassies and
consulates abroad.[29] Over the years, WAMY came to be perceived as a
much more hard-line organization than the Muslim World League.[30]

"Wahhabism Should Be Exported"

In short, King Faisal had renewed his predecessors' contract with the
descendants of Muhammad ibn Abdul Wahhab. The Saudi royal family
and the Wahhabi establishment had struck a political bargain: the latter
would back Saudi policies in fields that were not under its jurisdiction,
while the former would give the religious leaders free rein in—and funding for—its own ministries and institutions.

Before his death in 1969, the grand mufti, Muhammad ibn Ibrahim Al
al-Sheikh, had been one of Faisal's closest advisors. Like Faisal a descendant of ibn Abdul Wahhab, Sheikh Muhammad had not shied away from
controversy and had been quite willing to intervene in some of the most

sensitive struggles between Saud and Faisal. In one instance, on December 19, 1963, he had delivered an ultimatum to King Saud: withdraw Saudi troops that had set up around the Nasariyah Palace to threaten Faisal, or face a withdrawal of religious support.[31] The troops were withdrawn. Sheikh Muhammad had also advocated that the Saudis assume a more active role in the Middle East. Not long before his death, he stated, "Saudi Arabia should lead the Arab world and the ideology of Wahhabism should be exported."[32]

In its annual review for 1969, the British embassy in Jeddah concluded that the role of the *ulama* had not declined despite King Faisal's initial enthusiasm for greater internal reform. The embassy report bluntly noted, "The influence of the religious leaders (the *ulama*) and in particular the Grand Mufti (until his death in December) has not been eroded despite the widespread distaste, even among devout Saudis, for the bigotry they represent."[33] Wahhabi attitudes may not have been popular, but the *ulama* still exercised considerable influence.

Although Faisal did not name a permanent grand mufti to replace Sheikh Muhammad when he died in December 1969, the king instituted various advisory bodies to provide the *ulama* with an enhanced consultative role. In 1971, he created the Council of Senior Ulama and made Sheikh Abdul Aziz bin Baz its head (though the king himself determined the membership of this council and of a Standing Committee on Islamic Legal Rulings).

Sheikh bin Baz, a blind Wahhabi cleric who was born in Riyadh in 1909, would over the next two decades become one of the most significant religious authorities in the Saudi kingdom. Appointed the deputy rector of the new Islamic University of Medina in 1961, he was promoted to rector eight years later. Sheikh bin Baz was among the twelve leading *ulama* who signed the fatwa of March 29, 1964, which transferred most of King Saud's powers to Prince Faisal, and eventually led to Saud's removal.[34] He also headed the founding committee of the Muslim World League.

But bin Baz was not the most influential Wahhabi leader at this point. Sheikh Ibrahim bin Muhammad Al al-Sheikh, the eldest son of the late grand mufti, maintained a close relationship with Faisal, meeting with the king on a weekly basis.[35] Like his father, Sheikh Ibrahim believed that Saudi Arabia should take a leading role in the Arab world and not vacate this position to others, especially to Nasser's Egypt. His father had believed that Egypt had been defeated in 1967 because Nasser was a godless socialist. Now Sheikh Ibrahim was a major force pushing for the Saudis to get involved in the Arab war against Israel.

Faisal's relationship with Sheikh Ibrahim demonstrated the sort of precarious situation the king could be put in because of his power-sharing arrangement with the Wahhabi leadership. Indeed, the Saudi monarchy and the *ulama* had an ongoing, albeit quiet, struggle over their respective areas of authority. In this case, Sheikh Ibrahim, a religious authority, sought to exercise influence over an area that was not specifically under the *ulama*'s jurisdiction. More important, Saudi Arabia was simply not capable of taking the kind of confrontational role in the Arab war against Israel that Sheikh Ibrahim and some other religious leaders encouraged. The kingdom had proven its vulnerability to Egyptian air attacks during the Yemen conflict; only a deployment of eight U.S. Air Force F-100 aircraft had warded off further bombings. And Saudi Arabia did not have the population base of Egypt or Iraq, each of which could support a large military establishment.

Moreover, from King Ibn Saud's confidential conversations with American diplomats from 1947 to 1949 about the Hashemite threat, it was clear that inter-Arab political disputes loomed far larger in the eyes of the Saudi political leadership than the Arab-Israeli conflict. This pattern continued under King Faisal as well.

Thus, in 1965 the British embassy in Jeddah had reported, "Saudi Arabia's problems with the United Arab Republic were Faisal's main concern—Israel his least preoccupation."[36] And since the first Arab-Israeli War in 1948, Saudi Arabia had had only a peripheral role in the Arab-Israeli military confrontation. King Faisal had admitted that he was "loath to bring up the subject" of Israel with President Lyndon B. Johnson during a White House visit in June 1966.[37] Other, more pressing issues were on the Saudis' agenda.

Even in the 1967 Six-Day War, Saudi Arabia's involvement had been extremely limited. Before the Israeli preemptive strike against Egyptian airfields on the morning of June 5, 1967, the Egyptians had deployed ninety thousand troops on Israel's southern border, demanded the removal of UN peacekeepers, and blockaded Israel's southern port, Eilat.

Syria had already moved its army to the Golan Heights. Jordan had massed nearly all of its land forces, including artillery and armor, in the West Bank hills overlooking Israel's heavily populated coastal plain, and had even allowed Egyptian and Iraqi forces onto its territory as part of the joint war effort against Israel. But, as in 1948, the Saudi military contribution was almost entirely symbolic: a single Saudi brigade moved into southern Jordan only after the outbreak of hostilities, and stayed entirely out of combat.[38]

Like his father, King Faisal had an uncompromising view of Israel and was openly intolerant toward Jews. He went on record in the Arabic press supporting the blood libel, which charged that Jews practiced the ritual murder of Christian and Muslim children.[39] In discussions with U.S. ambassador George Ball after the Six-Day War, he had denied that any place in Jerusalem was holy to the Jewish people, claiming that the Western Wall and the Temple of Solomon had no deep religious significance to the Jews. According to the ambassador's notes from the meeting, Faisal added, "[The] last thing in [the] area, [that was] sacred to Jews ... was [the] rock on which Moses trod which [the] UAR had allowed [to] be shipped from Sinai to New York. Jews therefore can simply visit their holy place in New York."[40]

Faisal had warned Ball that an "unsatisfactory Jerusalem settlement would require him to declare *Jihad*."[41] Revealing the influence of the Saudi grand mufti, Sheikh Muhammad, the king was also known to have said during these years that he hoped "to pray in the morning in Mecca, in the afternoon in Madinah, and in the evening in Jerusalem, without ever leaving Arab lands." (In fact, he had not visited Jerusalem during the years it was under Jordanian rule, from 1948 to 1967).[42] Faisal had to balance these ideological predispositions with a keen sense of realpolitik, given the limits of what Saudi Arabia could do militarily.

After the defeat of Nasser in 1967, Faisal did have one option for increasing his involvement in the war against Israel—assisting several Palestinian organizations that were battling the Israelis, usually by acts of terrorism. It was only after the Six-Day War that King Faisal met with a member of Yasser Arafat's Fatah movement. Throughout 1968, the Saudis increased aid to the Palestinian fedayeen, who were staging sabotage and terrorist operations against Israel from Jordan. Assisting Fatah was also a way to counterbalance the Palestine Liberation Organization (PLO), which, before Fatah took over in 1969, was viewed as Nasser's creation.[43]

After 1969, helping the PLO was a way for the Saudis to counterbalance the Marxist Palestinian organizations, such as the Popular Front for the Liberation of Palestine (PFLP). In 1969, the PFLP had attacked the Trans-Arabian Pipeline (TAPLINE) on the Golan Heights, which carried Saudi oil from eastern Arabia to the Mediterranean Sea. When these same radical Palestinian groups—which had grown out of Nasserist pan-Arabism groups like the Arab Nationalist Movement (ANM) and had been suspected of sabotaging Saudi oil production—joined the PLO, the Saudis nevertheless kept assisting the Palestinian organization. The ANM—once led by Palestinians like George Habash, Wadi Haddad, and Naif Hawatmeh—had offshoots in Yemen and the Arabian peninsula.[44]

Why would Saudi Arabia continue to support the PLO even when it opposed that organization's member groups? Because its contributions to the PLO would serve as protection money to prevent Palestinian attacks against Saudi interests. The Saudis soon became Yasser Arafat's most dependable supporters in the Arab world.[45] Though he had not been a formal member, Yasser Arafat came out of the Muslim Brotherhood in Egypt, which Faisal had backed. Over time, Arafat became a regular at the annual meetings of the Constituent Council of Faisal's Muslim World League.[46] In addition, he won the honorary position of permanent deputy chairman of the Saudi-backed Organization of the Islamic Conference, which was created in 1969 at a summit meeting of the Islamic heads of state in Rabat, Morocco. Arafat gained his prominent role in the organization because the conference focused initially on the subject of Jerusalem.

This pro-Fatah policy, however, posed problems for the Saudis' northern neighbor, the Hashemite Kingdom of Jordan. The Jordanians faced a severe internal problem from the extensive Palestinian military activity in their kingdom. Indeed, in early September 1968, King Hussein had complained to Harrison M. Symmes, the U.S. ambassador in Amman, that "the Saudis at present are subsidizing Fatah on condition they not coordinate with any Arab government, including Jordan."[47] Within two years, Jordan was engaged in a full-scale civil war that pitted the Jordanian armed forces against the PLO, which was led by its largest component, Fatah. The civil war almost became a full regional conflict when Syria decided to invade Jordan in defense of the Palestinians. The Syrian forces withdrew from Jordan after one armed engagement, but the episode demonstrated the destabilizing effects of the Saudis' support for Fatah.

As it turned out, the Saudis did not buy complete immunity from Palestinian attacks. On March 1, 1973, eight Palestinian terrorists from the PLO's clandestine Black September group burst into the Saudi embassy in Khartoum and seized the Saudi ambassador as well as the U.S. ambassador to Sudan, his chargé d'affaires, and a Belgian diplomat.[48] After demanding the release of Palestinian prisoners in Jordan, Germany, and the United States, including Sirhan Sirhan, who had assassinated Robert F. Kennedy,[49] the terrorists received orders from the PLO headquarters in Beirut to execute the Americans and the Belgian. Subsequently, Yasser Arafat himself phoned to make sure that the terrorists had understood the execution order—and that nothing would be done to the Saudi ambassador.

By 1973, Saudi Arabia's noninterventionist position on Israel would prove difficult to maintain. As Egypt and Syria planned a simultaneous attack on Israel, King Faisal carefully considered using his main weapon: oil.

The Oil Weapon

Originally, Faisal's instincts on the oil issue had been the same as his father's; Ibn Saud, of course, had been unwilling to put Saudi Arabia's American oil connection at risk as part of his support for the Arab states' war with Israel. Although Faisal had briefly suspended oil supplies to the United States and Great Britain after the Six-Day War, he still believed that oil should not be used as a political weapon.[50]

But the oil situation had changed since Ibn Saud's time. In July 1968, a coalition of Iraqi army officers and the Iraqi branch of the Baath party, a pan-Arab socialist party founded in Syria, seized power in Baghdad; in mid-1972, the new regime, whose strongman was Vice President Saddam Hussein, nationalized the British-dominated Iraq Petroleum Company. In June 1973, the new Libyan regime of Colonel Muammar Qaddafi, which had toppled King Idris in September 1969, followed suit, nationalizing the assets of the Bunker Hunt Oil Company, a small, independent American oil producer.

Now, in Saudi Arabia, pressure was building to nationalize ARAMCO. In the early 1970s, King Faisal had assured the four ARAMCO partners

(Esso, Mobil, Chevron, and Texaco) that "only in Saudi Arabia were U.S. interests in the Middle East relatively safe." But he had also warned that with increased demands for Saudi participation in ARAMCO, it would be hard "to hold off the tide of opinion" because of U.S. support for Israel.[51] Even as he blamed Saudi demands for greater control over ARAMCO on the Israel issue, however, Faisal did not even hint of an oil embargo.

From the start of the Yom Kippur War on October 6, 1973, when Egypt and Syria jointly launched a surprise attack on Israeli military positions in the Sinai and the Golan Heights, through October 19, Faisal refused to support proposals for an oil embargo against the United States. As late as October 16, Faisal replied to Secretary of State Henry Kissinger's previous message notifying Riyadh about the American decision to airlift military supplies to Israel, but he did not mention any oil embargo. He said only that if Washington did not comply with Egyptian proposals for an Israeli withdrawal to the 1967 lines and with the Saudi request to halt all U.S. military aid to Israel, then Saudi-American relations would become "lukewarm."[52] The Saudi threat to the United States was still vague. Perhaps foreshadowing greater Saudi engagement in this Israel conflict, Faisal did dispatch a Saudi brigade to the Syrian front on the Golan Heights, but as usual, this force was insignificant compared with the armies the other Arab states had sent—a Saudi brigade was, for example, only about one-third the size of an Iraqi division, and Iraq sent two and a half divisions, some thirty thousand soldiers, to the Golan Heights.[53]

Only on October 20 did King Faisal decide to stop the export of oil to the United States. A day later he took this policy one step further, cutting off oil supplies to the U.S. Sixth Fleet in the Mediterranean. This was a particularly risky course of action, because Soviet planes were currently resupplying the USSR's Egyptian, Syrian, and Iraqi clients.

What, then, triggered the change in Saudi policy, and why did it come at this time? Earlier in the war, Egyptian and Syrian forces had vastly outnumbered Israel's small standing army. On the Golan Heights alone, Syria had enjoyed an eight-to-one advantage over Israel in tanks. Israeli airpower was ineffective until it could suppress its adversaries' air defenses. Moreover, since the Israeli army was made up largely of reserve units that needed several days to be called up, Israel's small front-line forces had been vulnerable to surprise attack from the Arab states' battle-ready active-service formations.

But as soon as Israel mobilized its reserve army and recovered the initiative, the tide of battle began to change. Israel's first effective counterattack against Egypt began on October 16, when Israeli forces, commanded by Major General (res.) Ariel Sharon, crossed the Suez Canal. Entire Egyptian divisions, principally the Egyptian Third Army, were about to be encircled. After impressive initial gains, Egypt was about to lose the war. This is the point at which the Saudis instituted the oil embargo. Israeli forces ultimately reached positions seventy to eighty kilometers from the outskirts of Cairo.

Apparently, King Faisal and the senior *ulama* had reached a tacit agreement whereby if the Egyptian war effort went badly, Saudi Arabia would unleash the oil weapon.[54]

According to this analysis, the moves against the United States came more from the Wahhabi religious establishment than from the Saudi royal family. The *ulama*'s role in matters of high policy had grown. Faisal must have known that the confrontation with the United States was dangerous, especially when the Saudi oil embargo targeted U.S. military forces overseas. In the past, the Saudis had been reluctant to get drawn into Arab-Israeli issues. That was clear from the British and American diplomatic record in the 1960s, and also from the Saudis' actions in past Arab-Israeli wars. Few expected that 1973 would be any different. Egypt's president, Anwar Sadat, would claim that he had never expected Faisal to actually use the oil weapon.[55]

Indeed, Saudi behavior in the 1973 Yom Kippur War indicated that something fundamental had changed. One could argue that Saudi Arabia did not get involved in 1948 and 1967 because in both instances Israel was fighting the Saudis' greatest adversary: first Hashemite Transjordan, and then Nasserist Egypt. In fact, British diplomats in Saudi Arabia raised such a possibility when analyzing the 1948 conflict: "Even Saudi Arabia's hostility to Israel seemed in practice to be to some extent subordinated to her Hashemite complex, since Israeli strength might be a useful counterweight to Jordan."[56] Such an analysis might be even more relevant for the 1967 conflict, for the Israeli victory in the 1967 Six-Day War forced the Egyptians to withdraw their expeditionary army from Yemen, effectively terminating the Nasserist threat to the Arabian peninsula. By 1973, Nasser was gone, replaced by Anwar Sadat, and the Egyptian threat to Saudi Arabia was over. That is when the Saudis backed Egypt, instituting an oil embargo against the United States—an embargo they lifted in the spring of 1974, after Egypt (and Syria) had reached a separation-of-forces agreement with Israel. Saudi oil had served Egyptian interests.

But such balance-of-power considerations do not fully explain Saudi behavior. The Faisal of the 1960s was determined to be a reformer; by the 1970s, he was much more conservative. The only real element of his 1962 reform program that he implemented was the abolition of slavery. And the conservative Faisal could be particularly influenced by his country's religious leadership, whose greater involvement in critical Saudi foreign policy decisions was the most likely explanation for the decision to embargo the United States. If the late Saudi grand mufti, Sheikh Muhammad ibn Ibrahim, advised Faisal that "Saudi Arabia should lead the Arab world," then the oil embargo against the United States was a major step toward accomplishing that goal. Egypt and Syria actually lost territory to the Israelis in the Yom Kippur War, but the Saudi diplomatic assault was not countered. In this sense, King Faisal emerged as the main victor on the Arab side.

Sheikh Muhammad ibn Ibrahim's second piece of advice to Faisal was that "the ideology of Wahhabism should be exported." After the latest Arab-Israeli conflict, the Saudis were in a far better position to fulfill that goal, for the Arab oil embargo had had a critical side effect: an explosion of oil prices, which meant that Saudi Arabia's national income mushroomed. Saudi oil revenue, which had already gone up to $4.3 billion in 1973 from $2.7 billion in 1972, now skyrocketed to $22.6 billion in 1974.[57] Through organizations like the Muslim World League, funds for the spread of Wahhabism, the Saudi version of Islam, increased accordingly. Wahhabism could become considerably more assertive.

Chapter 6

The Hothouse for Militant Islamic Radicalism

The struggle between Saudi Pan-Islamism and Nasserism had other side effects that lasted for decades, even after Nasser's death in 1970. The most significant anti-Nasserist force in the 1950s was the Muslim Brotherhood, the organization that the Egyptian-born schoolteacher Hasan al-Banna (1906–49) had founded in 1928 in order to create a completely different political and social order as Egypt emerged from foreign domination—a society based on Islamic law. By this point, the Muslim Brotherhood had grown into a formidable political opposition in Egypt; as of 1949, the organization had two thousand branches throughout the country. But more significant, it was now a dangerous militant movement with a "secret apparatus" that acquired arms and terrorized its enemies. In December 1948, a member of the Muslim Brotherhood murdered an Egyptian prime minister, Nuqrashi Pasha; Hasan al-Banna was assassinated less than two months later. In October 1954, a Muslim Brother made an attempt on Nasser's life.[1]

Many Egyptian members of the Muslim Brotherhood who had been driven out of Egypt by Nasser's regime found refuge in Saudi Arabia, and some received stipends from the Saudi government. Palestinian Muslim Brothers followed. Abu Jihad (Khalil al-Wazir), who before becoming one of the founders of the Fatah movement had been a member of the Muslim Brotherhood, left Egyptian-controlled Gaza to teach in Saudi Arabia. Yasser Arafat, who, though not formally a Muslim Brother, had fought as a sympathizer with their units in 1948, applied for a Saudi visa in 1957, but then decided to move to Kuwait.[2] (Decades later, Saudi Arabia would again become a refuge for the Muslim Brotherhood. When the Syrian Muslim Brotherhood split, after it was crushed by President Hafez al-Assad in 1982, at least one of its factions took refuge in Saudi Arabia.[3] Sudanese Muslim Brothers also came to the Saudi kingdom for political asylum. The number of Muslim Brotherhood refugees who fled to Saudi Arabia reached the thousands.[4]) Some of the Egyptian Muslim Brothers who arrived in Saudi Arabia in the late 1950s became prominent at the Islamic University of Medina, which was founded in 1961, following consultations between many of these foreign fundamentalists, the Wahhabi *ulama*, and other Saudi authorities.[5] With the help of these Egyptian refugees, the Saudis hoped to build up their Islamic University of Medina as an alternative to Cairo's famous al-Azhar, which had come under strict Nasserist control in 1961. Pakistani Islamic leader Mawlana Abu al-Ala Mawdudi was made a trustee of the new university.[6] Many of Egypt's future *ulama* were drawn to Saudi Arabia in these years; Sheikh Tantawi, who would eventually become the grand mufti of Egypt, spent four years at the Islamic University of Medina.[7]

The university was not under the jurisdiction of the Saudi Ministry of Education, but rather was controlled by the grand mufti, Sheikh Muhammad ibn Ibrahim Al al-Sheikh. The university's vice president was Sheikh Abdul Aziz bin Baz, the powerful conservative Wahhabi cleric who would himself become grand mufti in the 1990s. Students from the entire Muslim world attended its classes and were exposed to the ideas of Wahhabism and of the Muslim Brotherhood. Years later, 85 percent of its student body would be non-Saudi, making it an important tool for spreading Wahhabi Islam internationally.[8] Another important center for foreign students was King Abdul Aziz University, established in 1967. Both universities quickly became hothouses for the growth of Islamic militancy.

Other Muslim Brotherhood refugees made family fortunes in Saudi Arabia, including Muhammad Uthman Ismail, who became an intermediary between post-Nasserist Egypt and Saudi Arabia. In the late 1970s, some of these newly wealthy Muslim Brothers became key contributors to Egypt's Islamist movements.[9] In fact, in the 1990s Egyptian sources would charge in the Lebanese daily *as-Safir* that high-level Saudi officials also backed terrorist activity in Egypt.[10]

Saudi Arabia was a natural asylum for the Muslim Brothers. The kingdom had an interest in wielding influence in Egypt; after all, the Egyptians had invaded the Arabian peninsula twice and in both the nineteenth and twentieth centuries had fought the Saudis. Indeed, the Yemen war in the early 1960s, when Nasser's secular Arab nationalism went to war against Wahhabism, demonstrated the threat that Egypt could pose when it was in a position of complete ideological hostility to the Saudi state. Thus, for Saudi Arabia, investing in Egyptian Islamic movements and defeating Egyptian secular trends was an investment in security. And of course, Wahhabism and the Muslim Brotherhood had a great deal of ideological affinity. Both were *salafi* movements: they sought to restore an Islamic golden age—Islam as it had been under the Prophet Muhammad and his immediate successors, who were known as *al-salaf al-salihin*, or pious ancestors. Both were nurtured by their understanding of Ibn Taymiyya (1263–1328), whose writings Muhammad ibn Abdul Wahhab had found so compelling that he copied them by hand.

Ibn Taymiyya had written that with the Mongol invasions of Iraq in the mid–thirteenth century, whole parts of the Islamic world had reverted to a pre-Islamic state of spiritual darkness—*jahilia*—even after the Mongols converted to Islam. As a result, he said, it was permissible to conduct jihad against the Mongol state. The Wahhabis subsequently adopted Ibn Taymiyya's ideas to justify their wars against the Ottoman Empire. The Muslim Brothers took a similarly hostile attitude toward the secular regimes of the Middle East: they made war against President Nasser of Egypt and even his successor, President Sadat, because, like the Mongol rulers of the Middle East, they were false Muslims.

There were several instances of cross-fertilization between the two movements. As noted, Muhammad Rashid Rida, an admirer—even a promoter—of Wahhabism, served as a mentor for Hasan al-Banna, the founder of the Muslim Brotherhood. Rida was probably receiving financial assistance from Ibn Saud for his pro-Saudi positions ("There is money in the affair," one of Ibn Saud's advisors acknowledged).[11]

Saudi Arabia was also the refuge for Muhammad Qutb, the brother of the most important figure in the Muslim Brotherhood, Sayyid Qutb. In 1966, Sayyid Qutb was executed by Nasser; Wahhabi *ulama* and the Constituent Council of the Muslim World League, headed by the Saudi grand mufti, condemned the execution.[12]

Before his death, however, Sayyid Qutb had become the leading advocate for militant Islamic reform—not just in Egypt but the world over.

Hatred, "Deep and Fierce"

Sayyid Qutb, a prolific writer and thinker whose works included a six-volume commentary on the Koran, had argued that Egyptians were living in a modern state of spiritual darkness, or *jahilia*. Borrowing from Ibn Taymiyya, as well as from the Pakistani scholar Mawlana Abu al-Ala Mawdudi, who had written about the state of Muslims under British rule in India, Qutb claimed that Egypt had moved from the Dar al-Islam ("House of Islam") to the Dar al-Harb ("House of War"). The Arab regimes, he said, could legitimately become the object of a jihad.[13]

Qutb spent a number of years in America and subsequently became extremely anti-Western, believing in "excoriating the Western *jahilia*."[14] He associated Western civilization with the *jahilia* that the Prophet Muhammad had subdued at the dawn of Islam: "Man is at the crossroads and that is the choice: Islam or *jahilia*. Modern-style *jahilia* in the industrialized societies of Europe and America is essentially similar to the old-time *jahilia* in pagan and nomadic Arabia. For in both systems man is under the dominion of man rather than that of Allah."[15] In a later work, he concluded that in order to "throw off the yoke" of *jahilia*, society's "man-made idols" had to be demolished.[16] Over time, his focus shifted from the need to overthrow Arab secular governments to a call to struggle against the West itself.

Qutb predicted that eventually there would be a clash of civilizations between Islam and the West, and that because the West had become morally bankrupt, it would crumble.[17] Islam would assume the mantle of world leadership. Muslims, he said, had forgotten their own superiority (*al-taghallub*),[18] and thus jihad, an injunction of the Koran, had fallen into disuse.[19] He renewed the call for a militant jihad: "He who understands the nature of this religion [Islam] will understand the need for the activist push of Islam as a jihad of the sword alongside a jihad of education."[20]

From Saudi Arabia, Muhammad Qutb edited and published Sayyid Qutb's writings. He eventually taught Islamic studies at King Abdul Aziz University in Jeddah. His own writings, like his brother's, contained strong anti-Western themes; for example, he used the term *salibi* ("Crusader") for "Christian" and the term *al-salibiyah* for "Christianity," "Christendom," and the modern West as a whole, while his brother Sayyid had written about "the Crusader spirit that runs in the blood of all Occidentals."[21] Muhammad Qutb reminded readers of their new militant mission: "A handful of men, with faith, troubled the impotent British empire at the Canal. They did not need heavy arms for that. If we regain our disciplined faith, we shall, as did the early Muslims, defeat the great empires of the world. We can hold the balance between the great power of East and West."[22]

In 1954, Muhammad Qutb wrote that the Crusades were ongoing. But Western diplomats in Saudi Arabia failed to detect the implicit threat to the West when the Saudis themselves adopted this language. In a confidential 1966 memorandum on King Faisal's promotion of pan-Islam, a diplomat in the British embassy in Jeddah remarked:

> I take the relaxed view of Faisal's activities.... The American Embassy here, with whom we have discussed the subject at several levels, share this view. That is to say that the concept of Islam as an aggressive force has completely disappeared except among some older Saudis. An article in one newspaper a few weeks ago referred to Africa as the "Dar ul Harb" and to Islam's main enemies as communism, Zionism and "sulubbiya"— which I suppose can only be translated as "crusaderism"— referring of course to Christian missionary activity.[23]

Thus, according to the official Anglo-American view, Islamic activists' references to "crusaderism" merely reflected Saudi sensitivities to Christian proselytizing on Arabian soil. Yet those who carefully followed the literature of the Muslim Brotherhood came to a very different conclusion; in 1957, Wilfred Cantwell Smith of McGill University wrote, "Most westerners have simply no inkling of how deep and fierce is the hate of the West that has gripped the modernizing Arab."[24]

The "Emir of Jihad"

In the 1970s, the ideology of the Muslim Brotherhood and Saudi Wahhabism formed a potent mixture in Saudi Arabia's Islamic universities and in the international Islamic networks that King Faisal had established through the Muslim World League.

More and more Islamic radicals sought refuge in Saudi Arabia. Hassan al-Turabi of Sudan spent several years in exile in Saudi Arabia before being invited to join the government of President Jafar Nimeiri in 1977.[25] Sheikh Omar Abdul Rahman, the blind Egyptian cleric who would later be convicted for his involvement in the 1993 World Trade Center bombing, resided in Saudi Arabia from 1977 to 1980, teaching at a girls' college in Riyadh. He had been a bitter critic of Nasser, branding the Egyptian leader's regime as "un-Islamic" and even issuing a fatwa forbidding prayer at Nasser's 1970 funeral. He had been imprisoned several times by the Egyptian authorities for his activities.[26]

In the 1980s, the Saudis welcomed Ayman al-Zawahiri, despite his past involvement in Islamic radicalism and in the assassination of Anwar Sadat (for which he had served a jail sentence in Egypt). In 1986, al-Zawahiri left Saudi Arabia for Afghanistan; in the late 1990s, he would become Osama bin Laden's deputy and al-Qaeda's chief ideologue.[27]

Perhaps most significant, Abdullah Azzam, one of the most influential Islamic fundamentalist thinkers, sought refuge in Saudi Arabia. It is difficult to overstate the impact that this Islamic radical had.

Azzam was born in a Palestinian village near Jenin in 1941. In 1959, he traveled to Syria to study at Damascus University; he lived there through 1966, and during that time he joined the Muslim Brotherhood. In 1973, he completed his doctorate in Islamic jurisprudence at al-Azhar in Cairo, where he met the family of Sayyid Qutb. Subsequently, Azzam taught Islamic law at the University of Jordan in Amman, where he again became active in the Muslim Brotherhood. Because of his involvement in the Brotherhood, he was dismissed from his university position. So, like other Muslim Brothers, he moved to Saudi Arabia. There he joined Muhammad Qutb on the faculty of King Abdul Aziz University. At the university, Qutb and Azzam shared a young Saudi student named Osama bin Laden.[28]

Abdullah Azzam's most important contribution to the Islamic fundamentalist movement was to restore the centrality of the idea of jihad. In fact, he has been dubbed the "Emir of Jihad."[29] Analyzing the reasons for the relative decline of the Islamic world, he reached a clear conclusion: "Anybody who looks into the state of Muslims today will find that their great misfortune is their abandonment of *Jihad*."[30] In a famous Islamic legal opinion about defending Muslim land that comes under attack, he wrote, "In this condition the pious predecessors, those who succeeded them, the scholars of the four Islamic schools of thought...are agreed that in all Islamic ages, *jihad* becomes obligatory upon all Muslims." And in a booklet entitled *Defending the Land of the Muslims Is Each Man's Most Important Duty*, he clearly made the jihad a new Muslim priority.

Azzam was influenced in this period not only by the writings of his fellow Muslim Brothers but also by Wahhabi *ulama* in Saudi Arabia, particularly Sheikh Abdul Aziz bin Baz.[31] In his introduction to the booklet, Azzam stated, "I wrote this fatwa and it was originally larger than its present size. I showed it to our great respected Sheikh Abdul Aziz bin Baz. I read it to him, he improved upon it and he said 'it is good' and agreed with it." According to Azzam, Sheikh bin Baz then declared, in the mosques of Jeddah and Riyadh, that jihad was an obligation for every Muslim. Among the other leading Wahhabi *ulama* whom Azzam consulted was Sheikh Muhammad ibn Saleh al-Uthaiman, one of the highest religious authorities of Saudi Wahhabism, who went so far as to sign Azzam's fatwa.[32]

Azzam was also influenced by more classical sources. He cited this statement from Ibn Taymiyya: "If the enemy enters a Muslim land, there is no doubt that it is obligatory for the closest and then the next closest to repel him, because the Muslim lands are like one land. It is obligatory to march to the territory even without permission of parents or creditor[s]." Azzam called this the "General March," and elevated the importance of the obligation to defend Muslim lands, making it second only to the cardinal obligation of faith in Allah. "These are some of the evidences and reasons that corroborate the ruling on the General March when disbelievers enter a Muslim land," he wrote. "Verily, the repelling of the

disbelieving enemy is the most important obligation after *Iman* [faith]."
Citing Islamic sources, he stated, "There may arise such a situation in
which it is obligatory upon each and every one to march forward, when
Jihad is obligatory on all Muslims if the enemy invades one of our countries or he surrounds one of our territories. Then it is obligatory upon the
whole of creation to march out for Jihad. If they fail to respond they are
in sin." Neglecting the obligation to fight, according to Azzam, leads to
shirk (polytheism) and *kufr* (blasphemy)—two religious dangers that Wahhabism had always tried to eradicate. Picking up on this theme, he later
wrote, "Without *Jihad*, *shirk* (joining partners with Allah) will spread and
become dominant."[33]

The Soviet invasion of Afghanistan in December 1979 caused Islamic
fundamentalists like Abdullah Azzam to call for a jihad. For many of
Azzam's followers, the Afghan struggle replaced even the Palestinian cause
as an Islamic rallying point. One Islamic writer noted in the mid-1980s:

> It is a matter of obscured vision or shortsightedness or treason
> for Arabs and Muslims to be preoccupied with the Palestinian
> issue and to make [it] the pivotal point of the struggle between
> them and the Zionists, who are supported by Western imperi-
> alist capitalism, and to forget, that the toppling of the Ottoman
> state . . . with all its political, military and geographic, and even
> regional realities, was the major step toward the breaking
> down of the gateway to the East and the onslaught on the
> Islamic world.

According to this logic, a broader attack on the Islamic world—from
Somalia to Kashmir, and including Afghanistan—needed to be addressed.[34]

Azzam's ideology had an impact on many young Saudis besides Osama
bin Laden. Another famous Saudi follower of Azzam during his years in
Saudi Arabia was Abu Abdul Aziz, also known as "Barbaros," who would
lead Arab volunteers in Bosnia in the 1990s. He heard Azzam for the first
time in 1984. Like Azzam, he concluded that jihad had been in retreat:
"We forgot the concept of Jihaad in Islaam . . . the lights of Jihaad, its rules
and prescriptions (as detailed in the coded Islaamic legal text) faded (and
disappeared) from our daily reality."[35]

Azzam had the opportunity to put his ideas to work. After he left his university position in Jeddah, the Muslim World League sent him to teach at the International Islamic University in Islamabad, Pakistan. He ran the offices of the Muslim World League and the Muslim Brotherhood in Peshawar, Pakistan, in 1984, Initially he was responsible for providing teachers for the schools that promoted jihad.[36] One of his biographers commented that "he brought the spoiled Saudi youth from the streets of Riyadh and Jidda to the hills of the Hindu Kush."[37]

Others joined his cause in Pakistan. Another Muslim Brother, the Jordanian Muhammad Abdurrahman Khalifa, came to head the Muslim World League office in Peshawar; Khalifa would later marry one of Osama bin Laden's daughters.[38] Wael Hamza Julaidan, a Saudi, also became a Muslim World League employee in Pakistan; he would later join bin Laden's terrorist network. Wadih el-Hage, an American convert to Islam who was born in Lebanon, went to Peshawar as well; he, too, would work for bin Laden.[39] In short, the Muslim World League offices in Pakistan were a feeder for what would become Osama bin Laden's terrorist network. Interestingly, another who joined Dr. Azzam in Pakistan was Sheikh Omar Abdul Rahman, the blind Egyptian cleric who had taught for several years in Saudi Arabia—and who would be involved in the first terrorist action against the World Trade Center.[40]

In 1984, Abdullah Azzam established the Maktab Khadamat al-Mujahideen, or Services Center, in Peshawar to recruit Arabs and arrange funding for the war against the Soviets in Afghanistan. Money poured in from Saudi intelligence, the Saudi Red Crescent, private Saudi princes, and the Muslim World League.[41] Pakistan's Inter-Service-Intelligence (ISI) provided the new recruits with training and base facilities, while the U.S. Central Intelligence Agency supplied a good deal of the weaponry, deferring to the Pakistanis on how to distribute the arms.

The war against the Soviets in Afghanistan may have looked like a multinational effort, with Afghan guerrillas backed by Arab volunteers and armed with Western weapons, but the effort also required significant financial backing, and that came from Saudi Arabia and its Islamic charities. Abdullah Azzam's ideological conviction helped mobilize volunteers for the Afghanistan struggle, and without the Saudis, the Afghans would have lacked the resources to turn back the Soviets.

Abdullah Azzam's Ideology of Jihad

Azzam's ideology continued to evolve. In 1988, he toured the United States to raise funds. Anticipating that the Islamic forces would defeat the Soviets, he sensed that this victory would be a historic turning point for Islam—and not just in regard to the Soviet Union. In a speech in Oklahoma, he declared, "Oh Brothers, after Afghanistan, nothing in the world is impossible for us any more—there are no superpowers or mini-powers, what matters is our willpower."[42] A year later, in another speech, Azzam made clear that his movement could even target the United States: "You have to be willing to risk Holy War wherever you can carry it out, even in America."[43] It appeared that Azzam hoped to replicate Islam's military victories of the seventh century; just as the early Muslim armies had defeated the two great powers of the day, the Byzantine and Persian empires, Azzam saw his new jihad crushing the Soviet Union and the United States.

In February 1989, the Soviet Union pulled out of Afghanistan, but the victory was only a starting point for Abdullah Azzam. He envisioned a worldwide jihad: "This duty shall not lapse with victory in Afghanistan, and the *jihad* will remain an individual obligation until all other lands which formerly were Muslim come back to us and Islam reigns within them once again. Before us lie Palestine, Bukhara, Lebanon, Chad, Eritrea, Somalia, the Philippines, Burma, South Yemen, Tashkent, Andalusia."[44] Andalusia was the old Arabic name for Spain, which had been a long-term aspiration for Muslims ever since it had become part of the Christian world in the fifteenth century. Earlier Islamic militants, including the Muslim Brotherhood, had targeted the secular regimes in their own countries. The Palestinian terrorists within the PLO focused on Israel, although they began to operate beyond the boundaries of the Middle East. But the jihad of Abdullah Azzam introduced an entirely new order of magnitude to Islamic militancy, for the armed operations that he advocated had no geographic limits.

Undoubtedly, Abdullah Azzam's radical political thinking, which received consistent support from the Saudis, had already had a profound influence on world events. Indeed, his ideology had played a key role in the defeat of a world superpower. But the doctrines he propagated—which were influenced in no small part by the militant Islamic activism of the

Saudi Wahhabi establishment—would have an even more significant impact on world affairs, for his writings ultimately justified the indiscriminate terrorism that al-Qaeda would come to practice. "Many Muslims," he wrote, "know about the *hadith* in which the Prophet ordered his companions not to kill any women or children, etc., *but very few know that there are exceptions to this case* [emphasis added]. In summary, Muslims do not have to stop an attack on *mushrikeen*, if non-fighting women and children are present."[45]

Azzam acknowledged that Muslims generally should avoid killing children and noncombatant women, but his distinction between noncombatants that were just *kufar* (infidels), who should be afforded such protection, and *mushrikun* (polytheists), who should not, created theological categories that allowed, in certain cases, for mass murder of civilians. Simply put, in creating these categories, Azzam provided the religious justification for mass murder and set the stage for the globalization of Middle Eastern terrorism.

On November 24, 1989, Abdullah Azzam and two of his sons, Muhammad and Ibrahim, were killed by a car bomb in Peshawar. The perpetrators were never found, but the intelligence services of the pro-Soviet regime in Afghanistan were probably behind the attack. His strongly worded will outlined his ideological legacy: "Those who believe that Islam can flourish and be victorious without Jihad (fighting) and blood are deluded and have no understanding of the nature of this religion."[46] The Muslim World League in Mecca issued condolence notices for the loss of one of its most notable men, and the organization's head, Abdullah Umar Nasif, praised Azzam for his contribution to jihad. For a while, Azzam's son-in-law, the Algerian Boujema Bounouar, also known as Abdullah Anas, served as his successor; Anas, in fact, brought Azzam's jihad doctrines to Algeria. And Azzam's brother, Fayiz Azzam, continued fund-raising efforts in the United States.[47] But the effective successor of Abdullah Azzam was his Saudi student Osama bin Laden.

A New Militant Hybrid

King Faisal's Muslim World League had clearly become a critical instrument for advancing Saudi national policies. In 1974, when it had an annual budget of $50 million, it had co-opted major Islamic political activists like Sayyid Qutb's ideological mentor from Pakistan, Mawlana Abu al-Ala Mawdudi.[48] Its staff was also made up of members of the Muslim Brotherhood.[49] And by bringing into its ranks Islamic militant ideologues like Mawdudi and Abdullah Azzam, the Saudi-backed Muslim World League spread radical Islamic activism. The leap from ideological identification with Islamic militants to active support for jihad turned out to be not very great.

The second Saudi organization for international Islamic action was the World Assembly of Muslim Youth, which, as noted, published and distributed texts on Islam. Besides the usual introductory religious books, it also spread works on specialized subjects, including jihad. But the most prominent of its books were the writings of Sayyid Qutb, Mawlana Mawdudi, and Muhammad Qutb.[50] The World Assembly of Muslim Youth's stated objective was "to serve the ideology of Islam through the propagation of tawhid"—*tawhid* being the belief in the oneness of God, the primary Islamic tenet emphasized by Wahhabism. Thus, a Saudi organization dedicated to the international spread of the Wahhabi creed incorporated the writings of the Qutbs and Mawdudi into the message of Wahhabism.

Regardless of the historical differences between the rise of the Muslim Brotherhood and that of Wahhabism, the movements nonetheless shared important similarities. Ayman al-Zawahiri, who started his Islamist career in the Muslim Brotherhood, once said that Sayyid Qutb's works "affirmed that the issue of *unification* [the oneness of God] in Islam is important and that the battle between Islam and its enemies is primarily an ideological one over the issue of *unification* [emphasis added]." Thus, according to al-Zawahiri, the Islamic principle of *tawhid*—enshrined as the centerpiece of Wahhabism—was a paramount cause for Qutb, for there was a battle between those who correctly adopted strict monotheism and those who, in al-Zawahiri's words, "claim to be intermediaries between the Creator and mankind." And since the eighteenth century, Wahhabi scholars had labeled veneration of saints and the introduction of intermediaries in prayer as *shirk* (polytheism), which needed to be eradicated from Islam—even militarily. Al-Zawahiri concluded, "Sayyid Qutb's call for loyalty to God's oneness and to acknowledge God's sole authority was the spark that ignited the Islamic revolution against the enemies of Islam at home and abroad."[51]

In the 1970s and 1980s, the Wahhabi movement and the Muslim Brotherhood developed a working relationship, even though the Muslim Brotherhood had no Saudi branch. The noted French expert on Islam Olivier Roy observed, "In the 1980s a kind of joint venture was established between the Saudis and the Arab Muslim Brothers." The Saudis frequently used Muslim Brotherhood networks to spread their Islamic message.[52] Moreover, by supporting the Brotherhood, Saudi Arabia bought protection for itself—something of a modus operandi for the Saudis when dealing with potential adversaries. The Muslim Brotherhood, meanwhile, obtained from the Saudis and the Muslim World League positions for its members and funds for its operations. As a result of this partnership, Saudi Arabia became one of the main centers exporting the new Islamic fundamentalism of the 1970s and 1980s.

How did this interaction affect the intellectual environment in Saudi Arabia? In the late 1970s, a new hybrid of Saudi Wahhabism and Muslim Brotherhood ideology began to emerge. This is no surprise, given that Saudi Arabia harbored and funded so many of these Muslim Brotherhood activists, giving them jobs in its universities and its Islamic organizations. Several works at the time exemplified the kind of thinking that was emerging.

One example was a strongly anti-Western book entitled *The Methods of the Ideological Invasion of the Islamic World*, written by two Saudi lecturers at the Islamic University of Medina for students of Islamic law and *da'wa* (missionary work).[53] In their introduction, the authors argued that the West raised the flag of secularism: "In the economic field that means the flag of capitalism, in the political field that means the principles of democracy, and in the social field it waves the principles of freedom." The West, they claimed, was invading Islamic society in order to undercut the values of Islam. To counter this ideological invasion, the authors argued, strong Islamic states must be established, and the *ummah*, the Islamic nation, must be strengthened. They described secularism in education and the mass media as "aggression against Islamic legitimacy." To the authors, the West was nothing less than the enemy of Islam; there could be no coexistence.

Strong anti-Christian themes filled the textbooks of the late 1970s. One work, published in 1977, was entitled *The Facts That the Muslim Must*

Know About Christianity and Missionary Activity. The light-green booklet might be dismissed as the work of fringe elements except that on its cover is the seal of the Kingdom of Saudi Arabia and the sponsorship of the General Presidency for the Directorate of Religious Research, Islamic Legal Rulings, Islamic Propagation, and Guidance. This office—one of the Saudi *ulama*'s governmental strongholds—published books for those specializing in Islamic law or engaged in spreading Islam abroad. Since 1974, the directorate had been headed by Sheikh Abdul Aziz bin Baz, the Wahhabi cleric who would become Saudi Arabia's grand mufti in the 1990s. In short, the book represented official Saudi thinking.[54]

The tone of the book was set by its dedication: "To the martyrs of Islam, from the victims of Crusader Hostility Enmity." The text began by reminding the "people of the book"—usually taken to be Christians and Jews—that they and the Muslim world have been in agreement regarding their opposition to polytheism. But then the author began to distinguish between original Christianity and modern Christianity, claiming that the latter was no longer a monotheistic faith: "And they converted it into paganism and polytheism and fables and they call it the Christian religion, by lying and by falsehood."[55]

The author based his charge that Christianity was a form of polytheism on his critique of the Trinity: "They [the Christian missionaries] know that it is impossible to connect and to reconcile between Islam and Christianity and reconcile the *tawhid* [oneness of God] and the *tathlith* [the Trinity]." He wrote about the "attacks on Islam by 'Crusaderdom' in coordination with and planned by international Jewry" and discussed an overall Christian attack on Islam "under the new American umbrella."[56]

According to the author, "The Crusader wars that were ignited by the enemies of Islam continue. We suffer from its influence in the Philippines, in Lebanon, Ethiopia, Nigeria, Sudan, Chad, Bulgaria, Thailand, Palestine, and others. These wars will continue until Allah will take possession of the earth, or until the reasons for these wars will be uprooted."[57] Such an attack on the Christian world was not uncommon in official Saudi religious circles at the time. Sheikh bin Baz himself wrote in 1974 that Christianity was a form of blasphemy and a distortion of the Koran. He claimed that there could not be any fraternity between "the infidels [meaning Christians] and the Muslims."[58]

The author, in fact, was echoing classic Wahhabi arguments, for by labeling Christians polytheists, the author removed the protection that Islam traditionally afforded to "people of the book." And in Wahhabi history, stating that a group of individuals were polytheists was like issuing them a death warrant. But the author was aware of the potential power of the book's message, for he carefully warned that readers "should not turn to rage and violence but rather should arm themselves with conscience and . . . act to undermine these [Christian] plans by all legitimate means."[59]

The anti-Christian message in this official Saudi text was not uncommon; indeed, it appears to have penetrated religious circles. Years later, Khaled Muhammad Batrafi, a Saudi columnist for the London daily *al-Hayat*, asked in a newspaper article, "Why do we hate the People of the Book?" Batrafi complained that a preacher he had known had called for the "annihilation of Christians and Jews." When Batrafi had confronted the preacher, saying that according to Islam, the "people of the book" were to be protected, the preacher retorted, "The People of the Book of our day are not the People of the Book of the days of the Prophet." These religions, the preacher said, currently had polytheistic tendencies—for instance, the Holy Trinity—and were thus no longer monotheistic faiths.[60]

What is remarkable about this official Saudi text—including its anti-Americanism and repeated references to the ongoing Crusades—is how familiar it is. For in recent years Osama bin Laden and his al-Qaeda followers have articulated many of these same themes in interviews and religious rulings. Yet this book was published twenty-four years before the attack on the World Trade Center and the Pentagon. Osama bin Laden hadn't yet set foot in Afghanistan; he was only a university student in Saudi Arabia. But clearly the arguments being voiced in militant Wahhabi circles in the Saudi kingdom of the late 1970s helped set the stage for the leap to terrorism that the world witnessed two decades later.

Chapter 7

Wahhabism Reasserts Itself

On March 25, 1975, King Faisal was receiving a delegation that included the Kuwaiti oil minister, Abdul Mutalib Kazimi. Suddenly the king's nephew Prince Faisal ibn Musaid burst into the chamber, pulled out a revolver, and murdered his uncle, the king of Saudi Arabia. Following the assassination, Faisal's brother Khalid, the crown prince, became the new monarch. The experienced Fahd, who had served as minister of education and then minister of the interior, was appointed crown prince, while Abdullah, the commander of the Saudi National Guard, was named second deputy prime minister, making him second in line to the throne.[1]

To this day, ibn Musaid's motives for this act of regicide remain unclear. Many pointed out that he was engaged to a daughter of the ousted King Saud, and that his mother came from the Rashidis of northern Arabia, whom Ibn Saud had vanquished. But this explained little. Others linked the assassination to religious riots in 1965, a decade before; while demonstrating against the opening of the first Saudi television station, ibn Musaid's fundamentalist brother, Khaled ibn Musaid, was killed by the Saudi security services. Their father blamed his own brother, King Faisal, for the killing.[2] Subsequently, Faisal ibn Musaid went to the United States, where he grew his hair long and became involved in drugs; he was arrested with LSD in Colorado and was quickly returned home because of his excessive Westernization. But then, in the early 1970s, he gradually embraced an extreme form of Wahhabism and joined a group that dressed like the Ikhwan of the 1920s: they grew beards, and wore white turbans and short white robes.[3] King Faisal's murder may have been a belated act of revenge, but it could have had a religious dimension.

The Saudi security services interrogated Faisal ibn Musaid and many members of the Rashidi family but could never determine the assassin's true motives.[4] Finally, he was beheaded in Riyadh, in front of a crowd of twenty thousand.[5]

The episode was a shocking reminder that threats to the Saudi royal family did not have to come from other nations, or even from outside the family. Perhaps, as some claimed, Faisal ibn Musaid was simply deranged, but given the climate in Saudi Arabia in that era, the argument that religion motivated the assassin is at least plausible. Indeed, four years after the assassination, the Saudi regime would receive a clear challenge from the Wahhabi religious establishment.

A New Internal Challenge

November 20, 1979, marked the beginning of the fifteenth Muslim century. (The Muslim calendar traces its starting point to when the Prophet Muhammad fled to Medina from persecution in Mecca.) Early that morning, at the dawn of a new Muslim century, several hundred armed men seized control of the Grand Mosque in Mecca, taking hundreds of pilgrims hostage. Leading the attacks on Islam's holiest site were two Saudis, Juhaiman ibn Muhammad al-Utaibi and Muhammad ibn Abdullah al-Qahtani. The morning they seized Mecca's Grand Mosque, al-Qahtani declared himself to be the *mahdi*—literally, "the guided one"—who according to both Sunni and Shiite traditions is a messianic figure who will appear at the end of time to restore righteousness.

Al-Utaibi and al-Qahtani were different from the usual Saudi opposition leaders. They were not inspired by a foreign power as the Saudi Nasserists a decade earlier had been, though some of their followers included Egyptians and Yemenis. They did not represent an oppressed ethnic or religious minority, like the Saudi Shiites of the Eastern Province or the foreign workers in the Saudi oil industry. They did not even come from a geographically deprived area like the Asir province, near the Yemen border, or from a politically frustrated constituency, like the Hijazis, who resented the rule of the more backward Najdis.

Rather, these men were products of mainstream Saudi institutions. Both al-Utaibi and al-Qahtani had studied under the establishment religious leadership at the Islamic University of Medina; the former had attended the lectures of Sheikh Abdul Aziz bin Baz, the ultraconservative chancellor who would later become grand mufti of Saudi Arabia. And al-Utaibi, in particular, had strong Wahhabi credentials; he came from the family of a Saudi Ikhwan warrior who had been killed by Ibn Saud's forces at the battle of Sibila in 1929, although his particular branch of the al-Utaibi tribe had remained loyal to the Saudi monarch.[6] He had, moreover, served for eighteen years in the Saudi National Guard, the domestic security force that had evolved from the Ikhwan, and was under the command of Prince Abdullah bin Abdul Aziz.

Al-Utaibi and al-Qahtani saw the rapidly modernizing Saudi society as moving away from the true Islam, and their movement challenged the Islamic credentials of the Saudi regime. Significantly, despite their status as leaders of an opposition movement, al-Utaibi and al-Qahtani had allies within the Wahhabi elite. A year before the attack on the mosque, Saudi authorities at the Interior Ministry, after bringing in al-Utaibi for questioning (along with ninety-eight other suspects), had summoned Sheikh Abdul Aziz bin Baz to give his opinion about the group. The sheikh refused to label the acts of his former student's group as treasonous.[7] In fact, bin Baz and other conservative *ulama* interceded on behalf of al-Utaibi and al-Qahtani's organization.[8] And according to al-Utaibi, Sheikh bin Baz had accepted the arguments in the group's first pamphlet as well founded, even while objecting to its criticisms of the Saudi government.[9] Another Saudi religious leader, Sheikh Salih ibn Muhammad ibn Lahidan, even encouraged the movement.[10]

Undeniably, traditional Wahhabism had a profound influence on al-Utaibi and al-Qahtani's thinking; indeed, they even called the movement the Ikhwan. As much as they were reacting specifically to the influences of modernization, their movement really represented long-standing Saudi grievances. Al-Utaibi's complaints about Saudi Arabia sounded much like those of his Wahhabi ancestors. The original Ikhwan had protested Ibn Saud's ties to the infidel British and had called for continuing the Wahhabi jihad into the Hashemite territories of Transjordan and Iraq; now al-Utaibi's Ikhwan movement focused on similar issues. He believed that Muslim governments and the *ulama* were too close to the Christians: "Is it possible to declare the Jihad on the kifr states while we maintain our ambassadors in their territory, and keep their diplomats, experts and professors in our countries? How can we preach Islam while we take Christians as professors? How can we accept to see Christian flags beside the Muslim ones?"[11]

This was not just an old Ikhwan position, however; it went all the way back to the founding fathers of Wahhabism. According to Muhammad ibn Abdul Wahhab's grandson Sheikh Sulaiman bin Abdillah, Muslims could not have any contact whatsoever with the *kufar* (infidels); "employment, consultations, trust, visiting, advice, friendship, emulation, cordiality, and affability towards them"—all of these were forbidden.[12]

Thus, after al-Utaibi's group seized the Grand Mosque, Saudi Arabia's Wahhabi *ulama* had a serious problem dealing with the Ikhwan movement. King Khalid went to the *ulama* for their legal opinion, but it took them four days to issue a religious ruling. And the fatwa they finally provided avoided making any judgments about al-Utaibi's ideology, focusing instead on the mosque takeover itself.[13] Nevertheless, the *ulama*'s ruling authorized Saudi forces to kill members of al-Utaibi's group if they did not surrender. The Saudis, backed by foreign troops, stormed the Grand Mosque, and finally on December 3 they subdued the last of al-Utaibi's men. Al-Utaibi himself surrendered, and he and his remaining followers were ultimately put to death.

But the crisis for the Saudis did not end. The rebellion had badly shaken the Saudi establishment, since al-Utaibi's group had targeted the Saudi royal family for its corruption. Nor were al-Utaibi's rebels the only threat to the Saudi state's Wahhabi credentials. In fact, al-Utaibi's radical criticisms reflected a more general backlash against the effects of the 1970s oil boom on Saudi society. As a result of the boom, Westerners had poured into the Saudi kingdom, threatening the conservative Wahhabi way of life. The struggle between the forces of modernization and conservatism, always a part of Saudi history, reemerged.

In addition, a day before the attack on the Grand Mosque, Saudi Shiites, who made up 40 to 50 percent of Saudi Arabia's oil-rich Eastern
Province, publicly held an *ashura* procession to memorialize the death of
the Prophet Muhammad's grandson Hussein.[14] Shiites in Iran and in
other Arab states observed the *ashura* annually, but such processions were
strictly forbidden in Saudi Arabia, where anti-Shiite laws reflected the
views of its Wahhabi clerics. Thus, these Shiites were directly challenging the Saudi Wahhabi establishment. Rioting erupted when Saudi police
tried to disperse the Shiites, and continued for three days; oil installations
were also sabotaged.

Even the resolution of the Grand Mosque crisis created problems for
the Saudi leadership. There were widespread reports that French commandos had helped vanquish the al-Utaibi group; had the Saudi royal
family allowed non-Muslims into the holiest site of Islam?

With such questions being asked, and facing so much criticism, the
Saudis needed to bolster their legitimacy as Islamic leaders. In short, they
had to address the religious interests of the *ulama*, who, even in refusing
to brand al-Utaibi's ideology as heresy, had proven indispensable to the
Saudis in resolving the Ikhwan problem militarily. Thus, King Khalid and
Crown Prince Fahd expanded the *ulama*'s authority in "supervising the
kingdom's Wahhabi character."[15]

After the attack on the mosque, it was just as important for the *ulama*
themselves to demonstrate a greater role in Saudi affairs, for implicit in
al-Utaibi's critique on the Saudi regime was that the *ulama* had allowed
corruption within the Saudi state.[16]

A Saudi journalist at Harvard University, Sulaiman al-Hattlan, described the repercussions from the 1979 attack on the Grand Mosque in
Mecca:

> Though the government killed the extremists, it then essen-
> tially adopted their ideology. After the Mecca incident, Saudi
> authorities began imposing crushingly strict and pointless
> rules. Women were banned from appearing on television.
> Music was not allowed to be played in the Saudi media. Stores
> and malls closed during the five daily prayers. Members of the
> religious police were granted more power to intervene in

people's personal lives. The Saudi government did all this to please the Islamists, perhaps fearing further extremist threats.[17]

Indeed, the Saudi leadership gave the *ulama* much greater authority in the kingdom's affairs. The government backed the *ulama*'s demands for stricter observance of Wahhabi laws.[18] Signifying the rising power of the *ulama*, in 1980 the royal family fired the director of public security and replaced him with a member of the Al al-Sheikh family—the descendants of Muhammad ibn Abdul Wahhab.[19] The governor of Mecca was also replaced at this time.

In the highly strict religious environment that took hold after 1979, Sheikh Abdul Aziz bin Baz's influence grew. Bin Baz was one of the thirty *ulama* who approved of military action to vanquish his group, so he unquestionably came through for the Saudis in their struggle over the Grand Mosque. At the same time, however, he was a source of religious inspiration for al-Utaibi, as well as for Abdullah Azzam, who, as noted, would develop during the Afghan conflict a new doctrine of worldwide jihad, which he would transmit to his student Osama bin Laden. Sheikh bin Baz would prove to be a key figure in the development and direction of Wahhabism in the next decade and a half.

Bin Baz was born in 1909 in Riyadh. At age six he contracted an eye disease and was blinded. He received his Islamic education from descendants of ibn Abdul Wahhab, including the last grand mufti of Saudi Arabia, Sheikh Muhammad ibn Ibrahim Al al-Sheikh, who was his instructor for ten years.[20] He worked as a judge and later taught Islamic law in Riyadh, until becoming vice chancellor of the Islamic University of Medina in 1961, which spread Wahhabism and the doctrines of the Muslim Brotherhood to students from the entire Islamic world. Nine years later he became chancellor. In 1974, he was appointed president of the Directorate of Religious Research, Islamic Legal Rulings, Islamic Propagation, and Guidance, the Saudi governmental body that oversaw the legal rulings of Saudi clerics and the contents of mosque sermons.

Sheikh bin Baz's religious views were highly conservative. In 1966, he wrote an essay published in two newspapers claiming that, as taught in the Koran, the sun orbits around the earth and not the reverse.[21] Nevertheless, he had enormous moral authority in Saudi Arabia. One of the hallmarks of his writings was tremendous hostility to Christianity and Judaism. He explained, "According to the Koran, the Sunnah, and the consensus of Muslims it is a requirement of the Muslims to be hostile to the Jews and the Christians and other *mushrikun* [polytheists]." He added that various verses in the Koran prove "with absolute clarity that there is a religious requirement to despise the infidel Jews and Christians and the other *mushrikun*," and that this hostility should continue "until they believe in Allah alone."[22] He stressed on another occasion that Islam must have a global reach in order to fight Christian missionary activity in East Asia.[23] His language was somewhat ambiguous as to whether Christians and Jews were just infidels or belonged to the more inferior category of polytheists.

Sheikh bin Baz placed special stress on the importance of jihad. He wrote, "Jihad is the most preferable form of righteousness *(afdal al-qurbat)*."[24] According to bin Baz, only through the jihad against infidels could Muslims remove all obstacles and spread the *da'wa* (Islamic mission) worldwide. He explicitly justified jihad by the sword *(jihad bi-l-sayf)* as an important instrument for the spread of Islam, citing the historical Islamic conquests.[25] In short, one of Saudi Arabia's highest official authorities was echoing the radical writings of Abdullah Azzam and his followers, who were resisting the Soviets in Afghanistan.

Bin Baz's thinking on jihad represented a radical change in doctrine. According to the previous approach, jihad could be declared only by an authoritative leader for all Muslims, such as a new caliph for Sunni Islam. This put the idea of jihad off into the distant future, making it almost an eschatological concept. In the meantime, missionaries and proselytizers would spread Islam. Bin Baz was reversing the order by bringing jihad from a future era to the present, so that jihad opened the door for *da'wa*, rather than *da'wa* preceding the final jihad.

Although Sheikh bin Baz understood jihad to mean holy war—battle— he also promulgated a new kind of jihad: the financial jihad *(jihad bi-l-maal)*.[26] This idea would have profound consequences, for in the 1980s and 1990s, Saudi philanthropists adopted the approach and supported Wahhabi causes around the world.

External Challenges:
The Fall of the Shah and the Iran-Iraq War

Saudi Arabia faced external threats as well. In particular, three closely related developments in the late 1970s and 1980 jolted the Saudi kingdom and its Wahhabi foundations.

The first challenge occurred even before the 1979 takeover of the Grand Mosque in Mecca. In Iran, a Revolutionary Shiite Muslim regime overthrew the shah of Iran, stunning the Saudi leadership. The new Iranian elites under Ayatollah Khomeini were more than willing to challenge Saudi Arabia as leader of the Islamic world, for they knew how the Wahhabis viewed Shiite Islam. Saudi Arabia needed to respond actively on behalf of its own version of Islam. Iraq's invasion of Iran in September 1980 only sharpened the rift between Sunni Arab states and the Shiite clerics of Iran; Saudi Arabia backed the Iraqi war effort, making Revolutionary Iran a strategic-military rival as well as an ideological rival.

New pressures on Saudi Arabia emerged in the course of Arab-Israeli diplomacy, and the rise of Revolutionary Iran forced the Saudis to shift their position within the Arab world. Clearly, the Saudis needed to shore up a new consensus of Arab states against the Iranian threat and hence could not afford to tolerate splits in the Arab world on Arab-Israeli issues. For example, King Khalid and Crown Prince Fahd initially supported Egypt, their strategic partner, in its negotiations with Israel. In September 1975, not long after Faisal's assassination, they backed Egypt in the negotiations for the Sinai II Agreement, by which Israel withdrew forces from the strategic Gidi and Mitla passes in the Sinai peninsula. While Syria opposed Sinai II, fearing that Egypt might eventually reach a separate peace with Israel, the Saudis still backed the American-sponsored accord. In fact, Saudi Arabia worked to overcome Syrian opposition. When the Lebanese Civil War broke out in 1976, Saudi Arabia led the Arab states in recognizing Syria's authority in Lebanon, hoping to convince the Syrians to acquiesce to Egypt's new understanding with Israel.[27]

But opposition to Egypt grew too strong in the Arab world in 1977, when Egyptian president Anwar Sadat visited Jerusalem, and in 1979, when Egypt actually signed a peace treaty with Israel. In a more radicalized Middle East, Saudi diplomacy could not bridge the gap between

Egypt, on the one hand, and states like Libya, Syria, and Iraq, on the other. These splits were also reflected inside the Saudi royal family; Crown Prince Fahd still wished to help the Egyptians, while Prince Abdullah was more sympathetic to the Syrians. Significantly, Kamal Adham, the architect of the Saudi-Egyptian rapprochement under King Faisal, was fired as head of Saudi intelligence at this time.

It thus came as no surprise that after the peace treaty was signed, Saudi Arabia joined a coalition of sixteen Arab states to break off diplomatic relations with Sadat's Egypt and also cut off its economic assistance. The Saudis had been reluctant to go this far, but regional pressures had mounted at a conference of Arab nations in Baghdad. PLO chairman Yasser Arafat, who had received generous financial backing from King Faisal, now attacked his son Saud al-Faisal, the new Saudi foreign minister, as a "disgrace to his father."[28] In the environment of Baghdad, Arafat felt that he could afford to threaten his Saudi backers openly: "Do not force us to become a band of assassins."[29]

Saudi Arabia had other factors to consider in its international relations. At the time, the Saudi kingdom was seeking to modernize its air-defense capabilities by procuring new American F-15 fighters and AWACS early-warning aircraft. But the sale was highly controversial in the United States (it would receive congressional approval only after months of pro-Saudi lobbying efforts). In 1978, the Carter administration had sold sixty-two F-15 fighters to Saudi Arabia, arguing that the sale would moderate Saudi policy toward Israel. But the Saudis, of course, subsequently opposed the Israeli-Egyptian peace treaty. A new Saudi peace initiative was essential if the new arms package was to get past the U.S. Congress.

On August 7, 1981, Crown Prince Fahd issued an eight-point plan to establish an alternative peace strategy for the Arab states. The Fahd Plan did not back the Egyptian-Israeli peace, but rather suggested an entirely different approach that was essentially unworkable. It outlined vague principles of a peace settlement without giving any details about how to implement such principles. Israeli and Egyptian negotiators had already worked out a detailed plan for implementing an Arab-Israeli peace; U.S. secretary of state Alexander Haig later noted that the Fahd Plan "had no concept of a direct Arab-Israeli negotiating process."[30] The Saudi plan, moreover, did not explicitly call for peace with Israel, but rather envisioned peace for "all the states of the region," leading to contradictory Saudi statements about Riyadh's readiness to recognize the Jewish state. Fahd continued to back the PLO as the representative of Palestinian interests, despite its refusal to renounce terrorism.

In short, the Saudis were not prepared to divert from the common Arab position, which meant their policy remained hostage to the most radical Arab line. The overthrow of the shah and the rise of the Iranian regime—Shiite clerics antagonistic to Wahhabism—had changed the way the Saudis operated. With this new force in the Islamic word, Saudi Arabia could no longer risk supporting Arab-Israeli peacemaking if the other Arab nations refused to begin a process of reconciliation with Israel. The Fahd Plan quickly failed—in 1982, the Arab states adopted a watered-down version of the plan[31]—and Saudi Arabia refocused its diplomatic energies on more immediate threats.

The second major challenge Saudi Arabia faced was linked directly to the fall of the shah of Iran: Iraq's invasion of Iran on September 22, 1980. In the 1975 Algiers Agreement, Saddam Hussein, then vice president of Iraq, had acquiesced to Iran's territorial claims along the two nations' common border along the Shatt al-Arab waterway, and in exchange, Iran halted its support for the Kurdish revolt against Baghdad in northern Iraq. But once the shah of Iran was overthrown, in February 1979, the balance of power between the two states changed. Ayatollah Khomeini purged the Iranian armed forces of thousands of suspected pro-monarchical officers and lost access to American spare parts for the Iranian air force. Saddam Hussein, who had become Iraq's president in 1979, exploited Iran's new vulnerability, threw out the Algiers Agreement, and sent his army into Iran. Henceforth, this clash between its two neighbors was Saudi Arabia's primary concern.

Saudi Arabia was naturally drawn into a close relationship with Iraq against Revolutionary Iran. But the Saudi-Iraqi connection was not a simple matter. Iraq had been ruled since 1968 by the Baath (Renaissance) party, a pan-Arab Marxist political party originally founded by a Syrian Christian Arab, Michel Aflaq. The Baath was antireligious; it had no sympathy for Islam and was hence well suited for ruling religiously heterogeneous Arab societies like Syria and Iraq, which had large non-Sunni Muslim populations as well as a substantial Christian presence. Arab minorities were

drawn to secular movements of this sort in which they could fully participate without being Muslims. The Baath was also pro-Soviet. It is not surprising, then, that Sheikh bin Baz once called the Baath party *hizb al-shaitan*
(the party of Satan).[32]

Saudi religious circles had serious problems in particular with the Syrian Baath under President Hafez al-Assad, who took power in 1971. Assad
was an Alawite. The Alawites were an influential Syrian minority sect that
was an offshoot from Shiite Islam. Alawites accorded divine status to
Muhammad's son-in law Ali, making them, in the view of most Muslims,
heretics. Like other Baath leaders, who sought to secularize Syrian society, Assad clashed with the Muslim Brotherhood, killing twenty thousand
members in the Hama massacres of 1982. Many survivors had sought
refuge in Saudi Arabia.

In contrast, Iraq's Saddam Hussein was a Sunni Muslim holding back
the threat of militant Shiism. Not only did he prevent Iranian Shiites
from invading the Sunni Arab world, but just as important, he kept down
the Shiite majority in his own country (Shiites constituted nearly 65 percent of the Iraqi population).[33] The Saudis thus could reconcile their
Wahhabism with support for the Iraqi Baath regime.

Saudi Arabia's involvement in the Iran-Iraq war marked another significant shift. The Iran-Iraq war was not confined to the Arab world, for
Iran was ethnically Persian, not Arab. The Saudis' preoccupation with
Iran reflected a shift in their foreign policy focus—from the Arab world
to the wider Islamic world. Even before the outbreak of the Iran-Iraq
war, in fact, the Saudis had begun to look to other Islamic nations for
support. For example, in 1975 Saudi Arabia provided $948.9 million in
aid to its ally Egypt—more than half of all Saudi foreign aid to Islamic
countries. But just a year later, Saudi aid to Egypt was slashed to
$496.8 million, or only about a quarter of total Islamic aid; meanwhile,
the Saudis sharply increased their aid to Pakistan, to $514.8 million from
$74.8 million in 1975.[34] Pakistan had become a Saudi strategic ally in the
1960s, when King Faisal allied himself with other Islamic nations to
counter Nasser's pan-Arabist movement. Now, as the Saudis tried to
counter Revolutionary Iran's radical Islamic message, Pakistan—a mostly
Sunni Muslim state that bordered Iran—became an even more important ally.

Indeed, Saudi Arabia's relationship with Pakistan was a model for how the Saudis formed alliances in this new era. The Saudis exploited the political and financial backing that they had, since the time of King Saud, given Pakistan's largest Islamist party, the Jamaat-i-Islami.[35] Saudi money found its way into the educational networks of the Jamaat-i-Islami, which also became active in the Saudi-dominated Muslim World League.[36] In fact, segments of the Jamaat-i-Islami came to accept Wahhabism.[37]

Saudi Arabia was even drawn into Pakistani domestic politics. Prime Minister Zulfikar Ali Bhutto turned to the Saudi ambassador to Pakistan to exercise the Saudi kingdom's "religious-cum-financial influence" over the Pakistani opposition, which included these Islamic groups.[38] Crown Prince Fahd approved of the new Saudi role.[39]

Thus, Pakistan became a model of how Saudi Arabia's Islamic networks abroad could be used to serve the national-security interests of the Saudi state.

For all the changes that had occurred in the Saudis' foreign policy, even more changes would occur under a new king. King Khalid died in June 1982, and Crown Prince Fahd became the new monarch. His half brother Abdullah was elevated to crown prince. Fahd's full brother Prince Sultan, the Saudi defense minister, became second deputy prime minister, putting him next in line for the throne; Prince Sultan was very close to his brother, and he became a key ally for King Fahd within the royal family. Both Fahd and Sultan were the sons of Ibn Saud and Husa bint Ahmad al-Sudairi, who held her seven sons together as a tight clique within the royal family. Fahd could use this group as an internal lobby for his policies.

The Beginnings of the American Buildup

As crown prince, Fahd had been probably the most pro-American of the senior princes.[40] As king, he would face strategic realities in the Middle East that would require a far more intimate relationship with the United States and a massive increase in the American presence in the kingdom—certainly a major step for a kingdom rooted in a Wahhabi religious perspective.

Surprisingly, despite the presence of the huge ARAMCO oil concession, the United States did not have large military forces in the Arabian peninsula similar to its bases in Europe and the Western Pacific. U.S.

military aircraft had been deployed only intermittently and in small numbers in the past. In part this was the result of an American-British arrangement from World War II, whereby the United States was the primary strategic power in Europe and the Far East while Britain covered the Middle East and the Indian Ocean.[41] This basic division survived into the Cold War, even as the British retreated, in stages, from their overseas role: from the Suez Canal, Aden, and finally the Persian Gulf.

Then, in the 1970s, the U.S. government looked to the "twin pillars" of the Persian Gulf—the Saudi kingdom and the shah of Iran—to maintain stability in the region. The British withdrew their last forces from the Gulf in 1972. The United States was withdrawing from Vietnam, and making clear that it could no longer be the global policeman; regional powers would have to assume greater responsibility for global security.

With the fall of the shah, however, only the Saudi pillar remained, and the United States realized it could not rely on Saudi Arabia alone. In 1979, the United States created a Rapid Deployment Joint Task Force, made up of air, land, and naval units, to project American power in the Persian Gulf. By 1983, the United States had established a new unified command for the area, the U.S. Central Command (USCENTCOM), similar to the unified commands that had existed for years in other potential theaters of combat: USEUCOM for Europe and USPACOM for the Far East. In the years ahead, USCENTCOM would come under the command of American generals like Norman Schwarzkopf, Anthony Zinni, and Tommy Franks.

Meanwhile, the United States began modernizing and enlarging the Saudi Arabian air force and its military bases. Saudi defense spending soared from $9.6 billion in 1978 to $22 billion in 1982, but at least 60 to 65 percent of this funding went to infrastructure projects.[42] Between 1972 and 1988, the U.S. Army Corps of Engineers directed five huge military construction projects, including King Khalid Military City, at a total cost of $14 billion.[43] These immense military facilities were designed to allow the rapid deployment of U.S. forces, in the event the Soviets tried to invade Iran from newly occupied Afghanistan. Indeed, the Soviet invasion of Afghanistan added new urgency to America's plans to project power in the Middle East. On January 23, 1980, President Jimmy Carter declared, "Any attempt by an outside force to gain control of the Persian Gulf region will be regarded as an assault on the vital interests of the United States of America and such an assault will be repelled by any means necessary, including military force." In Europe and in the Western Pacific, the United States had erected a vast infrastructure of bases and forward-deployed U.S. forces, but no such infrastructure was in place in the Middle East—the United States had closed its bases in Libya and Saudi Arabia in the 1960s. The Carter administration began to close the gap by gaining access to military facilities *around* Saudi Arabia: in Kenya, Oman, and Somalia. It also pre-positioned military equipment on U.S. ships that were to be kept "over the horizon" until a military crisis on the Arabian peninsula occurred.

Yet these were insufficient. In order to fulfill the Carter Doctrine to protect the oil of the industrial world, America needed a naval and air presence in the Persian Gulf itself. As a result, the 1980s saw a major American buildup in Saudi Arabia, which would ultimately allow the massive U.S. deployments in Saudi Arabia during the 1991 Gulf War. The significant American presence undoubtedly enhanced Saudi Arabia's external security, but it also resulted in greater internal challenges for the Saudi regime.

Saudi Arabia and other Arab Gulf states paid a price for backing Iraq against Iran. In the early 1980s, the Iranian air force attacked oil facilities and oil tanker traffic. On June 5, 1984, a Royal Saudi Air Force F-15 downed an Iranian F-4 Phantom on the Saudi side of the Gulf. By 1987, Iranian speedboats were regularly attacking Saudi oil tankers in the Persian Gulf, and Iran was conducting naval maneuvers in Saudi territorial waters.

Moreover, Iran frequently targeted Saudi Arabia's neighbor Kuwait. After repeated Iranian air attacks on its shipping, Kuwait turned to the United States. On May 19, 1987, President Ronald Reagan approved a plan to provide a U.S. naval escort to Kuwaiti tankers in the Persian Gulf. But since 1981, the six-state Gulf Cooperation Council (GCC), of which Saudi Arabia and Kuwait were members, had opposed foreign intervention in Gulf waters, declaring that the defense of the Gulf was for "the sons of the Gulf." Now this policy had to change. Sensitive to widening the American air and naval role, but certainly not willing to forgo Washington's protection, in 1986 Saudi Arabia proposed the "Fahd Line" in the Persian Gulf: the United States would be responsible for the security of the Gulf's international waters, while the Saudis and the GCC states remained committed to protecting their own territorial waters. For sound strategic military reasons, America was increasingly encroaching on the Arabian peninsula; it was no longer "over the horizon."

Wahhabi Islam Responds

The fall of the shah had another important effect on Saudi Arabia: in 1979, oil prices climbed again. Saudi oil revenues skyrocketed from $32.2 billon in 1978 to $48.4 billion in 1979, and by 1981 had reached $102.1 billion.[44] Thus, Saudi Arabia had the financial wherewithal to pursue an activist policy on behalf of the international interests of Islam—however the Saudis chose to define those interests. And once again, the Muslim World League became one of the Saudis' main vehicles for spreading Wahhabism.

It was Sheikh bin Baz who set the tone for this new activism in his capacity as head of the Muslim World League's Constituent Council. He argued that the Islamic states had a responsibility to encourage the mujahideen and the proselytizers of Islam in Afghanistan, in the Philippines, and everywhere else. This was clearly a call for both religious and military support.[45] Bin Baz and other *ulama* were increasingly taking positions on issues of foreign and security policy that were not formally under their jurisdiction. The Saudi *ulama* were not adopting the Iranian clerical model of placing themselves above the Saudi government; the original alliance between the Saudi royal family and Muhammad ibn Abdul Wahhab recognized the supreme of authority of the Saudi ruler *over* the religious establishment, as their imam. Nevertheless, some of the *ulama* seemed to think they could share power equally with the ruling family. Bin Baz, in fact, would eventually argue that the two governing elites in Saudi Arabia were on a par with each other. But whether the Saudi leadership followed the lead of the *ulama* or took action in response to its own view of its interests, Saudi Arabia's Islamic activism discernibly increased. King Faisal had used the Muslim World League in the 1960s to meet the challenge of Nasserism. Now King Fahd would use Islamic diplomacy to counter Revolutionary Iran, and to reestablish his own Islamic credentials as well.

The old Wahhabi-Shiite rivalries of the nineteenth century were again in full swing. Iranian-Saudi clashes in Mecca and Medina had accompanied the annual pilgrimage since 1979, and in one incident in July 1987, Saudi forces had killed about four hundred pilgrims (mostly Iranians) during a violent struggle between Iranian demonstrators and Saudi security forces. Iranians were outraged.

The stakes were considerable. Saudi Arabia had to keep Sunni Muslim states like Pakistan aligned on its side against Revolutionary Iran, but in fact many members of the Pakistani Jamaat-i-Islami initially identified with the zeal of the Iranian revolution. Indeed, Saudi Arabia and Iran waged a proxy war for influence in Pakistan through militant Sunni and Shiite religious organizations.[46] Moreover, as events in 1979 had shown, the large, restive Shiite population in Saudi Arabia's Eastern Province could be triggered by Iranian incitement.

In October 1987, as King Fahd's regional rivalry with Iran was growing more heated, the Muslim World League's third General Islamic Conference assembled. At the conference—attended by some six hundred representatives from 134 countries (those figures indicating the organization's enormous global outreach)—Iran was condemned.

The Iranians, viewing the General Islamic Conference as a mechanism for spreading Wahhabism and attacking Shiism, counterattacked. Ayatollah Khomeini characterized the Saudis as "these vile and ungodly Wahhabis" and said that they were "like daggers which have always pierced the heart of Muslims from the back." The Speaker of the Iranian parliament, Hashemi Rafsanjani, spoke of "Wahhabi hooligans" and described the Saudi royal family as an "evil clique."[47] Of particular concern to the Saudis were the sympathetic audiences for Iranian propaganda in the Arab Gulf states. In Bahrain, Shiites made up more than 60 percent of the population; in Kuwait, 30 percent; in the United Arab Emirates, 16 percent.

Both sides traded tirades. The Iranian president, Ali Khamenehi, declared that Saudi Arabia was unfit to protect Mecca and Medina, the holy cities of Islam. Ayatollah Montazeri denounced the Saudis as "a bunch of English agents from Najd" and then declared that just as Jerusalem would be liberated from the "claws of usurping Israel," Mecca and Medina would be liberated from the "claws of the Al Sa'ud."[48] Iran was not just a security threat; it attacked the very legitimacy of the Saudi regime and its right to present itself as the guardians of Islam's holiest sites.

But the Saudis were well prepared to counter this Shiite ideological assault. By 1987, the Muslim World League had been in existence for

twenty-five years. It had extensive international experience and connections, with thirty offices worldwide. Its Supreme World Council of
Mosques had contributed tens of millions of dollars for mosque construction worldwide, the money coming from the Saudi government (the
Saudis' contributions accounted for most of the Muslim World League's
budget). It dispatched nearly a thousand missionaries worldwide, trained
and financed Muslim clergy from around the world, and paid for about a
thousand Muslims every year to make the hajj to Mecca. And of course,
by the mid-1980s, the Muslim World League was one of the main conduits for Saudi funding of the war against the Soviets in Afghanistan.[49]

As Saudi Arabia countered the Iranian Shiite threat, Wahhabism gained
strength again within the kingdom. Even while King Fahd pushed for
modernization and established a closer alliance with the United States, his
government seemed to be becoming even more religiously strict. The
Iranian challenge was, of course, one reason the Wahhabi elites accrued
more power in Saudi Arabia, but King Fahd had other reasons for granting the *ulama* more authority. To begin, he wanted to counter his reputation as a pro-American monarch, which could have weakened his standing
within religious circles. More important, he had acquired a reputation as a
pleasure seeker who spent his time in his palaces in Spain, Switzerland, and
France. His losses in the casinos of the French Riviera back in 1974 were
well publicized, earning him reproval from his older brother, King Faisal.[50]

Fahd fought his impious image in several ways. First, he changed his
title: instead of being referred to as "His Majesty," in October 1986 he
adopted a more religious title, "servant of the holy places" *(khadim al-haramain)*.[51] And by the late 1980s, he seemed to be pulling away from his pro-
American positions, after backing many of the Reagan administration's
policies—including America's support for such anticommunist forces as
the Contras in Central America and the mujahideen in Afghanistan. In
1986, for example, the Saudi government condemned the United States
for its air strike on Libya. The following year, when the USS *Stark*, an
American frigate in the Persian Gulf, came under attack from an Iraqi
Mirage fighter, the Saudis did not comply with a U.S. request to intercept
the Iraqi aircraft; thirty-seven American sailors were killed in the attack.
Remarkably, even after the attack on the *Stark*, Saudi Arabia refused to
allow U.S. aircraft to use Saudi air bases to provide air cover for American

naval convoys in the Persian Gulf.[52] Finally, in March 1988, it was disclosed that Saudi Arabia, which had presented itself as a bastion of anticommunism, had acquired CSS-2 ballistic missiles from Communist China. The United States was supposed to protect the Saudis in the Gulf, but this secret missile purchase looked like a vote of no confidence in the U.S. military umbrella.

Internally, Fahd adopted a number of measures that could hardly be called progressive. He expanded the hours of religious studies within Saudi Arabia's "secular" educational system. His government also imposed a stricter separation of the sexes in Saudi universities. Women's employment opportunities were reduced.[53] And in 1984, Fahd actually publicly endorsed Sheikh bin Baz's warning to young Saudis not to travel to Europe and the United States ("the heretical countries"), because such travel could turn them toward the path of evil—this despite the king's frequent and extended foreign visits.[54]

In addition, Fahd compensated for his image as a pro-Western "modernizer" by expanding the activities of the Saudi religious police (mutawain). As a result, the many Westerners in Saudi Arabia who went to work for the oil industry encountered a changed atmosphere. One Western observer in Dhahran wrote, "Human rights and conventional civilized practices are now taking a back seat to the over-zealous Muslim religious and national movement that affects everyone's daily life. Hit broadest by the movement are (1) Christian church gatherings; (2) women; (3) westernized Muslims; and (4) westerners and Filipinos." He also reported that crucifixes, holy water, and church bulletins were no longer permitted. Protestant workers had been deported for holding religious services in private homes in Riyadh. Some of these measures were not new; because of pressure from the ulama, the sale of Christmas trees had been banned in 1967.[55] But now these new measures were not confined to the public domain. The religious police had become more intrusive during this period. Even Westerners in the ARAMCO enclaves did not have immunity from Islamic punishments.[56]

All of Fahd's actions revealed that the Saudi state was indeed still under strong Wahhabi influence, as it had been since its founding. Often the needs of the Saudi leadership came into conflict with the policies of the Wahhabi religious elite. But no Saudi monarch could long survive without the support of those religious leaders. Even the forward-thinking

Fahd was forced to shift back toward giving the *ulama* a major role in Saudi affairs. Thus, the regime that had first invited an enlarged Western military presence now rebuked America and cracked down on Westerners living in Saudi Arabia. Also, to preserve the backing of the Wahhabi elite, the Saudi leadership heavily invested in the religious institutions that spread Wahhabi Islam worldwide.

Legitimacy had a price tag. It was paradoxical that the well-traveled King Fahd, known in the past as one of the strongest voices for Saudi Arabia's modernization and its pro-American orientation, would become the Saudi monarch who oversaw the export of Wahhabism on a global scale.

Chapter 8

Wahhabism's Global Reach

U nder the reign of King Fahd, Saudi Arabia extended its religious influence globally. Part of this expansion resulted from
Fahd's need to bolster his religious credentials, given his reputation for gambling on the French Riviera and enjoying the good life in
his many palaces in Europe. His palace in Marbella, Spain, had a hundred rooms; he owned a $50 million yacht; and his Boeing 747 was fitted
with chandeliers, an elevator, gold bathroom fixtures, and a sauna.[1] Fahd
was known for his experience and his competence, but reports of his personal indiscretions proliferated.[2] There were stories that in his youth he
drank scotch freely, ordered pounds of caviar, and frequented the night-
clubs of Beirut.[3]

Appearances matter for Saudi kings. After all, Fahd, like all Saudi
monarchs before him, was also the imam, or religious leader, of the Wahhabi movement. In the early 1960s, King Saud's tarnished religious reputation roused the *ulama* and eventually led to his ouster. In addition, there
were widespread rumors of the royal family's corruption, that Fahd and
his brothers earned under-the-table commissions from many of the kingdom's arms purchases.[4] The British newspaper the *Observer* alleged, for
example, that $300 million in commissions was paid as part of the sale of

seventy-two Tornado aircraft to the Royal Saudi Air Force in the mid-1980s.[5] Fahd was also increasingly dependent on the American military, given the threat posed by Iran and, to a lesser extent, the Soviet-backed regime in South Yemen.

So in order to retain a free hand in foreign affairs, King Fahd's government had to satisfy the needs of the Wahhabi clerics. Saudi Arabia, therefore, embarked on a massive campaign to bring Wahhabi Islam to the world. Between 1982 and 2002, 1,500 mosques, 210 Islamic centers, and 2,000 schools to educate Muslim children were established in non-Muslim countries alone. Staggering sums of money were involved. According to internal Muslim World League documents, in just a two-year period in the 1980s, the Saudis apparently spent $10 million on mosque construction in the United States.[6] Academic chairs for Islamic Studies were donated at Harvard Law School and at the University of California–Santa Barbara. The Saudis supported Islamic research institutes at American University (in Washington), Howard University, Duke University, and Johns Hopkins University. Islamic academies went up in Moscow and in Washington, D.C.[7]

At the core of this campaign to spread Wahhabi Islam—and thus Saudi influence—were the Islamic charities and organizations; under King Fahd, Saudi Arabia continued to lavishly endow these charities. The Saudis donated billions to the Muslim World League, which had been founded under King Faisal.[8] In addition, the Saudi royal family launched donation campaigns for al-Haramain—an international charitable foundation whose stated purpose was to promote "correct beliefs" in the hearts of Muslims—as well as for the International Islamic Relief Organization (IIRO) and the World Assembly of Muslim Youth (WAMY). The Muslim Brotherhood refugees who had sought asylum in Saudi Arabia provided critical manpower for the international efforts of several of these organizations, particularly the Muslim World League. The Saudi clergy, including Sheikh Abdul Aziz bin Baz, maintained their own Islamic support networks as well.[9]

These Saudi charities allowed the kingdom to spread its political and, especially, religious agenda worldwide in the 1980s and 1990s. For example, the charities were pivotal conduits for funding the most extreme Palestinian organizations, including Hamas (the Islamic Resistance Movement).[10] Hamas was a natural Saudi ally, having grown out of the Gaza branch of the Muslim Brotherhood in 1987. The Saudis, in short, were donating enormous sums, and contributions on such a massive scale can create certain expectations: the recipient might well adapt his positions toward the donor's to assure continuing assistance. Indeed, in the 1980s and 1990s, the Saudis pumped funding into Egypt's al-Azhar, and as a result that great center of Islamic learning adopted a more religiously conservative approach.[11] Thus, whether strings were explicitly attached to Saudi aid or not, the effect was probably the same for Saudi Arabia. A significant opportunity rose to spread the doctrines of Wahhabism on an unprecedented global scale.

The Afghan Intervention and the Rise of the Taliban

Saudi Arabia's initial Afghan links were driven by religious considerations as much as by its strategic interest in defeating the Soviet Union. The Saudis provided approximately $4 billion in aid to the Afghan guerrilla groups from 1980 through 1990—*excluding* the grants given by Islamic charities and through the private funds of princes. In the early 1980s, the Saudis had two primary Afghan partners. One was Abdul Rasul Sayyaf, an Afghan Islamic scholar who had lived many years in Saudi Arabia. He was sent to Peshawar, the Pakistani frontier town near the Khyber Pass into Afghanistan, in order to promote Wahhabism among the Afghan refugees. He actually set up a Wahhabi party, the Ittihad-e-Islami.[12]

In the immediate aftermath of the Soviet Union's 1979 invasion, Abdul Rasul Sayyaf brought in Arab volunteers to aid the Afghan resistance, internationalizing the war against the Soviets in its initial phase. He seems to have modified his behavior to satisfy his Wahhabi donors. Besides growing a long beard, he changed his first name from Abdul Rasul (literally, "servant of the Prophet") to Abdul Rab (literally, "servant of God"). According to Wahhabi sensibilities, a believer can see himself only as a servant of God, not as the servant of any human being, including Muhammad. Indeed, to elevate any individual to a status normally associated with the Divine undermines the monotheism (*tawhid*) of Islam.[13] In 1984, the Saudis awarded Sayyaf the King Faisal Prize for distinguished service to Islam, which was indicative, according to one observer, of his "impeccable Wahhabite credentials."[14]

Afghanistan and Its Neighbors

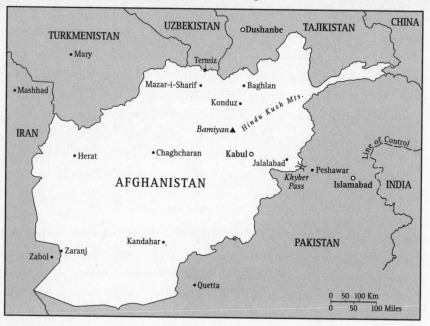

The other key Afghan figure was Gulbuddin Hekmatyar, head of the Hezb-e-Islami, which was close to Pakistan's radical Jamaat-i-Islami (the party of Mawlana Abu al-Ala Mawdudi) and to the Muslim Brotherhood.[15] As one expert on Islamic movements noted, these two organizations would receive the "lion's share" of Saudi aid to Afghanistan in the 1980s.[16] What made this remarkable was that these were not the best forces fighting the Soviets. The successes in the battlefield belonged to Ahmed Shah Massoud, who led the forces of Burhanuddin Rabani. But Hekmatyar and Sayyaf were ideologically loyal. That Hekmatyar was anti-American did not appear to upset the Saudis in the late 1980s.[17]

The Saudis also relied on non-Afghans: most notably, Abdullah Azzam and Osama bin Laden. Azzam ran the Muslim World League and Muslim Brotherhood offices in Peshawar, Pakistan.[18] In 1984, as noted, he created a Services Center (Maktab Khadamat al-Mujahideen) to prepare new recruits for the Afghan jihad and to coordinate the flow of contributions. Assessments vary regarding the number of Arabs who joined the Afghan jihad, but it is clear that the largest contingent came from Saudi Arabia. The Saudis certainly encouraged their people to join the Afghan cause: Saudi Arabia's national airline gave a 75 percent discount for volunteers heading to Afghanistan.[19] According to estimates from Saudi intelligence sources, beginning in 1979 as many as twenty-five thousand Saudis received training abroad, including in the Afghan war.[20]

Azzam's funding for these thousands of volunteers came from Saudi intelligence, the Saudi Red Crescent, the Muslim World League, and, privately, from Saudi princes.[21] One reason the Saudis offered Azzam so much support was self-interest: it was better to have Arab volunteers pouring into the Afghan jihad than to have them drawn to Iran's Revolutionary Shiism in places like Lebanon.

The Saudi investment in Peshawar was huge. In 1988, the Muslim World League claimed that it had opened 150 Koran study centers and 85 Islamic schools for Afghan students.[22] Two Saudis were among Dr. Azzam's key aides. One was Wael Hamza Julaidan, who headed various offices of the Muslim World League and the Saudi Red Crescent in Pakistan. Azzam's second Saudi partner in Peshawar was his former student Osama bin Laden.[23] After Abdullah Azzam was killed in a car bomb attack in 1989, bin Laden gradually took over the Maktab Khadamat al-Mujahideen. That same year he converted it into the al-Qaeda organization.

After the Soviets were defeated in Afghanistan, al-Qaeda began to evolve, and within a few years it had become a worldwide consortium of Islamist terrorist groups. One analysis broke down the nationalities of the Arab members of al-Qaeda as follows: 5,000 Saudis, 3,000 Yemenis, 2,800 Algerians, 2,000 Egyptians, 400 Tunisians, 350 Iraqis, 200 Libyans, and dozens of Jordanians.[24] Saudi nationals were clearly the leading component of the Afghan Arabs as they made their transition from fighting the Soviets to international terrorism.

Osama bin Laden came out of the Saudi establishment. His father, Muhammad bin Laden, despite his poor Yemeni origins, was head of the largest construction company in Saudi Arabia, and in fact was a close personal friend of King Faisal. His company extended and maintained the Grand Mosque in Mecca. Even after Muhammad bin Laden's death in 1968, the two families maintained widespread social contacts. In fact, Osama bin Laden and Prince Turki al-Faisal, a son of King Faisal, knew each other during bin Laden's university days. Turki would make use of his relationship with bin Laden after the prince became the Saudi intelligence chief in September 1977. After the Soviet invasion of Afghanistan, he put bin Laden in charge of moving Arab volunteers who wanted to fight the Soviets from Saudi Arabia to Peshawar, Pakistan.[25] (Prince Turki also had direct contact with Abdullah Azzam, whom he met in Saudi Arabia and on at least two occasions in Pakistan.)[26] Moreover, Prince Muhammad bin Faisal, Turki's older brother, used the bin Laden family as a front for funneling aid to the Afghan cause; he would later use the bin Laden connection to move funds to Islamist militants in Algeria in the 1990s.[27]

In the 1980s, Osama bin Laden became a major figure in the Saudi-supported jihad in Afghanistan. He described himself as the Saudis' "representative in Afghanistan" in an unpublished interview given to a French journalist from *France Soir* in April 1995.[28] After getting the order from Prince Turki, he set up some of the infrastructure for the Afghan Arabs inside the border areas of Pakistan, but in 1985 he moved into Afghanistan and joined up with Hekmatyar's pro-Saudi forces. Even after the Soviet defeat in 1989, he continued to set up bases in Afghanistan to train Arab volunteers. The war against the lingering pro-Soviet regime in Kabul was not over. Bin Laden used his own wealth and Saudi donations to spread Wahhabism among the Afghans.[29] In any case, most of the Arab volunteers in Afghanistan came from Saudi Arabia, so Wahhabi practices were already ingrained in them. For many non-Saudi volunteers, the transition to a more severe religious environment was fairly natural; for example, Ramzi Yousef—who would mastermind the 1993 World Trade Center attack—joined the Afghan jihad in 1986, but his father had already been drawn to Wahhabism in Kuwait.[30]

After the Soviets withdrew from Afghanistan in 1989, the Saudis' financial contributions continued. In March 1990, they transferred $100 million to their Afghan ally Hekmatyar.[31] But by 1992, the pro-Soviet Najibullah government in Kabul had fallen, and new dilemmas emerged. The victorious Afghan factions began fighting one another. Supporting a jihad against Soviet occupation of a Muslim country was one thing, but to support a jihad between armed Afghan groups would be an entirely different matter. The United States wanted all aid to Hekmatyar and Sayyaf terminated. They were seen as extremists who also dealt in the narcotics trade. And from the Saudis' perspective, both these Afghan groups betrayed Saudi Arabia when they backed Iraqi president Saddam Hussein after his August 1990 invasion of Kuwait.[32] Still, the Saudis did not write their Afghan clients off entirely; the director of Saudi intelligence, Prince Turki, maintained a dialogue with Hekmatyar as late as November 1991.[33] But Saudi Arabia was open to the idea of building relationships with new Afghan partners.

The Taliban (literally, "students"), the militia that became a political force in Afghanistan in 1994, were not initially Wahhabis. Sunni Muslims constituted 80 percent of the population of Afghanistan, but they were from the Hanafi school of Islamic law, whereas the Wahhabis came from the Hanbali school. Taliban traditions came from the Deobandi schools of nineteenth-century India, which were not particularly extreme; militant jihad was not their priority.[34] But in the wake of the Afghan war, the Taliban became more radical. Saudi funding poured into the Jamaat Ulama Islami (JUI), the Deobandi religious movement in Pakistan, as well as JUI's Pakistani competitor, Jamaat-i-Islami.

In the 1980s, radicalized JUI *madrasa*s and other advanced religious academies sprang up near the Afghan-Pakistani border and became training centers for the Taliban. These schools were initially funded from *zakat*, Islamic charitable donations provided by Pakistanis, but later, nongovernmental organizations from Saudi Arabia and other Gulf states became important backers.[35] A leader of one of Pakistan's hard-line sectarian Sunni parties called the *madrasa*s "a supply line for jihad."[36] Eight Taliban ministers came from one school alone, Dar-ul-Uloom Haqqania.[37] Visiting Haqqania, Thomas Friedman of the *New York Times* noticed direct evidence of Saudi aid: a sign on a classroom wall read, "A Gift of the Kingdom of Saudi Arabia."[38] According to analysts, the Taliban became a "hybridization" of Deobandism and salafism (supporting Islam as it had been under the Prophet Muhammad and his immediate successors), which the Wahhabi presence of the 1980s had made possible.[39]

But why, after 1992, when the pro-Soviet Najibullah government fell, did the Saudis continue to support the Taliban? After all, they no longer had a strategic interest in Afghanistan. True, there was potentially an economic interest, given that Delta, a Saudi oil and gas company, was a partner of the California-based UNOCAL company in the effort to erect pipelines from the Caspian Sea through Afghanistan and Pakistan to the Indian Ocean. But this sole economic consideration was not a compelling reason for the Saudi regime's involvement, particularly because it was not entirely clear that Riyadh supported developing Caspian Sea oil and gas that could compete with Saudi-owned energy resources in the Persian Gulf. More important, with the Saudis funding political parties in Pakistan—which, unlike Saudi Arabia, had real stakes in the question of which government ruled its neighbor Afghanistan—the kingdom had considerable leverage on the Pakistanis and did not need to remain engaged in Afghanistan because of Pakistani interests alone. No, the Saudis must have had motivations of their own for backing the Taliban into the 1990s.

The Saudi *ulama*, apparently, strongly advocated the Taliban connection. Indeed, Sheikh Muhammad bin Jubair, who has been called the "exporter of the Wahhabi creed in the Muslim world" and who sat on the Council of Senior Ulama with Sheikh Abdul Aziz bin Baz, personally pushed the idea that the Saudis should give the Taliban even more support. As in the days of the war against the Soviets, much of the hands-on coordination of Saudi aid was under the control of the Saudi intelligence chief, Prince Turki al-Faisal.[40] But there was still a strong Islamic component. In his first meeting with the Taliban leader, Mullah Omar, Prince Turki brought along with him Abdullah al-Turki, who would later become the secretary-general of the Muslim World League.[41]

The Saudi royal family maintained many of the initial contacts with the Taliban. In 1994 and 1995, Pakistan's JUI leader, Mawlana Fazlur Rahman, a close domestic ally of Prime Minister Benazir Bhutto, repeatedly invited Saudi princes to Kandahar, Afghanistan, to hunt exotic game birds. For these hunting trips, the Saudis would arrive on huge transport aircraft with their own luxury four-wheel drive vehicles. After the hunt, the Saudis would leave these vehicles—and donations—for their Taliban hosts; the Taliban made good use of the Saudi vehicles for their military campaign. Prince Turki also visited Kandahar regularly during this period, providing funds, vehicles, and fuel just before the final Taliban push on Kabul in July 1996.[42]

Given the Saudis' active support for the Taliban—which the Saudi religious leadership backed—it is little wonder that in the 1990s the Afghan rebels moved even closer to Wahhabism. But there was another reason that Wahhabism penetrated the Taliban: Osama bin Laden. After the Taliban captured Kabul in 1996, bin Laden's influence over the Taliban grew. He moved his residence to Kandahar, near the home of the

Taliban leader, Mullah Omar. Bin Laden had all-night conversations with the Taliban, and he provided substantial funds. He sent his Arab Afghan forces into battles to support the Taliban against rival Afghan militias. And he allowed his training camps to be used by Kashmiri terrorist organizations backed by the Taliban's key local ally, Pakistan.[43]

As bin Laden gained influence, the Taliban's acts reflected radical Wahhabi ideas. Historically, Afghan Sunni Muslims had not attacked the Shiite Muslim minority, but anti-Shiite reprisals began even before the Taliban takeover and grew more systematic under the Taliban regime. Bin Laden's Wahhabi fighters helped the Taliban massacre the Hazaras, a Persian-speaking Shiite group living in northern Afghanistan.[44] Whole Shiite sections of Afghanistan found themselves blockaded, their access to supplies cut off. Sources representing the Northern Alliance of militias, which held out against the Taliban, suggested that the new regime's policy was to starve out the Hazaras.

The situation for the Shiites worsened. The Taliban wanted to clean out the Shiite population from northern Afghanistan. They placed Mullah Niazi in command of the city of Mazar-i-Sharif, and Niazi declared to the Shiites, "Last year you rebelled against us and killed us. From all your homes you shot at us. Now we are here to deal with you. The Hazaras are not Muslims and now we have to kill Hazaras. You either accept to be Muslims or leave Afghanistan."[45]

The Taliban essentially gave the Shiites three choices: convert to Sunni Islam, move to Iran, or be killed. Tens of thousands of Mazar-i-Sharif residents fled for their lives; the Taliban killed many of these refugees from the air. Between five and six thousand Shiites were killed in this Taliban campaign, according to United Nations and Red Cross sources.[46] Additionally, a Taliban unit entered the Iranian consulate in Mazar-i-Sharif and murdered eleven people. The Taliban captured another forty-five Iranians as well. In response, in October 1998, Iran massed 200,000 troops on the Iranian-Afghan border until captured Iranians were released and Iranian bodies returned.

This anti-Shiite policy was not new in the world of Wahhabism, of course. The 1802 Wahhabi attacks on Shiite shrines in Kerbala left thousands dead. The Wahhabi clerics of modern Saudi Arabia viewed the Saudi Shiite population of the Eastern Province as heretics, not true Muslims.

Ibn Saud's Ikhwan had wanted them exterminated; the *ulama* had once advocated their forced conversion to Sunni Islam. Unlike other Arab states, the Saudi state even through the 1990s did not permit Shiites to build mosques or in any other way practice their religion publicly. The Taliban came to follow the Wahhabi approach to Shiism, rather than the practice followed in other parts of the Islamic world.

Wahhabi predispositions appeared in other areas of Taliban behavior. In September 1998, the Taliban captured the Bamiyan Valley, an area where monumental Buddhist statues had stood for nearly two thousand years. These statues had been one of the greatest archaeological treasures of Afghanistan and had withstood the country's many conquerors. But in the spring of 2001, the Taliban blasted the head of one colossal statue, and the midsection of a second statue came under rocket attack. The destruction of idols and religious shrines had also been common among the Wahhabis; this was how they justified their attacks on shrines in Mecca and Medina after their conquest in the 1920s.[47]

Although the Taliban regime eventually took control of about 90 percent of Afghanistan, by and large the international community refused to accord it diplomatic recognition. The Northern Alliance held Afghanistan's seat at the United Nations. Only three states recognized the Taliban: Pakistan, the United Arab Emirates, and Saudi Arabia.

Wahhabism in the Former Soviet Republics and in the Russian Federation

The breakdown and eventual collapse of the Soviet Union opened up another front for Saudi Wahhabism. In 1990, after Islam had been suppressed for years by the Soviet regime, mosques were springing up across Central Asia: fifty new mosques were erected in Kyrgyzstan, whereas just fifteen had gone up the year before; thirty mosques went up in Turkmenistan, after only five the previous year.[48] The pattern repeated itself in other Muslim republics.

And as a result of perestroika, many Soviet Muslims could travel to Saudi Arabia. Some even took religious instruction in Saudi schools. But more important, these Soviet Muslims made contact with Saudi charities that would provide them with funds after the Soviet Central Asian republics gained their independence. With the establishment of diplomatic relations between Saudi Arabia and the Soviet Union and the opening of a Saudi embassy in Moscow, many Saudi charities stepped up their activities. Using the Saudi embassy's section for Islamic affairs, the Muslim World League and its subsidiaries dramatically increased their activity in Russia and the Central Asian republics.

Several Central Asian movements came under Wahhabi influence. In Uzbekistan, for example, Juma Namangani and Tahir Yuldeshev, who became fluent in Arabic and interested in the Wahhabi creed, gained access to Saudi foundations, and in 1990 built a mosque and a *madrasa* in their Uzbek town. They went on to form Islamic revolutionary organizations like Adolat; the Uzbek government charged that both were involved in the attempted assassination of Uzbekistan's president, Islam Karimov, on February 16, 1999. Yuldeshev, who traveled to Saudi Arabia, Iran, Pakistan, and Turkey, settled in Afghanistan in 1998, and the Taliban gave him a residence in Kandahar near the homes of Mullah Omar and Osama bin Laden. According to Russian officials, the Saudi intelligence agency and Islamic charities aided Yuldeshev.

Such funding would not have been unusual; the Pakistan-based journalist Ahmed Rashid recalls how many of the young members of the new militant Islamist groups in the early 1990s "were proud to claim that their funds came from Saudi Arabia."[49] In Tajikistan, during the period of Soviet rule, some members of the Islamic Renaissance Party were connected to Gulbuddin Hekmatyar's pro-Saudi Afghan militia.[50] In the Tajik civil war that raged from May 1992 until the middle of 1993 between the Tajik government and Islamist armed insurgent groups, many of which were based in Afghanistan, an estimated 50,000 people, mostly civilians, were killed, while 600,000 were displaced internally.[51] Uzbekistan's Namangani joined the Islamist insurgents and formed a battalion of 200 to 350 fighters. According to Robert Baer, a former CIA operative, Saudi Arabia used the Muslim World League to supply funds and clandestinely ship weapons to the Tajik Islamist leader, Abdullah Nuri.[52] Later, in July 1996, Nuri brokered a meeting between Osama bin Laden and Iranian intelligence.[53]

Many of the Islamist movements in the former Soviet republics wanted to create independent Islamic republics. In March 1990, a writer for the Muslim World League, Sayyid Hassan Mutuhar, asserted in the organization's weekly newspaper, *Muslim World News*, "Like Palestine, Afghanistan, Kashmir, and Southern Philippines, the question of Central Asia and its Muslim-majority republics has assumed a special significance." He continued, "The current popular 'revolts' in Azerbaijan and Tajikistan aiming at complete independence and the simmering resistance in Kazakhstan, Kirgizia, Turkmenia, and Uzbekistan, in juxtaposition with the mounting repression by Moscow's war lords and party thugs in those territories, are—from any viewpoint—sufficient grounds to invoke the principle of *Jus Quasitum* (the right to recover), so expressly dealt with in the Holy Qur'an."[54] In other words, after the Soviet defeat in Afghanistan—which Mutuhar called the Soviet Union's Waterloo—the Islamic world had a real opportunity to take back lost Muslim land.

Of course, the idea of retaking lost Muslim land appealed to the most militant Wahhabis. And indeed, the Saudis assisted some of these Islamist reform organizations in Central Asia, most notably the Hizb ut-Tahrir (HT), which was founded in 1953 in Saudi Arabia and Jordan. The movement had certain similarities with Wahhabism. It was violently opposed to Sufism and worship at Sufi shrines. And it was fiercely opposed to Shiism; the HT intended to expel all Shiites from Central Asia if it came to power.[55] But it also envisioned restoring a Sunni caliphate over all of Central Asia, bringing this entire area under one Muslim leader. Moreover, the HT's Palestinian founder, Sheikh al-Nabhani, believed that the strategy for spreading Islam ought to emulate the stages followed by the Prophet Muhammad: first, spreading the message of Islam secretly; second, coming out in the open about the religion's aims; and only third, preaching a call for jihad. This interpretation did not comport with the more radical Wahhabi understanding of jihad, as articulated by Saudi Arabia's Sheikh bin Baz, who wanted to reverse the sequence and start the jihad.

Thus, a Central Asian leader of the HT admitted that the organization, which had originated "in the revivalist Wahhabi movement in Saudi Arabia," "soon developed differences with the Wahhabis and split. HT wanted to work with people in each country separately and bring about sharia [observance of Islamic law] in a peaceful manner." But the Wahhabis, he explained, were extremists who wanted guerrilla war and the creation of an Islamic army.[56]

Ayman al-Zawahiri, a deputy of Osama bin Laden, outlined the geo-political significance of jihad in the former Soviet republics:

> The liberation of the Caucasus would constitute a hotbed of *jihad* (or fundamentalism as the United States describes it) and that region would become the shelter of thousands of Muslim mujahidin from various parts of the Islamic world, particularly Arab parts. This poses a direct threat to the United States represented by the growing support of the *jihadist* movement everywhere in the Islamic world. If the Chechens and other Caucasian mujahidin reach the shores of the oil-rich Caspian Sea, the only thing that will separate them from Afghanistan will be the neutral state of Turkmenistan. This will form a mujahid Islamic belt to the south of Russia that will be connected in the east with Pakistan, which is brimming with mujahidin movements in Kashmir.

Another goal, according to al-Zawahiri, was the "fragmentation" of the Russian Federation itself. This would "topple the basic ally of the United States" in the war against the "Islamic Jihadist reawakening."

Some might dismiss al-Zawahiri's position as the statements of a radical Islamic associate of Osama bin Laden, but at the same time, one must ask whether Saudi Arabia had a national interest in this radical activity in Central Asia. Why did the Saudis intervene where they did?

The emergence of the Caspian basin as a new energy source at the end of the Cold War posed potential challenges for the Saudis and other traditional energy producers in the Persian Gulf. True, the oil and gas reserves of the Persian Gulf still dwarfed those of the Caspian. But the Caspian's energy reserves could threaten Saudi Arabia's unique position as the country that could most easily use its excess capacity to make up any world shortfalls. In short, Russian and Central Asian energy could undercut Saudi Arabia and some of the other oil-producing Gulf states. From this perspective, Saudi interests would certainly be served by a state of continuing instability in the Caucasus that delayed the development of Central Asian energy resources and pipeline routes.

Indeed, the Saudis intervened not just in the Muslim republics of the former Soviet Union but also in Russia itself. If one looks at the pattern of intervention, the target areas appear to be the strategically sensitive Northern Caucasus.

The first well-known area of confrontation in the Russian Federation was Chechnya. The first phase of Russia's war against the Chechens raged for two years, from 1994 through 1996. The revolt was led by a former Soviet general, Shamil Bassayev, who was not a product of "international Wahhabism" and did not appear to be affected by Saudi religious practices in any way. But an Islamist contingent in Chechnya known as the al-Ansar mujahideen came from Afghanistan and was led by Ibn al-Khattab, who some believe was a Jordanian from an area near the Saudi-Jordanian border. Other sources claim that he was a Saudi citizen, born in 1970, who had developed a close relationship with Osama bin Laden during the Afghan war.[57] Indeed, bin Laden's people claimed that al-Khattab was, in fact, a Saudi.[58] In an interview with a Chechen newspaper, al-Khattab said only that he came from "Arabia." But he did have ties to Saudi Arabia: a fund-raising website listed the Benevolence International Foundation—originally a Saudi-based charity—as a vehicle for contributions.[59] Also, al-Khattab apparently practiced a rigid type of Islam, one close to Wahhabism. He videotaped his cruel treatment of Russian captives in order to help his fund-raising efforts with international Muslim organizations, especially in Saudi Arabia.[60]

The Wahhabi presence in Chechnya became even more pronounced. In July 1998, a Wahhabi militia in the town of Gudermes clashed with Sufi Muslims from nearby villages after the Chechen Wahhabis tried to destroy a local Sufi shrine.[61] Leading the Wahhabi force at Gudermes was Brigadier General Arbi Barayev, who would emerge as one of the most brutal Chechen warlords. The internal security situation in Chechnya rapidly declined as the area became a base for terrorist operations and kidnapping within neighboring areas of Russia; in the period just after the Russian-Chechen agreement of 1996, at least 1,100 kidnappings occurred.[62] In 1998, for example, Barayev abducted three British telecommunications workers and then beheaded them, insisting that by carrying out the execution he could earn more money from his "Arab friends" than he could by accepting a ransom.[63] In June 2001, Russian federal forces killed

Barayev, so his nephew Movsar Barayev took command of his militia; in late October 2002, the new commander would lead an attack on a Moscow theater and take about nine hundred civilians hostage.

By 1999, the militant Islamist opposition had undermined President Aslan Maskhadov's control of the Chechen government. In March, the Russian Interior Ministry's envoy to Chechnya was abducted at the Grozny airport. President Maskhadov lashed out at the Wahhabi presence in Chechnya, reminding his fellow Chechens that they belonged to traditional Sufi Muslim orders: "We are Nakshband [members of a fourteenth-century Sufi order] and Kadari [members of a eleventh-century Sufi order] and Sunnites, and there is no place for any other Islamic sect in Chechnya."[64] He specifically condemned Saudi Arabia for financing the Wahhabi opposition. Maskhadov's arguments against Wahhabism were religious as well as political; he rejected the Wahhabi attempt to cleanse Islam in Central Asia of such traditions as veneration of saints: "We cannot tolerate a situation when the enemies of Islam trample under foot the century-old traditions of the Chechyn people, desecrate the names of our saints, kidnap and kill people. In the past 400 years history has given us the chance to build our own free state. But people who have sold their souls for dollars are standing in our way."[65] The Russians, who initially had confidence in Maskhadov and his ability to stand up to Islamist forces, eventually viewed him as an unreliable peace partner and even suspected him of colluding with the very extremists he criticized.

The war in Chechnya was reignited in August 1999, when Chechens staged an uprising in the neighboring republic of Dagestan.[66] The stakes were great in Dagestan, because the republic controlled 70 percent of Russia's shoreline on the oil-rich Caspian Sea; oil pipelines from Azerbaijan crossed Dagestan before moving through Chechnya and other Russian territories to the Black Sea.[67] Then Chechen rebel leader Shamil Bassayev broadened the war aims, proclaiming a jihad to liberate neighboring Muslim-dominated areas from Russian tyranny.[68] On November 16, 1999, the secretary-general of the Muslim World League, Abdullah bin Salah al-Obaid, declared that Dagestan, like Chechnya, had the right to be an independent state. He condemned Russian incursions into "Islamic territories," arguing that all the Islamic regions of the former Soviet Union had a right to be as free as the republics of Yugoslavia.[69] In essence, a

Islamic Resurgence in Chechnya and Dagestan

Saudi-directed international organization agreed to a strategy to dismember the Russian Federation. And when a series of Russian apartment buildings were bombed in Volgodonsk, Buinaksk, and Moscow in August 1999, killing about three hundred civilians, the Chechens seemed to have adopted a new strategy: taking the war to the heart of Russia.[70]

Dagestan was particularly vulnerable to penetration by outside radical forces. According to one estimate, 80 percent of those who embarked on the hajj to Saudi Arabia from the Russian Federation came from Dagestan. From 1994 to 1996, many Dagestan Muslims served in the Chechen war against the Russians and came under Wahhabi influence.[71] Most important, like Afghanistan in the early 1980s, Dagestan was poor. Economically failing states were notoriously easy to penetrate. The jobless were easier to recruit; monetary aid had even more political influence. And Wahhabism did make certain inroads in Dagestan during this period. One Wahhabi leader, Bagauddin Magomedov, described his flight from Chechnya to Dagestan in 1997 as a *"hijra,"* clearly drawing a comparison to the Prophet Muhammad's flight from Mecca to Medina. In two towns Magomedov established a small "Wahhabi republic," a highly disciplined society that engaged in collective prayer and study. Magomedov's group studied the works of Sayyid Qutb, Mawlana Abu al-Ala Mawdudi, Hasan al-Banna, and Muhammad ibn Abdul Wahhab. In June 1998, Russian interior minister Sergei Stepashin told a Commonwealth of Independent States (CIS) conference in Tashkent that "expressions of fundamentalism... or Wahhabism... have become a serious issue in the CIS." He announced that Russia and Azerbaijan were undertaking a joint study of the expressions of Wahhabism in Dagestan.[72]

The Russian Federal Security Service (FSB) charged that the Chechen rebels in Dagestan were receiving financial aid from the Saudi-based al-Haramain organization.[73] In 1997, this organization backed extremist groups in Dagestan, and in 1999, it started operating out of Azerbaijan. In May 2000, Azerbaijan closed down the Saudi-based charity's offices; a Justice Ministry official said that the activities of the al-Haramain organization "posed a threat to Azerbaijan's statehood." Saudi Wahhabis even seemed to be joining the fighting: the Russian federal forces announced that a Saudi-born "Wahhabite" named Abu Omar Muhammad al-Seif, reportedly a member of al-Haramain, had been killed in a clash between their units and militants in Chechnya.[74]

Two more of Russia's north Caucasian republics came under assault in 2001: Karachay-Cherkessia and Kabardino-Balkaria. Vladimir Ustinov, Russia's prosecutor-general, stated that Russian authorities had arrested eleven Wahhabis who had tried to overthrow these republics' legitimate governments and establish a "Wahhabite regime." Russian police had uncovered caches of weapons and also "Wahhabite literature," Ustinov said. According to Ustinov, there were 1,500 Islamic religious organizations in the Trans-Volga federal district: "With direct and indirect support from abroad, Wahhabis—the most radical Muslims—are gradually expanding their sphere of influence in these organizations."[75]

Russia has had great difficulty stopping the intrusion of Wahhabi radicals. Some of these groups have established bases outside of Russian territory. In Georgia's Chechen-populated Pankisi Gorge, about five hundred Wahhabis assisted Chechen refugees and other local residents, trying to generate a Wahhabist movement, according to a Georgian government representative. One American observer who actually visited the Pankisi

Gorge in August 2000 noted that this Wahhabism was prone to incite violence: "The version of 'Wahhabism' spread in the Caucasus, like Osama bin Laden's, allows other Muslims to be considered polytheists who can be robbed and killed."[76] Wahhabism was also promoted by Saudi charities. The Saudi-based IIRO was active in the Pankisi Gorge, funneling money to the al-Ansar mujahideen, which was led by al-Khattab, in 1999 and 2000.[77] At the same time, Azerbaijan encountered Wahhabi infiltration; Azerbaijan's deputy minister of national security affairs announced, "Over the last years 300 citizens of Azerbaijan had training in 'Wahhabist' centers in Daghestan." For Russia, this was becoming a problem on an international scale.[78]

President Vladimir Putin's envoy to the Volga Federal District, Sergei Kirienco, warned that hundreds of Muslim leaders had returned from training in Saudi Arabia, as well as other Islamic states, and were spreading Wahhabism to Russia's Muslims. Traditional Islam, he said, needed to be strengthened in Russia. But Russia was not offering sufficient financial support for more moderate forms of Islam that had been indigenous to Russia. Thus, the forms of Islam that the Saudis backed enjoyed a huge advantage.[79]

Wahhabi charities in Saudi Arabia funded religious centers and schools in Tartarstan, Bashkortostan, and other republics throughout central Russia. The Russian leadership was concerned for the future territorial integrity of Russia itself. After all, out of 143 million Russians, 20 million were Muslims; seven out of the Russian Federation's twenty-one republics had Muslim majorities. "If extremist forces manage to get a hold of the Caucasus," President Putin concluded in 2001, "this infection may spread up to the Volga River, spread to other republics, and we will either face the full Islamization of Russia, or we will have to agree to Russia's division into several states."[80]

There was one last area where Saudi Wahhabism was making its mark. By 2000, suicide bombings by Sunni Muslims had become prevalent in two struggles—in particular, the Palestinian suicide bombers from Hamas and Islamic Jihad attacked Israel, and Chechen suicide bombers attacked the Russian army.[81] Saudi Wahhabi clerics—Sheikh Hamud bin Uqla al-Shuaibi, Sheikh Hamid bin Abdul al-Ali, and Sheikh Sulaiman bin Nasr al-Ulwan—gave these attacks their blessing. Although these clerics were not in the highest levels of the Saudi *ulama*, their religious opinions were widely read and even posted on the Hamas website. Sheikh bin Baz had begun to legitimize Palestinian terrorism back in 1989 when he declared the Palestinian struggle a jihad. In the mid-1990s, one of bin Baz's colleagues, the highly respected Sheikh Muhammad ibn Saleh al-Uthaiman, had actually blessed Hamas's suicide bombings.[82]

The Battle for Bosnia and the Balkans

In March 1992, a month before the last remnant of the pro-Soviet regime fell in Afghanistan, Bosnia-Herzegovina declared its independence from Yugoslavia, and Serb militias opened fire on its capital, Sarajevo. About four thousand Arab Islamist veterans of the Afghan war made their way to Bosnia, the vast majority of them from Saudi Arabia and other countries of the Arabian peninsula.[83]

The most notable of these Saudi Afghans was Abu Abdul Aziz—also known by his *nom de guerre*, "Barbaros." Like Osama bin Laden, he was influenced in Saudi Arabia by Abdullah Azzam, who taught in the late 1970s at King Abdul Aziz University in Jeddah. Barbaros joined Azzam in Peshawar in 1984. Before going on to Bosnia, in 1992, he consulted with leading members of the Wahhabi *ulama* in Saudi Arabia, including Sheikh bin Baz, who supported his entering the Balkan struggle against the Serbs.[84] In his leadership capacity in the Muslim World League, bin Baz called on all Islamic organizations to assist the Bosnian Muslims in their war against "the enemies of Allah."[85]

By the end of 1992, an estimated four hundred Saudi volunteers were fighting with Muslim forces in Bosnia. These were in addition to Afghan veterans from Egypt, Pakistan, Sudan, and Algeria. Because of the serious ideological and religious differences between the Arab soldiers and the native Bosnians, in 1993 a separate El-Muzhahidun regiment was formed. Barbaros commanded this unit, which was disbanded after the signing of the Dayton Accords in 1995.[86] This unit had questionable military value. It constituted only 2 to 3 percent of the Bosnian government army, and as Bosnian capabilities improved, the unit's importance declined.[87] Moreover, many of the Saudis came to fight for only one- or two-month periods and then returned to Saudi Arabia. But the Arab force acquired a reputation as fierce fighters, known to have severed the heads of the "Christian

Serbs" and mutilated their enemies' bodies.[88] These acts, however, frequently undermined the cause of the Bosnian Muslims, who presented themselves as the victims of Serb brutality.

Saudi money had more influence in the Bosnian struggle. Money was raised at the highest levels of the Saudi kingdom. King Fahd's brother Salman bin Abdul Aziz, the governor of Riyadh, chaired the Supreme Commission for the Collection of Donations for Bosnian Muslims. On August 11, 1995, King Fahd himself sponsored a telethon in Saudi Arabia that raised more than $100 million.[89] These charities were instrumental in moving volunteers and especially supplies to the Bosnian front. The World Assembly of Muslim Youth (WAMY) dispatched Muslim troops to fight the Serbs and flew wounded Saudi volunteers to Germany for medical attention.[90] The Saudi-based International Islamic Relief Organization (IIRO) funneled financial aid (most of which came from Saudi individuals and companies) and relief workers to Bosnia. Saudi officials confirmed that the charities also provided arms and backing for the Arab volunteers.[91]

The IIRO was pivotal in allowing Afghan veterans to penetrate other parts of the Balkans as well. For example, in 1992, Muhammad al-Zawahiri, the brother of al-Qaeda's Ayman al-Zawahiri, came to Tirana, the capital of Albania, and worked as an engineer for the IIRO. But al-Zawahiri was really working on behalf of his brother's Egyptian Jihad organization just as it was merging with bin Laden's al-Qaeda. In 1993, Osama bin Laden appointed Ayman al-Zawahiri to direct al-Qaeda operations in the Balkans.[92]

Another Saudi-based charity that opened offices in Albania was the al-Haramain organization. One of its employees, Ahmed Ibrahim al-Nagger, was deported in 1999 from Albania to Egypt, where he was later sentenced to death for terrorism. He was an associate of al-Qaeda. In 2002, Secretary of the Treasury Paul H. O'Neill blocked the bank accounts of the Bosnian branch of al-Haramain because it had diverted funds to terrorists, including al-Qaeda. The United States took the same measures against the al-Haramain branch in Somalia. Al-Haramain workers were arrested in Albania because of their connections to Egyptian terrorist groups.[93]

Both the Saudi volunteers and the Saudi charities propagated Wahhabism to the Bosnian Muslims. They were disappointed with the type of

Islam that they encountered in Bosnia. As one UN officer noted, "Bosnian Moslems were Europeans. Some were religious, but most were not. After fifty years of Communism, many did not even know how to pray. They drank, smoked, danced, ate pork, and lived like their Serb and Croat neighbors."[94] The Wahhabis sought to cleanse the European form of Islam practiced in Bosnia and bring it closer to what they knew from the Middle East. Arab volunteers in Bosnia smashed cafés, urged Bosnian women to wear the veil, and encouraged men to grow beards.[95]

The Saudi charities stayed active in the Balkans even when the postwar reconstruction efforts were under way, but the clash between the Saudi donors' Wahhabism and the Balkan recipients' form of Islam became ever more glaring. For example, Balkan mosques had been decorated according to centuries-old Ottoman traditions, with ornaments and other unique architectural features that were not used in the mosques of the Arabian peninsula. So when the leaders of the Saudi charities, who felt it was their mission to spread Wahhabism, financed the reconstruction of mosques damaged in the war, they were sure to remove the ornate decorations. While rebuilding the Gazi-Husrevbeg mosque in Sarajevo—considered one of the greatest Islamic structures in southeastern Europe—the Saudi agency overseeing the project plastered over centuries-old frescoes and ceramic tiles. In Kosovo, the Saudis even destroyed mosques, some of them from the five-hundred-year period during which the Ottoman Empire ruled Kosovo. In two notable cases, older mosques were dismantled and replaced with much larger concrete mosques that had no offensive ornamentation.[96]

Thus, just as the Wahhabi-influenced Taliban destroyed Buddhist statues in Afghanistan's Bamiyan Valley, the Wahhabis in the Balkans had no problem tearing down the symbols of other cultures, no matter their archaeological and cultural value. But in this case, they were destroying *Islamic* culture. Saudi Wahhabism sought to restore the puritanical Islam of the seventh century, skipping over the centuries of Islamic civilization under the Ottoman Empire.

A clear cultural clash was under way. The head of the UN mission in Bosnia noted, "There is a conflict here between a Saudi-sponsored Wahhabi interpretation of Islam and an Ottoman perception."[97] Indeed, one Bosnian official confessed, "We have a big problem with the Saudis; they are spreading around huge amounts of money to help rebuild Bosnia. But they are also building mosques and spreading a version of Islam that is alien to our Bosnian Islam."⁹⁸ On December 29, 1999, the Kosovapress News Agency, the media arm of the former Kosovo Liberation Army, declared:

> For more than a century, civilized countries have separated religion from the state. . . . We now see attempts, not only in Kosovo but everywhere Albanians live, to introduce religion into public schools. . . . Supplemental courses for children have been set up by foreign Islamic organizations who hide behind assistance programs. Some radio stations . . . now offer nightly broadcasts in Arabic, which nobody understands and which may lead many to ask, are we in an Arab country? *It is time for Albanian mosques to be separated from Arab connections and for Islam to be developed on the basis of Albanian culture and customs* [emphasis added].⁹⁹

At the same time, the connections between the Saudi charities in the Balkans and international terrorism came into focus. In October 2001, a NATO force raided the offices of the Saudi High Commission for Aid to Bosnia in Sarajevo. The commission, founded in 1993 by Prince Salman bin Abdul Aziz, was supposed to help Bosnian war orphans, and had raised $600 million. But the NATO raid turned up maps of Washington, D.C., with bull's-eyes on U.S. government buildings, a computer program explaining how to use crop-duster aircraft (a method of spreading chemical weapons), and photographs of past American targets of terrorist attacks. Suspects connected with the Saudi agency were arrested and held by the United States at Guantanamo Bay, Cuba, along with other al-Qaeda suspects from the U.S. war in Afghanistan.¹⁰⁰

Meanwhile, Bosnian police raided the Sarajevo and Zenica offices of the Benevolentia charity, which was suspected of having ties with al-Qaeda.¹⁰¹ Benevolentia was a branch of the Islamic Benevolence Committee, which had had its headquarters in Jeddah, Saudi Arabia, until 1993. Then the Saudi government shut down the Jeddah office after complaints from Algeria and Egypt that Benevolence was funding their Islamist oppositions.¹⁰² But other branches of Benevolence remained intact.

Finally, Bosnian intelligence officials began to look more closely at the activities of the Saudi-based al-Haramain organization. A Bosnian intelligence report noted that al-Haramain had a "clear lack of any concrete humanitarian projects" in Bosnia. According to the report, it was likely that al-Haramain "was a fictitious cover." The intelligence report concluded that al-Haramain "acted as a channel for financing the activities of terrorist organizations," noting also that al-Haramain's Somalia offices employed members of Osama bin Laden's terrorist organizations and financed their operations.[103]

Wahhabism in America

Since the mid-1960s, Saudi-led Wahhabi organizations have been active in the United States. The Muslim Students Association (MSA), founded in 1963 at the University of Illinois, frequently features publications of the World Assembly of Muslim Youth (WAMY) on its website. The main works of Wahhabism, including an English translation of Muhammad ibn Abdul Wahhab's *Book of Tawhid*, have also been featured on the website of the University of Southern California's MSA chapter.

Professor Sulayman Nyang, a Sufi Muslim critic of the "Wahhabization of the Islamic movement" in America, has traced the social and intellectual history of the MSA and other U.S. Muslim movements in the 1960s. According to Nyang, the MSA was initiated by Muslims from the Indian subcontinent who were followers of Mawlana Abu al-Ala Mawdudi and by Arab students who identified with the Muslim Brotherhood and the ideas of Sayyid Qutb. And as one observer remarked, during the 1960s and 1970s "no criticism of Saudi Arabia would be tolerated at the annual conventions of MSA," for during this period, "official approval of Wahhabism remained strong."[104]

Back in the Middle East in the 1970s, Mawdudi and the Muslim Brotherhood enjoyed increasing Saudi financial backing. Moreover, many Egyptian Muslim Brothers who fled from Nasser in the 1960s made fortunes in Saudi Arabia and Qatar before moving to southern California. But while they were refugees in the Gulf, they became Wahhabis. As noted, many Muslim Brothers received positions in the Saudi educational system, especially at the Islamic University of Medina. In the United States, they became active in Muslim organizations. The first indication of their commitment to Wahhabism was their opposition to certain Islamic practices that Wahhabi clerics opposed, such as celebrating the birthday of the Prophet Muhammad.

In the late 1970s, as Muslims returned to their religion, they became active in the Islamic Society of North America (ISNA), which was established in 1981. At the same time, Nyang writes, ISNA Muslims rejected Sufism, which certainly could have been the result of Wahhabi influence. These ISNA attitudes were very similar to those of the American Muslims who founded MSA. Top ISNA leadership had been active in MSA or had links with the Muslim World League. Sayyid Muhammad Syeed was MSA president from to 1980 to 1983 and "pioneered its transformation into the Islamic Society of North America," according to his official ISNA biography.[105]

Muzammil H. Siddiqi, who received his B.A. in Islamic and Arabic Studies from the Islamic University of Medina in 1965, served as ISNA's president from 1996 to 2000. Previously he had been an MSA chairman and had worked with the Muslim World League.[106] He was known for extremist statements in which he called for an Islamic state to replace Israel. At a Washington rally, he warned Americans that "the wrath of God will come" in response to U.S. Middle East policies.[107] Siddiqi's successor, Sheikh Muhammad Nur Abdullah, came to the United States from Sudan but was educated in Saudi Arabia, receiving his B.A. in Islamic Law at the Islamic University of Medina and his M.A. at Umm al-Qura University in Mecca.[108] ISNA was an umbrella organization representing many different Islamic groups, but still its leadership seemed to come from a common background and consequently could be expected to be sympathetic toward the Saudi religious perspective.

ISNA's pro-Saudi religious orientation spilled over to its politics. While some prominent Arab-American organizations initially approved of the 1993 Oslo Agreement between Israel and the PLO, ISNA and MSA condemned any peace treaty with Israel.[109]

To spread Wahhabism in the United States, the Saudis used a tool that had proven very effective in other parts of the world: money. The North American Islamic Trust (NAIT) safeguarded the assets of both the MSA and ISNA. NAIT also helped Muslim communities build mosques, and in this area NAIT became highly dependent on Saudi funding. One

Hutton-Deutsch Collection/CORBIS

Under British hegemony: In the early twentieth century, Saudi Wahhabi warriors embarked on a brutal expansionist campaign in which up to 400,000 Arabs were killed or wounded. Only British power held the Wahhabis in check. Here London officials broker a treaty between the Saudi king, Ibn Saud (1880–1953), and Iraq's King Faisal I in 1930.

Bettmann/CORBIS

The modern map: In the mid-1920s, the Saudis clashed with Sharif Hussein of Mecca and the British-backed Hashemites. The modern Middle East took shape in the aftermath of the conflict, as the British installed Sharif Hussein's sons (seated) in positions of power: Faisal (left) would become king of Iraq; Abdullah, eventually, king of Jordan; and Ali, briefly, king of the Hijaz.

The U.S. moves in: Fearing that World War II had depleted oil reserves in Texas and Oklahoma, the United States upgraded its diplomatic and military involvement in Saudi Arabia. Here King Ibn Saud meets with President Franklin Delano Roosevelt in early 1945, aboard the USS *Quincy* in Egypt's Great Bitter Lake.

The Arab cold war: In the 1960s, Egypt's President Nasser (right) tried to expand into the Arabian peninsula, threatening the authority of Saudi Arabia's King Saud (left). To counter Nasser's Arab socialism, Saudi leaders turned to Wahhabi Islam, granting Wahhabi religious leaders tremendous power. Nasser also persecuted the radical Muslim Brotherhood, driving many of its members to Saudi Arabia. These events laid the groundwork for Saudi support of modern global terrorism.

Exporting Wahhabism: Wahhabi clerics helped oust King Saud in 1964 and install his half brother Faisal (right), a direct descendant of Wahhabism's founder. King Faisal began the worldwide export of Wahhabism through such Islamic institutions as the Muslim World League. In 1973, under pressure from Wahhabi clerics, Faisal instituted a complete oil embargo against the United States, which Secretary of State Henry Kissinger, shown here, tried to get the king to lift.

King Faisal's sons: King Faisal was assassinated in 1975, but his sons would exert a great deal of influence. Prince Saud (left) became foreign minister in 1975, and Prince Turki (right) became head of Saudi intelligence in 1978. Prince Turki, who knew Osama bin Laden, oversaw Saudi involvement in Afghanistan against the Soviets—the campaign out of which al-Qaeda grew.

Saudi "charities" (part I): In 2002, federal prosecutors indicted Enaam Arnaout, head of the Benevolence International Foundation's American offices, for connections to al-Qaeda. A former secretary-general of the Saudi-based World Assembly for Muslim Youth (WAMY) founded Benevolence in Saudi Arabia and appointed Arnaout as U.S. director. Arnaout is shown here (on right) with Osama bin Laden (in front) in Afghanistan in 1988.

Saudi "charities" (part II): U.S. authorities have linked WAMY, one of Saudi Arabia's largest Wahhabi charities, to terrorist funding. Perhaps it was no surprise, then, that in October 2002, Khaled Mishal, one of the top leaders of Hamas—the militant Palestinian movement responsible for so many suicide bombings—was WAMY's guest at its convention in Riyadh.

REUTERS/Photo by Saudi News Agency

A change: After a 1995 stroke, King Fahd (right) handed control of the government to younger brother Crown Prince Abdullah (left). Under Abdullah's leadership, Saudi Arabia began to distance itself from the United States.

REUTERS/Dalati Nohara

REUTERS/Photo by Sharif Karim

The supposed peace initiative: In early 2002, articles in the *New York Times* predicted that Abdullah would offer a bold new Arab-Israeli peace plan at the Beirut Arab Summit. His proposal, though, turned out not to be a breakthrough at all, but looked like a PR effort to divert attention from Saudi links to terrorism. In Beirut, in fact, Abdullah embraced a key deputy of Iraq's Saddam Hussein, Izzat Ibrahim (left). Western analysts were also concerned about how Abdullah had greeted Hizballah leaders in 2000 (right).

REUTERS

The grand mufti: For decades, Saudi Arabia's most powerful Wahhabi cleric was Sheikh Abdul Aziz bin Baz (above), who became the kingdom's grand mufti. While the conservative bin Baz maintained the flame of Wahhabism, he also had the authority to control its violent outbursts. But bin Baz died in 1999, and his successor, Sheikh Abdul Aziz bin Abdullah Al al-Sheikh, lacked that authority. The more extreme Wahhabi clerics went unchecked, and the incitement escalated; some clerics even justified the September 11 attacks.

REUTERS/Stan Honda/POOL

The smirk: In October 2001, Saudi Arabia's Prince al-Waleed presented New York City mayor Rudolph Giuliani with a $10 million check for the Twin Towers Fund. Yet as Giuliani later wrote, the prince and his entourage seemed to be smirking as they toured Ground Zero. When al-Waleed blamed the attacks on the U.S. government's Middle East policy, the mayor returned the Saudi check, refusing to accept any justification for the destruction of September 11.

Alex Wong/Getty Images

The PR campaign: Saudi Arabia's public relations efforts have consistently tried to portray the Saudis as America's partner and to obscure their ties to terrorism. Adel al-Jubeir, Crown Prince Abdullah's foreign policy advisor, became the most visible spin doctor, often appearing on American network television.

knowledgeable source familiar with Saudi connections in America estimated that *half* the mosques and Islamic schools in the United States were
built with Saudi money.[110]

Of course, the main question that arises from these contributions is
whether those who accept Saudi funds feel pressured to adhere to Wahhabism. The Saudi embassy in Washington has denied that such strings
are attached to Saudi donations. Yet American Muslims have reached different conclusions. Imam Hasan al-Qazwini, who heads the Islamic Center of America in Detroit, Michigan, and refuses to accept Saudi funds,
has stated, "The expectation is that communities receiving money should
view Wahhabism with more respect."[111] NAIT, for one, has a definite religious perspective. Its book service shows something of its orientation; it
promotes the writing of the founder of Wahhabism, Muhammad ibn
Abdul Wahhab.[112] It also distributes the works of Sayyid Qutb and
Mawlana Abu al-Ala Mawdudi.

Other, even more extreme organizations in America advance an
agenda sympathetic to Saudi Wahhabism. The chairman of the Michigan-
based Islamic Assembly of North America (IANA), which was set up in
1993, admitted to the *New York Times* in 2001 that half of IANA's money
came from the Saudi Arabian government, the rest from Saudi private
donors.[113] In May 2001—four months *before* the September 11 terrorist
attacks—the IANA's website featured justifications for "martyrdom operations," including crashing an airplane "on a crucial enemy target."[114]
IANA mostly ran seminars featuring speakers like Bilal Philips, a Jamaican
who converted to Islam and did his undergraduate work at the Islamic
University of Medina, followed by graduate studies in Islamic philosophy
at King Saud University in Riyadh, where he lived for a few years. He
clearly reflected a Saudi perspective. Additionally, IANA, like the Muslim
World League, had active Wahhabi proselytizing programs directed
toward America's prison population; the Muslim World League judged
that the number of American prisoners converting to Islam was constantly
on the rise.[115]

IANA maintained close working relations with a Pittsburgh-based
Arabic journal, *Assirat al-Mustaqeem*, begun in 1991, whose articles frequently condemned Americans, Jews, and other Muslims as "infidels" or
"apostates." The term "Zionist-crusaders" was also used. The journal's

religious message was based on praise for the value of jihad: "Anyone who believes that *jihad* is not a duty or seeks to abrogate it is an infidel and an apostate." In 1998, the magazine mourned the nineteen mujahideen killed by an American retaliatory missile strike against Afghanistan after two U.S. embassies in East Africa were bombed.[116] This radical perspective reflected the makeup of *Assirat*'s advisory board; the board consisted of clerics from only two Middle Eastern countries—Saudi Arabia and Yemen. *Assirat*'s publisher, Bandar al-Mushary, eventually returned to Saudi Arabia to teach at King Fahd University. Mohsen al-Mohsen, editor from 1996 to 2000, went back to Saudi Arabia to teach at the Imam Muhammad bin Saud Islamic University. Both men helped set up the Tawhid Foundation, a student organization in Pittsburgh whose spokesmen largely defended the content of *Assirat*.

During the war against the Soviet occupation of Afghanistan, the United States became an important center for fund-raising campaigns on behalf of the Saudi-backed Afghan Arabs. Between 1985 and 1989, Abdullah Azzam, working out of Pakistan, actually set up a support network in the United States. He visited dozens of American cities, spreading his philosophy of jihad. He set up major fund-raising offices, called Alkifah Centers, in Atlanta, Boston, Chicago, Brooklyn, Jersey City, Pittsburgh, and Tucson; thirty other U.S. cities had subsidiary offices.[117]

One of Azzam's most important protégés in the United States was Wael Hamza Julaidan, a Saudi national from a well-connected family in Medina. A student at the University of Arizona, he was president of the university's Muslim Student Association, and in 1983 and 1984 he served as the president of the Islamic Center in Tucson.[118] Soon he was drawn to join the Afghan struggle; in 1985 he left the United States. In the second half of the 1980s, in fact, he served the Afghan mujahideen as one of the heads of the Saudi Red Crescent Society in Pakistan, where he worked directly with Abdullah Azzam and Osama bin Laden.[119]

In the early 1990s, the Islamic Center in Tucson moved to Islamic extremism; rhetoric creeping into Friday sermons, delivered during prayers, urged its members to defend Islam from the "infidels." There were signs that it had become an al-Qaeda recruiting center. After Wael Hamza Julaidan left for Pakistan, Wadih el-Hage, a naturalized U.S. citizen who came from a Lebanese Christian background (and converted to

Islam), joined the Tucson mosque. Wadih el-Hage would later become Osama bin Laden's personal secretary in Sudan and be convicted of plotting the simultaneous 1998 bombings of the U.S. embassies in Kenya and Tanzania. Hani Hanjour, a Saudi student from Taif who attended the University of Arizona, joined the Islamic Center of Tucson in 1991. Drawn during this period to militant Islam, he returned to Saudi Arabia after about fifteen months in Arizona, but he came back to the United States in 1996 and enrolled in flight school in Scottsdale, Arizona. Five years later, after one brief visit to Saudi Arabia in 1999, Hani Hanjour piloted American Airlines Flight 77 on September 11, 2001, into the Pentagon, killing 184 Americans.[120]

Another Saudi-based charity, the Islamic Benevolence Committee, set up offices in the United States in the 1990s. Benevolence, headquartered in Jeddah, Saudi Arabia, was originally established to provide humanitarian assistance to Afghan civilians during the war against the Soviets. But it set up its first offices in the United States in 1992, after the Afghan jihad had ended. Benevolence had diversified its activities. As noted, just after it opened its U.S. branch offices, the Saudi government actually shut down its Jeddah headquarters, in February 1993, after Algeria and Egypt complained that Benevolence was funding their Islamist oppositions.[121] Yet the Chicago office of Benevolence kept operating through 2001. Its workers did not just raise money; from 1995 through 1998, one of its employees made radical speeches across the United States supporting jihad in Afghanistan and Chechnya.[122] When U.S. authorities finally raided the Chicago office, they found videos and literature that glorified martyrdom; according to the Benevolence newsletter, seven of its employees had been killed in the previous year in Bosnia and Chechnya.[123]

It soon became clear that Enaam M. Arnaout (also known as Abu Mahmud), who had been appointed in the early 1990s to run Benevolence's Chicago office, had had a personal relationship with Osama bin Laden for more than a decade. Arnaout maintained an apartment in Pakistan that had been used by one of bin Laden's wives. Moreover, he allowed a bin Laden operative, Mamduh Salim, to use Benevolence as a cover for his travel documents. Salim was connected to the 1998 al-Qaeda attacks on the U.S. embassies in East Africa. Another bin Laden operative, Muhammad Bayazid, involved in the al-Qaeda effort to obtain weapons of mass destruction, used Benevolence's Chicago address in his application for a driver's license.[124]

In early October 2002, U.S. federal authorities indicted Enaam Arnaout on seven counts of conspiracy and racketeering.[125] Earlier in the year, the U.S. Department of the Treasury had blocked Benevolence's bank accounts. According to his indictment, Adel Batterjee, the founder of Benevolence in Saudi Arabia, had told Arnaout in telephone conversations to leave the United States and relocate his family to Saudi Arabia; apparently he assumed the Saudi kingdom would be a safe asylum for someone the U.S. government was investigating for involvement in terrorism.[126]

Still other Saudi organizations were based in the United States. The IIRO, the operational arm of the Muslim World League, operated through two different organizations in America: the International Relief Organization (IRO) and the Success Foundation. The IRO, like IIRO branches elsewhere, was involved in terrorism: from 1996 through 1998, the IRO made donations to the Holy Land Foundation for Relief and Development, which years later would have its assets frozen by the U.S. government because it regularly transferred funds to Hamas.[127]

These American-based Saudi institutions disseminated some of the worst Wahhabi hate literature in the United States. WAMY, for example, distributed a book entitled *The Difference Between the Shi'ites and the Majority of Muslim Scholars*, which continues the Wahhabi practice of delegitimizing Shiite Islam: "The cornerstone of the Shi'i faith, as well as its dimensions and evidence, are false and baseless." It sets forward the thesis that Shiism was the product of a Jewish conspiracy. Furthermore, the Institute of Islamic and Arabic Sciences in America (IIASA) in Fairfax, Virginia, a branch of Imam Muhammad bin Saud Islamic University that trains more than four hundred students to serve as religious leaders in U.S. mosques, has released such Saudi texts as *The True Religion*. That book, printed by the Saudi Arabian Ministry of Islamic Affairs and Endowments, claims that "Judaism and Christianity are deviant religions" and states that befriending "the unbelievers" negates Islam. Another IIASA text published in the United States, *A Muslim's Relations with Non-Muslims, Enmity or Friendship?*, describes those who call for brotherhood and equality among religions as "parasites" and states that the Koran "forbade taking Jews and Christians as friends."[128]

Global Patterns of Wahhabi Activism

When one looks at how Saudi Islamic activism functioned in different parts of the world, several patterns repeat themselves.

First, the main instruments for this activism were Saudi Arabia's huge Islamic charity organizations—the Muslim World League; its operating arm, the International Islamic Relief Organization (IIRO); al-Haramain; and the World Assembly of Muslim Youth (WAMY). Since their inception, these organizations have been headed by individuals who came from the apex of the Saudi Arabian power structure—including government ministers and members of the Saudi *ulama*.

Second, the geopolitical interests of the Saudi state were not the only factors driving Saudi Islamic activism. In Afghanistan, the Saudis backed the groups who were *ideologically* closest to Wahhabism and not necessarily those militias that had the best combat record against the Red Army. Indeed, the *ulama* in Saudi Arabia were key in convincing the Saudi leadership to support the Taliban. In the Balkans, ideology led the Saudis to become involved not only financially and militarily but also *religiously*, for the Saudis stayed involved after the conflict was over to influence the character and design of Balkan mosques and to spread their puritanical form of Islam. In short, these charities' primary function was to spread Saudi Arabia's religious message. The IIRO, for example, was the Saudis' chosen instrument for spreading Wahhabism in northern Iraq.[129] And al-Haramain's website issued an online newsletter with Wahhabi literature: articles on *tawhid* (the oneness of God) and *shirk* (polytheism), as well as biographical materials about Muhammad ibn Abdul Wahhab.

Third, across the globe, the Saudi charities promoted terrorism. The IIRO and WAMY assisted the extreme Palestinian group Hamas. Osama bin Laden's brother-in-law Muhammad Jamal Khalifa headed the IIRO's office in the Philippines, through which he assisted the Abu Sayyaf terrorist organization. Muhammad al-Zawahiri, the brother of al-Qaeda's Ayman al-Zawahiri, worked for the IIRO in Tirana, Albania—but behind the scenes, he was working for an extremist Egyptian organization tied to al-Qaeda. In the late 1990s, the Kenyan government blacklisted the IIRO because of its ties to terrorists.[130] Finally, the IIRO in the Pankisi Gorge was funneling money to the al-Ansar mujahideen, the contingent led by al-Khattab that was fighting the Russians in Chechnya and Dagestan.

The al-Haramain organization also seems to have backed terrorist groups. The Russian Federal Security Service closely monitored al-Haramain's support for Islamic extremist groups in Chechnya and Dagestan. Because of al-Haramain's alleged links with such groups, Azerbaijan closed down its offices. In the Balkans, the Bosnian government also shut al-Haramain's office, because, as a Bosnian intelligence memo concluded, the organization had acted "as a channel for financing the activities of terrorist organizations." The Bosnian memo suggested that al-Haramain's Somalia office employed members of Osama bin Laden's terrorist organizations and financed their operations. And al-Haramain employees were arrested in Albania because of their terrorist connections. Law enforcement authorities in Kenya suspected al-Haramain's involvement in threats to the U.S. embassy in Nairobi.[131] Moreover, it seems that al-Haramain's funding of terrorism reached as far as the Far East; al-Qaeda's top representative in Southeast Asia told the CIA that his organization's operations were financed through al-Haramain, according to a transcript of his interrogation.[132]

Additionally, the Saudi-based Benevolence International was tied to militant groups in Algeria and Egypt; its offices in Sarajevo were suspected of backing terrorist activities. And, as noted, when a NATO force raided the Sarajevo offices of the Saudi High Commission for Aid to Bosnia in 2001, they found photographs of potential terrorist targets in Washington, D.C.

There are two ways of interpreting Saudi charities' global involvement in terrorism: first, that these organizations were themselves victims of determined terrorist groups who penetrated the charities and used them as a front; or, alternatively, that the charities were rogue operations. If the charities were linked to terrorist groups in only one or even two locations, then the first argument might be plausible. But because the Saudi charities have been linked to terrorist groups all around the world, it is more than likely that these Saudi-headquartered organizations made a conscious decision to back international terrorism.

For Saudi Arabia, however, this worldwide financial network was not about terrorism, but rather about jihad. And what began in Afghanistan—

supporting Muslims rebelling against their Soviet oppressors—evolved in the 1990s into a much wider global struggle involving the Balkans, Tajikistan, Uzbekistan, Kashmir, and parts of Russia. The multinational terrorist organization al-Qaeda emerged out of these conflicts, and because the Saudis had supplied not just money in many of these struggles but also manpower, it was no surprise that Saudi nationals would eventually represent the largest component of the al-Qaeda network.

Ultimately, the West itself would become a target of the new jihad. The addition of the United States to the list of potential adversaries was a direct by-product of the 1991 Gulf War.

Chapter 9

Countdown to September 11

The Gulf War and Wahhabism's
New Outburst in the 1990s

No event had a greater impact on internal developments in Saudi Arabia in the past quarter century than the 1991 Gulf War. For most of the 1980s, the Saudis' primary adversary was Revolutionary Iran. Iranian aircraft had crossed the Persian Gulf and attempted to attack Saudi oil facilities, while Iran pressed its brand of Revolutionary Shiism on the Shiite populations along the Arabian side of the Gulf, including the restless Shiites in Saudi Arabia's oil-rich Eastern Province. Tehran challenged the very legitimacy of the Saudi regime. So during the Iraq-Iran war that raged on from 1980 through 1988, King Fahd and the Saudi leadership backed the Iraqi war effort with huge sums of money in order to hold Iran at bay. Indeed, it is estimated that in the course of the Iraq-Iran war, total Saudi and Kuwaiti assistance to Saddam Hussein's Iraq was $40 billion.[1]

Yet with the Iraqi invasion of Kuwait on August 2, 1990, everything changed. Saudi Arabia's ally from the 1980s became, overnight, its primary enemy. The invasion of Kuwait was particularly threatening to the Saudi kingdom because Saddam Hussein's army clearly was larger than necessary to conquer just Kuwait. Three Republican Guard divisions, backed by units of Iraqi special forces, had seized Kuwait in hours, and by

August 6, another eight divisions had joined the initial invasion force.[2] And Iraq had many more forces in reserve; the Iraqi army, which could field a total of ten divisions back in 1980 when it launched its eight-year war against Iran, had since mushroomed to about forty divisions, many with combat experience. In short, the Iraqi army could move into eastern Saudi Arabia with little warning.[3]

This was CIA director William Webster's assessment in early August 1990 to President George Bush. Secretary of Defense Richard Cheney and General Norman Schwarzkopf, the commander in chief of the U.S. Central Command, presented even more dire intelligence to King Fahd, Crown Prince Abdullah, and other senior Saudi princes: surveillance photos indicated that Iraqi armor had *already* crossed over into Saudi Arabia.[4] Wild conspiracy theories being spread in the Middle East at the time had it that the Iraqi attack was one component of a much broader plan to dismember Saudi Arabia: Iraq would take the oil-rich Eastern Province; Yemen, which had recently hosted Iraqi officers, would capture Saudi Arabia's Asir province; and Jordan would recover its Hashemite patrimony in the Hijaz, regaining control of Mecca and Medina after sixty-five years.

President Bush offered King Fahd U.S. forces to defend Saudi Arabia: "We are prepared to deploy these forces to defend the kingdom of Saudi Arabia. If you ask us we will come. We will seek no permanent bases. And when you ask us to go home, we will leave."[5] The princes present were cautious about the U.S. offer, understanding its many implications. They spoke among themselves, saying, "We must be careful not to rush into a decision." King Fahd apparently understood from the ominous U.S. intelligence pictures what was at stake. He responded to their caution: "The Kuwaitis did not rush into a decision, and today they are all guests in our hotels!"[6] Hard decisions needed to be made quickly.

King Fahd turned to the Saudi high command. It became immediately clear that Saudi Arabia could not defend itself. The Saudi army reported that it suffered from a "pitiful lack of uniformed men."[7] In the 1980s, Saudi Arabia had ten thousand Pakistani soldiers, some of whom had seen action in border skirmishes with Yemen, but most of the Pakistanis had been sent home in 1989. Additionally, the maintenance of its heavy armored vehicles "was extremely poor." The reports to King Fahd from the well-equipped Royal Saudi Air Force were not much more encouraging; its commander determined that defending Saudi Arabia from the air was "futile."[8]

King Fahd could not decide on a huge American military deployment inside the Saudi kingdom by himself, or with the top members of the royal family. He needed to consult with Saudi Arabia's religious establishment, the *ulama*. And so Fahd called 350 Islamic scholars to Mecca, many of whom had been disturbed that Saudi Arabia was still dependent on foreign protection after spending $200 billion for defense since 1970.[9]

It was left to Sheikh Abdul Aziz bin Baz, the most powerful religious authority in the Saudi kingdom, to issue a fatwa approving the arrival of U.S. forces: "Even though the Americans are, in the conservative religious view, equivalent to non-believers as they are not Muslims, they deserve support because they are here to defend Islam."[10] Bin Baz went one step further, calling the war against Iraq a jihad.[11] On this basis, American forces arrived in Saudi Arabia on an unprecedented scale—eventually, a half million U.S. soldiers.

The American-led coalition won the Gulf War and pushed Iraq out of Kuwait. U.S. defense planners might have thought that the participation of military units from Arab states—including Egypt, and especially Syria, the historical bastion of Arab nationalism—in the coalition against Iraq would allay Saudi sensitivities about the enormous American deployment in Saudi Arabia. It was not, after all, a purely American presence in Saudi Arabia, but rather a huge *international* coalition approved by the United Nations Security Council. Of course, many Saudis considered Syria's president, Hafez al-Assad, illegitimate, since he was an Alawite; the Alawites were a Syrian minority that had broken off from Shiism in the Middle Ages and that accorded the Prophet's son-in-law Ali a divine status. True, the Shiites recognized the Alawites as true Muslims in the early 1970s, but this did not raise their stock with Saudi Arabia's Wahhabi clerics.

Some areas of Saudi Arabia had in the past accepted foreigners. Dhahran, for instance, had been an American air base from 1946 through 1962. And the U.S. Air Force had assisted the Saudis after the fall of the shah of Iran in 1979 by deploying F-15 fighter aircraft and AWACS early-warning aircraft.

But now, thousands of U.S. troops roamed Saudi cities like Riyadh. Americans went to Saudi supermarkets. American combat pilots were flying out of Saudi air bases in every corner of the kingdom—Tabuk in the northwest, Taif in the southwest, and Dhahran in the northeast. The United States even established an army radio station, which could be picked up across the entire kingdom.[12] Non-Muslim Western forces did not, however, venture into the area of the Hijaz, where the holy cities of Mecca and Medina were located. Nonetheless, Iraqi radio propaganda played on the fears of ultrareligious Saudis that the Americans had occupied their country.

The vast American presence fed internal tensions in Saudi Arabia. Even before the soldiers arrived, a struggle had been brewing in Saudi society. On the one hand, there were the Westernized technocrats, a small but influential minority of Saudis who had been educated in the United States and Europe; on the other were the Islamists, who were far more numerous and sought to tighten the Wahhabi clerics' grip on Saudi society. Indeed, in November 1990, when the American military buildup was just beginning, forty-seven Saudi women began driving their own cars—openly challenging the strict Saudi law that prohibited women from driving motor vehicles.[13] Saudi Islamic traditionalists felt their liberal rivals had acquired too much power through their control of major media outlets,[14] and now, with the Western military buildup, the Islamists felt they were on the defensive. The liberals felt emboldened. In fact, a month after the women's driving protest, forty-three modernists submitted a petition to the Saudi government calling for political reforms.[15]

Saudi anti-Americanism thrived. For most of the Cold War, Saudi Arabia was staunchly anticommunist, but not for the same reasons that motivated the American policy of containment of the Soviet Union. The real threat to Saudi Arabia was not communism per se but rather that the Soviets supported secular Arab socialism, led by Egyptian Nasserism, in the Middle East. Soviet power, therefore, advanced Marxist atheism among Arabs, and this challenged the Wahhabi religious establishment. Moreover, Moscow was backing new Arab military regimes that had overthrown pro-Western, traditionalist Arab monarchies. But Nasserism had lost its steam after Israel's victory in 1967, and after the collapse of the Soviet Union, Arab socialism looked weaker than ever. Now the power that could most induce secular trends in Saudi Arabia, and undermine its Wahhabi religious orientation, was the United States. Thus Saudi Arabia's Wahhabi traditionalists saw the massive American military presence as a direct threat.

Backlash Against the West

Wahhabism had been strongly anti-Western even in the early years of the Saudi kingdom. King Ibn Saud had had to deal with clerics who accused him of drawing too close to the British or relying excessively on non-Muslims to extract oil. But the anti-Western sentiment had grown much stronger over the years. Since the 1970s, Saudi universities, under strong Islamist influence, had used texts that contained strong anti-Christian themes. And in 1973, the Wahhabi *ulama* pressured King Faisal to impose an oil embargo on the United States. In the aftermath of America's Gulf War deployment, this hard-line view that branded the Christian West "Crusaders" and considered the United States an adversary became even more prevalent.

The vast majority of U.S. forces left Saudi Arabia when the Gulf War ended in 1991, but a religious backlash ensued nonetheless. It began in May 1991 with a Letter of Demands to King Fahd that was signed by four hundred members of the *ulama* and professors from Saudi universities.[16] These religious leaders demanded the repeal of Saudi laws that conflicted with Islam, the redistribution of wealth, and a foreign policy that did not rely on alliances but embraced Islamic causes. Although they did not sign the letter, Sheikh Abdul Aziz bin Baz and his fellow cleric Sheikh Muhammad ibn Saleh al-Uthaiman supported its contents in secret letters to the king.[17]

A second Memorandum of Advice, signed by 109 Islamic scholars, went to King Fahd in mid-1992. It spoke of the scholars' dissatisfaction with many aspects of the Saudi system, from the judicial system to foreign policy. The memorandum specifically claimed that the role of the *ulama* in Saudi government and society had become too marginalized and insisted on a greater share of power for the Saudi religious leadership.[18]

King Fahd firmly rejected this second document. He called on the Council of Senior Ulama, the highest religious body in Saudi Arabia, to condemn it in a formal statement. Sheikh Bin Baz signed the statement, but he was one of only ten members to denounce the Memorandum of Advice. In December 1992, Fahd dismissed seven elderly religious leaders for refusing to go along.

One of the most prominent religious supporters of the Letter of Demands and the Memorandum of Advice was Sheikh Safar al-Hawali. Born in 1950 in the Asir region just south of the Saudi city of Taif, Sheikh al-Hawali graduated from the Islamic University of Medina, that notable hotbed of Muslim Brotherhood and Saudi Wahhabi thought. After receiving his doctorate in Islamic studies from Umm al-Qura University in Mecca in 1986, he began teaching in the university's department of theology and was ultimately promoted to head of the department. Al-Hawali also became a leading spokesman for strict Wahhabi positions. In 1990, just after the Iraqi invasion of Kuwait, he addressed a large group in a mosque in northern Riyadh, questioning the official view that Iraq was a real danger. He believed that the true threat to Saudi Arabia came from the United States, which had used the Iraqi crisis as a pretext to take over the oil resources of the Gulf region. "The real enemy is not Iraq," he said. "It is the West.... While Iraq was the enemy of the hour, America and the West were the enemies of Judgment Day."

Millions of copies of al-Hawali's taped address were distributed all over Saudi Arabia and abroad. Cassette tapes were a proven way of skirting the state-controlled media and still having a nationwide impact; this was the way Ayatollah Khomeini reached the masses of Iran in the days of the shah. Recordings of this and other sermons by al-Hawali would have a profound influence on Saudi public opinion for years to come, particularly among his student-age followers in Saudi Arabia's southwest, where al-Hawali was born.

In 2002, a *Boston Globe* reporter visited King Khalid University in Abha, Saudi Arabia, in the region from which twelve of the fifteen Saudi September 11 hijackers came. Several of the hijackers attended King Khalid University. The reporter found students at the Islamic Law Department lining up to buy cassette tapes of militant Islamic clerics. Among the most notable taped sermons that gripped the students, including the hijackers when they studied there, were those by Sheikh Safar al-Hawali.[19]

The content of his message is thus particularly important. In another recorded sermon, al-Hawali stated that a clash of civilizations between Islam and the West was inevitable. Globalization, he said, would accelerate the secularization of Islamic societies. But the upcoming clash was not just a struggle of ideas, for he specifically added that "blood is unavoidable." To al-Hawali, the coming battle with the West was "the new phase of the Crusade war."[20] He envisioned a decisive role for Muslim youth in this struggle. Sheikh al-Hawali—careful about what he said with regard to Saudi Arabia—did not question the authority of the Saudi leadership, but he said that the Saudi kingdom had become subordinate to its "enemy," the United States.[21] Al-Hawali was also a vociferous critic of Israel and paid a great deal of attention to the backing it received from Christian fundamentalists in the United States.

Another powerful religious figure who grew in national prominence after the Gulf War was Sheikh Salman al-Auda. He, too, signed the letter and memorandum submitted to King Fahd, but more important, his popular taped sermons made him, in the words of one Saudi opposition figure, "the most influential preacher in Saudi Arabia."[22] Al-Auda, born in 1955, grew up in the province of Qasim, in Central Arabia, near the town of Buraida, the traditional stronghold of Wahhabism in the Najd. Like al-Hawali, he was a product of Saudi Arabia's Wahhabi-controlled higher education system. He completed his undergraduate studies in Islamic law at the Imam Muhammad bin Saud Islamic University in Riyadh, whose rector, Abdullah bin Abdul Muhsin al-Turki, became head of the newly created Ministry of Islamic Affairs right after the Gulf War. Al-Auda continued his graduate studies at the university's Qasim branch.

A major theme in al-Auda's works was the collapse of states—one of his famous and widely distributed sermons, in fact, was called "The Fall of States."[23] But he did not focus on Saudi Arabia. His book *The End of History*, published in the mid-1990s, dealt largely with how the Islamic world should fight the West. He observed that the West was already in an advanced state of decay: "The West, and above all the United States, and Western culture, in general are undergoing a historical process that is deterministic. This process leads to its total collapse, sooner or later."[24] His proposed strategy was for Muslims to cut themselves off from the West "and accelerate the collapse,"[25] and to undertake "actions that will facilitate the collapse of the American economy." He also reminded readers that "*jihad* is the highest Islamic goal"[26] and that it was necessary "to bring about the certain fall of the West."[27]

His concept of jihad involved using all means possible: "all aspects of life are a battlefield."[28] For him, the rifle, the airplane, ideology, and the economy were all weapons. He envisioned the struggle leading to the worldwide spread of Islamic belief: "Islam has the power and the capability to establish an international regime on the foundations of Islamic justice."[29] He also hoped that he could witness this victory:

> I seek that Allah the highest will provide us with comfort by giving us the privilege to see the realization of the fate of the dominant infidel nations of the West, and that he will bring joy to our hearts, and those of our descendants, by our witnessing the fall of these entities that took control over the Muslims...and I plead with him to take revenge. Allah will take revenge against the tyrants with his sword in this world and in the world to come.[30]

Of course, al-Auda had a very specific conception of which Islam should prevail: Wahhabism. He explained that what saved Saudi Arabia from reverting to a state of *jahilia*, or pre-Islamic darkness, was the eighteenth-century movement of Muhammad ibn Abdul Wahhab. The Saudi state, he said, must protect this movement's continuity and propagate Islam— that is, its Wahhabi version.[31] Like a classical Wahhabi, he called on the Saudi government to expel the kingdom's Shiite population.[32]

In this, al-Auda echoed al-Hawali, for both sheikhs urged Saudi Arabia and its *ulama* to carry the message of *tawhid* (Wahhabism's strict monotheism) to the world.[33] The *da'wa* (the call) of Wahhabism had to be carried beyond the borders of the Saudi kingdom.[34]

Undeniably, al-Auda's and al-Hawali's views were widely disseminated, but questions remain: Were these ideas representative of the thinking in the mainstream Wahhabi religious establishment in Saudi Arabia? Or were these essentially deviant views and the rantings of fringe elements?

The two sheikhs had clearly come out of the Saudi establishment. Both were products of the kingdom's university system. Official Saudi ministries even circulated Sheikh al-Auda's pamphlets throughout the Saudi kingdom.[35] Moreover, the establishment *ulama* did not utterly reject the claims that the two sheikhs put forward in the 1991 Letter of Demands. As noted, top Saudi clerics—including the single most powerful cleric, Sheikh Abdul Aziz bin Baz—while not actually signing the peti-

tion, appeared to lend it support in separate letters to King Fahd. A
even though King Fahd strongly rejected the 1992 Memorandum of
Advice, ten members of the *ulama* refused to repudiate the two activists.
Sheikhs al-Auda and al-Hawali had not by any means drifted to the mar-
gins of society.

Nonetheless, the Saudi regime soon could not tolerate the two hard-
line clerics' sermons. On September 9, 1994, Saudi authorities arrested
al-Hawali, and four days later, al-Auda. But even then, the Saudi regime
seemed more interested in control than in content. It did not want popular religious preachers obtaining national stature through means, like cassette tapes, that the Saudi government could not monitor and control.
Moreover, it is significant that what prompted the arrests were the clerics' complaints about the Saudi government's support for the South in the
Yemen civil war; they reminded the regime that the South Yemenis were
"communists." It was necessary, they claimed, to defeat *shirk* (polytheism),
Wahhabism's greatest adversary. Implicitly, they were saying that the
Saudi kingdom was supporting a polytheistic Arab regime. In other words,
the two clerics became a real threat to the regime only when they attacked
the kingdom's policies. The arrests of al-Hawali and al-Auda were just two
of well over a hundred made at this time.

Back in 1993, King Fahd had asked the Council of Senior Ulama to
issue a legal opinion about al-Hawali's and al-Auda's activities. In a secret
ruling, the *ulama* asked the two activist clerics to cease their practices—
but did not specifically define which practices were to be stopped. Nor did
the religious ruling state whether the two men would be banned from lec-
turing or attending closed meetings. Nor, in 1994, did the *ulama* issue a
new fatwa condoning the arrests of al-Hawali and al-Auda or condemning their religious positions.[36] In fact, the Committee for the Defense of
Legitimate Rights (CDLR), a Saudi fundamentalist group based in London, claimed that it possessed a legal opinion by Sheikh bin Baz that was
sympathetic to both al-Hawali and al-Auda.

The CDLR was yet another dissident group headed by individuals
close to the Saudi establishment. Sheikh Abdullah al-Masari, who signed
the initial letter forming the CDLR, was a student of the previous grand
mufti of Saudi Arabia, Sheikh Muhammad ibn Ibrahim Al al-Sheikh.
Sheikh bin Baz was a fellow student.[37] Eventually, al-Masari's son,

Muhammad al-Masari, became the leading force in the CDLR; he established an office in London, from which he sent regular fax bulletins back to Saudi Arabia. But the CDLR did not advocate the violent overthrow of the Saudi royal family. The organization even appeared to have sympathizers in official circles, for it had access to inside information and was able to obtain the fax numbers of senior members of the royal family. In any case, these religious dissidents had similar educational and religious backgrounds to Saudi Arabia's religious leadership.

In 1994, it became even clearer that the Saudi leadership was most concerned about attacks on the regime itself. Sheikh bin Baz—whom King Fahd had promoted to grand mufti of Saudi Arabia, a position that had been vacant since 1969—specifically denounced the "recording of poisonous allegations on cassettes and their distribution to the people."[38] The more extreme elements in the *ulama* were making disparaging remarks about Saudi princesses. The head of Saudi intelligence, Prince Turki al-Faisal, followed bin Baz's statements about the clerics with a rare public appearance in a mosque at which he specifically spoke about their efforts to slander his relatives. He challenged the clerics to prove their charges.[39] Again, however, this did not indicate that young radical clerics like al-Hawali and al-Auda had crossed any ideological red lines. The Wahhabi foundations of the Saudi regime were still intact; it was simply that the clerics had undermined the royal family's political authority.

In fact, it seemed that in the wake of criticism from hard-line clerics, the Saudi government adopted a more conservative approach. Within a month to six weeks, it released all but twenty-seven of the detainees, including al-Hawali and al-Auda. And Western visitors to the Saudi kingdom could discern a more religiously severe atmosphere, particularly in the Wahhabi stronghold of Buraida (the hard-line al-Auda had emerged from a nearby town). A local Saudi commented that the religious police had recently been strengthened in order to strictly enforce Wahhabi traditions: "The wartime economic boom is over. The family is under attack, so they let the zealots run loose. The new head of the Mutawwaeen was just given $18 million to train these three thousand idiots, most of them lower-class rejects from our good schools who can't get real jobs anywhere else."[40] This strongly opinionated Saudi used the word in Arabic for that which is religiously forbidden—*haram*—to describe the emerging situation in Buraida and the rest of the Najd: they had become *"haramstan."*[41] During this period, the Saudi regime demonstrated its determination to carry out the strictest of Islamic punishments: beheading. The number of beheadings in Saudi Arabia tripled from 59 in 1994 to 191 in 1995.[42] These executions were used not only in cases of murder and armed robbery but also for religious crimes like "sorcery."

If this was indeed the environment, then the more hard-line Wahhabi clerics had assuredly intimidated the Saudi government into adopting more extreme internal policies. A pattern from the Saudi past was being repeated: when faced with an internal religious dissent from the *ulama* or even from hard-line religious elements that were not officially part of the establishment, the Saudi government made concessions that reinforced Wahhabi Islam's grip on the society as a whole.

Foreign policy was also affected. Even after the United Nations coalition's victory in the Gulf War, the American presence in Saudi Arabia could not possibly return to its prewar level. The cease-fire between Iraq and the coalition was based on UN Security Council Resolution 687, which ordered Iraq to dismantle its biological, chemical, and nuclear weapons capability. Iraq was also forbidden to manufacture missiles with a range greater than 150 kilometers. The UN Special Commission (UNSCOM) needed to verify that the weapons were indeed destroyed, and American military pressure, along with ongoing UN economic sanctions, was the means to get Iraq to comply with Resolution 687. Moreover, the coalition had created two zones where Iraqi aircraft were prohibited from flying, to protect Iraq's Shiite minority in the south and its Kurdish minority in the north, and the coalition—and especially the United States—needed to maintain an air presence to enforce the no-fly zones. Therefore, the United States had to continue to use Saudi air bases. The real test of Saudi Arabia's post–Gulf War foreign and defense policy came in the fall of 1994. On October 10, Iraq deployed twenty thousand troops from two of its elite Republican Guard divisions some twenty kilometers from the Kuwaiti border; another fifty thousand troops waited in reserve in the Basra region.[43] It looked like a replay of the 1990 crisis that led to the Gulf War. An effective coalition response was needed to deter another Iraqi invasion of Kuwait.

But by 1994, the Gulf War coalition of 1991 was collapsing. Among the members of the Saudi-led Gulf Cooperation Council, the only states that came to Kuwait's defense were Bahrain and the United Arab Emirates, which deployed air-, land-, and sea-based forces. Saudi Arabia took no similar action. Qatar, Oman, Egypt, and Syria also remained on the sidelines. By October 12, the United States had deployed nineteen thousand U.S. Marines and seventeen thousand additional U.S. troops in Kuwait and the Gulf region.[44]

The Clinton administration requested that the Saudis agree to host a U.S. armored brigade. President Bill Clinton appeared to be in a strong position to obtain Saudi support. Since 1993, his administration had dedicated enormous political resources in Arab-Israeli peacemaking. It was hard to accuse him of having ignored the Middle East. Under his administration's "Dual Containment" policy—that is, containment of both Iran and Iraq—the Arab-Israeli peace process was supposed to help the United States form an anti-Iraq coalition consisting chiefly of Saudi Arabia and the Arab Gulf states. Clinton personally visited the kingdom to secure Saudi support, but the Saudis refused.[45] Saudi policy had clearly changed.[46] And these decisions were not made quietly; the Kuwaiti public was furious about the lack of support from Kuwait's regional allies.[47]

What had caused the change in Saudi policy toward the United States? It was not the stalemate in the Arab-Israeli peace process, as some frustrated Clinton administration officials later argued. One year earlier, Israel had signed the Oslo Agreement with the PLO in Washington, and by the fall of 1994, the peace process was in high gear. Israel had completed the first Oslo accord, called the Gaza-Jericho Agreement; PLO chairman Yasser Arafat had entered the Gaza Strip; and Israel had just signed a peace treaty with Jordan. Indeed, in 1990, when the United States had gotten permission to deploy, no Arab-Israeli peace process existed at all. There simply was no correlation between the condition of the Arab-Israeli peace process and American access to Saudi bases.

Clearly, the Saudi reluctance to accept new U.S. forces was the result of the post–Gulf War political environment in Saudi Arabia. The Wahhabi revival, and the religiously conservative clerics' unbridled anti-Americanism, had made the Gulf War partnership more difficult to maintain. When the primary threat to Saudi Arabia was external, large-scale U.S. forces were an asset, but when Saudi Arabia faced internal threats, any new American troops became a liability.

Osama bin Laden and the Saudi Clerics

Saudi Arabia's refusal to allow an enlarged American military presence did not end the activities of the new extremist clerics. There was also a new player in this struggle. Osama bin Laden had returned to Saudi Arabia after the Soviet withdrawal from Afghanistan. Right after the Iraqi invasion of Kuwait, he had proposed to Saudi authorities that they use his Afghan Arabs to defend the Saudi kingdom. But his proposal was not taken seriously, and the massive American troop deployment to Saudi Arabia soon got under way. At that point, he began to drift away from the Saudi regime.

Marking the beginning of this break was his arrival in Sudan in April 1991. From April 25 to April 28, radical Islamic groups that had been sympathetic to Iraq during the Gulf War convened in Khartoum at the invitation of Sudan's Islamist leader, Hassan al-Turabi. Fifty-five countries were represented, including the Middle Eastern nations. Many of the Islamic radical groups had received Saudi financial backing—groups from the Palestinian Hamas organization, to Rashid al-Ghannushi's al-Nahda party in Tunisia, to Gulbuddin Hekmatyar's Afghanistan faction. Fathi al-Shikaki of the pro-Iranian Palestinian Islamic Jihad was also there. Even nominally secular activists joined, including Egyptian Nasserists and Yasser Arafat, the head of the PLO. The attendees were united in their anti-Americanism.[48]

The Popular Arab and Islamic Conference that emerged from this meeting sought to broker relationships between its members; in January 1993, it issued a communiqué of cooperation between Arafat's Fatah movement and Hamas, signed by al-Turabi.[49] Osama bin Laden himself certainly used the conference to develop new relationships. He established a close relationship with al-Turabi. Moreover, it is likely that bin Laden's operational connections with Egyptian fundamentalist organizations like Ayman al-Zawahiri's Egyptian Islamic Jihad evolved in this period (although he had known al-Zawahiri in Afghanistan). Terrorist groups developed relations of mutual support in logistics, falsification of documents, and explosives. This type of networking came to characterize the growth of al-Qaeda.

A follow-up conference from March 30 to April 2, 1995, was attended by the Algerian Front Islamique du Salut (FIS), Hamas, Palestinian Islamic Jihad, and, for the first time, Hizballah, the pro-Iranian Lebanese Shiite militia that was formed in 1982.[50] There, bin Laden met with Imad

Mughniyeh, who was responsible for Hizballah's overseas operations.[51] Mughniyeh, who began his career in terrorism working for Yasser Arafat's Force-17 "presidential guard" in Beirut, rose quickly after joining Hizballah; he masterminded the 1983 bombing of the U.S. Marine Corps barracks in Beirut that killed 241 Americans, after which the United States withdrew from Lebanon.

Mughniyeh's experience must have fascinated bin Laden, who hoped to drive the United States out of the Arabian peninsula. Bin Laden's statements at the time made clear that he was still a strong adherent of Wahhabi Islam; nonetheless, he overcame his ideological reservations about Shiite Islam to forge a cooperative relationship with Hizballah, which received support from Iran's Revolutionary Shiite regime.[52] Hamas had already broken the Sunni-Shiite fundamentalist barrier in Lebanon in 1992, and the Iranians had labored to establish their own Sunni fundamentalist group among the Palestinians, the Palestinian Islamic Jihad.

Bin Laden may have been in Sudan and engaged in discussions about Islamic movements globally, but he was still very much influenced by the internal discourse in Saudi Arabia. Despite his years in university in Jeddah, he was no an Islamic scholar. He therefore tended to cite Saudi clerics like al-Hawali and al-Auda.[53] He used Sudan as a new alternative base for his Arab forces; close to five hundred of them joined him in his new African headquarters.

In this period, bin Laden's anti-Americanism became operational. He dispatched some of his Arab Afghans to Somalia, where U.S. forces had been recently deployed. In October 1993, when the Somalis shot down three American Black Hawk helicopters over Mogadishu, they demonstrated war-fighting skills that they had probably acquired from outsiders, perhaps from bin Laden's forces. Bringing down Soviet helicopters in Afghanistan had become one of the specialties of the Afghan mujahideen and was a critical factor in the defeat of the Soviets. The situation in Mogadishu deteriorated. Eighteen American soldiers were soon killed, convincing the United States to pull out of Somalia. In 1998–99, bin Laden boasted that his men were involved in the fighting in Somalia.[54]

Another characteristic of the 1993–94 period was the effort of militant Islamic groups to transfer the most daring of their terrorist activities from the Middle East to the heart of Europe, and even to North America. In

February 1993, a group affiliated with bin Laden placed a truck bomb in the World Trade Center in New York City. In December 1994, the Algerian Groupe Islamique Armé (GIA), which consisted of many Afghan Arabs, hijacked an Air France plane, intending to plunge it into the Eiffel Tower. But since none of the terrorists could fly the aircraft, they agreed to let the pilot land it in Marseilles, where it was stormed by French police.[55] While the GIA served, at times, as an al-Qaeda satellite, it is difficult to establish whether bin Laden was involved in this mission.

Bin Laden began releasing statements through the London offices of the Advice and Reform Committee, an umbrella organization of several Saudi Arabian radical groups. He openly attacked the Saudi regime, so much so that Riyadh revoked his Saudi citizenship in 1994. On August 3, 1995, he issued "An Open Letter to King Fahd," a ten-page document in which he argued that Fahd's regime was not sticking "to the teachings of Sunni Islam" as interpreted by Muhammad ibn Abdul Wahhab.[56] In other words, Saudi Arabia was not sufficiently committed to Wahhabism.

Bin Laden attacked the Saudis' defense policy, their squandering of the kingdom's oil income, and their dependence on non-Muslims for protection; he supported his arguments with quotations from the writings of Muhammad ibn Abdul Wahhab.[57] Fahd had tied Saudi Arabia's foreign policy "to the Crusaders and to despotic Muslim countries," he said. Even after the Saudis refused to accept new U.S. forces in 1994, he continued to attack "the presence of the troops of the Crusaders and the Jews, who are profaning the holy places."[58]

Bin Laden concluded that Fahd's regime was un-Islamic and called on the king to resign. But significantly, he did not call for the violent overthrow of the whole royal family. Rather, he described the "source of the disease" in Saudi Arabia as "you, your defense minister, and your interior minister"—that is, Fahd and his full Sudairi brothers, Princes Sultan bin Abdul Aziz and Naif bin Abdul Aziz. Bin Laden noticeably refrained from criticizing Crown Prince Abdullah. He recalled King Saud being deposed and replaced by King Faisal. He reminded Fahd of his involvement in Saud's removal in the early 1960s, emphasizing that Saud "was tens of times less corrupt than you."[59] He was clearly trying to manipulate court tensions to serve his own interests, either to earn Abdullah's backing or to force Sultan and Naif to reverse their previous stance on his activities—even, perhaps, seeking their political and financial backing.

On November 13, 1995, a car bomb exploded outside the Saudi National Guard building in Riyadh. Five Americans were killed, along with two Indian nationals, and there was a total of sixty-seven casualties—none of them Saudis.[60] Apparently the blast had been detonated at 11:30 A.M., when most Saudis would be at midday prayer.[61] Months later, the Saudi authorities announced that they had arrested four suspects. Three stated that they were veterans of the Afghan war against the Soviets. In their public confessions, which were televised, all four said that they had been inspired by bin Laden, and one stated that the American presence in Saudi Arabia warranted a jihad. The four were beheaded in May 1996.[62]

Bin Laden did not take credit for the Riyadh attack. But organizations claiming responsibility for the bombing shared his political agenda: the withdrawal of all U.S. forces from Saudi Arabia, or the release of Sheikh Omar Abdul Rahman, a conspirator in the 1993 World Trade Center bombing, and Mousa Abu Marzouk, the Hamas leader who had just met bin Laden in Khartoum. In 1997, bin Laden told an Arabic periodical, *al-Huquq*, that what mattered most in the bombing was that "no Saudi was hurt, only Americans were killed."[63] Bin Laden's ideological justification for his anti-Americanism was clearly intended for Saudi consumption. In his 1996 "Declaration of War Against Americans Occupying the Land of the Two Holy Places," he focused squarely on the U.S. military presence in Saudi Arabia: "The crusaders were permitted in the land of the two Holy Places." His document was subtitled "Expel the Infidels from the Arabian Peninsula"; in another version, it was subtitled, "Expel the Polytheists from the Arabian Peninsula."[64] In either case, the language "infidels" *(kufar)* and "polytheists" *(mushrikun)* placed the United States in a religious category that made it a valid target of jihad: "The sons of the land of the two Holy places know and strongly believe that fighting (jihad) against the Kuffar in every part of the world is absolutely essential." Bin Laden anticipated that Muslim enthusiasm for this campaign would be unprecedented, since Muslims would be "defending the greatest of their sanctuaries."

He expected Muslim youths to become martyrs in this struggle against the Americans: "Those youths know that the reward in fighting you, the USA, is double than [*sic*] the reward in fighting someone not from the

People of the Book." In bin Laden's theology, the Americans were an even more appropriate target of holy war than peoples who were not protected at all under Islam. He tied Israel into his anti-American diatribe, believing that Israeli control of Jerusalem came about because of U.S. support. For this reason he spoke of the "Zionist and Christian Crusader Alliance." But it would become clear from his successive declarations in this period from 1996 to 1998 that Israel was, at best, a tertiary concern; bin Laden was fixated on getting the United States out of the Arabian peninsula.

Bin Laden also blamed Washington for the Saudi decision to arrest Sheikhs al-Hawali and al-Auda. And he criticized the Saudi government for not taking seriously the religious reforms put forward in the 1992 Memorandum of Advice. He clearly still saw himself as part of the internal Saudi discourse. But at the same time, he made clear that the Saudi government was about to engage in *shirk*, or polytheism: "To support the infidels against the Muslims is one of the ten 'voiders' that would strip a person from his Islamic status (turn a Muslim into a Mushrik, non believer status)." As in his 1995 "Open Letter" to Fahd, he attacked the Sudairi branch of the royal family: King Fahd, Prince Sultan, and Prince Naif. To delegitimize King Fahd further, he charged, "The king himself wore the cross on his chest," making Fahd one of the "crusaders." But again, not a word was said about Crown Prince Abdullah.

Two years later, on February 23, 1998, bin Laden released a third major declaration in the newspaper *al-Quds al-Arabi*, which included an important point of clarification. Released in the name of the newly declared "World Islamic Front," the 1998 statement, which called for a "Jihad Against Jews and Crusaders," laid out the basic grievances motivating bin Laden and established a clear order of priorities.[65] First and foremost, he charged that "for over seven years the United States has been occupying the lands of Islam in the holiest of places, the Arabian peninsula." Second, bin Laden called attention to "the great devastation inflicted on the Iraqi people." Third, he brought in the "occupation" of Jerusalem, presumably in order to tie together the Jews and the "Crusaders." This time, however, bin Laden did not criticize the Saudi royal family.

The real question is whether bin Laden's rhetoric and ideological orientation had any real influence in Saudi Arabia. Did he mobilize new followers, or did his ideas fall on deaf ears?

Certainly, his anti-Americanism would resonate in Saudi Arabia. The idea that the United States was the enemy had been a subject of al-Auda's popular speeches, of course. Other Saudi clerics had expressed concerns about the continuing U.S. military presence in the kingdom. And for the previous two decades, it had not been uncommon in Saudi religious circles to refer to the Christian world and the West as "Crusaderdom." No, bin Laden's language did not fall on deaf ears.

In the late 1990s, bin Laden could undoubtedly find Saudi religious leaders with whom he shared views. Strong anti-Christian themes were prevalent in Saudi religious circles. In 1997, Sheikh Abdul Muhsin al-Kadi gave a sermon in which he stated that Christianity was a "distorted and twisted religion." He warned the faithful, "The hearts of the Crusaders who despised us still [beat] in their chests [of today's Christians], and the weapons with which they fought us are still in their hands."[66]

In the more central mosques of Mecca, the messages from the religious leaders were not much different. Sheikh Ali Muhammad al-Barum spoke in the Manar al-Islam mosque, attacking the idea of interreligious understandings: "The idea of intertwining religions and the claim that the Jews and the Christians believe in religions of truth ... are sinful arguments and deceitful ideas unacceptable to the religion of [Islam]. ... It is forbidden for man to bring together Islam and blasphemy, monotheism and polytheism ... Allah's straight path of righteousness and the satanic path of heresy."[67] The sheikh was lending credence to the argument that Christians and Jews engaged in polytheism, which according to Wahhabism was a belief with which there could be no peaceful coexistence.

Less than a year later, this strong Wahabbi intolerance of any sort of interfaith dialogue appeared in yet another sermon in Mecca. Sheikh Adnan Ahmad Siami, speaking about Pope John Paul II's visit to the Umayyad mosque in Damascus, Syria, declared:

> This pope, the head of the Catholic Church, and those behind him calling for the unification of the religions, are the descendants of the Spanish Inquisitors who tortured the Muslims most abominably. ... They are the descendants of those who led the Crusades to the Islamic East, in which thousands of Muslims were killed and their wives taken captive in uncount-

able numbers. They are the perpetrators of the collective massacres in Bosnia-Herzegovina ... in Kosovo, in Indonesia, and in Chechnya. ... Can we expect compassion from these murderous wolves?

Mosque sermons, in this period, were also full of strong anti-Jewish themes. The clerics claimed that in every generation the Jews repeated the same acts, like murdering prophets and violating agreements with the Prophet Muhammad. A sermon in a Taif mosque asserted, "The present behavior of the brothers of pigs and monkeys, their treason, their violation of agreements, the ritual impurity they bring to places of worship ... are connected to the deeds of their fathers' fathers that lived at the beginning of Islam."[68] Another sermon, delivered in a different Taif mosque, took these anti-Jewish themes one step further: "The ingathering [of the Jews] from all the corners of the Earth to the land of Palestine is one of the signs of the Day of Judgment. ... The purpose of this ingathering is that it will become possible to torture them and kill them to the very last one along with the False Messiah."[69]

The sheikhs delivering these extreme sermons in the late 1990s were fully aware that according to Islam, Christians and Jews were "people of the book" and hence protected. Sheikh Marzuq Salem al-Ghamadi dealt with this point in his talk in the al-Rahman mosque in Mecca: "If the *kufar* [infidels] live among Muslims according to the conditions established by the Prophet, that's one thing." He then detailed those conditions: the *kufar* must pay the *jizya* (the poll tax for every non-Muslim) to the Islamic treasury, their churches or monasteries could not be repaired, they must remain unarmed, their church bells must never ring, and so on. He closed by noting that if these conditions for non-Muslims were violated, they would have no protection. The listeners knew, however, that these strict conditions were not met anywhere, which meant that Christians and Jews were not protected.[70]

In short, a cross section of Saudi sermons delivered in this period demonstrates that for religious leaders in the mosques, both non-Muslim monotheistic religions—Christianity and Judaism—were illegitimate. Both were seen as enemies that still sought to harm Muslim peoples. At best, their members were described as *kufar* (infidels), although sometimes

Saudi preachers placed them in the even worse category of *mushrikun* (polytheists).

The Saudi school system reinforced the message coming from the mosques. In 2000, ninth- and tenth-graders read a text published by the Ministry of Education that declared, "Jews and Christians are the enemies of believers[;] they will never approve of Muslims, beware of them."[71] Another textbook for the same age group stated, "It's allowed to demolish, burn, or destroy the bastions of the *kufar*—and all that constitutes their shield from Muslims—if that was for the sake of victory for the Muslims and the defeat for the *kufar*."[72] A text for tenth-graders, Sheikh Saleh al-Fawzan's *Monotheism*, was filled with anti-Christian and anti-Jewish bigotry; the text stated that before Judgment Day, "Muslims will kill all the Jews."[73] Sheikh al-Fawzan was part of Saudi Arabia's Islamic elite; a student of Sheikh bin Baz, he was also a member of the Council of Senior Ulama and the Muslim World League's Jurisprudence Committee.[74] He even had his own call-in radio show and was a prolific writer.[75]

Thus, for those who accepted and internalized the messages presented in the Saudi curriculum, the leap to what bin Laden was saying at the time was not very great.

The Saudis Fail to Stop the Hatred and Terror

What did the Saudi government do to combat these dangerous trends in its mosques and to fight the escalating acts of terrorism directed against Americans and other foreigners in the Saudi kingdom? In October 1994, King Fahd announced the establishment of a Supreme Council of Islamic Affairs; the minister of defense, Prince Sultan bin Abdul Aziz—and not the Saudi clerics—directed the new council. Shortly thereafter, Fahd appointed a new minister of Islamic affairs to oversee religious guidance and endowments (*awqaf*).

The new bodies were intended to help the Saudi regime regulate what went on in the kingdom's mosques.[76] But when one examines the extraordinary level of invective that continued in sermons, it becomes clear that the Saudi regime failed to restrain its clerics—if in fact it sought to do so in the first place.

In terms of Saudi policy on the mosques, one important exception proved the rule. On March 13, 1998, the grand imam of the Prophet's

Mosque (Masjid al-Nabawi), in the city of Medina, Sheikh Abdul Rahman al-Hudaifi, delivered the Friday sermon. In it, he echoed common
Saudi religious declarations from the time. To begin, he attacked Christianity: "There is no similarity between Christianity and Islam. Islam is a
pure and clean religion believing in the oneness of Allah...whereas
Christianity is a deviation from the right path." Regarding Judaism, he
stated that the Talmud was "the holy book of the Satanish Jews." Then,
in classic Wahhabi terminology, al-Hudaifi attacked the Shiites as those
who "attempt to destroy Islam." As far as he was concerned, there could
be no reconciliation between the Sunnis and the Shiites.[77]

There was one special problem with Sheikh al-Hudaifi's vitriolic sermon and, specifically, his anti-Shiite rhetoric. Joining the Friday prayers
in Medina was Hashemi Rafsanjani, the former president of Iran, who
was an official guest of Saudi Arabia. Crown Prince Abdullah had been
laboring for two years to bring about a Saudi-Iranian rapprochement.
The sermon's anti-Shiite epithets ruined everything for which Abdullah
had worked; shortly thereafter, Tehran issued its anti-Wahhabi reaction.
In this case, the Saudis decided to fire Sheikh al-Hudaifi.[78] But the trig-
ger was his anti-Shiite diatribe, not his anti-Christian or anti-Jewish
hatred. Al-Hudaifi almost certainly would have remained free to
continue with his hatred-filled sermons—as virtually all hard-line Saudi
clerics were at the time—had Rafsanjani not been in attendance that particular day.

Significantly, Sheikh al-Hudaifi's 1998 sermon also had an important
message for the United States: "The world powers are the sworn enemies
of the Kingdom of Saudi Arabia." He suggested that the Americans
should learn a lesson from Afghanistan; the jihad of the Muslims "brought
about the total destruction of the superpower of the day." The implicit
message was clear: America was next.

Saudi Arabia's failure to handle terrorism was even more noticeable
and far more dangerous. The first sign of how Saudi Arabia actually dealt
with the terrorist challenge came in April 1995. The United States
received information that a specific flight of Lebanon's national airline,
Middle East Airlines, would carry Imad Mughniyeh of Hizballah, the
mastermind of the 1983 Beirut bombing that killed 241 U.S. Marines.
The flight, from Khartoum to Beirut, was scheduled to make a stopover

in Jeddah, Saudi Arabia.[79] The FBI dispatched agents to arrest Mughniyeh; President Clinton's national security advisor, Anthony Lake, had
coordinated the operation with the Saudi ambassador to Washington,
Prince Bandar bin Sultan.[80] At the last minute, however, the Saudi government blocked the Lebanese airliner from landing. Mughniyeh got
away. The Clinton administration strongly protested the incident; in his
understated diplomatic way, Secretary of State Warren Christopher
explained, "We expressed our concern that we had not had the cooperation we hoped to have."[81]

What was motivating the Saudi leadership? How did the government
hope to deal with the threat of terrorism?

In November 1995, King Fahd suffered a stroke, and Crown Prince
Abdullah effectively began running Saudi Arabia. Under Abdullah, Saudi
foreign policy changed. He stressed the need to improve Saudi Arabia's
regional relationships to avoid having to rely on the American military.[82]
The Clinton administration clearly hoped that its allies in the Middle East
would support the Dual Containment policy in regard to Iran and Iraq.
But this policy could not be sustained, for after the 1997 election of
Muhammad Khatami as president of Iran, Abdullah initiated dialogue
with the Iranian leadership. In the 1960s, when faced with the rise of
Palestinian terrorism in the Middle East, Saudi Arabia had bought off the
Fatah movement, and later the PLO, rather than confront those groups.
Whether this was now Abdullah's plan for dealing with the terrorism, the
net result was the same: Saudi Arabia even risked its relations with Wash-
ington to avoid cracking down on Hizballah or any similar group. On
March 3, 2000, in fact, Crown Prince Abdullah visited Beirut and openly
met with a delegation from Hizballah, Mughniyeh's organization.

This meeting was staggering, coming as it did after the bombing of
Saudi Arabia's Khobar Towers on June 25, 1996. The blast from the truck
bomb killed 19 American servicemen and injured another 373 people. No
Saudis were hurt in the attack. Several signs indicated that this was not
the work of forces loyal to bin Laden. One of the organizations that took
credit was a Shiite group that called itself Hizballah al-Khalij ("Hizballah
of the Gulf"). Three months earlier, on March 29, 1996, Saudi border
officials had stopped a car entering from Jordan. The car had driven
across Jordanian territory from Syria, originating from Lebanon's Bekaa

Valley, the main base for Hizballah. In the vehicle were thirty-eight kilo-grams of explosives. The driver was a Saudi Shiite.[83]

The initial evidence reinforced the Hizballah theory; the truck used in the bombing was traced to one individual who reportedly admitted to being trained by Iranian Revolutionary Guards. The FBI normally has jurisdiction in investigating the deaths of Americans in foreign countries, but it took at least two and a half years before the Saudi authorities would seriously cooperate with the American authorities, especially when it came to interrogating suspects.[84] Similarly, after the 1995 National Guard Head-quarters bombing, the kingdom had quickly executed the Saudi suspects before the FBI could speak with them.

Perhaps the Saudi government did not want U.S. investigators open-ing an inquiry into Islamist groups inside Saudi Arabia. Whatever tech-nical assistance the United States might initially supply, the investigation might uncover embarrassing connections between leading families in the Saudi establishment and some of the more extreme dissident groups. After all, into the 1990s bin Laden himself had had close connections with Prince Turki al-Faisal, the Saudi intelligence director.

Indeed, the Saudis knew that they were being closely scrutinized for financial contributions to Islamic groups engaging in international ter-rorism. In 1993, for example, the French minister of the interior, Charles Pasqua, had met with his Saudi counterpart, Prince Naif bin Abdul Aziz, to force Naif to limit the financial backing that Saudi private businessmen were providing to the Algerian Islamic group FIS and other armed orga-nizations.[85] And in 1994, President Bill Clinton had made a brief stopover in Saudi Arabia to complain that private Saudi funds were reaching Hamas.[86] But Clinton's pleas had little effect.

In the Khobar Towers investigation, the Saudis could have been con-cerned that the Americans would not accept the Hizballah connection and would instead investigate Sunni extremist groups, including those backed by Saudi citizens. Even if the United States accepted the Hizballah theory, it might question the status of Shiite Muslims in Saudi Arabia's Eastern Province. And there was also an international context. President Clinton had stated that he would make sure that "those responsible are brought to justice." Years later, the investigation revealed that the bombers had trained in Lebanon, Syria, and Iran. Indeed, on June 21, 2001, a U.S.

federal grand jury in Alexandria, Virginia, indicted thirteen Saudi militants suspected of being involved in the attack; the indictment made it clear that the militants were part of a group called Saudi Hizballah, explaining that "these Hizballah organizations were inspired, supported, and directed by elements of the Iranian government."[87] An American retaliatory strike on Iran, after it had been tied to the Khobar bombing, could draw Saudi Arabia into a conflict that it preferred to avoid—particularly because American operations against Iran might require the U.S. Air Force to use Saudi air bases.

A Ransom to Be Left Alone?

As the evidence mounted that the Iranian-Hizballah theory was the most plausible explanation for the 1996 Khobar attack, it became clear that Saudi Arabia was no longer on the target list of bin Laden or the organizations that backed him as it had been back in 1995. Many radical Muslim groups at this time were pulling back from confronting their home governments because they sensed that they were engaging in *fitna*—a Muslim civil war, which was forbidden.[88] Something had changed. Perhaps the most revealing point in his 1996 Declaration of War is that bin Laden urged his fellow Muslims not to start a civil war in Saudi Arabia.[89] He explicitly stated, "Muslims must not be engaged in an internal war amongst themselves as this will lead to the following grave consequences." He warned that this kind of internal conflict could destroy Saudi Arabia's oil industries, the kingdom's greatest asset.

Bin Laden understood the value of the vast oil infrastructure in the Arabian peninsula: "I would like to alert my brothers, the Mujahideen, the sons of the nation, to protect this [oil] wealth and not to include it in the battle as it is a great Islamic wealth and a large economical power essential for the soon to be established Islamic state." Even while referring to this future Islamic entity, he did not incite Islamic guerrillas to remove the Sudairi branch of the Saudi royal family from power. Recall, too, that his February 1998 statement, "Jihad Against Jews and Crusaders," dropped all disparaging remarks about King Fahd, the Sudairis, and the Saudi royal family in general. Bin Laden's tone had entirely changed. He now wanted to sustain the jihad against the United States without damaging Saudi Arabia internally. In practice, this meant that bin

Laden carried his conflict with the United States outside of Saudi Arabian territory: to Africa, Yemen, and finally the United States.

In early 1996, Sudan faced severe pressure from Washington concerning its emergence as a new major center of international terrorism. Sudan had provided refuge to the terrorists who had attempted to assassinate Egypt's President Mubarak in Ethiopia; Hamas and Hizballah, moreover, ran training facilities near Khartoum. But the Sudanese appeared ready to reverse course. They had just turned over the master terrorist "Carlos" to France. Now they were in discussions with the United States to extradite Osama bin Laden.[90] Both governments preferred that he be expelled to Saudi Arabia for prosecution; in fact, the head of the Saudi General Intelligence Department, Prince Turki al-Faisal, later confirmed that the Sudanese president, General Omar Bashir, had "conditionally" offered to hand bin Laden over to the Saudis in 1996.[91] The Clinton administration, which maintained extensive contacts with Riyadh on the bin Laden issue, understood that the Saudis would not go along because they feared a backlash from Islamist elements in the kingdom. It was better to have Osama bin Laden outside of Saudi Arabia. In the end, Sudan expelled him to Afghanistan on March 18, 1996.

High-level U.S. intelligence officials became convinced that Saudi Arabia had struck a deal with bin Laden. Dick Ganon, who served as director of operations of the State Department's Office of Counterterrorism, observed in October 1998, less than three months after leaving his post, "We've got information about who's backing bin Laden, and in a lot of cases it goes back to the royal family."[92] U.S. intelligence sources confided that two Saudi princes were channeling funds to bin Laden. A senior source in the Clinton administration believed that the Saudis began making regular payments to bin Laden in 1995—the year the National Guard Headquarters was struck.[93] "There's no question they did buy protection from bin Laden," the source said. "The deal was, they would turn a blind eye to what he was doing elsewhere. 'You don't conduct operations here, and we won't disrupt them elsewhere.'" Another report claimed that U.S. and British officials had actually identified the two Saudi princes who funded bin Laden.[94]

According to an entirely different report, U.S. intelligence intercepts revealed that Saudi officials began supporting bin Laden and his al-Qaeda terrorist network in 1996. That year, the Saudi regime had "gone to the dark side."[95] Saudi money was supporting extremist groups in Afghanistan, Lebanon, Yemen, Central Asia, and the Persian Gulf.[96]

Whatever the details, these analyses were clear on one point: Saudi Arabia was paying a ransom to be left alone. Before bin Laden left Sudan for Afghanistan, at least three Saudi delegations approached him asking that he not strike at Saudi targets. They explained, "Your fight is with the United States, not with us."[97] In the end, the Saudis could tolerate Islamic extremists, including bin Laden, as long as they engaged in terrorism *outside* the kingdom, even if directed at the United States.

Two events revealed bin Laden's new approach. First, al-Qaeda bombed two U.S. embassies in Kenya and Tanzania in 1998, killing more than 240 people and wounding 4,500. A British intelligence report established that the two al-Qaeda operatives, who drove a Toyota truck right up to the U.S. embassy in Nairobi, were Saudi citizens.[98] Another Saudi national, Khaled al-Midhar, helped plan the bombings.[99] Second, in October 2000, al-Qaeda used a small boat to bomb the USS *Cole* while it was in port in Aden, Yemen; seventeen American sailors were killed. Yemen's president, Ali Abdullah Saleh, confirmed that the rubber skiff that ripped the hole in the USS *Cole* came from Saudi Arabia.[100] U.S. officials maintained that it was purchased in the Saudi port of Jizan and smuggled to Yemen.[101] They also received information that a Saudi merchant family had financed the *Cole* bombing.[102] Those who planned the *Cole* attack apparently escaped from Yemen and sought sanctuary in Saudi Arabia.[103] Their choice made sense, since the commander of the operation against the USS *Cole*, Abdul Rahim al-Nashiri, was himself a Saudi citizen who had founded the first al-Qaeda cell in Saudi Arabia.[104] He had also been involved in planning the attacks on the East African embassies in 1998.

Al-Qaeda was establishing a formidable presence in Saudi Arabia as the campaign against American targets intensified. Robert Baer, a CIA Clandestine Service officer, obtained hard intelligence from a source in Qatar that detailed the names of some six hundred Islamic extremists in Saudi Arabia and Yemen who were linked to bin Laden.[105] In short, bin Laden had succeeded by 1998 in using the Saudi kingdom as a base of operations against American targets, but he no longer attacked Saudi Arabia itself.

Additional evidence against Saudi Arabia became apparent only in retrospect, after the September 11, 2001, terrorist attacks. Six of the fifteen
Saudis involved in the hijackings went through a process of religious
recruitment while they were in Saudi Arabia. Some were introduced to
al-Qaeda through the mosques of Khamis Mushayt, in southwest Saudi
Arabia near the Yemeni border.[106] There is serious doubt whether any of
the fifteen Saudi hijackers ever set foot in Afghanistan, except for one or
two cases.[107] Thus, much of the preparatory phase of the training for the
eventual suicide attacks on America occurred in Saudi Arabia itself.
Indeed, as U.S. federal prosecutors have disclosed, in July 2001 U.S. intelligence intercepted communications from a Yemeni-American, Mukhtar
al-Bakri, who had trained in an al-Qaeda camp in Afghanistan and was
staying in Saudi Arabia for two months. In an e-mail sent from a Jeddah
internet café to a contact near Buffalo, New York, al-Bakri said that certain people *inside of Saudi Arabia*, with whom he was presumably in contact, had "visions" about a "big meal" that would be impossible for all but
the faithful to bear.[108] U.S. investigators later recognized the e-mail as a
coded message for an impending terrorist attack; it came out of Saudi
Arabia, not Afghanistan or Sudan, about two months before the World
Trade Center and the Pentagon were hit.

The Ideological Roots of the New Terrorism

In 1999, Sheikh Abdul Aziz bin Baz, the main religious figure who had
the authority to legitimize Saudi Arabia's tactical embrace of the West—
including the U.S. Gulf War deployments—died. His successor, Sheikh
Abdul Aziz bin Abdullah Al al-Sheikh, was a descendant of Muhammad
ibn Abdul Wahhab, but he still did not enjoy bin Baz's stature with the
more hard-line Wahhabi clerics and thus could not hold them in check,
as bin Baz occasionally had.

But even before bin Baz's death, and especially in the aftermath of the
Gulf War, the strong anti-Western orientation that had been voiced by
Wahhabi clerics in the past had been reinvigorated. The prevalent religious
attitudes in Saudi Arabia delegitimized the members of other religions,
particularly Christians and Jews, placing them in religious categories that
made them eligible for the severest treatment, including physical elimination. In fact, in the 1990s, religious and educational elements of the

Saudi *establishment* were consistently putting forward the key components of Osama bin Laden's religious justification for attacking America:

(1) There was no basis for interfaith dialogue with religions based on blasphemy, polytheism, or heresy. The Christian world was still engaging in the crusades against Islam.

(2) Christians and Jews were infidels *(kufar)* or even polytheists *(mushrikun)* and therefore not protected peoples but rather in perpetual conflict with Islam.

(3) It was permissible (in the words of an official Saudi Ministry of Education textbook) "to demolish, burn, or destroy the bastions of the *kufar.*"

Thus, Osama bin Laden was preaching nothing new. An entire generation of Saudis was brainwashed with this hatred; bin Laden merely set out to mobilize predisposed Wahhabi Muslims for a war against the West.

The Saudis also used their international charitable networks to assist the most extreme Islamic organizations that accepted hard-line Wahhabi views. There is substantial evidence that this included support for Osama bin Laden. Of course, by employing its international Islamic charities and relying on private contributions to extreme Islamic groups, the Saudi government could distance itself from the terrorist organizations—even while paying "protection money" to those who could cause the Saudis harm.

Too much of this information came out only in retrospect. Saudi Arabia for the most part maintained plausible deniability throughout the 1990s. Thus, the Saudi foreign minister could, in March of 1996, attend an international "Summit of Peacemakers" convened in Egypt in the wake of four successive suicide bombings in Israel by Islamic extremists from Hamas and Islamic Jihad. The Saudi kingdom made common cause with the other attendees—including the United States, Great Britain, France, and Russia—in expressing its "strong condemnation of terror in all its abhorrent forms." But in reality, Saudi Arabia was working in an entirely different direction—a direction that would become clear only after September 11, 2001.

Chapter 10

The Hatred Continues

Within weeks of the attacks on the World Trade Center and the Pentagon, the Saudi political leadership sounded as if it was in a state of denial about the involvement of Saudi citizens and the possibility of any Saudi responsibility. In October, for example, Saudi Arabia's minister of Islamic affairs, Sheikh Saleh Al al-Sheikh, asserted, "There is no proof or evidence that Saudis carried out these attacks"[1]—though, of course, the United States had identified fifteen of the nineteen September 11 hijackers as Saudi nationals. Then the Saudis tried to link Osama bin Laden to other countries. Saudi defense minister Prince Sultan, for instance, told the Kuwaiti daily *al-Siyasah* that he doubted whether "bin Laden and his supporters [were] the only ones behind what happened," since "another power with advanced technical expertise" had to have been behind the attack.[2] His full brother, Interior Minister Prince Naif bin Abdul Aziz, said bin Laden seemed to be "a tool" of others rather than the mastermind of the September 11 attacks, particularly because the Saudis who the United States claimed were involved in the attacks didn't seem to "have the capability to act in such a professional way."[3] Given the past history of Saudi Arabia's official connections with bin Laden, such statements had the ring of a cover-up.

The United States certainly expected that its allies around the world would respond forcefully to what had happened on September 11. Speaking before a joint session of Congress on September 20, 2001, President George W. Bush clearly identified who stood behind the attack: "a collection of loosely affiliated terrorist organizations known as al-Qaeda." He identified its leader, Osama bin Laden, by name. Then, describing America's upcoming military campaign, he told the international community, "We will pursue nations that provide aid or safe haven to terrorism. Every nation, in every region, now has a decision to make. Either you are with us, or you are with the terrorists."[4] Bush spoke about the need for "a lengthy campaign," including "covert operations" and efforts to "starve terrorists for funding." On the ideological sources of terrorism, the president was less clear, stating only, "Americans are asking, why do they hate us?"

Still, Bush's message was forceful, and given that fifteen of the nineteen hijackers were Saudi citizens, one might have expected the American president's words to cause the Saudis to change course. After all, what was being preached in Saudi mosques and by members of the Saudi religious establishment could easily send the message that the Saudis were, in Bush's words, "with the terrorists."

Yet significant Saudi Arabian religious figures continued with the same anti-Western themes that had been a part of the kingdom's religious orientation for the past two decades. It was as though nothing had happened.

War Against the West: The Saudis Justify September 11

One notable Saudi religious figure who continued to speak out against America and the West was Sheikh Hamud bin Uqla al-Shuaibi. After September 11, Sheikh al-Shuaibi ruled against Saudi participation in America's war against terrorism in Afghanistan: "Whoever supports the infidel against Muslims is considered an infidel." Furthermore, he stated that it was "a duty to wage jihad on anyone who supports the attack on Afghanistan." This was essentially a call to wage jihad on the United States itself.[5]

According to al-Shuaibi's fatwa, the United States was a *kufr* state—that is, a state living in blasphemy. Both Christians and Jews were defined as infidels. Anyone who helped America would be a *murtadd*—that is, an apostate, someone who has left the Muslim faith. Sheikh al-Shuaibi called President Bush and Prime Minister Tony Blair criminals and defined their war against terrorism as a "Crusade." He called on all Muslims to help their brothers in Afghanistan against the Anglo-American forces.[6] And he warned them, "Abandonment of jihad is *kufr* [blasphemy]."

This hard-line fatwa was not the only indication of Sheikh al-Shuaibi's position. Indeed, he became the first major Saudi religious leader to condone the destruction of the World Trade Center and the Pentagon. Not long after the attack on the United States, there appeared on the Internet a book whose Arabic title translates as *The Foundations of the Legality of the Destruction That Befell America*.[7] Notably, al-Shuaibi wrote the preface to this anti-American text that justified the murder of thousands of innocent people—a book in which the author, another Saudi cleric, Sheikh Abdul Aziz bin Salih al-Jarbu, asserted, "Osama bin Laden is a natural continuation from Muhammad ibn Abdul Wahhab."[8]

In his preface, Sheikh al-Shuaibi revealed a clearly pro-Taliban orientation—"because they created a fully Islamic state, implemented Islamic law, proof of which is the destruction of the Buddhist statues, and the removal of graves, and the prohibition that they instituted against worship of graves." These were classic Wahhabi criteria. In an earlier fatwa, Sheikh al-Shuaibi had explained why the Taliban regime was the legal government of Afghanistan; he praised the Taliban for helping the mujahideen, for taking no positions that conflicted with Islamic law, and for following the teachings of Islam rather than shifting toward secularism, as so many other Muslim nations had.[9]

Given his predispositions, the rest of the positions he outlined in his preface were not completely surprising. "It is an instructive and useful [book]," he wrote, "which gives us good advice and should be regarded as a weapon for the Muslims in opposing corrupt modern trends." Sheikh al-Shuaibi concluded, "We beseech Allah to render mujahidin everywhere victorious, and forsake America and those who help her and are allied with her, and bring further destruction upon her destruction." Here was a Saudi cleric who not only defended the attacks on the World Trade Center and the Pentagon, but even called for further destruction of the United States.

Nor did Sheikh al-Shuaibi simply justify heinous actions after the fact—his views probably inspired the Taliban and their al-Qaeda supporters also.

References to his writings, along with those of Sheikh al-Jarbu, were found in a book called the *Great Book of Fatwas*, which was lying in a Taliban office in Kabul at the time of the Northern Alliance forces' victory.[10] And in fact, in an October 2001 interview with al-Jazira television, Osama bin Laden cited Sheikh al-Shuaibi when he answered a question about how he could justify killing "a Jew, or a Christian, or a Catholic."[11] Prior to the strikes on the United States, moreover, Sheikh al-Shuaibi had already issued a fatwa supporting suicide attacks, which Hamas and the Chechen rebels adopted. If suicide attacks against Israel and Russia could be religiously justified, then it was not difficult to provide the religious justification for suicide attacks on New York and Washington.

Sheikh al-Shuaibi's militant writings drew attention to the question of his exact status as a Saudi religious leader. Significantly, Saudi authorities did not block his website, as they had done with other adversaries. The Saudi government had, in fact, made a large-scale effort to block websites that dealt with pornography, women's rights, gays or lesbians, non-Islamic religions, and political criticism.[12] There was no similar effort against Islamic extremism. And Sheikh al-Shuaibi's writings were photocopied and distributed outside many Saudi mosques.[13] Sheikh Saleh al-Sadlan, a university professor who served as an advisor to the Saudi royal family, refused to condemn Sheikh al-Shuaibi when asked by a *New York Times* reporter about al-Shuaibi's rulings. Rather, the establishment religious leader confined himself to the slightest possible criticism: "He made a mistake, but it was not a major one, and it does not detract from his reputation."[14]

And Sheikh al-Shuaibi had very strong religious credentials. He was born in 1925 near Buraida, the traditional stronghold of Wahhabism. Blinded at age seven from measles, he nevertheless advanced as a Wahhabi scholar, studying Islam under members of the Al al-Sheikh family, the descendants of Muhammad ibn Abdul Wahhab. In Riyadh, he was a student of King Faisal's grand mufti, Sheikh Muhammad ibn Ibrahim Al al-Sheikh. Sheikh al-Shuaibi's roster of students read like a "Who's Who" in Saudi religious affairs, including the current grand mufti, Sheikh Abdul Aziz bin Abdullah Al al-Sheikh, and Abdullah al-Turki, a former minister of Islamic affairs and the Muslim World League's secretary-general. In short, al-Shuaibi came from the Saudi mainstream.

Once Sheikh al-Shuaibi's positions became internationally known, however, they caused the Saudi royal family considerable embarrassment. He continued to state, "It is the duty of every Muslim to stand up with the Afghan people and fight against America."[15] On October 23, 2001, Prince Naif, the minister of the interior and a full brother of King Fahd, denied the validity of the fatwa on the front page of the Saudi-owned, London-based Arabic daily *al-Hayat*. But despite this statement, in reality official Saudi Arabia was dragging its feet about cooperating with America in the most important aspects of the war on terrorism. Bush administration officials noted that one month after the September 11 attacks, the Saudi government still refused to freeze the assets of Osama bin Laden and his associates.[16] And it took Saudi Arabia—one of only three nations, along with Pakistan and the United Arab Emirates (UAE), that recognized the Taliban regime in Afghanistan—a full two weeks after the World Trade Center and Pentagon were hit to sever diplomatic relations with the Taliban; indeed, the Saudi government waited three days *after* the UAE cut its ties with the Taliban, on September 22, to finally act.[17]

Even when some in the Saudi establishment tried to delegitimize the elderly Sheikh al-Shuaibi, the Wahhabi religious leadership reinforced his stature. The Saudi daily *al-Ukaz* reported that the secretariat of the higher *ulama* had claimed that Sheikh al-Shuaibi did not deal with *ifta*—that is, giving religious opinions or fatwas. His religious positions, the newspaper asserted, did not form the basis of religious practice. Even more damning, the newspaper stated that the senior *ulama* had determined that "his independent judgment cannot be relied upon." The article clearly put the radical views of Sheikh al-Shuaibi beyond the boundaries of acceptable Islam in Saudi Arabia.

But the story did not end there. The editor in chief of *al-Ukaz* called the Office of the Grand Mufti of Saudi Arabia and asked further about Sheikh al-Shuaibi. The mufti's office verified that he was not a formal member of "the fatwa-issuing body in the Presidency for Religious Research and the Issuing of Fatwa,"[18] but it did *not* call into question his status as an Islamic authority, express doubts about his level of scholarship, or condemn or disown him. Thus, after commenting on the narrow issue of whether Sheikh al-Shuaibi was a formal member of the fatwa-issuing body, the Office of the Grand Mufti clarified that "what was attributed to the secretariat and published in the context of a news item, is but additions and speculation from the reporter of this news item, Abdullah al-Uraifej, and its attribution to the senior ulama is a lie and a fabrication."[19] The Office of the Grand Mufti insisted that this *strong* clarification be published in *al-Ukaz*—on the same exact page and in the same font size as the original article that it sought to correct.

This strong rebuttal from the highest Saudi religious authority made it clear that Sheikh al-Shuaibi was not fringe, but rather part of Saudi Arabia's Wahhabi religious establishment.

In fact, Sheikh al-Shuaibi's harsh anti-Western positions could be found elsewhere in post–September 11 Saudi Arabia. Sheikh Abdullah bin Abdul Rahman Jibrin also justified the attack on the World Trade Center and refused to use any language of remorse about the deaths of innocent victims.[20] Only Sheikh Jibrin was actually a member of the General Presidency for the Directorate of Religious Research, Islamic Legal Rulings, Islamic Propagation, and Guidance—an official branch of the Saudi government.[21]

These attitudes were common in Saudi mosques as well. Speaking in one of the main mosques of Mecca on October 6, 2001, Sheikh Wajdi Hamzeh al-Ghazawi gave no indication of remorse over the attacks on America. He was also highly defensive about the term "terrorism":

> The [kind of] terror [in Arabic, "striking of fear"] that is permissible according to Islamic law is terrifying the cowards, the hypocrites, the secularists, and the rebels, by imposing punishments [according to the religious] law of Allah.... The meaning of the term "terror" that is used by the media ... is the jihad for the sake of Allah. Jihad is the peak of Islam. Moreover, there are religious scholars who view it as the sixth pillar of Islam.

This was a remarkable statement, since the only religious movement that defined jihad as the sixth pillar of Islam was the Kharajites, who withdrew from the Islamic community in the seventh century.

The sheikh continued his sermon: "Jihad—whether speaking about the defensive jihad for Muslim lands and Islam like in Chechnya, the

Philippines, and Afghanistan, or whether speaking about jihad whose purpose is the spread of religion—is the pinnacle of terror as far as the enemies of Allah are concerned."[22]

Such sermons could not be dismissed as the talk of peripheral clergy. In fact, on December 13, 2001, the U.S. government released a video of Osama bin Laden that illustrated the Saudi clergy's powerful influence on the perpetrators of the September 11 attacks. In the video, bin Laden asked those seated around him what was the "stand of the mosques," for he undoubtedly recognized that he could count on sympathy from Saudi religious leaders for what he had done against the United States. One Saudi in the video, Khaled al-Harbi, who had fought in Afghanistan, Bosnia, and Chechnya, told bin Laden about Sheikh al-Shuaibi's vision concerning the World Trade Center attack.[23] He added that he had just received a "beautiful fatwa" from Sheikh Sulaiman bin Nasr al-Ulwan of Saudi Arabia: that fatwa, according to the video, stated that the attacks on the World Trade Center were an act of jihad.[24] The tone of the Saudi preachers remained unchanged into 2002. On January 22, Sheikh Abdullah bin Matruk al-Haddad, a Saudi preacher from the Ministry of Islamic Affairs, appeared on the popular al-Jazira television program *The Opposite Direction*, saying, "The Western world focuses on Osama bin Laden and the Jihad, and ignores the Muslims' faith, their principles, and their values. Men like bin Laden will not allow the Islamic world to bow down to the infidel enemies' tyranny of the U.S."[25] He also described American Jews as the "brothers of apes and pigs," saying they had corrupted the United States.[26]

The imam of the Grand Mosque in Mecca, Sheikh Abdul Rahman al-Sudays, broadened this religious attack by talking about a worldwide conspiracy of Hindus, Christians, Jews, and secularists. Al-Sudays, who was close to the Saudi government—in 1997, King Fahd had sent him abroad to inaugurate new mosques in France and Spain; he had also spoken at the Islamic Center in Washington, D.C.[27]—declared, "The idol-worshiping Hindus indulge in their open hatred against our brothers in Muslim Kashmir, threatening an imminent danger and a fierce war in the whole Indian subcontinent." He attacked "the advocates of credit and worshipers of the Cross" and reminded his listeners that the Jews had been turned into "pigs and monkeys." The sermon was broadcast on Saudi Arabia's national television, TV1.[28]

Months after September 11, Crown Prince Abdullah finally recognized that such inflammatory language from Muslim preachers could damage Saudi interests in the new post-attack environment. In November, Abdullah called together the kingdom's leading clerics to brief them on his discussions with the Bush administration. He warned them on this occasion, "You know that we are in the midst of difficult days.... [Therefore] you must act with moderation and examine every word you say, as you are responsible to Allah and to the Islamic nation."[29] He made sure to have his remarks made public in the Saudi daily *al-Watan*. Did Abdullah understand that there was a connection between terrorism and religious incitement in the mosques? Or was he just concerned that Saudi Arabia was being closely watched since September 11 and had to tread carefully as a result?

In late January 2002, the crown prince tried to characterize bin Laden and those who supported him as a peripheral phenomenon in Saudi Arabia. In a joint interview with the *New York Times* and the *Washington Post*, he argued, "You have had in your own country Americans who have committed terrorist acts such as Timothy McVeigh, in Oklahoma.... A deviant is a deviant regardless of nationality." Yet the McVeigh comparison was inapt; the ideology driving the September 11 terrorists was *not* on the fringes of Saudi society, as McVeigh's had been on the fringes in America. In fact, Abdullah refused to acknowledge any Saudi responsibility for the attacks on America, explaining that the tragedy "was not the fault of either [the Saudi or U.S.] government but was a crime committed by an evil person."[30] In essence, Abdullah was saying that nothing going on in Saudi Arabia could have inspired Osama bin Laden or the fifteen Saudi hijackers to attack America. It was not completely surprising, then, that Saudi preachers failed to respond to his call to use more moderate religious language. Nor were there further efforts to crack down on extreme religious incitement, even though, since 1994, and especially after September 11, the Saudi government was supposed to monitor carefully these mosque preachers and their sermons.

The effort to describe Osama bin Laden as a Saudi Timothy McVeigh did not make a strong impression in the United States. True, elements of the U.S. government were initially predisposed to giving Saudi Arabia the benefit of the doubt; indeed, one week after September 11, the FBI warned members of the bin Laden family in the United States that they were in danger and then facilitated their departure on a chartered Boeing 727 from Boston's Logan Airport back to Saudi Arabia.[31] But Saudi Arabia was not off the hook as far as the American public was concerned. A revealing news story in the *Washington Post* on February 26, 2002, reported that a full 54 percent of Americans viewed Saudi Arabia as a state supporting terrorism, whereas only 35 percent shared the same perception of Syria—a nation that had for years been on the State Department's "Terrorism List." The Saudis would have to take action quickly in order to prevent a further slide downward in their public standing in the United States.

Creating a Diversion

Right after the September 11 attacks, the Saudis knew that they faced a difficult public relations challenge. The Saudi government paid an American advertising company, Burson-Marteller, $2.7 million to place ads in the American press depicting Saudi Arabia as a staunch U.S. ally.[32] They then stepped up their PR efforts in Washington, hiring Qorvis Communications on a $200,000-a-month retainer. Frederick Dutton, a former special assistant to President John F. Kennedy, received $536,000 to help manage the Saudi PR problem.[33] The Saudis paid another firm, Patton Boggs, $100,000 to educate U.S. congressmen and their staffs on issues of concern to the Saudi kingdom.[34]

Initially, Saudi leaders tried to divert attention away from the involvement of Saudi citizens in the attack and blame U.S. policy toward Israel for motivating the terror. This was vividly demonstrated on October 11, 2001, when Prince al-Waleed bin Talal visited Ground Zero with New York City mayor Rudy Giuliani. Al-Waleed gave Giuliani a check for $10 million made out to the Twin Towers Fund. While stating that he felt badly for the victims of the attack, al-Waleed appeared unmoved by what he saw. Giuliani later wrote that he had even detected a smirk on al-Waleed's face and on the faces of his entourage. And in a subsequent press release, al-Waleed argued that "we must address some of the issues that led to such a criminal attack," adding, "I believe the government of the United States of America should re-examine its policies in the Middle East and adopt a more balanced stance toward the Palestinian cause."[35] Prince al-Waleed's strategy backfired, however: Giuliani subsequently returned the Saudi check, refusing to accept any justification for the destruction of September 11.

In early November 2001, the Saudis dispatched Adel al-Jubeir to Washington. He had served as a political aide to Prince Bandar bin Sultan, the Saudi ambassador in Washington, but had since been promoted to foreign policy advisor for Crown Prince Abdullah. Al-Jubeir was to help coordinate the Saudis' public relations campaign and appear on American network television. He stated that the Saudi government needed to appropriate the techniques of an American political campaign and became more accessible to the press, frequently briefing editorial boards.[36] By late February 2002, however, it was clear that the Saudis were still in trouble in the United States. Soon enough, the *Washington Post* survey would justify Saudi concerns. A more radical step was needed.

It was precisely at this time that *New York Times* foreign affairs columnist Thomas L. Friedman, visiting Riyadh, was invited to a dinner with Crown Prince Abdullah. According to Friedman's column in the *New York Times* on February 17, 2002, Abdullah suggested a way to break the logjam in Arab-Israeli negotiations, which had broken down after the failed Camp David summit in July 2000. The crown prince spoke about a "full Israeli withdrawal" from the territories that had been at the center of the Arab-Israeli dispute since 1967, in exchange for "full normalization" of relations with the entire Arab world. Instead of dropping this as a new diplomatic bombshell at the upcoming Arab summit in Beirut, to be held at the end of March, Abdullah let Friedman float the Saudi proposal in his newspaper.

Friedman understood the potential significance of the Saudi proposal. He began his column by admitting that he had had a similar idea. Still, he was careful not to overstate the diplomatic significance of Abdullah's new formulation, which he called "an intriguing signal." The real centerpiece of the Abdullah plan was the term "full normalization." During the past decade of Israeli-Arab diplomacy, that was precisely the sort of peace that Israeli diplomats had been seeking with the Arab world. "Normalization" implied the kind of irreversible political ties that bonded such former enemies as France and Germany, for whom a return to hostile relations would be unthinkable. If Israel was trading strategic land for peace, then it wanted a peace that gave it protection. "Full normalization" was a way of saying that Saudi Arabia was ready for a permanent peace.

Up until Abdullah's talk with Friedman, Arab leaders had been extremely careful not to adopt the term "normalization." The preferred term had been "normal relations," which was diplomatic shorthand for the kind of cold peace Egypt had maintained with Israel since the 1979 peace treaty: the establishment of embassies and the exchange of ambassadors—and that's all.[37] In fact, Egypt had withdrawn its ambassador from Israel in 2001, showing how tenuous "normal relations" were.[38] Thus, it looked for a moment as though Abdullah was breaking ranks with the Arab consensus.

All of this was particularly surprising given Saudi Arabia's recent track record on Israel. Ever since the failure of the 1981 Fahd Plan, the Saudis had been very careful about floating diplomatic initiatives and had been reluctant to become involved in peacemaking. At the 1991 Madrid Peace Conference, for example, they were willing to send only "an observer," and even that observer was a representative of the six-state Gulf Cooperation Council (GCC), not of Saudi Arabia itself.[39] And they took this limited step only after the hard-line Syrians had agreed to come as a full participant. To the Saudis' credit, they joined the GCC states in post-Madrid Middle East multilateral talks—on water, arms control, and the environment—but Saudi Arabia never actually hosted talks, unlike Bahrain, Qatar, and Oman. Then, in December 1994, after Sultan Qabus invited Yitzhak Rabin to Oman—making it the first visit of an Israeli prime minister to the Persian Gulf—King Fahd joined the leaders of Syria and Egypt at a three-way summit in Alexandria in order to block further normalization between Israel and the Arab world.[40]

More to the point, a new Saudi peace plan would seem to violate the kingdom's commitment to its Wahhabi roots. In 1994, it had initially been reported that the Saudi grand mufti, Sheikh Abdul Aziz bin Baz, would provide a limited justification for the Israeli peace process, but he had subsequently clarified that any *hudna* (cessation of hostilities) was only temporary:

> The peace between the leader of the Muslims in Palestine and the Jews does not mean that the Jews will permanently own the lands which they now possess. Rather it only means that they would be in possession of it for a period of time until

either the truce comes to an end, or until the Muslims become strong enough to force them out of Muslim lands—in the case of an unrestricted peace.[41]

Bin Baz had since passed away, and simply put, he had not left a very flexible legacy for his successors to move toward "full normalization."

Moreover, Crown Prince Abdullah—who in recent years had assumed a number of responsibilities from his disabled brother, the king—was known to take an even harder line than Fahd. In 1998, Sheikh Ahmad Yasin, the leader of Hamas, which had already launched a series of deadly suicide bombings in Israeli cities, was admitted to Saudi Arabia for medical treatment after being released from prison in Israel in a complex prisoner exchange with Jordan. Crown Prince Abdullah made a highly visible visit to Sheikh Yasin's bedside in the hospital.[42] The visit, which was prominently reported in the Saudi press, had enormous political symbolism. Saudi Arabia had already been accused of financially backing Hamas terrorism, at least since 1996. Moreover, Osama bin Laden had adopted Hamas in his 1996 "Declaration of War," in which he called for Sheikh Yasin's release from prison. Both bin Laden and Yasin were part of the same Islamist network that had repeatedly met and coordinated in Sudan from 1991 through 1995. Abdullah presumably knew all this.

Although, given Abdullah's past proclivities, a new Saudi peace plan seemed unlikely, Abdullah's ideas continued to gain momentum. In a February 21 *New York Times* op-ed piece, Henry Siegman, who ran a Middle East project at the Council on Foreign Relations, claimed that unnamed "Saudi officials" had said that Abdullah would consider transferring "small areas of the West Bank to Israel." This reportedly included Saudi flexibility on the question of Jerusalem. Historically, Saudi Arabia and other Arab states had opposed such territorial flexibility, believing that the November 1967 UN Security Council Resolution 242 had required a full Israeli withdrawal from territories that Israel's forces had occupied in the June 1967 Six-Day War. But the British and American drafters of the resolution's withdrawal clause had intentionally left out the word "the" before the word "territories" so that Israel would not be expected to pull back from the entire area that had come under its control; most American secretaries of state had since backed Israel's interpretation, asserting that it had a right to "defensible borders." It is unclear whether Siegman had direct access to Abdullah, but he certainly had ties with Adel al-Jubeir, the crown prince's foreign policy advisor, who was in Washington coordinating Saudi Arabia's public relations effort and who had participated in the Council on Foreign Relations Middle East project.

Saudi Arabia was making a huge splash in the United States—and had successfully shifted itself from the box of states supporting terrorism to the box of peacemakers. On February 21, the *New York Times*'s lead editorial, which ran with Siegman's piece, acclaimed Abdullah's thinking as "an impulse worth pursuing." Six days later, the White House, while not ready to characterize Saudi Arabia's op-ed diplomacy as a breakthrough, said, "The president praised the crown prince's ideas regarding the full Arab-Israeli normalization once a full Arab-Israeli peace agreement is reached."[43] Secretary of State Colin Powell called the Abdullah ideas an "important step."

Internationally, word of Abdullah's idea sparked a diplomatic flurry. Javier Solana, the head of foreign and security policy for the European Union, raced off to Saudi Arabia to meet with Abdullah in late February. And on March 12, 2002, the United Nations Security Council adopted Resolution 1397, which called for an end to violence between Israelis and Palestinians; notably, it acknowledged in its preamble "the contribution of Saudi Crown Prince Abdullah."[44] His proposal was becoming a diplomatic fact. Of course, Abdullah had not yet presented a new Saudi initiative; he had only described some of his ideas to an influential American columnist in the *New York Times*. Abdullah had managed to draw enormous international attention—and credit—without putting anything tangible on the table. The real test would come at the Arab summit in Beirut at the end of March.

There were two possible explanations for what Prince Abdullah was doing. First, he might have decided to effect a 180-degree shift in Saudi Arabia's policy on peace with Israel. In other words, he would accept "normalization" and welcome Israeli tourism, businessmen, and cultural ties despite vocal Saudi opposition to Western cultural penetration of Saudi Arabia. Alternatively, the whole Abdullah plan might have been a brilliant public relations stunt. After all, Abdullah did not risk very much in floating an idea to an influential American columnist; he never had to present a real plan for "normalization" of relations with Israel.

In fact, when Crown Prince Abdullah did finally address the Arab summit in Beirut in March, his ideas turned out to be very different from the ones first heralded in the pages of the *New York Times* as a Saudi change of heart. Abdullah did not hint at any territorial flexibility: he expected "full Israeli withdrawal from all occupied Arab territories." Suddenly, he included "the return of refugees" as part of any solution to the conflict, though the refugees were not even mentioned in Friedman's original column. And most important, the word "normalization" could not be found anywhere in the final speech. Instead, the crown prince reverted to the old terminology of "normal relations." To make matters worse, in front of all the television cameras, Abdullah embraced Izzat Ibrahim, the vice chairman of Iraq's Revolutionary Command Council, which was headed by Saddam Hussein.

Unsurprisingly, when the Beirut summit finally formulated what it called "The Arab Peace Initiative," on March 28, 2002, the initiative also used the term "normal relations."[45] The centerpiece of Abdullah's bold peace idea, "normalization," which had sparked worldwide diplomatic activity, was gone.

The Paper Trail

Even while Crown Prince Abdullah was supposedly putting forward a bold new proposal to establish peace with Israel, the preachers in Saudi mosques were continuing their incitement against Jews, Christians, and even Hindus—despite the fact that the Saudi government was supposed to carefully monitor sermons in the mosques. Yet even more devastating to the notion that the Abdullah peace plan was for real were the revelations that came out of Israel about Saudi ties to the new wave of Palestinian terrorism, particularly through Hamas.

The original 1993 Oslo Agreement between Israel and the PLO had been crafted under the assumption, by both Israelis and Americans, that Yasser Arafat would fight the militant cells of Hamas and the Islamic Jihad among the Palestinians of the West Bank and the Gaza Strip, just as the Egyptians and Algerians had fought their Islamist opposition. But Arafat colluded with these groups and failed to break their organizations. Their military capabilities actually grew in the areas that Israel turned over to Arafat's jurisdiction. In 1994–95, Hamas and Islamic Jihad launched a campaign of suicide-bombing attacks in Israeli cities. In fact, more Israelis died from Palestinian terrorist attacks in the first three years after Oslo's implementation than in the prior *decade*.

With the outbreak of the second Palestinian intifada, the armed uprising of September 2000 that followed the failed July 2000 Camp David summit, Arafat's own forces joined Hamas and Islamic Jihad. By the end of March 2002, after eighteen months, 429 Israelis had been killed in terrorist attacks—132 during the month of March alone. A suicide bombing in Netanya on Passover Eve, March 27, left 29 Israelis dead and 140 injured, prompting Israel to launch Operation Defensive Shield to dismantle the infrastructure of terrorism in the Palestinian-controlled West Bank cities that had been the springboard of past terrorist attacks. In the midst of this military campaign, Israel discovered thousands of original Arabic documents that revealed the financial support system backing those engaged in suicide-bombing attacks in the heart of Israel. Unexpectedly, Saudi Arabia figured prominently in this material.

For example, in April 2002, Israeli forces entered Tulkarm Charity Committee offices and found a detailed spreadsheet of charitable payments that accounted for how $545,000 had been allocated to 102 Palestinian families. According to the table, this was the tenth payment round, meaning that a far greater sum of money had already been transferred. But this spreadsheet was not a Palestinian document. The logo at the top of the spreadsheet read, in Arabic, "Kingdom of Saudi Arabia, the Saudi Committee for Aid to the Al-Quds Intifada." This committee had been established in the fall of 2000 by Saudi Arabia's powerful minister of the interior, Prince Naif.

At the time, Prince Naif's committee was being accused of supporting terrorism, because it had just sponsored a telethon on April 11 that raised $109 million for "Palestinian martyrs." To those familiar with this terminology, it looked as if the Saudis were establishing a huge slush fund for suicide bombers. Facing a barrage of questions about the Saudi telethon, White House spokesman Ari Fleischer could respond only on the basis of what the Saudis had told the Bush administration: "As I said, we received assurances from the Saudi Arabian government that the money is going to the Palestinian people, and not to support terrorism." On American television, Adel al-Jubeir, himself fending off tough questions about the telethon, repeated this line, insisting that Saudi Arabia was involved only in "humanitarian assistance to the families who have suffered as a result of the Israeli occupation and the recent Israeli aggression." He said, "We do not support suicide bombers. Our objective is to put food on people's tables and medicine in their pharmacies."[46]

The problem with al-Jubeir's argument was that the Saudi spreadsheet found in Tulkarm did not indicate an overall humanitarian fund or provide a general distribution plan for food and medicine to the needy. Rather, the Saudi assistance was actually earmarked to families whose sons were "martyrs." One column specifically described the "act of martyrdom"—*amaliya istishadiya*—and mentioned the location in Israel where the act was committed. There could be no doubt whatsoever about the activities with which those listed were involved. In fact, the whole idea of an al-Quds Intifada fund was first proposed by Crown Prince Abdullah himself, at the emergency Arab summit of October 21–22, 2000, where he stated that the fund would make contributions to "the children of the Palestinian martyrs."[47] Despite the demurrals of al-Jubeir and other Saudi officials, Saudi officials at the highest levels knew exactly where the money was going.

And for those familiar with Palestinian politics, some of the "martyrs" listed on the spreadsheet were household names, such as number sixty-eight on the list, Mahmud Abu Hanud, the commander of Hamas in the West Bank. Saudi money had also been earmarked for families of notorious suicide bombers, including number fourteen, Abdel Rahman Hamad, the senior Hamas operative who was behind the June 1, 2001, bombing of Tel Aviv's Dolphinarium disco that killed twenty-three Israeli teenagers and wounded more than a hundred. Israeli citizens were not the only casualties of these attacks: another spreadsheet listed the name of Sufian Jabarin, a Hamas recruit who blew himself up on a Jerusalem city bus back in August 1995, killing, among others, Joan Davenny, a forty-seven-year-old schoolteacher from Connecticut.[48] Because terrorists like Jabarin knew that their families would receive a check after they committed the suicide attacks, the aid from the Saudis was clearly an incentive for them to commit murder and take their own lives. At the end of June, Secretary of State Colin Powell admitted on *Fox News Sunday*, "I think it's a real problem when you incentivize in any way suicide bombings."[49] And the terrorists' incentives came from Saudi Arabia.

What made matters worse for those defending the Saudis was what Israel revealed about the so-called Tulkarm Charity Committee, where the spreadsheets were found. Running the supposed charity was a leading Hamas member in Tulkarm, Husni Hawaja. When Israeli soldiers entered the committee's offices, they found a huge poster featuring the picture of the suicide bomber who had been responsible for the Passover Eve bombing in Netanya. There were also many smaller photographs of past Palestinian "martyrs." The Israelis discovered Hamas leaflets, including one with quotations from Abdullah Azzam, Osama bin Laden's Palestinian mentor, as well as index cards that called on Palestinian youth to conduct suicide operations. Israeli soldiers also found records indicating that the Tulkarm Charity Committee had received funding from the Texas-based Holy Land Foundation, whose assets were frozen in December 2001, according to President Bush, because it had funneled money to Hamas.[50] It became as clear as day that the Tulkarm Charity Committee was nothing less than a Hamas front.

Notably, Israeli forces also found two checks made out to the Tulkarm Charity Committee, in the amounts of $1,597.60 and for $4,247.73, from the Chase Manhattan Bank account of al-Rajhi Banking and Investment Corporation, whose head office was located in Riyadh, Saudi Arabia. Finding al-Rajhi Corporation checks was significant to those familiar with the war on terrorism on other fronts. Sulaiman Abdul Aziz al-Rajhi, the corporation's chairman of the board, headed one of the wealthiest and most prominent families in Saudi Arabia. The family ran the SAAR Foundation (SAAR were his initials) in Herndon, Virginia,[51] whose offices were raided by U.S. federal agents in October 2002 because the foundation had moved funds to two offshore institutions in the Bahamas that had been tied to al-Qaeda.[52] It was also reported that at least one of the September 11 hijackers, Abdul Aziz Alomari, had an account in the Jeddah branch of the al-Rajhi bank. Moreover, Wadih el-Hage, bin Laden's Lebanese-born aide, who had been convicted in connection with the 1998 bombings of the U.S. embassies in East Africa, had the name of Sulaiman al-Rajhi's brother

Saleh al-Rajhi in his telephone book.[53] Thus, there was a sound basis for investigating whether the Saudi entities connected to al-Rajhi that had been suspected of helping al-Qaeda were also funneling Saudi funds to Hamas, or at least laundering private assistance to Hamas, for the al-Rajhi Banking and Investment Corporation had allowed funds diverted through its U.S. banking connection to be used for a Hamas charity.

Israel discovered even further Saudi connections with Palestinian terrorism, particularly in regard to Islamic charities. For example, Israel found a report from the Jeddah-based International Islamic Relief Organization (IIRO), which had been a conduit for funds to al-Qaeda and which was alleged to have aided Hamas in the mid-1990s. This particular IIRO report detailed the distribution of $280,000 to fourteen different Islamic committees, all of which were identified with Hamas. One recipient, the Islamic Center in the Gaza Strip, had even been shut down in the past by Yasser Arafat's Palestinian Authority because of its Hamas connection. Another Hamas recipient, the Islamic Charity–Hebron, had also received money from Prince Naif's Saudi Committee for Aid to the al-Quds Intifada. Finally, the IIRO included the ubiquitous Tulkarm Charity Committee as one of its fourteen Hamas recipients.

Also among the seized documents was a handwritten memorandum by a key deputy of Yasser Arafat, Abu Mazen, complaining to the governor of Riyadh, Prince Salman bin Abdul Aziz, that funds from Prince Naif's committee were reaching Hamas and allied organizations. According to Abu Mazen, Saudi money was going to al-Jamiya al-Islamiya (the Islamic Society) in the Gaza Strip, an organization, he wrote, that "belongs to Hamas." He was right. In fact, Israel had independently verified that the graduation ceremonies for the Islamic Society's network of kindergartens had Palestinian children enacting the attacks of suicide bombers; the children wore military uniforms and mock explosive belts. The head of the Islamic Society, Sheikh Ahmed Bakhar, even urged Palestinian mothers to educate their children with a love for jihad. Thus, Saudi money was supporting the next generation of terrorism as well.

Finally, captured reports from Palestinian intelligence agencies added that the Saudis were directly transferring funds not only to Hamas but also to the pro-Iranian Islamic Jihad organization.[54] For instance, a report from the Bethlehem office of the Palestinian Preventive Security organization implicated the Saudis when it traced the sources of funding for Islamic Jihad. A document dated May 1, 2000, identified two separate conduits of financing: "The first begins in Damascus [and] goes through Jordan to Cairo-Amman Bank. The second starts in *Saudi Arabia* goes through Egypt and reaches Palestine through the same bank [emphasis added]." The Saudis were up to their necks in financing terrorism.

Brinksmanship

These documents were stunning, but the revelations did not halt the Saudis' effort to shift international attention away from their involvement in terrorism back to the conflict between Israel and the Palestinians. "These allegations are a smoke screen intended to distract attention away from the peace process," said the Saudi ambassador to the United States, Prince Bandar. "Israel wants to discredit Saudi Arabia, which has been a leading voice for peace."[55] The Saudis wanted to stay in the box of "peace-makers" and not fall back into the box of states supporting terrorism.

The opportunity to renew their diplomatic efforts came when Crown Prince Abdullah decided to visit President Bush in the United States at the end of the April 2002. The two leaders had a somewhat tense history. Two months earlier, Saudi sources had revealed to the *Washington Post* that in late August 2001, Abdullah had written an angry twenty-five-page letter to Bush complaining about U.S. policy on Israel. According to these Saudi sources, at that time Abdullah had extracted from Bush "a U.S. vision of peace that was acceptable to the Saudis, and that differed from any Israeli plan."[56] How did the Saudis yank the administration in their direction? It seems that Abdullah had threatened Bush with a return to the "summer of 1973," which could have been a reference to the planning stages of the Egyptian-Syrian joint attack on Israel but was more likely a hint that the Saudis could use the oil weapon against the United States.[57] The Saudi crown prince also shared Bush's response with the leaders of Egypt, Jordan, Syria, and the PLO.[58] In exposing this sensitive correspondence, the Saudis seemed to be more concerned with showing off their diplomatic muscle against the American president than with preserving a discreet line of communications.

In April 2002, before his summit with President Bush, Crown Prince Abdullah reportedly was deeply disturbed because Israeli forces had encircled Yasser Arafat's compound in Ramallah. Saudi Arabia had tried to gain leverage with the United States, but initially it could do nothing to change the Arafat situation. Perhaps this was because Arafat had become such a tough client to defend. Documents found in the Palestinian leader's compound indicated that he had directly financed suicide bombings by the Tanzim militia of his Fatah movement. His Arabic signature was found on letters authorizing payments to Tanzim operatives. Moreover, Arafat's links to Iran had been discovered in January 2002, when Israeli naval commandos intercepted a cargo ship bound for the Gaza Strip that was packed with more than fifty tons of Iranian munitions. Nevertheless, the Saudis, who had a diplomatic agenda that was at variance with American focus on terrorism, tried pressure tactics once more.

In anticipation of the summit meeting between the two leaders, Saudi diplomats briefed the major U.S. media outlets. The Saudis faced an additional problem: members of the diplomatic press corps were aware of the ongoing incitement coming out of Saudi religious circles. Indeed, 126 Islamic scholars in Saudi Arabia had released a statement identifying the Bush administration as "a first class sponsor of international terrorism" and saying that the United States and Israel "form an axis of terrorism and evil in the world." So now Saudi Arabia blamed Israel for the rhetoric coming from its own Wahhabi preachers: "According to the Saudis," the *Washington Post* reported, "the perception of the United States [as] unwilling or unable to control Israel is largely responsible for a new tide of extremist statements coming from Islamic clerics."[59]

The Saudi background briefings leading up to the Bush-Abdullah summit even openly threatened the president with the use of the Saudi oil weapon for the first time since 1973. The *New York Times*'s State Department correspondent, Patrick E. Tyler, reported that "a person familiar with the Saudi's [Crown Prince Abdullah's] thinking" had said, "There was talk within the Saudi royal family and in Arab capitals of using the 'oil weapon' against the United States, and demanding that the United States leave strategic military bases in the region."[60] The unnamed Saudi source added, "It is a mistake to think that our people will not do what is necessary to survive...and if that means that we move to the right of bin Laden, so be it; to the left of Qaddafi, so be it; or fly to Baghdad and embrace Saddam like a brother, so be it." The reason for this threat to side with America's enemies, the source explained, was that the Saudi government could no longer defend the relationship with the United States to the Saudi people.[61] As Tyler wrote in his *New York Times* article, the Saudis were using "undeniable brinksmanship" with the White House.

Ultimately, however, the Saudi brinksmanship with the United States failed. After his April 25 summit meeting with Crown Prince Abdullah at his Crawford, Texas, ranch, President Bush stated, "Saudi Arabia made it clear, and has made it clear publicly, that they will not use oil as a weapon."[62] Moreover, at Crawford, Crown Prince Abdullah put forward an eight-point peace plan—one that, again, did not include any mention of "normalization," and that called for Israel to resume political negotiations with the Palestinians even without demanding a cessation of violence.[63] Bush did not adopt this Saudi approach. True, in the short term the Saudi pressure appeared to work in one respect, for right after the Crawford summit, Israel suddenly ended its siege of Arafat's Ramallah compound. The outgoing head of the Israeli Mossad, Efraim Halevy, even disclosed that the Saudis had offered behind-the-scenes assistance to end the crisis over Arafat's compound, pressuring the Palestinian leader to accept the terms for an Israeli pullback.[64] Apparently, it was important for the Saudis to show they could be helpful and not just threaten. But in the longer term, Saudi Arabia, in spite of any credit it could gain for its tactical assistance to Washington, could not muscle the United States into accepting Arafat, for in June, President Bush effectively called for Arafat's replacement.

Even if the Saudis were attempting to focus attention on the Israeli-Palestinian issue, why did they resort to brinksmanship with Washington? One factor was Crown Prince Abdullah himself, who had already proven to be more hard-line than King Fahd. Whereas Fahd, aware that Saudi Arabia depended on the American military for protection, had issued no ultimatums to the Reagan administration during the first Palestinian intifada from 1987 to 1990, in the second intifada, which began in September 2000, Abdullah did not show the same concern for upsetting the Americans. At the October 2000 Emergency Arab Summit in Cairo, in fact, he blamed the Clinton administration for the failure of Camp David and issued strong anti-American warnings. Arab satellite channels actually broadcast the second intifada into Saudi living rooms.

Second, by tying the overall U.S.-Saudi relationship to the Israeli-Palestinian peace process, the Saudis had a way to respond to the increasing opposition in Saudi Arabia to the American military presence. In 1998 and 1999, the Saudis had restricted U.S. access to their air bases during American operations against Iraq.[65] More recently, as part of America's air war against Afghanistan, the Bush administration had tried to get enhanced access to Saudi air bases. But in the lead-up to the Afghan campaign, the Saudi defense minister, Sultan bin Abdul Aziz, had told a Saudi newspaper, *al-Ukaz*, "We do not accept the presence in our country of a single soldier at war with Muslims or Arabs."[66] As an alternative during the early part of its Afghan campaign, on September 29, 2001, the United States began using Qatar's al-Udeid air base.[67]

With Saudi clerics issuing opinions that Saudi Arabia should back their fellow Muslims against the Americans, expanding the American air presence on Saudi soil would not be politically easy for the royal family—particularly since Sheikh bin Baz, who had issued the fatwa permitting the 1991 U.S. Gulf War deployment, was no longer alive. And in any case, Crown Prince Abdullah reportedly wanted to reduce the U.S. military presence in Saudi Arabia, though the United States still made limited use of Prince Sultan Air Base, outside of Riyadh.[68]

With the Afghan campaign coming to a close, the United States could be expected to request the use of Saudi air bases for the next big American military operation: against Iraq. Rather than turning down the administration flatly again, the Saudis could tell U.S. officials in their private meetings that they could not allow the Americans to use Saudi air bases because the United States had failed to honor Saudi Arabia's calls for a peace settlement on Israel. In other words, the Saudis would have a convenient excuse for reducing the American military presence, one that would allow them to escape any responsibility for being an unreliable U.S. ally.

Radical Wahhabism Gains Strength in Saudi Arabia

A third factor behind the Saudi brinksmanship was the internal struggle going on in Saudi Arabia. Like other Saudi leaders before him, Crown Prince Abdullah had always had to respect the authority of the ruling Wahhabi elite—but after September 11 it seemed that this was an even more pressing concern for him.

In October 2001, Saudi Arabia's internal intelligence agency reportedly ordered a confidential poll of Saudi men between the ages of twenty-five and forty-one, finding that *95 percent* approved of Osama bin Laden's cause.[69] Even if the poll had some inaccuracies, it indicated overwhelming backing for bin Laden, which only empowered the more radical Wahhabi clerics. And indeed, in this new environment, the Saudi *ulama* became more assertive. At the very time that Abdullah was warning the *ulama* to be careful with their language, Sheikh Abdullah al-Turki, the secretary-general of the Muslim World League and a member of the Council of Senior Ulama, made a revealing comment. He asserted that the Saudi kingdom's ruling body was made up of both its civic leaders (the royal family) and its religious scholars (the *ulama*).[70]

Historically, Abdullah al-Turki was right—up to a point. Saudi Arabia was of course the product of an eighteenth-century partnership between Muhammad ibn Abdul Wahhab, the spiritual founder of Wahhabism, and Muhammad Ibn Saud, the emir, or ruler, of the Saudi clan. But it is important to recall that according to their political alliance, Muhammad Ibn Saud was also the imam of the emerging Wahhabi community. In other words, the original political covenant between Wahhabism and the Saudis acknowledged the supremacy of the Saudi leadership, even its religious supremacy. Abdullah al-Turki, meanwhile, was hinting at the desirability of having the royal family and the religious establishment share power equally.

Prince Turki al-Faisal, the former head of Saudi Arabia's external intelligence and a son of the late King Faisal, answered Sheikh Abdullah in an article in *al-Sharq al-Awsat* on January 20, 2002. He argued that "those responsible for the affairs of state are the rulers" while "scholars only act in an advisory capacity." He criticized Sheikh Abdullah al-Turki's new definition of the relations between the rulers and the *ulama* as being at variance with the interpretation of the majority of Islamic scholars.[71]

Of course, the late Sheikh Abdul Aziz bin Baz, the former grand mufti of Saudi Arabia, had also put forward the view that the two governing elites in Saudi Arabia were on a par with each other. Yet even while he elevated the theoretical importance of the *ulama* in governance, he also supported and even protected the Saudi royal family at critical times, as has been shown. In other words, over two decades, bin Baz maintained the flame of Wahhabism but also stood ready to serve as a check against its violent outbursts. Now he was gone and no one could fill that role. His successor as grand mufti, Sheikh Abdul Aziz bin Abdullah Al al-Sheikh, had issued an important fatwa condemning suicide bombings, but he was a minority voice. There were more popular clerics who had greater stature with the Saudi religious public; these clerics—al-Shuaibi and others—filled the vacuum created by the death of bin Baz.[72]

Clearly, after September 11, a struggle was under way in Saudi Arabia. For example, when the Saudi education minister, Muhammad al-Rashid, wanted to reform educational methods, he earned a harsh rebuke from a religious critic. Sheikh Saleh al-Fawzan—the hard-line author of anti-Christian and anti-Jewish textbooks, who was also a member of the Council of Senior Ulama—expressed his disgust with any talk of such reform: "Some of our people want us to become like the infidels who want us to renounce our religious beliefs and follow in their footsteps by changing our education curricula that are based on the Koran and the teachings of the Prophet."[73] Sheikh al-Fawzan warned against anyone who acts like "a parrot...who repeats the demands of the enemies of Islam."[74]

This internal struggle only intensified in the summer of 2002, when Saudi religious police prevented firemen from rescuing Saudi girls caught in a school fire in Mecca, because the girls did not have their head scarves and thus their faces were immodestly exposed; fifteen girls died and forty were wounded. In response, the Saudi government removed responsibility for girls' education from a religious official and put it in the hands of a secular academic.[75] This was only one case of a well-reported conflict between the religious establishment and the Saudi government.

Crown Prince Abdullah's pressures against the United States gave him some edge in this ongoing internal struggle. It was important for him to stand up to Washington, even if this involved some tactless diplomatic threats against the United States. To placate Saudis who opposed the West, Abdullah also had to embrace the Iraqis—which he did literally at the March 2002 Arab summit in Beirut, when he hugged Izzat Ibrahim, Saddam Hussein's envoy. (In doing so, Abdullah was putting his arms around one of the key officials associated with Iraq's genocidal chemical weapons attacks on its Kurdish population in 1988.) Moreover, visible success in obtaining an Israeli pullback in the West Bank and Gaza Strip would certainly enhance Abdullah's prestige in Islamic circles, even though they saw the primary threat to Islam to be the West as a whole, not only Israel. He needed to present himself as a religiously pious leader, in the mold of King Faisal, whom the *ulama* had encouraged to impose an oil embargo on the United States in 1973.

Abdullah was not in any position to begin a full-scale clash with the Wahhabi *ulama*, even if some insisted on a greater share of power. A struggle for Saudi succession lay ahead. King Fahd was incapacitated; upon Fahd's death, Abdullah was expected to become king, and he would be expected to name Sultan as his crown prince. Sultan was already voicing some of the most hard-line positions with respect to the United States. In October 2002, he went so far as to argue that Saudi Arabia would not make any move against Iraq even if it had to defy the UN Security Council: "We don't have the ability to oppose the resolution of the United Nations or the Security Council. But it's not obligatory on us to implement what is said. We give priority to the interests of our country, then of Muslims and Arabs."[76] Additionally, Sultan was defiant about the need for Saudi Arabia to change its schoolbooks: "We do not plan to change our educational policy and no one asked us to do so."[77]

The issue of succession did not end with Sultan. Fahd (born 1921), Abdullah (born 1923), and Sultan (born 1924) were well over seventy years old. Would Fahd's other Sudairi brothers, Princes Naif (born 1933) and Salman (born 1936), come next? Or would members of the next generation be groomed to succeed—like Prince Saud al-Faisal (born 1941), the foreign minister? The *ulama* had been a part of the decision-making process in Saudi successions in the past; they had been part of the effort to depose King Saud and to replace him with King Faisal. Abdullah could not afford to alienate them.

At this point, Saudi Arabia was not in a strong position to contend with the Islamic extremism that had grown over the past two decades from its soil. In addition to the royal family's continued dependence on the *ulama* for legitimization, the Saudi regime had far less money available than in the past. Saudi budgets were being slashed; Saudi civilians' per capita income had dropped from an all-time high of between $18,000 and $20,000 in the early 1980s to between $6,000 and $7,000.[78]

In the past, the Saudis had bought off their potential opposition, including the *ulama*. By now such policies had become far more difficult to implement. And as has been detailed, the Saudi regime failed to control the hard-line Wahhabi clerics after September 11; despite a warning from Crown Prince Abdullah, clerics continued to preach anti-Christian and anti-Jewish messages in the mosques with impunity. A young Saudi woman confessed to Thomas Friedman of the *New York Times* in mid-2002, "Our schools teach religious intolerance, most of our mosques preach hate against any non-Muslims."[79]

The mosques and schools were not the only problems. In early May 2002, at the meeting of religious affairs ministers from the Organization of the Islamic Conference in Kuala Lumpur, Malaysia, a leading member of the Saudi *ulama* was still justifying suicide bombings. While Malaysia's deputy prime minister, Abdullah Ahmad Badawi, frankly stated that holy war could not be won with violence and suicide bombers, Saudi Arabia's minister for Islamic affairs, Sheikh Saleh Al al-Sheikh, completely disagreed. Reflecting a more hard-line religious position, he asserted, "The suicide bombings are permitted," adding that "the victims are considered to have died a martyr's death."[80]

It is noteworthy that several months later, Sheikh Saleh's deputy, Sheikh Tawfiq al-Sediry, spun a story to Donna Abu-Nasr of the Associated Press that mosques in Saudi Arabia were not allowed to preach extremism or recruit for Osama bin Laden. The AP article appeared in major newspapers across the United States, which apparently did not bother to check the recent public support for suicide bombings articulated by al-Sediry's boss.[81] Unfortunately, the PR-minded Saudi officials were generally successful in marketing the image they wanted to convey to the Western press.

A few reporters were determined to discover what was really going on in Saudi Arabia, however. For example, an Australian reporter visiting the Khamis Mushayt area, where five of the September 11 hijackers were recruited, found that a year after the attacks on New York and Washington, the same radical religious leader who was suspected to have recruited them, Sheikh Ahmad al-Hawashi, was still in charge of the local mosque. A Saudi reformer in the area told the visiting Australian journalist, "There are a lot of suspect sheiks working in this area. They are intense and they are part of a radical movement. The universities are the same. We have become more *Wahabist*."[82]

The Threat Remains

In short, even after the horrific attacks on America, the religious environment that had incited fifteen Saudi nationals to commit mass murder remained militant; the incitement continued, and thus the threat remained. Indeed, in 2002, Saudi nationals continued to turn up as part of the al-Qaeda network: in Morocco, where three Saudis who planned to strike at U.S. and British warships in the Strait of Gibraltar were seized; in Lebanon, where Saudis were found in an al-Qaeda cell; and in Saudi Arabia's Empty Quarter area, where U.S. unmanned aerial vehicles conducted surveillance operations and searched for terrorist suspects.[83] Despite the ongoing instances of Saudi nationals' involvement in terrorist activities overseas, Prince Naif still felt confident that Saudi Arabia itself was not threatened; thus he asserted in late November that there were no al-Qaeda sleeper cells in the Saudi kingdom.[84]

Why did the incitement continue? Did the Saudis think they had immunity from future attacks? Did the Saudi royal family not have the political leverage to control the Wahhabi clerics? Or did the royal family simply refuse to apply the necessary pressures to change the hatred, and instead make pro forma declarations about moderation for Western consumption? In any case, the net result was the same: Saudi Arabia was still promoting anti-Western hatred—and by doing so, it helped feed the manpower pool for further attacks on America and its allies.

Saudi Arabia's entry into Arab-Israeli diplomacy in 2002 was a microcosm of Saudi behavior worldwide. The Saudis said all the right things, persuading many members of the world community—including the UN Security Council—that they sought to advance peace in the Middle East. At times they even provided behind-the-scenes diplomatic assistance to Washington, by pressuring Yasser Arafat and other Arab leaders who had benefited from Saudi assistance. But at the same time, Saudi charities were funneling money to Hamas, which was engaging in suicide bombings against Israeli civilian targets. By giving money to the families of suicide bombers, they "incentivized" the attacks, to use the language of Secretary of State Colin Powell.

And these charities were not fringe groups unrelated to the Saudi regime, but rather they revealed the real aims of the Saudi regime.

Members of the Saudi royal family actually funded the charities, and the Muslim World League and its operational arm, the IIRO, served essentially as ministries of the Saudi government, with access to Saudi embassies abroad, in most cases. At the apex of the al-Haramain foundation sat no less than the Saudi minister of Islamic affairs, Sheikh Saleh Al al-Sheikh, who chaired the foundation's administrative board and monitored its global activities.[85] The Saudi government knew exactly what these huge Wahhabi charities were doing.

The game the Saudis played with Israel and the Palestinians was really a sideshow, diverting attention from the Saudi role in September 11 and in continuing terrorism operations. But after the Abdullah initiative was exposed to be far different from what had initially been promised— particularly since the magic word, "normalization," was dropped—the Saudis had a tougher time portraying themselves as peacemakers.

If Saudi Arabia was making a show of its support for Israeli-Palestinian peace while simultaneously backing the suicide bombers of Hamas, then what about the larger questions of Saudi Arabia's role in al-Qaeda's global terrorism? For the same charities that funded Hamas had been tainted with serious allegations concerning their support for terrorism elsewhere: in the Balkans, East Africa, and the Philippines.[86] That the Saudis were prepared to continue with these games even after September 11 was the best indication that their leaders had not seen the need to change their ways after the attacks on America.

After September 11, Saudi Arabia remained a womb in which radical Islamic terrorism continued to grow, the Saudi kingdom providing not only its supporting ideology but also its financial support structure. Unfortunately, while the military campaign against terrorism appeared to be succeeding, particularly in Afghanistan, the diplomatic campaign against Saudi behavior had not really begun.

Chapter 11

Was Saudi Arabia Finally Changing?

The global impact of Saudi Wahhabi institutions in spreading the new terrorism worldwide became even more evident at the time of the 2003 Iraq War and its immediate aftermath. In the Balkans, a former Bosnian interior minister declared that Saudi religious teachings were "poisoning our youth;" he was commenting after a high-profile case in which a Bosnian Muslim youth, belonging to an extremist organization funded with Saudi aid, had murdered a Christian Croat man and his daughter on Christmas Eve.[1] It turned out that Jamel Zougam, one of the main suspects in the March 11, 2004, al-Qaeda bombings in Madrid regularly attended a Wahhabi mosque south of Tangiers, Morocco, along with other co-conspirators in the attack.[2]

The Saudis were also making new inroads in Kosovo and Africa, backing radical strains of Islam in Nigeria and in Tanzania. In Southeast Asia, a Bin Baz Islamic Center was established in Indonesia, where it was associated with strident Islamic teaching.[3] And a Philippine intelligence report described the creation in 2002 of a new Islamist organization, the Rajah Solaiman Movement, with a special operations arm financed by money from Saudi Arabia; it was linked to the older, pro-bin Laden Abu Sayyaf terrorist group. The newer organization sought the Islamization of the entire Philippines.[4]

More analysts of Middle Eastern events, looking back, were coming to the conclusion that the rise of the new global terrorism was directly tied to Saudi Arabia. Thus Wael Abrashi, the deputy editor of the Egyptian weekly *Ruz al-Yusuf*, (the functional equivalent of *Newsweek* in Cairo) asserted in mid-2003 that Saudi authorities had to admit that al-Qaeda was "a local Saudi organization" which, like the organizations it drew around it, "emerged from under the robe of Wahhabism."[5] Abrashi charged Saudi Arabia with backing the Islamic militancy that had afflicted Egypt for more than two decades: "I can say with certainty that after a very careful reading of all the documents and texts of the official investigations linked to all acts of terror that have taken place in Egypt, from the assassination of the late president Anwar Sadat in October 1981, up to the Luxor massacre in 1997, Saudi Arabia was the main station through which most of the Egyptian extremists passed."[6]

The rise of the new terrorism had come about, according to Abrashi's analysis, because of an important doctrinal shift. Since the founding of Wahhabism in the eighteenth century, its adherents had engaged in *takfir*: the condemnation of other Muslims, especially Shiites, as infidels (*kufar*). But now, Abrashi pointed out, movements inspired by this doctrine had progressed to a new stage in their thinking: They preached the necessity of the "annihilation and destruction" of those they accused of heresy. This set the intellectual and religious groundwork for a new militancy, of which al-Qaeda became the foremost exponent. At the same time, Saudi Wahhabi clerics began talking about the legitimacy of the mass murder of infidels. This prepared the background not only for justifying the September 11, 2001, attacks on New York and Washington, but also for escalating the war against the West.

For example, a prominent Saudi Islamic scholar, Sheikh Nasir Hamad al-Fahd, issued an Islamic ruling in May 2003 approving the use of weapons of mass destruction against the United States. The use of such weaponry was permissible, he explained, since it was directed against the infidels. Additionally, he considered a strike of this sort as a form of retaliation—in response to what he charged the U.S. government had done to the Muslims. Because of these evils, he argued, the Muslims have the right to kill ten million Americans.[7]

These ideas penetrated al-Qaeda periodicals and websites. One Saif al-Din al-Ansari (a nom de guerre), who wrote frequently in *al-Ansar*, said this about the extermination of infidels: "Just as the law of extermination was applied to the infidel forces among the nations in previous days and no one could escape it, so it will be applied to the infidel forces in our day and no one will escape it." He referred to pagan Arab people who, according to Islamic tradition, had been exterminated because of their rejection of Muhammad. By analogy, he concluded, "the American state, the Jewish state, and all other infidel countries will certainly be destroyed."[8]

Also, during 2003 and 2004, more evidence surfaced on the Saudi role in terrorist financing over the previous decade or more. A detailed memorandum on the stationery of the International Islamic Relief Organization (IIRO), discovered by Bosnian intelligence, recorded a meeting between bin Laden associates and representatives of a Saudi organization. The undated memorandum (which was probably written around 1988 or 1989, when related documents found with it were dated) includes a proposal for IIRO offices in Pakistan: "attacks will be launched from them."[9] Indeed, in 1995, a classified FBI intelligence report listed the IIRO and its mother organization, the Muslim World League, as important resources for the new generation of Sunni Islamic terrorists.[10] And it turned out that the head of the IIRO office in Peshawar, Pakistan, Abu Talal al-Qasimy, was a close protégé of bin Laden's deputy, Ayman al-Zawahiri. Al-Qasimy had also led the Egyptian mujahideen in Bosnia until his disappearance in 1995.[11]

Taken together with other reports of the IIRO's terrorist links in Albania, Chechnya, India, the Philippines, the West Bank, and the Gaza Strip, these reports led analysts to conclude that the IIRO was becoming the Saudis' chosen instrument for funding the global jihad. And this IIRO funding was linked in one way or another to the apex of the Saudi establishment. According to documents submitted to U.S. courts by his American attorneys, Saudi Arabia's defense minister, Prince Sultan, was a regular contributor to the IIRO: He gave $266,000 annually to the organization for sixteen years.[12] Indeed, former CIA operative Robert Baer contended that Prince Salman, the governor of Riyadh and full brother of King Fahd, controlled IIRO distributions "with an iron hand."[13]

Wahhabism in Iraq

The new Islamist militancy would have its most strategically significant impact in Iraq. In the run-up to the Iraq War, as the Bush administration sought to establish a link between al-Qaeda and the regime of Saddam Hussein, attention became increasingly drawn to a small Kurdish Islamist group called Ansar al-Islam. Secretary of State Colin Powell disclosed on February 5, 2003, that "Baghdad has an agent in the most senior levels of the radical organization, Ansar al-Islam, that controls this corner of Iraq. In 2000, this agent offered Al Qaida [sic] safe haven in the region. After we swept Al Qaida from Afghanistan, some of its members accepted this safe haven."

But who were Ansar al-Islam, and where did they come from?

The group originated when Kurdish Islamists reached out to the al-Qaeda leadership in Afghanistan in August 2001. Many underwent training in al-Qaeda camps; shortly thereafter they established Ansar al-Islam. The head of the group, Mullah Krekar, was a student of Sheikh Abdullah Azzam in Pakistan; Azzam was Osama bin Laden's ideological mentor. Krekar's Kurdish deputy, Abu Abdullah Shafae, trained with al-Qaeda in Afghanistan for ten years.[14] American sources maintained that the organization was created with $300,000 to $600,000 in seed money that came from al-Qaeda and had originated in Saudi Arabia. Ansar al-Islam prisoners claimed that they had received funds from Saudi Arabia, as well as from Iran and from the regime of Saddam Hussein. Sheikh Muhammad Muhammad Ali, one of the founders of the Iraqi National Congress, claimed that Ansar al-Islam's predecessor, an organization known as Jund al-Islam, had been funded by bin Laden, Saddam Hussein, and "the Wahhabi extremists."[15]

Beyond these various reports of Saudi financial support, there is strong evidence of Wahhabi religious influence on Ansar al-Islam. It exhibited the extreme intolerance of Christians and Jews that was characteristic of Wahhabis. In a guest house in Kabul, Afghanistan, documents were found that were associated with the Kurdish Islamists who would form Ansar al-Islam; one called for the creation of a Taliban-style society in Kurdistan, which would require members to "expel those Jews and Christians from Kurdistan, and join the way of jihad."[16] Additionally, the Kurdish Islamists vandalized centuries-old tombs of revered Muslim scholars in Kurdistan who had belonged to the Naqshabandi Sufi order; Wahhabism discourages the veneration of Muslim saints, forbidding prayers at their graveside. The smashing of tombs and shrines had been a Wahhabi trademark since the eighteenth century. In a July 28, 2002, press release, the Patriotic Union of Kurdistan (PUK) of Jalal Talabani compared one such assault on a place called Bakhi Kon, in the Hawraman Mountains, to the Taliban's destruction of the Buddhist statues in the Bamyan Valley in Afghanistan. Given the adoption of these Wahhabi practices by Ansar al-Islam, it was not surprising that Mullah Krekar once proudly described himself as a disciple of Muhammad ibn Abdul Wahhab.[17]

In line with this, Ansar al-Islam viewed the secular leadership of the Kurds—both the Kurdish Democratic Party that ruled northern Kurdistan and the PUK in the south—as "infidels." It attempted to assassinate the PUK prime minister, Barham Salih, in mid-2002. It treated PUK fighters with enormous brutality, massacring and mutilating forty-three PUK fighters on September 23, 2001. Ansar al-Islam also recruited non-Kurdish foreign fighters into Kurdistan—in particular, al-Qaeda Arabs seeking a new refuge in the isolated mountain areas of southeastern Kurdistan, along the Iraq-Iran border. But its main impact on Iraq was the introduction of suicide bombing, which had not previously been employed by Iraqi movements of any ideological orientation. One of the first and most notable of these attacks took place on March 26, 2003. It killed five people, including Paul Moran, a journalist with the Australian Broadcasting Company. The Ansar al-Islam suicide bomber, Abdul Aziz Saud al-Gharbi, was not Kurdish, but came from the ranks of its foreign volunteers. Notably, he was from Hail, in northern Saudi Arabia.[18]

The buildup of pro-Wahhabi organizations in Iraq in general, and Kurdistan in particular, had been an ongoing Saudi project for at least a decade. According to a March 12, 2001, press release from the Saudi embassy in Washington, the IIRO had spent more than $19 million in Kurdistan alone over the last nine years. Much of this investment was devoted to a geographic belt from the Kurdish town of Barzan down to Halabja: precisely the same area where Ansar al-Islam was flourishing.

Western reporters noted in 2002 the construction there of new white
Wahhabi mosques with the letters "IIRO" stamped on their outside walls.
In 2002, a senior Kurdish cleric complained, "The Wahhabis are stealing
our youth," referring to the effects of Saudi penetration into the area.[19] Yet
the IIRO wasn't alone. The World Assembly for Muslim Youth (WAMY),
according to another press release from July 4, 2001, was actively organizing what it called medical and educational services in Kurdistan. Al-
Haramain, a charitable foundation that billed itself as "your beating heart
and compassionate hand for your Muslim brethren," was, according to its
website, also active in Kurdistan. These Saudi charities may very likely
have gone beyond providing only religious and humanitarian support,
since each organization had been linked in the past to the financing of
Hamas, Abu Sayyaf, Chechen militant Islamist groups, and al-Qaeda.

The growth of the Wahhabi presence in Iraq and the rise of Ansar al-
Islam affected the interests of a number of parties. In the past, Saddam
Hussein had looked upon Iraqi Islamists in general with antipathy; after
all, he had emerged as Iraq's leader from the ranks of the generally secular Iraqi Baath Party. But with the American victory in the 1991 Gulf War
and the imposition of a "no-fly zone" over northern Iraq, his calculus had
to quickly change. As Kurdish groups in the area set up highly
autonomous institutions, Saddam needed an instrument to destabilize this
pro-American region that was beyond the control of his regime in Baghdad. The Syrian Baath had already made this ideological leap by allying
themselves with the militant Shiite organization Hizballah. Apparently,
Saddam Hussein appointed Colonel Saadan Mahmoud Abdul Latif al-
Aani, also known as Abu Wael, from the Iraqi secret police as his liaison
officer to Ansar al-Islam. According to one of his men, now in custody,
Abu Wael supplied hundreds of thousands of dollars, as well as weapons,
such as mortars, to the Kurdish Islamist group. Well before the outbreak
of the Iraq War in 2003, Abu Wael organized the recruitment of foreign
fighters from outside Iraq—including Jordanians, Turks, Syrians, Yemenis, Egyptians, and Lebanese—to join Ansar al-Islam.[20] Saudis would
become involved as well.

It would be a mistake to interpret this movement as confined to the
mountains of Kurdistan. Abu Wael's deputy told Jonathan Schanzer of the
Washington Institute for Near East Policy that the Iraqi leadership had

ordered Ansar al-Islam members to reposition themselves in Mosul and key Sunni Arab towns in western Iraq, such as Tikrit and Fallujah, in the event of an American attack on their Kurdish center of operations.[21] He also disclosed that the foreign fighters were trained at Salman Pak, twenty miles southeast of Baghdad. This indicated that they could be a force in the area that became known as the "Sunni triangle" if they received instructions to leave their Kurdish base.

American officials grew concerned about Ansar al-Islam because it became the nexus between Saddam Hussein's weapons of mass destruction and international terrorism. For example, the Bush administration received reports that Ansar al-Islam had been given VX nerve agent by the Iraqis and managed to move it overland with a courier into Turkey.[22] Reportedly, Ansar al-Islam had tested the toxin ricin on animals. According to the March 2004 report of the United Nations Monitoring, Verification, and Inspection Commission (UNMOVIC), the Iraqis admitted to having produced ricin. According to a captured al-Qaeda operative in Italy, the Iraqis had sold toxins to the terrorist network of Abu Mussab al-Zarqawi, who served as al-Qaeda's liaison officer to Saddam Hussein's regime.[23] Jordan's prime minister Ali Abu al-Rageb publicly claimed that al-Zarqawi was hiding out in an Ansar al-Islam camp.[24] If there was ever a terrorist group with international connections that would choose to use weapons of mass destruction against the infidels—as the militant Wahhabi clerics of Saudi Arabia had envisioned—it was Ansar al-Islam.

But with the Western coalition's rapid advance to Baghdad and the elimination of Saddam Hussein's regime, Ansar al-Islam and its collection of foreign fighters would serve as the core for another mission—leading terrorist attacks against the U.S. Army in Iraq after major operations had already come to an end on May 1, 2003. American military officers began briefing the international press that they were increasingly identifying the attackers as Wahhabis. *Newsweek* quoted one U.S. intelligence officer in mid-June as saying: "Now, all of a sudden, these Wahhabi guys have been appearing. We're hearing that word a lot more: Wahhabi."[25] There was evidence that Saudi volunteers had crossed the border into Iraq to fight in the Sunni-populated areas. A Saudi website carried the story of how two Saudis died in combat in the town of Fallujah while fighting U.S. troops.[26] Saudi opposition websites recorded the deaths of other Saudis fighting the

U.S. in November 2003. A tribal representative from the Sunni triangle warned during a December 2003 visit to Washington: "The Fallujah region is filling up with Wahhabis."[27] There appeared to be those who were willing to encourage Saudi mujahideen to join the fight: the May issue of *The Future of Islam*, the monthly publication of WAMY, carried a cover interview with Sheikh Ayed al-Qarni, a Saudi cleric who was also an advisor to King Fahd's youngest son, Prince Abdul Aziz bin Fahd, in which he urged Saudis to go fight in Iraq or to contribute money.[28]

During July 2003, a new militant Islamic organization began taking credit for attacks on U.S. troops throughout the Sunni triangle in Iraq: al-Jama'a al-Salafiya al-Mujahida.

This group appeared to be related to al-Qaeda. On its website, it called the September 11 attacks on the United States "blessed" and worthy actions in which the "enemies of Allah" were defeated. It stated that the attacks had brought hope and vitality to the forces seeking the awakening of Islam throughout the world. The organization held up both Osama bin Laden and Abdullah Azzam as ideal models for its supporters to follow in carrying out jihad against the West. It took credit for anti-American operations in Iraqi cities such as Mosul and Ramadi. Al-Jama'a al-Salafiya used classic Wahhabi terminology in defining democracy as an infidel religion and participation in parliamentary elections as forbidden *bid'a* (innovations), which would distort the proper Islamic form of governance. The group painted America as an infidel force that was not only leading a crusade in the name of Christianity against Islam, but was also seeking global hegemony for its new infidel religion—democracy. But it also aimed its hostility toward the Shiites, whom it viewed as unbelievers, with a version of Islam that was "evil."

Al-Jama'a al-Salafiya drew its religious inspiration from the writings of Ibn Taymiyya and Muhammad ibn Abdul Wahhab. But on its website, it highlighted the approval of suicide attacks given in religious edicts and writings of several important Saudi clerics: Sulaiman bin al-Ulwan, Ali al Khudair, and Hamud bin Uqla al-Shuaibi.[29] These same clerics were cited as authorities on the websites of militant Islamic movements among the Chechens, as well as of Hamas. Al-Jama'a al-Salafiya was not the only militant Sunni movement killing U.S. soldiers in Western Iraq: in Mosul, an armed Wahhabi group called Abu Ammash was uncovered.[30] But al-

Jama'a al-Salafiya seemed to have emerged from the same roots as others that were engaged in the reawakened global jihad.

While al-Jama'a al-Salafiya was understandably reticent about its sources of funding, its clearly Wahhabi agenda could be expected to open doors in Saudi Arabia—just as it had for the mujahideen of Afghanistan, Bosnia, Chechnya, and the Palestinians. Without mentioning this organization in particular, Deputy Secretary of State Richard Armitage admitted that "some money from Saudi private charities had gone to funding militants in Iraq."[31] Senior coalition military officials also spoke about money having been sent from Saudi Arabia to Iraqi mosques in order to fund the spread of Wahhabism.[32] Meanwhile, despite the organization's efforts at concealment, there was one noticeable Saudi link to the new efforts of militants in Iraq. The founders of al-Jama'a al-Salafiya were interviewed on the Saudi satellite channel, al-Arabiya. What stood out from the interview was that the leaders of the movement spoke Arabic with a distinctly Saudi accent. This led some observers to conclude that the leadership of the organization was made up of Saudi citizens.[33]

Why would the Saudis get involved in the jihad against the U.S. Army in western Iraq?

After the involvement of Saudi citizens in the attacks of September 11, such activity could only be disastrous for the Saudi state, which was trying to preserve its traditional ties to Washington. Yet there were plenty of countervailing Saudi interests involved here, which can only be evaluated through some conjecture. For instance, the Saudis could be only ambivalent about the entire American war effort against Saddam Hussein in 2003. On one hand, Saddam's Iraq had been a geostrategic adversary; his armored divisions invaded Kuwait in 1990 and threatened to move into northern Saudi Arabia, as well. On the other hand, during the Iraq-Iran War in the 1980s, Saddam's army had been a bulwark against Iranian expansionism and the spread of militant Shiite Islam into the Arabian states of the Persian Gulf, where Shiites made up significant portions of the population—especially in Bahrain, Kuwait, the United Arab Emirates, and the eastern province of Saudi Arabia. From the time of its birth, Wahhabism viewed Shiism as its ideological nemesis.

A clear-cut American victory in Iraq would thus have two principle effects. First, it would bring about the complete recovery of the Iraqi oil industry, driving down the price of oil and providing the United States with a new alternative source of oil with reserves on a scale that rival the Saudis'. Second, should democracy prevail in Iraq, any new government would reflect the true demographic makeup of Iraq, where Shiites make up at least 65 percent of the population. The Wahhabi kingdom would thus face a new Shiite state along its northern border, which could arouse separatist sentiments among the Shiites of the oil-rich eastern province of Saudi Arabia. The outcome that would best protect Saudi interests in regard to Iraq would be the elimination of Saddam Hussein and his replacement by a regime that would preserve the hegemony of the Iraqi Sunni Arabs, with the possible backing of a militant contingent of Iraqi Kurds who were also Sunni Muslims.

The Saudis did not necessarily have to get caught tampering in the internal affairs of Iraq. The actual number of Saudi volunteers crossing the border into Iraqi territory was disputed. The Saudi-Iraq border was partly monitored, forcing Saudi volunteers to enter Iraq through Kuwait or by flying to Syria and then crossing into Iraq.[34] Saudi opposition elements put the number of Saudis fighting in the Baghdad area at around five thousand. American sources generally spoke about foreign fighters coming from Syria and Iran; they mentioned Saudi Arabia only occasionally. Iraqi Shiites readily blamed the Wahhabis for attacks on their holy sites in Najaf and Karbalah. Having invested over a decade in the spread of Wahhabism in Iraq, the Saudis really didn't need large numbers of their own nationals to engage in combat: There were plenty of Iraqi Wahhabis available for resistance operations against the U.S. Foreign journalists noticed that repeatedly, in the last years of Saddam Hussein's rule, there was an upsurge of mosque construction in the Sunni communities of Iraq, and that mosque attendance had appeared to be on the rise. This was significant, as the Wahhabi mosques served also as recruiting centers for the mujahideen as they waged their campaign against US. forces.

In December 2003, elements associated with al-Qaeda published a detailed fifty-page analysis of the situation in Iraq and the role of the mujahideen in the struggle against the U.S. and its coalition partners. The book was presented as a follow-up to an earlier work written by Sheikh Yusuf al-Ayiri, a leading Saudi scholar who wrote al-Qaeda propaganda on the Internet. Eight pages of the newer work were dedicated to the

Spanish role in the war in Iraq, with special attention given to the Spanish parliamentary elections set for March 14, 2004. The al-Qaeda book focused on how to create a change in the Spanish government that would force the withdrawal of Spanish forces from Iraq. The author clearly states an interest in fostering a "domino effect" that would arouse opposition in Italy, Poland, and eventually the United Kingdom, to their support for the U.S. war effort in Iraq. The book called on the Iraqi "resistance" to strike repeatedly at Spanish troops in Iraq in order to secure the victory of the Spanish Socialist Party.[35] It did not suggest striking in the heart of Madrid, as an al-Qaeda-related group eventually did in March 2004, bringing about the same result that the book envisioned. But it demonstrated the intimate connection between al-Qaeda global strategy and the war effort of the mujahideen in Iraq.

Al-Qaeda Strikes Saudi Arabia: The New Saudi Counter-terrorist Campaign at Home and the Continuing Support for Terrorism Abroad

The Saudis have said that they endured their own version of the September 11 attacks in the triple suicide bombing in Riyadh on May 12, 2003, which killed thirty-five people, including nine Americans. What was striking about the attack and its immediate aftermath was the fact that previously, leading Saudis, especially Interior Minister Prince Naif, vociferously denied, despite all the evidence to the contrary, the existence of an al-Qaeda presence in the kingdom. Despite all the warning signs, the Saudis had been complacent about their security situation. Six days before the triple attack, they discovered a weapons cache in Riyadh that included hundreds of pounds of explosives. Indeed, in the months prior to the attacks, U.S. officials had asked the Saudi government to deploy armed uniformed guards around all Western targets, but the Saudis did not respond.[36] Perhaps they felt that they still had a degree of immunity; even the May 12 bombings were directed against three housing compounds for foreigners working in Saudi Arabia. The Saudi regime was not specifically targeted. Nonetheless, the Saudi leadership could not ultimately tolerate the conversion of their capital into a full-scale battleground. And, as the Saudi security services began to round up al-Qaeda suspects, the extent of their presence in the kingdom was fully revealed.

Al-Qaeda units in Saudi Arabia were not confined to just one city or province of the kingdom, but seemed to be everywhere. On May 20, 2003, three al-Qaeda suspects were arrested in the Red Sea port city of Jidda. In early June, another terrorist suspect was killed along with two Saudi security men in a gun battle in Hail, in north-central Saudi Arabia. On June 14, Saudi security forces were involved in a shootout with an al-Qaeda cell in Mecca; they also detained four women on terrorist charges. The Saudi security force waged a crackdown in June against Saudi radical clerics in Medina, including Sheikh Ali bin al-Khudair and Sheikh Nasir Hamad al-Fahd, the author of the May 2003 *fatwa* permitting the use of weapons of mass destruction against infidels. From these clerics and their associates they confiscated Kalashnikov rifles, boxes of ammunition, grenades, and forged IDs. And on July 3, 2003, a top al-Qaeda fugitive and three other suspects were killed in a shootout in Suweir, a small Saudi town in the northern al-Jawf region, close to the Iraqi border. After the shootout, Saudi security forces discovered not only weapons but also charity boxes containing up to 300,000 Saudi riyals.[37] Symbolizing the new crackdown, pictures of twenty-six terrorist fugitives were plastered across the front page of the Saudi daily *al-Watan* on December 7, 2003.[38] The banner headline over the photographs read *"matlubun"*: wanted.

Street battles with al-Qaeda cells continued into the next year as well. In another shootout in Riyadh on April 12, 2004, al-Qaeda operatives used rocket-propelled grenades against Saudi security forces. Around the same time, huge quantities of explosive materials, including five hundred kilograms of dynamite, were intercepted by Saudi security forces in the Najran area, along the Yemeni border.[39] In early 2004, Prince Turki al-Faisal, the Saudi ambassador to the United Kingdom and former intelligence head, summarized the Saudi counter-terrorist crackdown as follows: nearly six hundred arrested, seventy to ninety indicted for involvement in terrorism, 250–300 still under investigation. Most of those imprisoned were between the ages of fifteen and twenty-five.[40] These young men were not, for the most part, veterans of bin Laden training camps in Afghanistan—which indicated how the Saudi educational system had influenced youth to take part in militant operations.

Yet despite these battles, al-Qaeda spokesmen made it clear that they had not decided to declare war on the Saudi leadership. In November

2003, Abu Salim al-Hijazi, an al-Qaeda commander operating near Fallujah in western Iraq, gave an interview on an al-Qaeda website in which he explained that in a second Riyadh bombing on November 8, 2003, it was al-Qaeda's intention to kill Americans and Lebanese Christians—not Saudi Muslims. He stressed that al-Qaeda had instructed its members not to confront the governments of Islamic countries, since America was the main target of the organization. Yet he made it clear that he did not view the Saudis as legitimate Islamic rulers, explaining that fragile Middle Eastern regimes would collapse by themselves with the demise of the United States.[41] In a subsequent al-Qaeda analysis, Abu Hajer (Abdul Aziz al-Muqren, who was on Saudi Arabia's most wanted list), gave another reason for being careful about attacks in the kingdom: "It is also true that we must take advantage of this country [Saudi Arabia] *because it is the primary source of funds for most Jihad movements.*" (emphasis added)

Abu Hajer reminded his followers of their primary mission: "I have sworn to purge the Arabian peninsula of the polytheists [Christian Crusaders and Jews]." The Saudi regime and its armed forces were thus not their immediate adversaries.[42] This left open the possibility of resuming the "Faustian bargain" of the 1990s—al-Qaeda would leave the Saudis alone and focus on operations abroad if Saudi officials didn't interfere with the group's activities. Statements on al-Qaeda-oriented websites encouraged supporters to leave the Saudi regime alone, and instead to pursue jihad against America in Iraq. But in 2003, it did not seem that the Saudi leadership was willing to ignore any longer the threat posed by the al-Qaeda presence that had grown over the years on Saudi soil. Years of fostering global jihad appeared to have blown back to the Arabian peninsula and to have threatened the Saudi regime. The Saudis were forced to make hard choices.

As a result, was Saudi Arabia turning the corner on its past support for terrorism? Unfortunately, while the Saudis seemed determined to move against al-Qaeda cells *inside* the kingdom, there was substantial evidence that Saudi Arabia was still backing terrorism *outside* the kingdom. For example, six weeks after the May 12 attacks, on June 26, 2003, David Aufhauser, general counsel to the Treasury Department, appeared before the Senate Judiciary Committee and described Saudi Arabia as the "epicenter" of terrorist financing. Over a month later, on July 31, John Pistole, the acting FBI director for counter-terrorism, was asked in a hearing of the U.S. Senate's Government Operations Committee about Saudi efforts to halt terrorist financing. Pistole, who praised as "unprecedented" the level of Saudi cooperation with the FBI on investigating the May 12 bombings in Riyadh, could only say that regarding Saudi Arabia's actions with respect to terrorist financing, "The jury's still out." There was a clear difference between how Saudi Arabia was handling its internal threat and how it acted with respect to the problem of global terrorism.

This distinction was borne out by Saudi financing of Hamas in mid-2003. Israeli military intelligence estimated that Saudi Arabia was providing at least 50 percent of Hamas's income during June 2003.[43] According to another estimate, as much as 60 to 70 percent of Hamas's funds came from the Saudi Kingdom.[44] In August 2003, Sheikh Ahmed Yasin, the head of Hamas who was eliminated by Israel in March 2004, rather conspicuously went out of his way during a public address in the Gaza Strip to thank two prominent Saudi charities, IIRO and WAMY, for their assistance. In the past, Yasin had made sure to praise the Saudis in interviews he gave to the Saudi press. In November 2001, he described Saudi Arabia's material assistance to the Palestinian people to a Saudi newspaper, adding, "The majority of material and economic aid that reaches the Palestinian people, in all its sectors, comes from the Saudi Arabian Kingdom, and with the support of King Fahd bin Abdul Aziz and Crown Prince Abdullah."[45] This public praise of Saudi largesse continued in statements from the Hamas leadership in late 2003. In December 2003, in an interview in the London-based Arabic daily *al-Hayat*, Khaled Mashal, who had received assurances of continuing Saudi support from Crown Prince Abdullah during an October 2002 Riyadh visit, continued to lavish praise on the Saudis: "Over the years, the Saudi people provided more aid to our Palestinian people than any other Arab state."[46] This did not provide proof of Saudi payments to Hamas, but Mishal did not sound like someone who had lost Saudi financial backing for his organization.

Saudi Wahhabism was also making ideological inroads among the Palestinians in general and Hamas in particular. According to the Hamas website, in 2003 Saudi clerics still remained the main religious source for the justification of suicide bombing attacks.

Saudi Clerics Provide Religious Legitimacy for Hamas Suicide Attacks

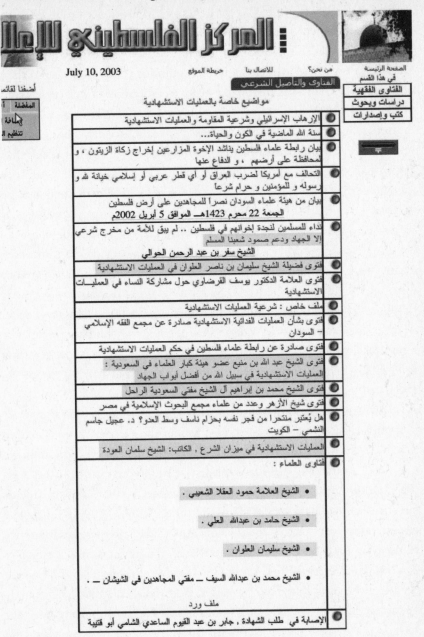

Israeli forces operating in the West Bank and the Gaza Strip also discovered other forms of ideological support for Palestinian extremism from Saudi Arabia. For example, the Hamas-oriented Koran and Sunna Society Palestine was a relatively new organization, set up in 1996; by 2003, it had branches in Bethlehem, Salafit, Abu Dis (next to Jerusalem), Jenin, and in the Tulkarm area. It distributed Saudi texts praising suicide attacks against "the infidels" and condemning those who dodge their obligations to join "the jihad." The Koran and Sunna Society was supported by WAMY.

In the Gaza Strip, there was the Dar al-Arqam Model School, a special project of Sheikh Ahmed Yasin. Here Saudi funds were less important than the spread of radical Wahhabi militancy. The school used texts with strongly anti-Western messages. They widely cited Sheikh Sulaiman bin Nasir al-Ulwan, one of the Saudi clerics whose statements supporting suicide attacks appeared on the Hamas website. He was also ideologically close to al-Qaeda; during a December 2001 al-Qaeda videotape, in which Osama bin Laden reenacts with his hands the crashing of hijacked aircraft into the World Trade Center, a Saudi mujahid appears who says he is bringing "a beautiful *fatwa*" for bin Laden from Sheikh al-Ulwan of Saudi Arabia. The exportation of radical jihad ideology to the Palestinians was reminiscent of the Saudi support for madrassas in western Pakistan during the 1980s, which gave birth to the Taliban. The Dar al-Arqam School was also partly supported by WAMY.

Nevertheless, Saudi spokesmen tried to make the case that they were clamping down on terrorist financing. Saudi ruling circles recognized that they had a serious problem on their hands. One commentator admitted that Saudi Arabia had been too permissive to terrorist groups: "we were slow, until the Riyal became an explosive device."[47] But Saudi anti-terror measures seemed halfhearted. Thus, on June 12, 2003, Adel al-Jubeir, the foreign policy advisor to Crown Prince Abdullah, held a press conference in Washington, where he announced that al-Haramain would be shutting down all its foreign offices. Yet within a few weeks, on July 5, 2003, Jane Perlez of the *New York Times* reported from Jakarta, Indonesia, that al-Haramain had put its large headquarters in a Jakarta suburb up for rent and simply "moved to a smaller house down the block."[48] Meanwhile, the al-Haramain office in Ashland, Oregon, was still up and running in September 2003, though its lawyer argued that it did not receive funds from its main office in Riyadh.[49]

Saudi National Charities and the Financing of International Terrorism

IIRO	WAMY	al-Haramain
International Islamic Relief Organization	World Assembly of Muslim Youth	Charitable Foundations of al-Haramain
Sheikh Abdul Aziz bin Abdullah Al al-Sheikh	Sheikh Saleh bin Abdul Aziz Al al-Sheikh	Sheikh Saleh bin Abdul Aziz Al al-Sheikh
(Grand Mufti, Saudi Cabinet Member)	(Minister of Islamic Affairs, Saudi Cabinet Member)	(Minister of Islamic Affairs, Saudi Cabinet Member)
Chairman of Constituent Council of World Muslim League	Chairman of WAMY Secretariat	Chairman of al-Haramain Administrative Council
DONATIONS FROM SAUDI ROYAL FAMILY	DONATIONS FROM SAUDI ROYAL FAMILY	DONATIONS FROM SAUDI ROYAL FAMILY

Global Links to Terrorism

IIRO	WAMY	al-Haramain
Documented link to Osama bin Laden in 1989, when al-Qaeda founded, on IIRO stationery	U.S. WAMY office in Northern Virginia under investigation (past director, Abdullah bin Laden)	Finances al-Qaeda operations in Southeast Asia
Bin Laden's brother-in-law, Muhammad Jamal Khalifa, runs Philippines offices—conduit to Abu Sayyaf	WAMY-Hamas connection noted in 1996	al-Haramain closed down by Bosnian government for "financing the activities of terrorist organizations"
Muhammad al-Zawahiri, brother of Ayman al-Zawahiri (#2 in al-Qaeda), employed in Albanian office	WAMY funds I'tilaf al-Hir of Sheikh Qardawi which directs money to Hamas	Azerbaijan closes down al-Haramain for Chechen terrorist activities
Kenya blacklists IIRO	WAMY hosts Hamas, Riyadh, Saudi Arabia, November 2002	al-Haramain employees arrested in Albania
IIRO employee implicated in planned terrorist attack in India		al-Haramain closed down in Somalia
IIRO in Pankisi Gorge (Georgia) conduit to al-Ansar in Chechnya		
Documented IIRO funding of Hamas, on IIRO stationery		

Dif Allah bin Salim al-Bilawi, the general supervisor for the operations of the charity organizations in the Ministry of Labor and Social Affairs, announced in early 2004 that new rules for charity operations would be published soon—after many Saudi charities had had to close their offices abroad on suspicion of financing terrorism.[50] But al-Bilawi also revealed the extent to which these charities had up until recently received direct governmental support: The Saudi government had supplied land for their offices, up to 85 percent of their construction costs were picked up by the government, and their electricity was subsidized. The Saudis had also actively encouraged the proliferation of Islamic charities: In 2001, there were 242 registered Saudi charities; in 1981 there had been only forty-nine.[51] The Saudi government thus had clear-cut leverage over the Saudi charities, which it was only beginning to use.[52] Clearly, however, to describe most of the Saudi charities as purely non-governmental organizations was untrue: They either received indirect aid from the Saudi government or, in the case of the three big charities (al-Haramain, IIRO, and WAMY), Saudi ministers sat on their board of directors. In short, the Saudi government bore direct responsibility for the problem of terrorist financing, and had its work cut out for it in 2004.

The Saudis also appeared to deal only partially with the issue of religious incitement in the aftermath of the May 12, 2003 bombings. The Saudis were taking some steps to curb the hatred that generated the new global terrorism, but the measures adopted seemed almost universally to be insufficient to deal with the magnitude of the problem they had created. Mixed messages came from Saudi officialdom. At the same June 12 Washington press conference, al-Jubeir announced with great fanfare that Saudi Arabia had fired several hundred clerics and suspended more than a thousand for preaching intolerance. Yet within weeks the Saudi deputy minister for Islamic affairs flatly denied that the move against the clerics had anything to do with curbing extremism. Indeed, Robert Jordan, the U.S. ambassador to Saudi Arabia, noted in 2003: "We have noticed lately in influential mosques the imam has condemned terrorism and preached in favor of tolerance, then closed the sermon with 'O God, please destroy the Jews, the infidels, and all who support them.'"[53] And while it was true that the Saudis managed to get Sheikh Ali bin al-Khudair, in late November 2003, to renounce his radical jihadi stance on prime-time Saudi television,[54] al-Khudair actually dealt largely with the doctrine of *takfir*—proclaiming Muslims to be infidels. His renunciation might help stop militant Muslim violence against other Muslims, but it simply did not address the problem of jihadi violence against Americans or others outside of Saudi Arabia. His statement seemed designed primarily to preclude attacks against the Saudi government and foreigners inside Saudi Arabia.

The Saudi battle with al-Qaeda exposed another disturbing development in the Saudi kingdom. At times, after various gun battles, it was revealed that individuals in the Saudi security services were caught fighting on the side of the militants. This raised the question of whether al-Qaeda had penetrated the Saudi defense establishment. Lt. General Moshe Yaalon, chief of staff of the Israel Defense Forces, expressed concern in September 2003 that al-Qaeda was trying to recruit Saudi pilots for suicide missions against Israel.[55] This scenario was raised by captured al-Qaeda operatives under interrogation outside of Israel. During the Iraq War, the Saudis redeployed their advanced F-15 S fighter aircraft from the Iraqi theater of operations to the Tabuq Airbase near Israel; as a result, there was growing concern in Israel that these aircraft, which could cross into Israeli airspace with little warning time, would be used for such a suicide mission. Israel's defense minister, Shaul Mofaz, expressed a broader concern several month later that al-Qaeda was trying to infiltrate Saudi Arabia's armed forces.[56]

Regardless of the way al-Qaeda might penetrate the Saudi military establishment, the terror group had demonstrated that it was not represented in Saudi Arabia by just a few cells, but had developed a widespread and massive presence that no one had fully appreciated before the May 12, 2003 bombings. With the April 21, 2004, suicide bombing attack in Riyadh against a Saudi police building, al-Qaeda indicated a readiness to turn on the institutions of the Saudi regime, and not only on foreign compounds. The global jihad that Saudi Arabia had fostered for more than two decades was coming back to threaten the very foundations of the Saudi kingdom.

Conclusion

Ending the Hatred

The world now knows an unprecedented and devastating threat: the new global terrorism. Of course, terrorist acts are nothing new in themselves, but in recent years terrorism has drastically broadened its scope and stepped up its aims. Ideologically motivated terrorist groups no longer confine themselves to one region. Indeed, the new terrorism has struck from Indonesia to Yemen; terrorist cells have been operating in the center of Europe and reached down into East Africa; they have extended their campaign from southern Russia into the heart of Moscow. Moreover, the new terrorism is far more lethal than anything that has come before it: a single attack can claim, and has claimed, thousands of victims. It is not a terrorism of limited aims, but rather a terrorism that seeks to bring about a total collapse of its opponents. The attacks of September 11, 2001, were perhaps the most graphic reminder of this new reality.

The horrific attacks on the World Trade Center and the Pentagon spurred the United States to action. President George W. Bush almost immediately declared war on terror—not on a nation or nations, nor on one or two terrorist organizations, but on "every terrorist group of global reach," which Bush vowed would be "found, stopped, and defeated."[1] The

233

war on terror achieved some successes in its early stages, particularly with the military victory in Afghanistan that ousted the Taliban regime. The United States and its allies have also targeted terrorists' sources of funding and weaponry.

Such actions have been somewhat effective and obviously are essential to any attempt at preventing future terrorist attacks. But by and large, the West's campaign has overlooked a critical component of terrorism—that is, the precise *source* of the terror, the *ideology* that motivates individuals and groups to slaughter thousands of innocent people, and perhaps even to take their own lives. True enough, ideology alone is not sufficient to launch terrorist attacks. Nevertheless, it is a necessary condition for terror, for terrorism is never spontaneous violence or the result of an impulsive act—it does not occur in a vacuum.

Simply put, deeply ingrained hatred motivated the rash of terrorist attacks of which September 11 was a part. Where did that hostility come from? In fact, the ideology of hatred underpinning the attacks of September 11, 2001, had roots that were more than 250 years old. As has been seen, this ideology of hatred was a product of Saudi Wahhabism. Muhammad ibn Abdul Wahhab developed this radical Islamic creed in Arabia in the mid–eighteenth century, and it grew and thrived on extreme intolerance toward those who did not adhere to its tenets.

The problem is not Islam as a whole, for Islamic civilization came to honor the contributions of other civilizations and recognized Christians and Jews over which it ruled as peoples deserving protection because they were "people of the book" *(ahl al-kitab)*. As far back as the year 632, the second caliph of Islam, Umar bin al-Khattab, allowed the Jews to return to their holy city, Jerusalem, after they had been banned for centuries, since the time of the Roman conquests. Umar respected the Church of the Holy Sepulcher and did not turn it into a Muslim shrine.

True, life for Christians and Jews under Islamic rule was hardly idyllic; as non-Muslims, they were required to pay discriminatory taxes. But there were significant historical periods in which Islamic rulers demonstrated an extraordinary degree of tolerance for minorities, given the era in which they lived. For example, an Islamic conqueror of Jerusalem, Saladin, permitted the Jewish people to resettle the holy city after they had been evicted by the Crusaders. Also, the Ottoman Empire gave sanctuary to Jewish refugees from the Spanish Inquisition, and under Ottoman rule, the Jewish people reestablished a majority in Jerusalem in 1864—well before the arrival of the British. No, Islam itself is not the problem.

Nor is Wahhabism per se the problem, since not every country touched by Wahhabism automatically engaged in international terrorism. Witness, for example, Qatar, which adopted Wahhabism in the late nineteenth century: though the Qataris hosted some extremist elements, including Sheikh Yusuf Qaradhawi of the Muslim Brotherhood, this tiny sheikhdom did not adopt the same extremist policies globally as its larger neighbor to the west, Saudi Arabia. Indeed, the U.S. State Department's 2002 *International Religious Freedom Report* notes that while Qatar has given de facto recognition to Catholic, Anglican, and Orthodox churches, public practice of Christianity is still banned in Saudi Arabia, and even Shiites are not permitted to build their own mosques in the Saudi kingdom.[2]

Rather, the problem is Wahhabism as it has developed in the milieu of Saudi Arabia. This radical and violent departure from the mainstream Islamic tradition remains, more than two and a half centuries after its founding, the dominant religious creed in Saudi Arabia. And the Saudi regime has been a key backer of Wahhabism's international terror network. Indeed, Saudi Arabia, supposedly an ally of the United States, emerges as a key to the new global terrorism, for the Saudi kingdom has provided not only the ideology that motivates terrorists but also manpower and seemingly endless supplies of money for terror operations. As radical as the Wahhabi creed is, the true danger results from Saudi state support for its ideology of hatred and Wahhabi-endorsed campaigns of terror.

The Legacy of Hatred

But can twenty-first-century terrorism really be linked to a creed developed in the mid–eighteenth century? To answer that question, one must look not just at Wahhabism's profound influence in modern Saudi Arabia but also at how Saudi Wahhabism has motivated violence throughout its history. Specifically, Wahhabi Islam provided the motivation for three waves of extreme violence that resulted in terrible atrocities in the Middle East.

The first wave took place in the late eighteenth and early nineteenth centuries, when Wahhabism revived the Islamic idea of jihad as military expansionism—a concept that had fallen out of favor with traditional Islam after the early Muslim conquests. Wahhabism also broke with Islamic tradition by legitimizing jihad against other Muslims who did not accept ibn Abdul Wahhab's creed. Wahhabism gave teeth to its tenets, arming itself through an alliance between its founder, Muhammad ibn Abdul Wahhab, and the head of the Saudi clan, Muhammad ibn Saud, in 1744.

In the name of Wahhabism, its adherents were extraordinarily brutal toward noncombatants, including women and children, delegitimizing them as *mushrikun*, or polytheists, who did not have any right to live. Most notably, in 1802 Wahhabi armies slaughtered thousands of Shiites in their holy city of Kerbala, situated in Ottoman Iraq. Wahhabi warriors also destroyed tombs and other Shiite shrines. Such brutality is, in fact, at the core of modern terrorism, for the early Wahhabi warriors acted on Wahhabism's claims that entire groups of people have no right to live and deserve to be slaughtered. Delegitimizing other religious groups and labeling them as infidels or, even worse, as polytheists—often based on the imprecations of mainstream Wahhabi clerics in Saudi Arabia—is precisely how Osama bin Laden's mass terrorism works.

The second wave of Wahhabi violence came with the formation of modern Saudi Arabia in the early twentieth century. The successor as the emir of the Saudi clan, Ibn Saud, reestablished his family's alliance with the Wahhabi movement, promoting the creation of a fanatical Wahhabi army called the Ikhwan. The Ikhwan waged a jihad against other Muslims in Arabia, including Sharif Hussein of Mecca, who established the Hashemite dynasty that ruled first in Arabia and then in Syria, Iraq, and Transjordan. As many as 400,000 Arabs were killed or wounded in these campaigns. Just as Saudi Wahhabi warriors had in Kerbala more than a century earlier, these soldiers of Wahhabism justified their atrocities by labeling their victims as polytheists. The Ikhwan were initially held in check by the Royal Air Force and other British military units, but ultimately it was Ibn Saud himself who had to turn against the Wahhabi warriors in order not to lose control of his nascent Saudi state.

Wahhabism's third wave began in the 1950s and lasted through the 1970s, when modern Saudi Arabia became a refuge for Islamic radicals who fled from persecution by militant pan-Arab secular rulers, especially Egypt's Nasser. This third wave, in fact, laid the groundwork for Saudi support of modern global terrorism. In this period, thousands of members of the Egyptian Muslim Brotherhood sought asylum and employment in Saudi Arabia. The Saudi government erected universities to serve the Muslim world, including the Islamic University of Medina and King Abdul Aziz University in Jeddah. The faculties of these schools consisted of both Wahhabi clerics and the Muslim Brothers. The ideologies of the two movements were fused so that eventually a new hybrid developed, best exemplified by Muhammad Qutb, the brother of the Muslim Brotherhood's martyred ideologue, Sayyid Qutb, and especially by Abdullah Azzam, a former member of the Jordanian branch of the Muslim Brotherhood. Both taught at King Abdul Aziz University and both had a young Saudi student named Osama bin Laden.

The ideology of hatred became pronounced during this period, as Wahhabi religious leaders renewed the call for jihad and delegitimized non-Wahhabis. Saudi Wahhabi clerics issued texts in which they determined that present-day Christians were not the "people of the book" that Islam was committed to protect, but rather hated *mushrikun* (polytheists). These texts spoke about a new "Crusaderism" more than twenty years before Osama bin Laden's men brought down the World Trade Center. The preachers in Saudi mosques echoed these themes in their sermons, which were frequently broadcast on Saudi state television. As late as 2001, a Saudi eighth-grade textbook would explain to Saudi schoolchildren that because Christians and Jews had become polytheists, Allah had turned them into "apes and pigs."[3]

Saudi Arabia in this period also created its large Muslim international charities, such as the Muslim World League, which exported the kingdom's Wahhabi version of Islam. These charities were not nongovernmental entities or international organizations like the International Red Cross. The secretary-general of the Muslim World League was a minister in the Saudi government; Saudi *ulama* sat on its main board. The Muslim World League was part of the *ulama*'s share of the division of governmental powers and resources with the Saudi royal family. The organization served as an arm of the Saudi government, condemning Nasser in Egypt and strengthening Saudi strategic ties with Pakistan by funding that country's Islamic movements. The explosion in oil prices in 1973 provided Saudi Arabia with vast financial resources that more than matched the budgetary needs of these semiofficial aid organizations.

In recent years, the connection between the Saudi government and its Wahhabi charities was graphically laid out in court testimony given in Canada by a local representative of the Muslim World League, Arafat al-Asahi:

> Let me tell you one thing. The Muslim World League, which is the mother of IIRO [International Islamic Relief Organization], is a fully government funded organization. In other words, I work for the Government of Saudi Arabia. Second, the IIRO is the relief branch of that organization which means we are all controlled in all our activities and plans by the Government of Saudi Arabia.[4]

It was the very same Muslim World League that sent Abdullah Azzam to Pakistan, where he fed Arab volunteers to help Afghanistan in its campaign against Soviet occupation. Azzam sought the help of the Saudi *ulama* in order to develop his doctrine of a renewed jihad, which he did not restrict to Afghanistan but rather made into a global mission. He took his doctrine of jihad one step further by providing the theological justification for the murder of innocent civilians: "Many Muslims know about the *hadith* in which the Prophet ordered his companions not to kill any women or children, etc., *but very few know that there are exceptions to this case* [emphasis added]. In summary, Muslims do not have to stop an attack on *mushrikeen*, if non-fighting women and children are present."[5]

The Saudi charities did provide legitimate humanitarian relief to Muslim populations who were engaged in armed struggles with non-Muslim powers: for example, in Afghanistan, Bosnia, Chechnya, Kosovo, and the Philippines. Also, to spread Wahhabi Islam, they funded mosque construction around the world and paid the salaries of local religious leaders. But the Saudi charities also facilitated the growth of Islamic militancy, subsidizing, for example, the flow of men and materiel to conflict areas. After the death of Abdullah Azzam in 1989, his successor, Osama bin Laden, used the charities to pay the salaries of his al-Qaeda operatives around the world. And the IIRO, in particular, was repeatedly identified as a conduit for funding to the Abu Sayyaf organization, which fought the government in the Philippines, to Hamas in the West Bank and Gaza, to al-Khattab's militia in southern Russia, and to terrorist networks in East Africa. And if IIRO was involved in terrorism in each of these areas, that meant the Saudi government was involved as well.

In short, the problem was not simply that Wahhabi religious leaders were promulgating anti-Western hatred that motivated new generations of terrorists, but that the Saudi regime itself was backing radical and violent Wahhabi organizations. Why did the Saudi regime emerge as a backer of Wahhabism's international terror network? The answer might lie in the geostrategic needs of the Saudi state. In the 1960s, Saudi Arabia had to combat its secular pan-Arab rivals, and in the 1980s it faced a rival in the Revolutionary Shiite regime in Iran. As a result, the Saudi regime adopted the cause of Wahhabi Islam in its foreign policy and created charities with global reach. Later, as the Saudis tried to offset the influence of Revolutionary Iran, the charities became a means of buying influence in nations that were critical for Saudi security interests, particularly Egypt and Pakistan. Finally, beginning in the late 1990s, as King Fahd's health started to fail, leading members of the Saudi royal family recognized a pending struggle for succession—a struggle in which the Wahhabi clerics would have a great deal of influence. Thus, clamping down on Wahhabi charities at this time would entail paying an enormous political price.

Bernard Lewis, the noted historian of the Middle East, has offered an analogy that graphically depicts how the Wahhabi ideology has gained such influence:

> Imagine if the Ku Klux Klan or Aryan Nation obtained total control of Texas and had at its disposal all the oil revenues, and used this money to establish a network of well-endowed schools and colleges all over Christendom peddling their particular brand of Christianity. This was what the Saudis have done with Wahhabism. The oil money has enabled them to spread this fanatical, destructive form of Islam all over the Muslim world and among Muslims in the West. Without oil and the creation of the Saudi kingdom, Wahhabism would have remained a lunatic fringe.[6]

In short, Saudi Arabia's brand of Wahhabism helped generate a unique anti-Western hatred, but the Saudi state provided the delivery system to carry that hatred worldwide.

Why the Hatred?

One of the common failings among analyses of modern terrorism, even those that try to ascertain the motivating forces behind terror operations, is that the focus is myopic. They look for recent events to explain the attacks on the United States, refusing to seek deeper historical reasons. They believe that some action on the part of the victim drove the perpetrator to act. As a result, commentators have come up with a number of misguided notions as to what is behind the new global terrorism.

Some think that the rage underpinning the September 11 attacks— as well as the bombings of the USS *Cole*, the U.S. embassies in East Africa, and more—must be tied to something in the recent history between the United States and Saudi Arabia. But when Muhammad ibn Abdul Wahhab began articulating his unique version of Sunni Islam, the United States of America did not even exist. Nor was Wahhabi violence ever a reaction to imperialist intruders. The first eruption of Wahhabi expansionism, in fact, predated European colonialism. Even the second major eruption of militant Wahhabism, which created the modern Saudi Arabian kingdom, did not come against a background of any serious colonial legacy; indeed, while Egypt had been under British military occupation and Syria and Iraq were League of Nations mandates administered by France and Britain, Saudi Arabia was never a colony or mandated territory.

And when American oil companies penetrated Saudi Arabia, they did not come with the full imperial packaging that the British brought to other oil producers in the Middle East; they did not rely on an invasive American military presence or large fleets nearby to gain their oil rights. When Standard Oil of California first struck oil in Saudi Arabia in 1938, isolationist America had no military presence in the Middle East whatsoever. There was no gunship diplomacy to exploit the economic resources of Saudi Arabia. America sought only freedom of access for its overseas corporations under the doctrine of the "open door"; it saw no need for a corresponding American empire.

Years later, in the 1970s, the United States did not use its military superiority to confront the Arab oil-producing countries as they unilaterally increased the price of oil and nationalized the American oil interests in Libya and Iraq. In Saudi Arabia, American oil companies quietly held "participation" talks that gradually increased Saudi ownership in ARAMCO until the oil group became fully Saudi-owned. Although the Americans meddled in Iranian politics in the early 1950s, after Western oil interests were nationalized, their response to Saudi Arabia's oil moves in the 1970s was only to arrange for the "recycling" of petrodollars back into American banks and industry. Americans believed in interdependence, not imperialism.

During the Cold War, it might have been tempting to hold on to bases in Saudi Arabia for the containment of the Soviet Union, but the United States let go of its Dhahran air base in 1962. American forces came back to Saudi Arabia only when the Saudi kingdom was under a direct military threat—from Egypt in the 1960s, from Iran in the 1980s, and from Iraq in the 1990s. As much as hard-line Wahhabi clerics—and bin Laden and his followers—came to denounce the American presence in Saudi Arabia, the United States was consistently a reluctant military partner, not an imperialist intruder. There was no arrogance of American power, as detractors of the United States try to assert. The blame for the hatred behind September 11 is not at America's doorstep. Rather, as has been seen, Saudi Arabia's own internal development accounts for how such hatred was spawned.

In late 2002, Sheikh Muhammad bin Abdul Rahman al-Arifi, the imam of the mosque of King Fahd Defense Academy, offered the sort of incendiary rhetoric that had become common among Saudi clerics. Envisioning the subjugation of Europe, he wrote, "We will control the land of the Vatican; we will control Rome and introduce Islam in it. Yes, the Christians, who carve crosses on the breasts of the Muslims in Kosovo— and before then in Bosnia, and before then in many places in the world— will pay us *Jiziya* [poll tax paid by non-Muslims under Muslim rule], in humiliation, or they will convert to Islam."[7] Of course, anyone recalling the history of the 1990s would immediately protest that NATO went to war in Bosnia and Kosovo to defend Muslims from Serb armies. Again, the United States and its European allies did nothing to merit this kind of rage from a Saudi cleric.

Others link the hatred toward America to the Arab-Israel issue. But trying to argue that al-Qaeda was motivated to strike at the West because of frustration over the Palestinian cause is simply not plausible. The Arab veterans of Afghanistan, many of whom were part of Osama bin Laden's networks, began striking outside of the Middle East—in the United States and Western Europe—in 1993–94, precisely when the Oslo Accords between Israel and the PLO were being signed and initially implemented. Israel dismantled its military government over the Palestinians and replaced it with the Palestinian Authority, led by Yasser Arafat. In any case, al-Qaeda's stated grievances against the West are far broader than the Arab-Israeli issue; chiefly they include the fall of the Ottoman caliphate, the American military presence in the Arabian peninsula, U.S. policy toward Iraq, and only then the question of Jerusalem and the Palestinians.

Saudi Arabs undeniably have had strong feelings about the Israeli-Palestinian conflict all these years. In practice, however, the Saudi state had only a peripheral military role in most Arab-Israeli wars. Saudi leaders from King Ibn Saud to King Faisal made clear in private conversations with U.S. officials that the primary threats that concerned them emanated from their Arab rivals—the Hashemites and later Nasser—and not from Israel. Ultimately, what really captured the imagination of young Saudis to rejuvenate the idea of jihad and volunteer to put themselves in real danger was not the Palestinian cause but the war in Afghanistan against the Soviet Union. The same motivation was noticeable in the 1990s when Saudis became the largest national contingent of the al-Qaeda network. The war against the West became much more of a rallying cry for Saudi volunteerism than the struggle against Israel alone. Indeed, the religious incitement fed to Saudi youth over the years by Saudi Arabia's educational system and by many preachers in Saudi mosques has focused as much on the Christian world as on the Jewish people, and in recent years the Hindus of India have become a target as well.

Cutting the Saudi Ties to Terrorism

The Saudis would try to argue that they never had anything to do with terrorism, but the historical record shows that this is not true. Even leaving aside the critical component of ideological motivation for a moment, one finds ample evidence of Saudi support for terrorist activities. The earliest Saudi links to terrorism were its ties in the 1960s with the Fatah movement, whose early leadership also had an association with the Muslim Brotherhood: Yasser Arafat was a sympathizer, while Abu Jihad was an actual member. Fatah threatened both Israel and Jordan back in 1970. Unlike Egypt and Jordan, which clashed militarily with terrorist organizations on their own soil that threatened their security, Saudi Arabia seems to have tried to buy off terrorist groups within the kingdom.

In the 1990s, Saudi support for the Palestinians extended to Hamas, which came directly out of the Muslim Brotherhood in the Gaza Strip. Saudi Arabia was verbally supporting the Israeli-Palestinian peace process, but at the same time funding those who most undermined it by means of suicide bombings. During these same years, Arab states like Algeria and Egypt complained that Saudi money was backing their Islamic oppositions. There is also considerable circumstantial evidence that the Saudis struck a Faustian bargain with Osama bin Laden sometime in 1995–96 in order to be sure that he would halt all attacks on the Saudi kingdom itself.

Given the weight of the evidence against Saudi Arabia as a supporter of international terrorism, a hard question emerges: What is the international community supposed to do about Saudi Arabia as a banker for international terrorist groups? The United Nations has already taken some steps in this direction. In September 2001, the UN Security Council adopted Resolution 1373, which made any support for international terrorism a violation of international law. The resolution was adopted under Chapter 7 of the UN Charter, the most severe category of UN resolutions, reserved for threats to international peace and security. For example, the 1990–91 Security Council resolutions on Iraq, which justified the launching of the Gulf War, were Chapter 7 resolutions. Backing global terrorism is therefore a violation of international law on a par with Iraq's violations of its arms-restriction commitments, which the Bush administration in the fall of 2002 determined was a legitimate reason for going to war. There is thus a firm international legal basis for compelling Saudi Arabia to halt its support for international terrorist groups.

How, then, to compel Saudi Arabia to obey international law? The Saudi kingdom does not need to be attacked militarily, but the United States and its allies cannot simply assume that this supposed friendly nation is not backing terrorism. Sophisticated public relations consultants in

Washington might whitewash Saudi Arabia, but the international community must carefully monitor the Saudis to be certain that they disengage from all aspects of their support for terrorism.

First, Saudi state support for terrorism must come to an end, particularly the use of its global charities for funding international terrorist organizations. The Saudis would protest that they have already taken steps since September 11, 2001, to keep better track of what their charities are doing.[8] Indeed, in December 2002, the Royal Embassy of Saudi Arabia in Washington issued a nine-page report detailing all the measures the Saudis had already adopted. But there was little reason to be reassured by its contents, given the glaring inconsistencies between its claims and other Saudi statements and actions.[9]

For example, the report boasted of a "joint anti-terrorism action" taken by the Saudi kingdom and the United States to freeze the assets of Wael Hamza Julaidan, one of the cofounders of al-Qaeda, whom the report called "a Saudi fugitive." But in fact, the day after the U.S. Treasury Department acted against Julaidan in early September 2002, in what Washington characterized as a joint Saudi-American move, Saudi Arabia's minister of the interior, Prince Naif, dissociated Saudi Arabia from this action and even criticized Washington, saying, "Those who make this accusation should provide convincing evidence."[10] The Saudi sensitivities to the case of Julaidan were understandable, for since February 2000 he had headed the Rabita Trust, another offshoot of the semiofficial Muslim World League.[11]

The report also asserted that according to Saudi Arabia's post–September 11 policy, "charitable groups have been closely monitored and additional audits have been performed to assure that there are no links to suspected groups." As recently as October 29, 2002, however, Khaled Mashal, one of the top leaders of Hamas, was the guest of another Saudi charity, the World Assembly of Muslim Youth (WAMY), at its convention in Riyadh. According to a captured internal Hamas memorandum dated November 11, 2002, the WAMY convention was held under the auspices of Crown Prince Abdullah himself.[12] During the visit, Mishal met privately with Abdullah. Saudi officials, according to the Hamas account, promised to continue their funding for the Palestinian intifada through "civilian channels." It seemed that the Saudi-Hamas connection was still very much alive, just weeks before the Saudi embassy's antiterrorism report was released in Washington.

Getting at the Source

It is essential to stop the Saudis from financing terrorist organizations, but moving beyond the nuts and bolts of state support for terrorism to the issue of incitement and hatred is just as critical. This is a far more difficult challenge for the international community, but it is a challenge that must be undertaken if the world ever hopes to put an end to the scourge of terrorism. The United States and its allies can achieve the most impressive military results in Afghanistan and elsewhere, including Iraq. They can also cut terrorists' financial lifelines by freezing hundreds of bank accounts. But unless the ideological motivation for terrorism is addressed and, indeed, extinguished, then the war on terror will not be won. Saudi Arabia is the breeding ground for Wahhabi extremism and consequently the source of the hatred that impels international terrorist organizations.

Hatred cannot be eradicated by an international treaty or through another resolution of the UN Security Council. It would take decades to negotiate an effective international treaty against incitement that would take into account the cultural and religious particularities of all the member states of the UN.

In any case, the international community should not get drawn into the business of evaluating religious practices in terms of international law. It is not up to the community of nations to enter into theological debates between Wahhabi Islam and the rest of the Islamic world over whether it is fitting to commemorate the birthday of the Prophet Muhammad. This is part of their internal discourse. Yet it *is* the business of the international community if any religious movement systematically disseminates hate literature and incites its adherents to take militant action against the members of another faith.

Is there a precedent for altering nations' behavior, outside of the mechanism of formally signed international treaties?

In the last decade and a half of the Cold War, the United States and its Western allies sought to transform their adversaries in the Eastern bloc by setting standards of international behavior. In the 1975 Helsinki Final Act, the Soviet Union and its allies agreed to observe a code of basic human rights, and in exchange they benefited from enhanced East-West trade and new military confidence-building measures. The Helsinki Final Act was not a binding international agreement; it was just a joint declaration about an agreed-upon code of conduct. But it at least set clear standards of acceptable international behavior as well as human rights standards. It empowered thousands behind the Iron Curtain to fight for freedom. Adherence to Helsinki principles by Eastern bloc states led to tangible rewards; abuse of these principles led to the threat of negative sanctions.

In order to address the systematic hatred emanating out of Saudi Arabia, the international community must make the Saudis adhere to minimal standards of international behavior demanded elsewhere in the world. But setting such standards is not, in fact, a challenge specific to Saudi Arabia; it applies to the Middle East as a whole. In recent decades, for example, the call to spread freedom and democracy has skipped over the Middle East, while reaching Latin America, the Far East, and Central Asia. The Middle East has been first and foremost a region of commercial opportunity, regardless of any consequences. Thus, during the 1980s, many Western states scrambled for a share of Iraq's civilian and military market, despite the growing evidence of Baghdad's massive abuse of the rights of its minorities, which culminated in the use of chemical weapons against its own Kurdish population in 1988. France, not the Soviet Union, sold Saddam Hussein the Osiraq nuclear reactor that the Israeli air force destroyed in 1981. Western firms extended the range of Iraq's Soviet-manufactured Scud missiles—missiles that struck Tehran, Riyadh, and Tel Aviv in the late 1980s and early 1990s.

Even the United States has so far refused to hold the Middle East to any minimal standards of behavior. The Clinton administration, for instance, dedicated enormous diplomatic resources to brokering a Syrian-Israeli peace treaty in the 1990s, yet it did not, as part of the diplomatic process, set firm rules precluding Syria from harboring and launching Hizballah units. The Palestinians copied the Syrian model when they did not prevent the suicide bombers of Hamas from striking at Israeli cities as negotiations were pursued. In an environment in which there was little accountability, the Middle East became a black hole in the effort to establish a more secure world order.

The Middle East in general, and Saudi Arabia in particular, can no longer be allowed to escape under the radar. Certainly, establishing an international code of conduct to which Saudi Arabia and the other Middle Eastern states must adhere will require an adjustment in how diplomacy is practiced. Diplomats usually deal with international law or the monitoring of armaments, not with incitement and hatred emanating from mosques and featured in textbooks or on national television networks. But this material must be monitored and collected, because such incitement leads to horrible violence. This is not true simply of Saudi Wahhabism, for incitement has set the stage for other recent conflicts. Richard Holbrooke, the chief architect of the Dayton Peace Accords in Bosnia, noted that the war in Yugoslavia erupted not because of "ancient hatreds" but rather because Belgrade television in the early 1990s repeatedly fed racist messages to the Bosnian Serbs.[13]

Clearly, the scope of diplomacy must be broadened to provide early warning that this sort of hostile environment is being created. The greatest pressure on Saudi Arabia to adhere to established standards against incitement and hatred will come not from international courts but from the wider court of international opinion. Consequently, the hatred-filled sermons and textbooks in Saudi Arabia must be collected and widely reported, not buried in basements of foreign ministries. This book has offered just a small sample of the sort of hard-line anti-Western rhetoric coming out of Saudi Arabia's mainstream; if such material is regularly presented to national legislatures, including the U.S. Congress and European parliaments, Saudi Arabia will begin to feel pressure to institute internal reforms.

There are brave, introspective Saudis who recognize the need to bring about a change in Saudi Arabia. Several Saudi columnists have attributed the fact that so many Saudi citizens were involved in the September 11 attacks to "the culture of violence that has infiltrated religious education" and that has thus "politiciz[ed] Da'wa [the propagation of Islam] and then militariz[ed] it."[14] These voices of coexistence should be encouraged, not stifled.

Failing to insist on minimal standards of international behavior in Saudi Arabia and encourage Saudi educational reform will have devastating consequences. Under present conditions, the Saudi leadership senses that it can get away with its own internal extremism. It faces no negative sanction. In a Middle East in which no state is held accountable to minimal standards of behavior, double games are inevitable. The Saudis make a show of pursuing certain policies for external consumption in Western capitals, but at the same time they are free to follow their own interests. Thus, they can launch a dramatic new peace initiative even while they fund those terrorist groups that make any peace accord impossible. The Saudi regime can pay U.S. public relations firms to portray Saudi Arabia as America's tolerant partner while Saudi preachers and state-controlled religious texts spew anti-Western invective and place Christians in the category of polytheists. Saudi officials can condemn pro forma the September 11 attacks on the United States while Saudi religious leaders openly justify them.

For the war on terrorism to be won, this duality cannot be allowed to continue. Saudi Arabia must be forced to make a choice. President Bush asked, after the destruction of the World Trade Center and the attack on the Pentagon, whether nations are with the United States or with the terrorists. Despite Saudi Arabia's insistence to the contrary, the record makes it frighteningly clear that the Saudi kingdom is, at this point, with the terrorists. Indeed, it is Saudi Arabia that has spawned the new global terrorism. Unless the Saudi regime feels pressure to change, the hatred that has motivated a horrifying series of worldwide terrorist attacks—including the attacks of September 11—will only go on. And as long as the hatred continues, the terror will go on.

Appendix

Saudi Support for Terrorism: The Evidence

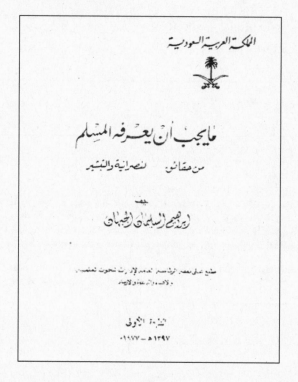

State-sponsored incitement: The anti-Western and anti-Christian hatred that began emerging from Saudi Arabia in the 1970s was not from fringe elements. For example, this 1977 booklet, *The Facts That the Muslim Must Know About Christianity and Missionary Activity,* argued that Christianity had been converted "into paganism and polytheism and fables." The booklet, which bore the seal of the Kingdom of Saudi Arabia on its cover, was issued by the General Presidency for the Directorate of Religious Research, Islamic Legal Rulings, Islamic Propagation, and Guidance—a branch of the Saudi government.

Excerpt 1: Sheikh Abdul Aziz Qari, Qabaa mosque, Medina (undated)

فلما بعث خاتم النبيين وإمام المرسلين سيدنا محمد ﷺ قامت الحرب التي أعلنها معسكر الكفر على دعوته ورسالته ﷺ. وكان مركزها ومدارها على هاتين الطائفتين وعلى اليهود منهم على وجه الخصوص.

وستظل هاتان الطائفتان هما قطبا رحى الصراع والحرب بين الإيمان والكفر إلى أن يأتي الأجل الذي ضربه الله عز وجل وحينئذ يكون انتهاء هذا الصراع وختامه بنزول عيسى بن مريم عليه السلام وكسر الصليب ومحوه من الأرض وقتل الأعور الدجال رئيس اليهود وطاغيتهم الأكبر ومسيحهم المنتظر.....

المغضوب عليهم هم اليهود، والضالون هم النصارى. وصفهم بذلك سيدنا رسول الله ﷺ في غير ما حديث ثبت عنه ﷺ وصف هاتين الطائفتين الكافرتين بهذين الوصفين، من تلك الأحاديث: حديث عدي بن حاتم رضي الله عنه وفيه قال له النبي ﷺ: ((المغضوب عليهم هم اليهود والضالون هم النصارى)). أخرجه الإمام أحمد في مسنده.

والقرآن الكريم وصف اليهود بأنهم أمة لعنهم الله وغضب عليهم ومسخ بعضهم قردة وخنازير، وجعل منهم عبدة للطاغوت.

Excerpt 2: Sheikh Ali Muhammad al-Barum, Manar al-Islam mosque, Mecca (September 2, 2000)

فمن الأمور التي تبث بين الناس ولا يكاد يفقه تلبيسها كثير من الأكياس ما يزعم بالتقارب بين الحضارات ودعوى اندماج الديانات فكل من اليهود والنصارى ـ كما قالوا ـ على دين حق، ونحن نقول: ﴿ومن يبتغ غير الإسلام ديناً فلن يقبل منه وهو في الآخرة من الخاسرين﴾ كل هذه دعاوى فاجرة وأفكار ماكرة لا تقبل في الدين، بل هي مردودة مصفوع بها وجه قائلها ولو كان من كان، في أي مكان كان أو أي قائل.....

عباد الله: لا يجوز للإنسان أن يقارب بين الإسلام والكفر، وبين التوحيد والشرك، بين الاستقامة، والإلحاد، وبين سبيل الله بين صراط الله المستقيم، وصراط الملاحدة الشياطين.

Friday sermons in the mosque: The incitement in Saudi Arabia has been ongoing, and it comes from some of the Saudi kingdom's main mosques. These excerpts from Friday sermons were downloaded from the Saudi-based website www.alminbar.net. The English translations—shown on right—were provided by the Middle East Media Research Institute (MEMRI).

Excerpt 1: **Sheikh Abdul Aziz Qari, Qabaa mosque, Medina (undated)**

"When the Prophet Muhammad was sent out, the 'Camp of *Kufr* [blasphemy]' declared war on his *da'wa* [creed] and his message. At the center of this war were these two groups [Christians and Jews], particularly the Jews. These two groups will continue to serve as the grindstones of the conflict and the war between belief and *kufr* until eternity comes as determined by Allah. Then the conflict will end when Jesus the son of Mary, peace be upon him, arrives to break the cross and wipes it off the face of the earth, and kills the blind *Dajjal* [false Messiah], the leader of the Jews, their grand tyrant, and the Messiah for whom they await. Until that day, the conflict between us, the Muslims, and the Jews and Christians will continue, and it will ebb and flow, one day ours, another day theirs....

"The Jews are the objects of Allah's [promised] wrath, while the Christians are those who deviate from the path of righteousness.... The Koran described the Jews as a nation cursed by Allah, a nation at which he was angry—some of whom he turned into apes and pigs and into worshipers of the *Taghout* [idol]."

Excerpt 2: **Sheikh Ali Muhammad al-Barum, Manar al-Islam mosque, Mecca (September 2, 2000)**

"The idea of intertwining religions and the claim that the Jews and the Christians believe in religions of truth ... are sinful claims and deceitful ideas unacceptable to the religion [of Islam].... It is forbidden for man to bring together Islam and blasphemy, monotheism and polytheism ... Allah's straight path of righteousness and the satanic path of heresy."

Excerpt 3: Sheikh Adnan Ahmad Siami, a mosque in Mecca (May 11, 2001)

قبل عدة سنوات قامت دعوة آثمة نصرها وللأسف بعض رجالات هذا الدين الإسلامي من علماء ومفكرين ودعاة، تلكم الدعوة الآثمة هي الدعوة إلى وحدة الأديان السماوية، ورفعوا لهذه الدعوة شعارات برّاقة خدّاعة، وهي (الإخاء الديني، الصداقة الإسلامية المسيحية، توحيد الأديان الثلاثة، الديانة العالمية)، ونشطت هذه الدعوة وامتدت استنادًا مكّن البابا في سنة 1986م في السابع والعشرين من شهر أكتوبر في قرية أسيس بإيطاليا أن يقيم صلاة مشتركة بين ممثلي الأديان الثلاثة، مسلمين ويهود ونصارى، وسميت هذه الصلاة بصلاة روح القدس، وهي أول مرة يؤم فيها كافر مسلمًا.

ليقدم البابا نفسه للعالم بهذه الصلاة بأنه القائد الروحي للأديان جميعًا، وأنه حامل رسالة (السلام العالمي) للبشرية، ويعلن بعدها أن يوم سبع وعشرين أكتوبر هو عيد لكل الأديان.

عبد الله - أتباع محمد ﷺ:

إن دعوة وحدة الأديان دعوة إلى إلغاء الفوارق الدينية بين الناس، فليس هناك مؤمن وكافر، الكل يدخل تحت وحدة الإخاء الإنساني، وينادي أصحاب هذه الدعوة إلى ضرورة طباعة التوراة والإنجيل والقرآن في غلاف واحد، وإلى بناء مسجد وكنيسة ومعبد في مكان واحد.

ولقد تسربت هذه الدعوة إلى ديار الإسلام، وطاشت بها أحلام، وعملت من أجلها أقلام، وفاهت بتأييدها أفواه، وانطلقت بالدعوة إليها ألسن من بعد أخرى، وعلت الدعوة بها سدّة المؤتمرات الدولية، وردهات النوادي الرسمية والأهلية.

عبد الله - أتباع محمد ﷺ:

إن لهذه الدعوة المشؤومة آثارًا كفيلة بزعزعة الإسلام في قلوب أهله، لا تنتهي بهم إلا إلى الدرك الأسفل من النار، من تلكم الآثار:

1. هدم عقيدة الولاء والبراء عند المسلمين، بل وإزالة شيء اسمه دين من اعتقاد المرء.

2. تصحيح مذاهب الكافرين والسكوت عليها.

3. السماح بالدخول في اليهودية والنصرانية دون أن حرج.

4. إلغاء الفارق العظيم بين المسلمين وغيرهم، والذي عليه محور الصراع بين الحق والباطل.

5. جعل دين الإسلام كسائر الأديان المحرّفة من حيث اتباعه، وأنه لا ميزة له على سائر الأديان.

6. هدم الإسلام في قلوب أصحابه لأن الذي يرضى أو يدعو إلى وحدة الأديان، يمسخ عن دينه، ولا يتنازل أولئك عن دياناتهم، لأنهم هم الذين يرعون الدعوة إلى وحدة الأديان.

7. عدم الدعوة إلى الإسلام، لأن المسلم إذا أراد أن يدعو إلى دينه فإنه مضطر لبيان حال الكافرين ضرورة شرعية وضرورة كونية، وإذا لم يفعل ذلك وأقر بجواز الدخول في أي دين فإنه لم يعد داعيًا إلى الإسلام بحقيقته التي أنزله الله على نبيه محمد ﷺ عليها.

8. تمهيد السبيل للتنصير أن يتغلّل كيفما شاء في بلاد المسلمين.

عبد الله:

إن زيارة البابا الأخيرة لسوريا، البلد الذي ينبض بالتوحيد وتصدع منائره بالأذان، وزيارته للجامع الأموي الذي هو حصن من حصون الإسلام، يُعدُّ مظهرًا من مظاهر هذه الدعوة لا شكّ، بل إنّ دعوته - عليه من الله ما يستحق - أصحاب الأديان الموجودة الآن بالشام إلى ضرورة التعايش السلمي، ما هي إلا دعوة جريئة ووقحة إلى توحيد الأديان ومبدأ الإخاء الديني الإنساني.

ألا وإن كثيرًا من المسلمين البسطاء لينظرون إلى زيارة البابا (رمز السلام العالمي) المشؤومة أنها ستكون فرصة للفت أنظار العالم كله إلى ما يجري في فلسطين، ويرجو هؤلاء المساكين من البابا أن يتخذ موقفًا إيجابيًا تجاه ما يحدث للفلسطينيين من اليهود. ناسين أو متناسين أن هذا البابا رأس الكنيسة الكاثوليكية، ودعاة توحيد الأديان من خلفه، هم أبناء أصحاب محاكم التفتيش في إسبانيا التي مارست مع المسلمين أفظع وأشنع سبل التعذيب، هم أبناء أصحاب المذابح المشهورة عبر التاريخ قديمًا وحديثًا، أبناء أصحاب مذبحة معرّة النعمان، هم أبناء الذين قادوا الحملات الصليبية على المشرق الإسلامي التي قتل فيها الآلاف من المسلمين، وسبي فيها ما لا يحصى من نسائهم.

هم أصحاب المذابح الجماعية في البوسنة والهرسك، هم أصحاب الجرائم التي لا تجد لها وصفًا لائقًا في قواميس لغات العالم أجمعها. هم أصحاب مجازر كوسوفا وإندونيسيا، والشيشان، هم أبناء من باركوا أصحاب مذبحة صبرا وشاتيلا، هم من باركوا ودعوا أصحاب مذبحة الحرم الإبراهيمي، وقصف المخيمات الفلسطينية، هم من دعوا قتلة الأطفال، وباركوا قتل محمد الدُّرة والطفلة الفلسطينية الرضيعة: إيمان حجو.

أيرجى من هؤلاء النذل القتلة أن يكونوا سببًا في الرحمة، إن الذي حمل البابا على هذه الزيارة عدم اكتفائه بأن يُسلب المسلمون أرضهم، فأراد أن يسلبهم دينهم فيخسروا الدنيا والآخرة.

Excerpt 3: **Sheikh Adnan Ahmad Siami, a mosque in Mecca (May 11, 2001)**

"Several years ago, a sinful call arose, which unfortunately garnered support from some clerics, intellectuals, and preachers of this Islamic religion, [a call] for the unification of the monotheistic religions. They flaunted an empty and false slogan of 'religious harmony,' Christian-Islamic friendship, and uniting the three religions into a global religion. . . .

"The call for the unification of the religions is a call for the abolition of religious differences among people: No more Believer and infidel. All will come under the unity of human harmony. . . . This accursed call has ramifications that most certainly will shake Islam in the hearts of its people, leading them to the lowest of the levels of Hell. Among these ramifications: (1) to destroy the belief in *al-walaa wa al-baraa* [loyalty (among Muslims) and disavowal (of responsibility for non-Muslims)] and even to abolish 'something called religion' from people's thought; (2) to present the infidels' schools of thought as correct, and to silence regarding them; (3) to permitting conversion to Judaism and Christianity with no shame whatsoever; (4) to the abolition of the vast difference between the Muslims and others—a difference underpinning the conflict between truth and falsehood; (5) to the transformation of the religion of Islam into a religion like the other, false religions, into a religion that has no advantage over the other religions . . . ; (7) to refraining from calling [people] to join Islam, because if the Muslim wants to do so, he must tell the truth about the infidels . . . ; (8) to facilitate the infiltration of Christian missionary activity.

"The pope's recent visit to Syria . . . to the Al-Umawi [Umayyad] mosque is, without a doubt, another manifestation of that call. The call by [the pope]—may Allah punish him as he deserves—to the people of the [different] religions in Syria to live in peaceful coexistence is nothing more than an audacious and impudent call for the unification of religions, in accordance with the principle of human religious harmony. . . . This pope, the head of the Catholic Church, and those behind him calling for the unification of the religions, are the descendants of the Spanish Inquisitors who tortured the Muslims most abominably. . . . They are the descendants of those who led the Crusades to the Islamic East, in which thousands of Muslims were killed and their wives taken captive in uncountable numbers. They are the perpetrators of the collective massacres in Bosnia-Herzegovina . . . in Kosovo, in Indonesia, and in Chechnya. . . . Can we expect compassion from these murderous wolves? What made the pope go on his visit was his dissatisfaction with the robbing of the Muslims' lands; he wanted also to rob their religion, so that they lose both this world and the Hereafter. . . ."

Excerpt 4: Sheikh Muhammad Saleh al-Munajjid, a mosque in al-Dammam
(undated)

وهذا الذي نريده أيها الأخوة, أن يزيل المسلمون غبار النوم عنهم, أن يتركوا الانغماس في الشهوات,
ويقوموا لتربية أولادهم على الجهاد, هذه هي الفائدة الكبيرة من الموضوع, تربية الأولاد على الجهاد وكره
اليهود والنصارى والكفار, تربية الأولاد على الجهاد وإحياء جذوته في نفوسهم, هذا هو المطلوب الآن
والاستعداد لما سيجد في المستقبل.

Excerpt 5: Sheikh Wajdi Hamzeh al-Ghazawi, al-Manshawi mosque, Mecca
(October 6, 2001)

وأما الإرهاب الذي يستخدم ـ معاشر المؤمنين ـ الذي يستخدم في وسائل الإعلام ويردده الناس، فإنهم
يقذفون به أصولاً ثابتة، ويهاجمون به ثوابت تدور على محاور خمسة، فهذه الكلمة إذا استخدمت فإنها
تدور ـ إشارة وتلميحًا بل وتصريحًا ـ حول محاور خمسة:
أولها: الجهاد في سبيل الله، فالجهاد ـ معاشر المؤمنين ـ ذروة سنام الإسلام، بل عده بعض أهل العلم ـ ولا
مشاحة في الاصطلاح ـ الركن السادس من أركان الإسلام، الجهاد ـ معاشر المؤمنين ـ سواء كان جهاد دفع
ومدافعة عن أراضي الإسلام والمسلمين كما هو الحال في الشيشان والفلبين وبلاد الأفغان، أو جهاد تبليغ
ونشر لدين الله عز وجل، هو قمة الإرهاب عند أعداء الله عز وجل، والمجاهد الذي لم يركن لمال ولا لدنيا
يصيبها، وإنما خرج يريد الشهادة أو النصر المؤزر ويرجع بالغنيمة هو إرهابي عند أعداء الله عز وجل،
فينبغي أن يتفطن لهذا ـ

Excerpt 4: Sheikh Muhammad Saleh al-Munajjid, a mosque in al-Dammam (undated)

"What we want, oh Brothers, is that the Muslims will rub the sleep from their eyes, and stop sinking in their desires and will rise to educate their children to jihad. This is the greatest benefit from this subject: educating the children to jihad and to hatred of the Jews, the Christians, and the infidels; educating the children to jihad and to reviving the embers of jihad in their souls. This is what is needed now and [what is needed] for preparing for what will be in the future."

Excerpt 5: Sheikh Wajdi Hamzeh al-Ghazawi, al-Manshawi mosque, Mecca (October 6, 2001)

"Jihad is the peak of Islam. Moreover, there are religious scholars who view it as the sixth pillar of Islam.

"Jihad—whether speaking about the defensive jihad for Muslim lands and Islam like in Chechnya, the Philippines, and Afghanistan, or whether speaking about jihad whose purpose is the spread of religion—is the pinnacle of terror as far as the enemies of Allah are concerned."

Justifying the terror: Not long after the September 11 attacks, a Saudi book justifying the terror appeared on the Internet. The book, entitled *The Foundations of the Legality of the Destruction That Befell America* (see cover, above left), featured an introduction by a prominent mainstream Saudi religious leader, Sheikh Hamud bin Uqla al-Shuaibi, whose students have included a number of important Saudi religious leaders, including the current grand mufti. In October 2001, Osama bin Laden cited Sheikh al-Shuaibi when he spoke of his justification for killing Jews and Christians. The English translation of Sheikh al-Shuaibi's introduction is at far right.

An Introduction by the Eminent Scholar Sheikh Hamud al-Uqla

Praise be to Allah, Lord of the universe and prayer, and peace be upon the noblest of the prophets and messengers, our Prophet Muhammad, and upon all his family and companions:

I have reviewed what His Eminence Sheikh Abdul Aziz bin Salih al-Jarbu, may Allah give him success, wrote in his book *The Foundations of the Legality of the Destruction That Befell America.* He, may Allah give him success, based his book upon specific [Islamic] principles, including the obligation to prepare morally and practically to fight the infidels and the illegality of forcing the Nation [of Islam] to accept a single opinion when such an opinion runs counter to Islamic law, particularly when such opinions are tainted by politics in the service of certain parties, and he mentioned that the principle of Muslim behavior with regard to infidels is war [on them].

He also spoke of the problems of making a *hudna* [truce] and everything that this concerns, and of a *hudna* that is invalid and contrary to Islamic law. He mentioned also the question of helping infidels, and its legal consequences according to Islamic law, which is unbelief and apostasy. He also spoke of the destruction that befell the edifice of the American economy and military, and clarified the legality of this act, if it were Muslims who carried it out, and that it is to be considered jihad for the sake of Allah.

He concluded his book with a review of some legally invalid views that are being disseminated and published by some dubious and defeated [Muslims] who deviate from the path of jihad, and he did very well in reviewing these erroneous views and responding to them.

It is an instructive and useful [book], which gives us good advice and should be regarded as a weapon for the Muslims in opposing corrupt modern trends. Sheikh Abdul Aziz, may Allah give him success, has done a great deed in fighting these trends, and these wrong, defeated statements, and has confronted them and given his utmost effort and good counsel to Islam and Muslims. This is how the *ulama* [Muslim scholars] and [Muslim] sheikhs should be during this time, acting as a single strong hand offering counsel and implementing that which is right, without fearing anyone, [in their struggle] for Allah, without cajoling, flattering, making concessions, or watering down their views.

Allah is victorious, and there is always a group within the Nation [of Islam] that holds on to the truth and is supported by Allah, and it cannot be hurt by its adversaries.

We beseech Allah to render mujahidin [jihad fighters] everywhere victorious, and forsake America and those who help her and are allied with her, and bring further destruction upon her destruction. He is the custodian of this [America's destruction], and is capable of it.

Allah's prayers on Muhammad and all his family and his companions.

Dictated by the Sheikh Hamud bin Uqla al-Shuaibi on the first of the month of Ramadan, 1422 A.H. [November 16, 2001].

بسم الله الرحمن الرحيم

المملكة العربية السعودية
رئاسة إدارة البحوث العلمية والإفتاء
مكتب المفتي العام

سعادة رئيس تحرير جريدة عكاظ   وفقه الله

السلام عليكم ورحمة الله وبركاته وبعد

فإشارة إلى ما نشر في الصحفــة السادســة مــن جريدتكــم في عددهـا رقــم
١٢٨٣٣ والصادر بتاريخ ١٤٢٢/٧/٢٨ هـ بعنوان ((أمانة كبار العلماء لــــ عكاظ
الأسبوعية (حمود العقلا الشعيبي لم يشتغل بالإفتاء واجتهاداته لايعتد بها)

وبعد عرض هذا الخبر على الأمانة العامة لهيئة كبار العلماء أفادت الأمانة أن ما صدر
من الأمانة هو أن فضيلة الشيخ حمود العقلا ليس عضو إفتاء في رئاسة البحوث العلميــة
والإفتاء وسبق له التدريس في المعاهد العلمية وفي كلية الشريعة فقط وذلك إجابة لسـؤال
من محرر الجريده عبر الهاتف عن الشيخ أما ماعدا ذلك مما نسب إلى الأمانة ونشر في ثنايـا
الخبر فكله إضافات وتخرصات من محرر هذا الخبر عبدالله العريفج ونسبته إلى أمانــه هيئـة
كبار العلماء كذب وبهتان.

نرجو من سعادتكم نشر هذا التعقيب والتوضيح في نفس الصحفه التي نشر فيهـا
هذا الخبر من دون نقص وان يكتب عنوانه بنفس البنط الذي كتب به بنط الخبر المنشور.

كما أرجو التأكيد على محرر هذا الخبر بعدم إختلاق وإضافة أية معلومات لم يصرح
بها وذلك لتحقيق المصداقيه في نقل الأخبار لقراء الجريده. وفق الله الجميع لكـل خــير.

والسلام عليكم ورحمة الله وبركاته .،،،

مدير إدارة العلاقات العامه والإعلام برئاسه
إدارة البحوث العلمية والإفتاء

سليمان بن محمد أبو عباه

الـرقـم :   التاريخ :   المشفوعات

Endorsing the extremists: Significantly, even after Sheikh al-Shuaibi's statements regarding the September 11 attacks drew international attention, Saudi religious authorities did not condemn him. Indeed, when a Saudi newspaper reported that the senior *ulama* (religious leaders) had determined that Sheikh al-Shuaibi's "independent judgment cannot be relied upon," the Office of the Grand Mufti—Saudi Arabia's highest religious authority—dismissed the paper's claim, calling the attribution to senior *ulama* "a lie and a fabrication." The office refused to call into question al-Shuaibi's status as an Islamic authority or express doubts about his level of scholarship. (*See* www.saaid.net/Warathah/hmood/2/oqla.jpg.)

In The Name of Allah the All-Merciful, All-Compassionate
The Arab Kingdom of Saudi Arabia
The Presidency of the Directorate for Religious Research and [the Issuing of] Fatwas
The Office of the Grand Mufti

To:
H.E. the Editor of the Newspaper al-Ukaz, *May Allah Help Him*

Greetings upon You and Allah's Mercy and Blessings

In reference to what was published in the sixth page of your newspaper No. 12833 issued on 28/7/1422 H [*hijra*] under the title "Secretariat of the Senior Ulama to the *Ukaz* weekly: (Hamud al-Uqla al-Shuaibi did not work on issuing fatwas and his independent judgment cannot be relied upon)."

After reviewing this news item by the general secretariat of the Council of the Senior Ulama the general secretariat wishes to clarify that His Eminence Sheikh Hamud al-Uqla is not a member of the fatwa-issuing body in the Presidency for Religious Research and the Issuing of Fatwas but has only previously taught at the academic institutions and the Sharia college, and this is in response to a question on the phone from the editor of the newspaper about the Sheikh. Apart from this, what was attributed to the secretariat and published in the context of the news item is but additions and speculations from the reporter of this news item, Abdullah al-Uraifej, and its attribution to the Senior Ulama is a lie and a fabrication.

We ask your Excellency to publish this follow-up and clarification on the same page the news item was published without cut and in the same typeset used for publishing the news item.

I would also wish to stress to the editor of the news item to avoid fabricating or adding any information not furnished so that the credibility of disseminating the news to the readers of the newspaper can be maintained. May Allah help us all and greetings to you with Allah's mercy and blessings.

Director of Public Relations and Information
Presidency of the Directorate for Religious Research and [the Issuing of] Fatwas
Sulaiman bin Muhammad Abu Abaa
1/8/1422 H.

[FILE_NUMBER]
[CLASSIFICATION_TERM]

التاريخ /

بسم الله الرحمن الرحيم

الاخ العقيد علي دغل الله مدير العمليات المركزيه حفظه الله

تحية الوطن وبـعد .   سـرى ع. ب /   (٦٢١)

الموضوع :مصادر اموال الجهاد الاسلامي في بيت لحم.

فاد المصدر رقم ٢٠/ب بناءا على معلومات حصل عليها من ابرزة اجتماعه في القدس المتوجه انز

مصادر تمويل اجهاد الاسلامي في منطقة بيت لحم تأتي من مصدرين . الاون دمشق وتمر عبر الاردن ثـ

الى بنك القاهره عمان .وانمصدر الثاني السعوديه وتمر عبر مصر ثـ انى فلسطين وعلى نفس البنك

(القاهره عمان) .

***فادت ايضا خلا ان الاموال تأتي باسماء اشخاص مختلفه و مؤسسـات حسب الظروف

واكدت انها تصل بشكل مستمر وشهرى .

***سوف نحاول المصدر معرفة اسماء اشخاص معينين تأتي الاموال باسمائهم ونكل المصدر ـ نخول

التشديد على الموضوع في تلك اللحضه حتى لا تثار الشك .

للعلم سيادتكم

مسؤول الاجراء/ابتسام عليان

مدير وحدة العمليات   نائب المدير المعني   مدير مديرية بيت لحم

نقيب/سامد خليل   رائد/خالد الطيطي   مقدم/ابراهيم رمضان

The money trail: This Palestinian intelligence document, which Israeli forces captured from the Bethlehem office of the Palestinian Preventive Security organization in 2002, establishes that Saudi Arabia is a source of funding for the Islamic Jihad organization. A major conduit of financing, the document reports, "starts in Saudi Arabia goes through Egypt and reaches Palestine."

The checks: Israeli forces discovered Saudi canceled checks in the offices of the Tulkarm Charity Committee, a known front for the Hamas organization. These checks come from the Chase Manhattan Bank account of the al-Rajhi Banking and Investment Corporation, whose head office is in Riyadh, Saudi Arabia. The al-Rajhi family, one of Saudi Arabia's wealthiest and most prominent families, has several times been linked to terrorist funding. In October 2002, for example, U.S. federal agents raided the Virginia offices of the family's SAAR Foundation because the foundation had moved funds to two offshore institutions in the Bahamas that had been tied to al-Qaeda.

The spreadsheet: At the Tulkarm Charity Committee's offices, Israeli forces also found this spreadsheet, which details how $545,000 was allocated to 102 Palestinian families whose sons were "martyrs" of the intifada. That is, the money went to the families of suicide bombers and other Hamas operatives. For example, number fourteen on the list, Abdel Rahman Hamad, was responsible for a June 2001 bombing that killed twenty-three and wounded more than a hundred Israelis. And the source of the funding? The logo at the top of the spreadsheet (in Arabic) makes it clear: "Kingdom of Saudi Arabia, the Saudi Committee for Aid to the Al-Quds Intifada," the logo reads. This committee had been established in the fall of 2000 by Saudi Arabia's powerful minister of the interior, Prince Naif bin Abdul Aziz.

The funding continues: This captured report from the Saudi-based International Islamic Relief Organization (IIRO) records $280,000 in payments to fourteen Palestinian charities that were known as Hamas front organizations. Included in the list is the Tulkarm Charity Committee. Investigators have also demonstrated that IIRO has substantial links to Osama bin Laden's al-Qaeda network in Albania, Chechnya, the Philippines, and Tanzania. The head of the IIRO office in Canada testified in court, "The Muslim World League, which is the mother of IIRO, is a fully government funded organization. In other words, I work for the Government of Saudi Arabia."

The Saudis send "large amounts to radical[s]": In this handwritten letter, a key deputy of the PLO's Yasser Arafat complains to Prince Salman bin Abdul Aziz, the governor of Riyadh and a full brother of Saudi Arabia's King Fahd, about Saudi donations to al-Jamiya al-Islamiya (the Islamic Society) in the Gaza Strip. The Arafat deputy, Abu Mazen, states bluntly that the Islamic Society "belongs to Hamas." The English translation is at far right.

The Embassy of the State of Palestine   30 December 2000
Riyadh
[*Emblem of the PLO*]
PERSONAL

To: Your Royal Highness the Emir Salman bin Abdul Aziz, may Allah protect you, the
Governor of the district of Riyadh and the Chairman of the popular committees for assistance to the jihad warriors of Palestine [in the original, *Mujahedi Falastin*].

Greetings,
It is my pleasure to send Your Royal Highness my greetings for the blessed 'Id al-Fitr.
I pray that Allah may bless you and grant you health and happiness. I have also pleasure
in sending Your Royal Highness the greetings of your brother, President Yasser Arafat, and
his blessings for a merry holiday.
I hereby wish to inform you that he [Arafat] has spoken with me on the telephone and
asked me to transmit to you his request that you mediate and interfere, and express his view
concerning the ongoing situation in our homeland. The Saudi committee responsible for
transferring the donations to beneficiaries has been sending large amounts to radical committees and associations, *among which the Islamic Society [al-Jamiya al-Islamiya] which
belongs to Hamas* [emphasis added], the al-Islah association [an association known to be a
Hamas institution in Gaza], and to the brethren who engage in jihad in all regions. This
fact badly influences the internal situation; it also results in strengthening these brethren,
and has therefore a negative impact on all sides. Moreover, the committee does not send
any money or assistance to the members of Fatah.
He [Arafat] has asked me about the outcome in connection with the arrival of the
[Palestinian] Committee about which I have written to Your Royal Highness and to His
Royal Highness the Minister of Interior [Naif bin Abdul Aziz, who heads the Saudi Committee for Assistance to the al-Quds Intifada]. The Committee will be chaired by Dr. Riad
al-Za'anun, and its purpose will be to coordinate [matters] with the brethren, and store all
accurate information on computer diskettes, which will be handed to the people in charge,
in order to assure a fair distribution. The Committee consists of professional members, and
its sole purpose is to facilitate the task of the Saudi Committee, for the sake of public benefit and of the longed-for goal.
I hope that Your Royal Highness will agree to assist us in connection with the arrival
of this Committee, in order that we can achieve the goal set by His Royal Highness the
Emir Abdullah bin Abdul Aziz and His Royal Highness the Emir Naif bin Abdul Aziz,
may Allah protect them, namely that the assistance reach the true beneficiaries, in order
to assure the control of the Palestinian Authority over its people and over the situation,
which is close to catastrophe within the homeland, and in order to avoid the disaster of the
Palestinian Authority losing its honor and its power.
May Allah protect Your Royal Highness from any evil, and may Allah safeguard the
security, stability, and prosperity of the Saudi Arabian Kingdom, under the auspices of him
who keeps the two holy places [that is, the king of Saudi Arabia, who watches over the
mosques of Mecca and Medina], His Royal Highness the Crown Prince, Their Royal
Highnesses the princes, and our brethren, the sons of the Saudi people.
I shall once again express my greetings, my gratitude, and my deep appreciation,

Your brother, the Ambassador of the State of Palestine to the Kingdom [of Saudi Arabia]
Delegate of the Palestinian National Authority
[Signature] *Abu Mazen*

Teaching hatred: As Abu Mazen revealed, the Saudis were funding the pro-Hamas Islamic Society, and by doing so, they were also grooming the next generation of terrorists. Indeed, the Islamic Society's head, Sheikh Ahmed Bakhar, urged Palestinian mothers to educate their children with a love for jihad. And at the graduation ceremonies for the Islamic Society's network of kindergartens, Palestinian children enacted the attacks of suicide bombers. Children wore military uniforms and mock explosive belts, wielded imitation Kalashnikov rifles, and burned the Israeli flag (top). One young girl (bottom) enacted dipping her hands in the blood of a dead Israeli.

The truth emerges: In early December 2002, the Saudi embassy in Washington announced that with new monitoring mechanisms in place, Saudi charities had had no ties with suspected terrorist groups since September 11, 2001. But this internal Hamas document, dated November 11, 2002, reveals the embassy's claim to be untrue. In late October 2002, Hamas leader Khaled Mashal traveled to Riyadh, Saudi Arabia, to attend a conference convened by Crown Prince Abdullah himself for WAMY, one of the largest Saudi Wahhabi charities. According to this document, which was captured by Israeli forces, Saudi officials assured Mishal that Saudi support for the Palestinian intifada would continue.

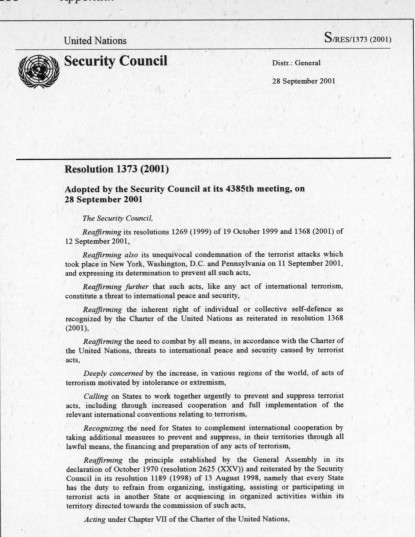

United Nations   S/RES/1373 (2001)

Security Council   Distr.: General

28 September 2001

Resolution 1373 (2001)

Adopted by the Security Council at its 4385th meeting, on 28 September 2001

The Security Council,

Reaffirming its resolutions 1269 (1999) of 19 October 1999 and 1368 (2001) of 12 September 2001,

Reaffirming also its unequivocal condemnation of the terrorist attacks which took place in New York, Washington, D.C. and Pennsylvania on 11 September 2001, and expressing its determination to prevent all such acts,

Reaffirming further that such acts, like any act of international terrorism, constitute a threat to international peace and security,

Reaffirming the inherent right of individual or collective self-defence as recognized by the Charter of the United Nations as reiterated in resolution 1368 (2001),

Reaffirming the need to combat by all means, in accordance with the Charter of the United Nations, threats to international peace and security caused by terrorist acts,

Deeply concerned by the increase, in various regions of the world, of acts of terrorism motivated by intolerance or extremism,

Calling on States to work together urgently to prevent and suppress terrorist acts, including through increased cooperation and full implementation of the relevant international conventions relating to terrorism,

Recognizing the need for States to complement international cooperation by taking additional measures to prevent and suppress, in their territories through all lawful means, the financing and preparation of any acts of terrorism,

Reaffirming the principle established by the General Assembly in its declaration of October 1970 (resolution 2625 (XXV)) and reiterated by the Security Council in its resolution 1189 (1998) of 13 August 1998, namely that every State has the duty to refrain from organizing, instigating, assisting or participating in terrorist acts in another State or acquiescing in organized activities within its territory directed towards the commission of such acts,

Acting under Chapter VII of the Charter of the United Nations,

01-55743 (E)

To stop Saudi support for terrorism: UN Security Council Resolution 1373 made any support for international terrorism a violation of international law. The resolution was adopted under Chapter 7 of the UN Charter, the most severe category of UN resolutions, reserved for threats to international peace and security. Backing global terrorism is therefore a violation of international law on a par with Iraq's violations of its arms-restriction commitments, which the Bush administration in the fall of 2002 determined was a legitimate reason for going to war. There is thus a firm basis for compelling Saudi Arabia to halt its support for terrorist groups.

1.   *Decides* that all States shall:

(a)   Prevent and suppress the financing of terrorist acts;

(b)   Criminalize the wilful provision or collection, by any means, directly or indirectly, of funds by their nationals or in their territories with the intention that the funds should be used, or in the knowledge that they are to be used, in order to carry out terrorist acts;

(c)   Freeze without delay funds and other financial assets or economic resources of persons who commit, or attempt to commit, terrorist acts or participate in or facilitate the commission of terrorist acts; of entities owned or controlled directly or indirectly by such persons; and of persons and entities acting on behalf of, or at the direction of such persons and entities, including funds derived or generated from property owned or controlled directly or indirectly by such persons and associated persons and entities;

(d)   Prohibit their nationals or any persons and entities within their territories from making any funds, financial assets or economic resources or financial or other related services available, directly or indirectly, for the benefit of persons who commit or attempt to commit or facilitate or participate in the commission of terrorist acts, of entities owned or controlled, directly or indirectly, by such persons and of persons and entities acting on behalf of or at the direction of such persons;

2.   *Decides also* that all States shall:

(a)   Refrain from providing any form of support, active or passive, to entities or persons involved in terrorist acts, including by suppressing recruitment of members of terrorist groups and eliminating the supply of weapons to terrorists;

(b)   Take the necessary steps to prevent the commission of terrorist acts, including by provision of early warning to other States by exchange of information;

(c)   Deny safe haven to those who finance, plan, support, or commit terrorist acts, or provide safe havens;

(d)   Prevent those who finance, plan, facilitate or commit terrorist acts from using their respective territories for those purposes against other States or their citizens;

(e)   Ensure that any person who participates in the financing, planning, preparation or perpetration of terrorist acts or in supporting terrorist acts is brought to justice and ensure that, in addition to any other measures against them, such terrorist acts are established as serious criminal offences in domestic laws and regulations and that the punishment duly reflects the seriousness of such terrorist acts;

(f)   Afford one another the greatest measure of assistance in connection with criminal investigations or criminal proceedings relating to the financing or support of terrorist acts, including assistance in obtaining evidence in their possession necessary for the proceedings;

(g)   Prevent the movement of terrorists or terrorist groups by effective border controls and controls on issuance of identity papers and travel documents, and through measures for preventing counterfeiting, forgery or fraudulent use of identity papers and travel documents;

2

3.   *Calls* upon all States to:

(a)   Find ways of intensifying and accelerating the exchange of operational information, especially regarding actions or movements of terrorist persons or networks; forged or falsified travel documents; traffic in arms, explosives or sensitive materials; use of communications technologies by terrorist groups; and the threat posed by the possession of weapons of mass destruction by terrorist groups;

(b)   Exchange information in accordance with international and domestic law and cooperate on administrative and judicial matters to prevent the commission of terrorist acts;

(c)   Cooperate, particularly through bilateral and multilateral arrangements and agreements, to prevent and suppress terrorist attacks and take action against perpetrators of such acts;

(d)   Become parties as soon as possible to the relevant international conventions and protocols relating to terrorism, including the International Convention for the Suppression of the Financing of Terrorism of 9 December 1999;

(e)   Increase cooperation and fully implement the relevant international conventions and protocols relating to terrorism and Security Council resolutions 1269 (1999) and 1368 (2001);

(f)   Take appropriate measures in conformity with the relevant provisions of national and international law, including international standards of human rights, before granting refugee status, for the purpose of ensuring that the asylum-seeker has not planned, facilitated or participated in the commission of terrorist acts;

(g)   Ensure, in conformity with international law, that refugee status is not abused by the perpetrators, organizers or facilitators of terrorist acts, and that claims of political motivation are not recognized as grounds for refusing requests for the extradition of alleged terrorists;

4.   *Notes* with concern the close connection between international terrorism and transnational organized crime, illicit drugs, money-laundering, illegal arms-trafficking, and illegal movement of nuclear, chemical, biological and other potentially deadly materials, and in this regard *emphasizes* the need to enhance coordination of efforts on national, subregional, regional and international levels in order to strengthen a global response to this serious challenge and threat to international security;

5.   *Declares* that acts, methods, and practices of terrorism are contrary to the purposes and principles of the United Nations and that knowingly financing, planning and inciting terrorist acts are also contrary to the purposes and principles of the United Nations;

6.   *Decides* to establish, in accordance with rule 28 of its provisional rules of procedure, a Committee of the Security Council, consisting of all the members of the Council, to monitor implementation of this resolution, with the assistance of appropriate expertise, and *calls upon* all States to report to the Committee, no later than 90 days from the date of adoption of this resolution and thereafter according to a timetable to be proposed by the Committee, on the steps they have taken to implement this resolution;

7.   *Directs* the Committee to delineate its tasks, submit a work programme within 30 days of the adoption of this resolution, and to consider the support it requires, in consultation with the Secretary-General;

3

8.   *Expresses* its determination to take all necessary steps in order to ensure the full implementation of this resolution, in accordance with its responsibilities under the Charter;

9.   *Decides* to remain seized of this matter.

Notes

Introduction: The Roots of Terror

1. Romesh Ratnesar, "Do We Still Need the Saudis?" *Time*, July 31, 2002.
2. Linda Robinson, Peter Cary, et al., "Princely Payments," *U.S. News and World Report*, January 14, 2002. Dick Gannon, who served as director of operations of the State Department's Office of Counterterrorism until July 31, 1998, claimed, "We've got information about who's backing bin Laden, and in a lot of cases it goes back to the [Saudi] royal family." Gannon asserted that the reason was that "there are certain factions in the Saudi royal family who just don't like us." Bruce B. Auster and David E. Kaplan, "Saudi Royalty Gives Money to bin Laden," *U.S. News and World Report*, October 19, 1998. Whether the payments resulted from anti-Americanism or from a need for protection money, there is little question that these Saudi princes were not prevented from taking this step. Seymour M. Hersh attempted to make the same argument with reports of U.S. National Security Agency electronic intercepts: "The intercepts have demonstrated to analysts that by 1996 Saudi money was supporting Osama bin Laden's Al Qaeda and other extremist groups in Afghanistan, Lebanon, Yemen, and Central Asia, and throughout the Persian Gulf region. 'Ninety-six is the key year,' one American intelligence official told me. 'Bin Laden hooked up to all the bad guys—it's like the Grand Alliance—and had a capability for conducting large-scale operations.' The Saudi regime, he said, had 'gone to the dark side.'" Seymour M. Hersh, "Annals of National Security: King's Ransom," *New Yorker*, October 22, 2001.
3. Susan Schmidt, "Sept. 11 Families Join to Sue Saudis," *Washington Post*, August 16, 2002.

4. Thomas E. Ricks, "Briefing Depicted Saudis as Enemies: Ultimatum Urged to Pentagon Board," *Washington Post*, August 6, 2002.

5. Michael Isikoff and Evan Thomas, "The Saudi Money Trail," *Newsweek*, December 2, 2002.

6. Tariq Ali makes this point in *The Clash of Fundamentalisms: Crusades, Jihads, and Modernity* (London: Verso Books, 2002), 298. The quotation is taken from a *News from Bangladesh* op-ed. See www.bangladesh-web.com/news.

7. "Brother Slams Moussaoui's Islam," CNN.com/World, September 20, 2002. See europe.cnn.com/2002/WORLD/europe/09/20/france.sept11.book/.

8. Youssef M. Ibrahim, "The Mideast Threat That's Hard to Define," *Washington Post*, August 11, 2002.

9. Mohamed Charfi, "Reaching the Next Muslim Generation," *New York Times*, March 12, 2002; also, Ahmad Sobhi Mansour, "Medieval Theocracies in a Modern Age," *al-Ahram Weekly*, October 15–21, 1998.

10. Sahr Muhammad Hatem, "Our Culture of Demagogy Has Engendered bin Laden, al-Zawahiri, and Their Ilk," *al-Sharq al-Awsat* (London), December 21, 2001, translated in *MEMRI Special Dispatch Series*, No. 331. See www.memri.org/bin/articles.cgi?Page=archive&area=sd&ID=SP33102.

11. Khaled Abou El Fadl, UCLA School of Law, "Islam and the Theology of Power: Supremacist Puritanism in Contemporary Islam Is Dismissive of All Moral Norms or Ethical Values," *Middle East Report 221*, Winter 2001. See www.merip.org/mer/mer221/221_abu_el_fadl.html.

12. Sheikh Muhammad Hisham Kabbani, "The Doctrine of Ahl al-Sunna Versus the Wahhabi-Salafi Movement," Islamic Supreme Council of America, 1996. See www.islamicsupremecouncil.org/extremism/SalafiDoctrine.pdf.

13. Hajj Salih Brandt, "Die Hintermanner in Daghestan" in *Islamische Zeitung*, September 21, 1999. See www.islamische-zeitung.de/salih_2109.html.

14. Jusuf Wanandi, "Forget the West, Indonesia Must Act for Its Own Sake," *The Age*, November 12, 2002.

15. Simon Elegant, "The Family Behind the Bombings," *Time*, November 18, 2002.

16. U.S. Department of Justice website. See www.usdoj.gov/ag/trainingmanual.htm.

17. See www.saaid.net/book/kotop.htm.

18. More recently, an Egyptian fundamentalist book published clandestinely in 1981 complained, "Despite its crucial importance for the future of our faith, the *jihad* has been neglected, maybe even ignored by men of religion of our age." Emmanuel Sivan, *Radical Islam: Medieval Theology and Modern Politics* (New Haven: Yale University Press, 1985), 127. Similarly, "Barbaros," a Saudi Islamic warrior in Bosnia, noted in the 1990s that Muslims had forgotten the concept of jihad, asserting that the lights of jihad had "faded." *Assirat al-Mustaqeem*, August 1994. See www.jihaadulkuffarin.jeeran.com/file382.htm.

19. Sheikh Abdullah bin Muhammad bin Humaid, *Jihad in the Qur'an and Sunna* (Saudi Arabia: Maktaba Dar-us-Salam), 24.

20. Sheikh Wajdi Hamza al-Ghazawi, October 6, 2001. See www.alminbar.cc/alkhutab/khutbaa.asp?mediaURL=5628; translation available at memri.org/bin/opener.cgi?Page=archives&ID=SR01002.

21. *ARAMCO Handbook: Oil and the Middle East* (Dhahran: Arabian-American Oil Company, 1968), 46.

22. George Rentz, "The Saudi Monarchy," in Willard A. Beling, ed., *King Faisal and the Modernization of Saudi Arabia* (London: Croom Helm, 1980), 17; Anthony Cave Brown, *Oil, God, and Gold: The Story of ARAMCO and the Saudi Kings* (Boston: Houghton Mifflin, 1999), 142.

23. Nawaf E. Obaid, "Improving U.S. Intelligence Analysis on the Saudi Arabian Decision-Making Process" (Master's Thesis, John F. Kennedy School of Government, Harvard University, 1998), 34.

24. Ralph Peters, "Turn East from Mecca: Islam's Future Will Be Decided on Its Frontiers," *Washington Post*, December 1, 2002.

25. James Bennet, "Arafat and Peres Agree to Meet Today in Gaza in First High-Level Talks Since July," *New York Times*, September 26, 2001.

26. Caryle Murphy, "A Hatred Rooted in Failings," *Washington Post*, September 16, 2001.

27. Included among the many articles stressing that Israel was the source of anti-Western hatred were: Tony Karon, "Why Didn't We Know," *Time*, September 14, 2001; Gary Kamiya, "The Bloody Jordan River Now Flows Through America," Salon.com, September 17, 2001; and Jim Muir, "Explaining Arab Anger," BBC News, September 19, 2001.

28. Hisham Melhem, CNN, October 8, 2001.

29. Noted by the editor of *Al-Quds al-Arabi*, as cited in Peter Beinart, "TRB from Washington: Fault Lines," *New Republic*, October 1, 2001.

30. "Text of Fatwah Urging Jihad Against Americans." See www.ict.org.il/articles/fatwah.htm.

31. U.S. Department of Justice website. See www.usdoj.gov/ag/manualpart1_1.pdf.

32. F. Gregory Gause III, "The Kingdom in the Middle: Saudi Arabia's Double Game," in James F. Hoge Jr. and Gideon Rose, eds., *How Did This Happen?: Terrorism and the New War* (Oxford: Public Affairs, 2001), 109–122.

33. F. Gregory Gause III, "Be Careful What You Wish For: The Future of U.S.-Saudi Relations," *World Policy Journal*, Vol. XIX, No. 1, Spring 2002, 45.

34. Thomas Fuller, "Driving Al-Qaeda: Religious Decrees: Terrorism Expert Lays Out the Evidence," *International Herald Tribune*, January 31, 2002.

35. Rohan Gunaratna, interviewed by Stephanie Walker and Sean Costigan, June 27, 2002. See www.ciaonet.org/pub/gur01.html.

36. Stephen Schwartz, *The Two Faces of Islam: The House of Sa'ud from Tradition to Terror* (New York: Doubleday, 2002).

37. " 'Why We Fight America': Al-Qa'ida Spokesman Explains September 11 and Declares Intentions to Kill 4 Million Americans with Weapons of Mass Destruction," *MEMRI Special Dispatch Series*, No. 388, June 12, 2002.

38. Michael Scott Doran, "Somebody Else's Civil War," *Foreign Affairs*, January–February 2002, 24.

39. Jeffrey S. Helmreich, "Beyond Political Terrorism: The New Challenge of Transcendent Terror," *Jerusalem Viewpoints*, November 15, 2001.

40. Aziz al-Azmeh, *Islams and Modernities* (London: Verso Books, 1996), 144.

41. Mansour, "Medieval Theocracies in a Modern Age."

42. Gilles Kepel, *Jihad: The Trail of Political Islam* (Cambridge: Harvard University Press, 2002), 254–55.

43. "Why We Fight America," *MEMRI Special Dispatch Series.*

44. Sermon given on September 13, 1997. See www.alminbar.cc/alkhutab/khutbaa.asp?mediaURL=1455.

45. Sermon given on September 2, 2000. See www.alminbar.cc/alkhutab/khutbaa.asp?mediaURL=2761.

46. Charles M. Sennott, "Saudi Schools Fuel Anti-U.S. Anger," *Boston Globe,* March 4, 2002.

47. Douglas Frantz and Desmond Butler, "Imam at German Mosque Preached Hate to 9/11 Pilots," *New York Times,* July 16, 2002.

48. Neil MacFarquhar, "A Few Saudis Defy a Rigid Islam to Debate Their Own Intolerance," *New York Times,* July 12, 2002.

Chapter 1: Violent Origins

1. Hamid Algar, *Wahhabism: A Critical Essay* (Oneonta, NY: Islamic Publications International, 2002), 6–7.

2. Joel Kraemer, "The Jerusalem Question," in Joel Kraemer, ed., *Jerusalem: Problems and Prospects* (New York: Praeger Books, 1980), 34.

3. R. A. Nicholson, *A Literary History of the Arabs* (Cambridge: Cambridge University Press, 1969), 466.

4. Moojon Momen, *An Introduction to Shi'i Islam: The History and Doctrines of Twelver Shi'ism* (New Haven: Yale University Press, 1985), 125.

5. Wilfred Cantwell Smith, *Islam in Modern History* (New York: Mentor, 1957), 62.*f*

6. Ghassan Salame, "Islam and Politics in Saudi Arabia," in *Arab Studies Quarterly,* Vol. 9, No. 3, 310.

7. Al-Azmeh, *Islams and Modernities,* 145.

8. Albert Hourani, *Arabic Thought in the Liberal Age, 1798–1939* (Oxford: Oxford University Press, 1970), 37.

9. The full verse in another translation is: "When the sacred months are over slay the idolaters wherever you find them" (Chapter 9, verse 5). See *The Koran,* translated with notes by N. J. Dawood (London: Penguin Books, 1999), 133 [hereafter "Koran"]. The Arabic word for "idolaters" in the Koran is *mushrikun.*

10. Algar, *Wahhabism: A Critical Essay,* 18.

11. L. Carl Brown, *Religion and State: The Muslim Approach to Politics* (New York: Columbia University Press, 2000), 16.

12. Carl Brockelmann, *History of the Islamic Peoples* (New York: Routledge, 2000), 352.

13. Madawi al Rasheed cites a biography of Muhammad ibn Abdul Wahhab written by A. Abu Hakima. See Madawi al Rasheed, *A History of Saudi Arabia* (Cambridge: Cambridge University Press, 2002), 17.

14. Frank E. Vogel, *Islamic Law and Legal System: Studies of Saudi Arabia* (Leiden: Brill, 2000), 207.

15. Phillip Khuri Hitti, *History of the Arabs* (New York: St. Martin's Press, 1963), 740.

16. Jamil al-Zahawi, "The True Dawn: A Refutation of Those Who Deny the Validity of Using Means to God and the Miracles of Saints." See www.ummah.net/Al_adaab/fajr.html.

17. Ayyub Sabri Pasha, "The Beginning of the Spread of Wahhabism." See www.ummah.net/Al_adaab/wah-36.html.

18. Ayman al-Yassini, *Religion and State in the Kingdom of Saudi Arabia* (Boulder: Westview Press, 1985), 28; Anwar Alam, *Religion and State: Egypt, Iran, and Saudi Arabia* (New Delhi: Gyan Sagar Publications, 1998), 177.

19. Al-Yassini, *Religion and State in the Kingdom of Saudi Arabia*, 28.

20. *Travels of Ali Bey* (Philadelphia: Printed for John Conrad at the Shakespeare Buildings, 1816).

21. Bernard Lewis, "The Revolt of Islam," *New Yorker*, November 19, 2001.

22. H. A. R. Gibb, *Mohammedanism* (Oxford: Oxford University Press, 1969), 117.

23. Daniel Pipes, *In the Path of God: Islam and Political Power* (New Delhi: Voice of India, 2001), 50.

24. Rudolph Peters, *Jihad in Classical and Modern Islam* (Princeton: Markus Wiener, 1996), 187, note 52.

25. Bernard Lewis, "Politics and War," in Joseph Schacht and C. E. Bosworth, eds., *The Legacy of Islam* (Oxford: Clarendon Press, 1974), 176; Doran, "Somebody Else's Civil War," 32.

26. Koran, 2:190–92. Dawood translates this as: "Fight for the sake of God those that fight against you, but do not attack them first. God does not love aggressors."

27. James Reston Jr., "Seeking Meaning from a Grand Imam," *Washington Post*, March 31, 2002.

28. Ignaz Goldhizer, *Muslim Studies*, Vol. II (London: George, Allen & Unwin, 1971), 352.

29. Abdulaziz A. Sachenda, "Activist Shi'ism in Iran, Iraq, and Lebanon," in Martin E. Marty and R. Scott Appleby, eds., *Fundamentalisms Observed* (Chicago: University of Chicago Press, 1991), 426.

30. Alexander Ignatenko, "Ordinary Wahhabism: Peculiarities of the Teaching of 'Monotheists,'" in *RJ Politics*, December 4, 2001, translated from Russian by Olga Yurchenko.

31. Sheikh-ul-Islam Muhammad bin Abdul-Wahhab, *Kitab al-Tawhid* (Riyadh: Dar-us-Salam Publications, 1996). See Chapter 24, particularly page 97.

32. Ibid., 83.

33. Ibid., 51. See Chapter 9, entitled "Whoever Seeks Blessing Through a Tree, a Stone, or the Like."

34. Koran, 47:15, 56:35–38.

35. Ibn Razik, cited in Alexei Vassiliev, *The History of Saudi Arabia* (New York: New York University Press, 2000), 106.

36. Described by the Saudi chronicler Uthman bin Abdullah bin Bishr, in Algar, *Wahhabism: A Critical Essay*, 24.

37. Vassiliev, *The History of Saudi Arabia*, 97.

38. *Travels of Ali Bey*, 152.

39. Vassiliev, *The History of Saudi Arabia*, 78.

40. Ibid., 97.

41. Yitzhak Nakash, *The Shi'is of Iraq* (Princeton: Princeton University Press, 1994), 57.
42. *Travels of Ali Bey*, 153.
43. F. E. Peters, *The Hajj: The Muslim Pilgrimage to Mecca and the Holy Places* (Princeton: Princeton University Press, 1994), 201.
44. Pasha, "The Beginning of the Spread of Wahhabism."
45. Brockelmann, *History of the Islamic Peoples*, 354.
46. Algar, *Wahhabism: A Critical Essay*, 27.
47. Ibid.
48. Donald Hawley, *The Trucial States* (London: George Allen & Unwin, 1970), 101.
49. Ibid., 117.
50. J. B. Kelly, *Arabia, the Gulf, and the West: A Critical View of the Arabs and Their Oil Policy* (New York: Basic Books, 1980), 61.
51. Madawi al Rasheed, *Politics in an Arabian Oasis: The Rashidis of Saudi Arabia* (London: I. B. Tauris, 1997), 35.
52. Hitti, *History of the Arabs*, 741.
53. Stanford Shaw, *History of the Ottoman Empire and Modern Turkey* (Cambridge: Cambridge University Press, 1976), 270.

Chapter 2: Countering the Wahhabi Menace

1. Halil Inalcik, *The Ottoman Empire: The Classical Age 1300–1600* (New York: Praeger Publishers, 1973), 57.
2. Bernard Lewis, *The Political Language of Islam* (Chicago: University of Chicago Press, 1988), 49.
3. Nakash, *The Shi'is of Iraq*, 142–43.
4. Arabs from the Hijaz sought Ottoman naval protection from the Portuguese in the early sixteenth century, as did Muslims from India.
5. Jamil al-Zahawi, "The True Dawn: A Refutation of Those Who Deny the Validity of Using Means to God and the Miracles of Saints." See www.ummah.net/Al_adaab/fajr.html.
6. Bernard Lewis, *What Went Wrong?: The Clash Between Islam and Modernity in the Middle East* (London: Oxford University Press, 2002), 31.
7. Vassiliev, *The History of Saudi Arabia*, 143.
8. Katherine Sim, *Desert Traveller: The Life of Jean Louis Burckhardt* (London: Phoenix Press, 1969), 299.
9. Jacques Benoist-Mechin, *Arabian Destiny* (London: Elek Books, 1957), 53.
10. Vassiliev, *The History of Saudi Arabia*, 155.
11. This description comes from the nineteenth-century writer E. Rehatsek, who wrote "The History of the Wahhabys in Arabia and India," *Journal of the Bombay Branch of the Royal Asiatic Society*, Vol. 14, 1880, 274–401, cited in Vassiliev, *The History of Saudi Arabia*, 156.
12. William Gifford Palgrave, *Personal Narrative of a Year's Journey Through Central and Eastern Arabia (1862–63)* (London: Macmillan and Co., 1883), 160.
13. Ibid., 184.
14. Sir Richard F. Burton, *Personal Narrative of a Pilgrimage to Al-Madinah and Mecca* (New York: Dover Publications, 1964), 360.

15. G. P. Badger, *History of the Imams and Seyyids of Oman* (London, 1871), cited in Kelly, *Arabia, the Gulf, and the West*, 226.
16. Joshua Teitelbaum, *The Rise and Fall of the Hashemite Kingdom of Arabia* (New York: New York University Press, 2001), 9, 37–38. The Ottomans became increasingly involved in the selection of the sharif. For example, years later, the famous founder of the Hashemite dynasty, Sharif Hussein ibn Ali, who was born in Istanbul in 1853, became the Ottoman-appointed sharif of Mecca in 1908; his descendants would later become the rulers of Jordan and Iraq.
17. Bernard Lewis, *What Went Wrong?*, 89.
18. Ahmad bin Zayani Dahlan, *Fitnatu-l-Wahhabiyyah*. See www.village.flashnet.it/users/fn034463/fitnah.html.
19. Algar, *Wahhabism: A Critical Essay*, 77.
20. Frederick F. Anscombe, *The Ottoman Gulf: The Creation of Kuwait, Saudi Arabia, and Qatar* (New York: Columbia University Press, 1997), 17.
21. Said K. Aburish, *The Rise, Corruption, and Coming Fall of the House of Saud* (London: Bloomsbury, 1994), 13.
22. Charles M. Doughty, *Travels in Arabia Deserta*, Vol. II (New York: Dover Publications, 1888), 455.
23. Ibid., 459.
24. Ibid., 368.
25. Alexander Bligh, "The Saudi Religious Elite (Ulama) as Participant in the Political System of the Kingdom," *International Journal of Middle East Studies*, Vol. 17, 1985, 37–50.
26. Ahmed Rashid, "Fires of Faith in Central Asia," *World Policy Journal*, Vol. 28, No. 1 (Spring 2001).

Chapter 3: "White Terror"

1. Gary Troeller, *The Birth of Saudi Arabia* (London: Frank Cass, 1976), 11.
2. Helmut Mejcher, *Imperial Quest for Oil: Iraq 1910–1928* (London: Ithaca Press, 1976), 4–6.
3. H. V. F. Winstone, *Captain Shakespeare* (London: Quartet Books, 1976), 102–3.
4. Algar, *Wahhabism: A Critical Essay*, 22.
5. Vassiliev, *The History of Saudi Arabia*, 225.
6. Ibid., 229.
7. H. R. P. Dickson, *Kuwait and Her Neighbors* (London: Allen and Unwin, 1956).
8. Fouad al-Farsy, *Saudi Arabia: A Case Study in Development* (London: Stacey International, 1978), 76–77.
9. Ibid.
10. Vassiliev, *The History of Saudi Arabia*, 129.
11. David Fromkin, *A Peace to End All Peace: The Fall of the Ottoman Empire and the Creation of the Modern Middle East* (New York: Holt and Company, 1989), 425.
12. Dickson, *Kuwait and Her Neighbors*, 274–75.
13. Kelly, *Arabia, the Gulf, and the West*, 238.

14.   Reader Bullard, British Consul-General, September 21, 1924, India Office; see Joshua Teitelbaum, "Pilgrimage Politics: The Hajj and Saudi-Hashemite Rivalry, 1916–1925," in Asher Susser and Aryeh Shmuelevitz, eds., *The Hashemites in the Modern World* (London: Frank Cass, 1995), 78.

15.   Ibid.

16.   Al-Azmeh, *Islams and Modernities*, 145.

17.   Aburish, *The Rise, Corruption, and Coming Fall of the House of Saud*, 24.

18.   Al Rasheed, *A History of Saudi Arabia*, 231.

19.   F. E. Peters, *The Hajj*, 358–59.

20.   Salame, "Islam and Politics in Saudi Arabia," 313.

21.   Vassiliev, *The History of Saudi Arabia*, 273.

22.   Martin S. Kramer, *Islam Assembled: The Advent of Muslim Congresses* (New York: Columbia University Press, 1986), 106.

23.   Ibid., 111.

24.   Ibid., 109.

25.   Ibid., 116.

26.   Al-Farsy, *Saudi Arabia*, 35.

27.   Aaron S. Kleiman, *Foundations of British Policy in the Arab World: The Cairo Conference of 1921* (Baltimore: The Johns Hopkins Press, 1970), 30–31.

28.   William Roger Louis, *The British Empire in the Middle East: 1945–1951* (Oxford: Oxford University Press, 1984), 176.

29.   Philip S. Khoury, *Syria and the French Mandate: The Politics of Arab Nationalism* (Princeton: Princeton University Press, 1987), 229.

30.   Hourani, *Arabic Thought in the Liberal Age, 1798–1939*, 231, 237.

31.   Elie Kedourie, *Arabic Political Memoirs and Other Studies* (London: Frank Cass, 1974), 144–45.

32.   Kramer, *Islam Assembled*, 110.

33.   Hourani, *Arabic Thought in the Liberal Age, 1798–1939*, 360.

34.   Daniel Benjamin and Steven Simon, *The Age of Sacred Terror* (New York: Random House, 2002), 57.

Chapter 4: Building the Modern Saudi State

1.   Document 14, "British Treaty with Ibn Saud," in J. C. Hurewitz, ed., *The Middle East and North Africa in World Politics*, Vol. 2 (New Haven: Yale University Press, 1979), 58.

2.   Vassiliev, *The History of Saudi Arabia*, 273.

3.   Al-Azmeh, *Islams and Modernities*, 144.

4.   "Account of Mr. Bird's Interview with King Ibn Saud, January 7, 1943," United Kingdom, Public Record Office, Foreign Office, FO 371/35417 E 140/69/25.

5.   Document 20, "Situation in Saudi Arabia," September 12, 1941, American Legation, Cairo, to the Secretary of State. Also see Enclosure No. 3, "Tribal System in Saudi Arabia," Colonel De Gaury, Mr. Hare, in Ibrahim al-Rashid, ed., *Saudi Arabia Enters the Modern World*, Vol. IV (Salisbury: Documentary Publications, 1980), 90–91.

6.   Document 101, "The Visit of His Royal Highness Emir Faisal al Saud to Baghdad," July 13, 1932, U.S. Legation, Baghdad, to the Secretary of State, in Ibrahim al-Rashid, *Saudi Arabia Enters the Modern World*, Vol. IV, 125.

7.   Nadav Safran, *Saudi Arabia: The Ceaseless Quest for Security* (Cambridge: Harvard University Press, 1985), 58.

8.   Ibid., 61.

9.   Martin Gilbert, *Churchill: A Life* (New York: Henry Holt and Company, 1991), 260–61.

10. Gerald De Gaury, *Faisal: King of Saudi Arabia* (London: Arthur Barker, 1966), 67.

11. H. St. John B. Philby, *Arabian Oil Ventures* (Washington, D.C.: The Middle East Institute, 1964), 73–74.

12. "The Acting Secretary of State to the Ambassador in Great Britain, June 16, 1932," *Foreign Relations of the United States, 1933*, Vol. II (Washington, D.C.: U.S. Government Printing Office, 1978), 990; "The Secretary of State to the Charge in Great Britain, April 26, 1933," ibid., 998.

13. Telegram, Political Resident to Secretary of State for India, January 11, 1934; "Qatar Oil Concession," January 12, 1934, FO 371/1778 E 292/81/91; and Document 110, "British Interests in the Persian Gulf: Report of the Political Department of British India," June 25, 1935, in Hurewitz, *The Middle East and North Africa in World Politics*, Vol. 2, 476.

14. William A. Eddy to the Secretary of State, "Complaints by Certain Arabian Fanatics That King Abdul Aziz Is Surrending His Land to Unbelievers," December 4, 1944, in Ibrahim al-Rashid, *Saudi Arabia Enters the Modern World*, Vol. IV, 201–3.

15. Alam, *Religion and State: Egypt, Iran, and Saudi Arabia*, 181–83.

16. Ibid.

17. Phillip Mattar, *The Mufti of Jerusalem: Al-Hajj Amin Al-Husayni and the Palestinian National Movement* (New York: Columbia University Press, 1988), 60.

18. Elie Kedourie, "Great Britain and Palestine: The Turning Point," in Elie Kedourie, ed., *Islam in the Modern World and Other Studies* (New York: Holt, Rinehart, and Winston, 1980), 96, 150.

19. Document 17, "Syrian Policy," Note by the Prime Minister and Minister of Defense, May 14, 1941, in Gavriel Cohen, *Churchill and Palestine 1939–1942* (Jerusalem: Yad Itzhak Ben Zvi, 1976), 82.

20. "Account of Mr. Bird's Interview with King Ibn Saud, January 7, 1943."

21. Document 35, "Visit of His Majesty King Abdul Aziz ibn Saud to Dhahran," January 31, 1947, in Ibrahim al-Rashid, *Saudi Arabia Enters the Modern World*, Vol. V, 97.

22. "Audience with His Majesty King Abdul Aziz, Childs to Marshall, December 4, 1947," *Foreign Relations of the United States, 1947*, Vol. V, 1336–37.

23. Document 41, "Audience with His Majesty December Third," Childs to Marshall, December 4, 1947, in Ibrahim al-Rashid, *Saudi Arabia Enters the Modern World*, Vol. V, 114.

24. "Acting Secretary of State [Lovett] to Childs, December 12, 1947," *Foreign Relations of the United States, 1947*, Vol. V, 1340.

25. "Childs to Acheson, November 17, 1949," *Foreign Relations of the United States, 1949*, Vol. VI, 1621.
26. James P. Piscatori, "Islamic Values and National Interest: The Foreign Policy of Saudi Arabia," in Adeed Dawisha, ed., *Islam in Foreign Policy* (Cambridge: Cambridge University Press, 1983), 38.
27. Safran, *Saudi Arabia*, 67.
28. Transmittal of Saudi Pamphlet Entitled "The Saudi Army in Palestine," October 4, 1951, Dispatch 125, Palestine, Washington, D.C.: U.S. National Archives, NA RG 59 786A.55/10-451.
29. "Celebrations Marking the Return of Last Saudi Contingent from Palestine," Childs to the Department of State, February 27, 1950, Washington, D.C.: U.S. National Archives, NA RG 59 786A.54/2-2750.
30. United Kingdom, Public Record Office, Foreign Office, FO371/75509 XC/1 55632.
31. United Kingdom, Public Record Office, Foreign Office, FO371/75507 XC/A 55632.
32. "Saudi Arabia: Annual Review for 1950," March 19, 1951, United Kingdom, Public Record Office, Foreign Office, FO 371/ 91757 55458.
33. "Memorandum of Conversations, by the Ambassador in Saudi Arabia [Childs], March 23, 1950," *Foreign Relations of the United States, 1950*, Vol. V, 1147.
34. Ibid., 1149
35. Parker T. Hart, *Saudi Arabia and the United States: Birth of a Security Partnership* (Bloomington, IN: Indiana University Press, 1998), 58.
36. "Saudi Arabia: Annual Review for 1950."
37. "The Ambassador in Saudi Arabia [Childs] to the Secretary of State, April 3, 1950," *Foreign Relations of the United States, 1950*, Vol. V, 1155.
38. Ibid., 1173.
39. "The Ambassador in Saudi Arabia [Childs] to the Consulate General at Dhahran, May 7, 1950," *Foreign Relations of the United States, 1950*, Vol. V, 1173.

Chapter 5: Reactivating Wahhabism

1. Bligh, "The Saudi Religious Elite (Ulama) as Participant in the Political System of the Kingdom," 44–45.
2. Abbas R. Kelidar, "The Problem of Succession in Saudi Arabia," *Asian Affairs: Journal of the Royal Society for Asian Affairs*, February 1978, 24.
3. Michael Herb, *All in the Family: Absolutism, Revolution, and Democracy in the Middle Eastern Monarchies* (Albany: State University of New York Press, 1999), 102.
4. *Internal Security in Saudi Arabia*, United Kingdom, Public Record Office, Foreign and Commonwealth Office, FCO8/1483, 1970.
5. "Saudi Arabia: Annual Review for 1964," in Robert L. Jarman, ed., *Political Diaries of the Arab World: Saudi Arabia*, Vol. 5 (Chippenham: Antony Rowe, 1998), 525.
6. Ibid.
7. De Gaury, *Faisal: King of Saudi Arabia*, 131.

8.   Vassiliev, *The History of Saudi Arabia*, 367.
9.   *Internal Security in Saudi Arabia.*
10.   Jacob M. Landau, *The Politics of Pan-Islam: Ideology and Organization* (Oxford: Clarendon Press, 1990), 284.
11.   Kepel, *Jihad*, 52.
12.   Martin S. Kramer, "Muslim Statecraft and Subversion," in Haim Shaked and Daniel Dishon, eds., *Middle East Contemporary Survey, 1983–84* (Boulder: Westview Press, 1986), 166.
13.   Piscatori, "Islamic Values and National Interest: The Foreign Policy of Saudi Arabia," 40; Abdullah M. Sindi, "King Faisal and Pan-Islamism," in Beling, *King Faisal and the Modernization of Saudi Arabia*, 186; Mordechai Abir, *Saudi Arabia: Government, Society, and the Gulf Crisis* (London: Routledge, 1993), 52.
14.   Al-Yassini, *Religion and State in the Kingdom of Saudi Arabia*, 66.
15.   Abir, *Saudi Arabia*, 44.
16.   Bligh, "The Saudi Religious Elite (Ulama) as Participant in the Political System of the Kingdom," 39, 43.
17.   Sarah Yizraeli, *The Remaking of Saudi Arabia* (Tel Aviv: The Moshe Dayan Center for Middle Eastern and African Studies, Tel Aviv University, 1997), 202–7.
18.   Michael Field, *Inside the Arab World* (Cambridge: Harvard University Press, 1994), 337.
19.   Abir, *Saudi Arabia*, 16.
20.   See Foreign Office Minutes, dated January 23, 1935, in Anita L. P. Burdett, ed., *Islamic Movements in the Arab World, 1913–1966*, Vol. 3 (Chippenham: Antony Rowe, 1998), 52.
21.   Ibid.
22.   Bligh, "The Saudi Religious Elite (Ulama) as Participant in the Political System of the Kingdom," 44.
23.   Abir, *Saudi Arabia*, 18.
24.   Gad Gilber, *The Development of Higher Education Systems in Seven Arab States, 1965–1988* (Haifa, Israel: Technion, 1993), 13.
25.   Teitelbaum, *The Rise and Fall of the Hashemite Kingdom of Arabia*, 7.
26.   Ibid., 14.
27.   Field, *Inside the Arab World*, 337.
28.   Al-Yassini, *Religion and State in the Kingdom of Saudi Arabia*, 72.
29.   See interview with Dr. Abdul Wahab A. Noorwali, Assistant Secretary-General of the World Assembly of Muslim Youth, in Khouloud Soliman, "WAMY Team in Afghanistan Risks Life to Deliver Aid," *Saudi Gazette*, November 20, 2001.
30.   Ian Black, Deborah Pugh, Simon Tisdall, Kathy Evans, and Leslie Plommer, "Militant Islam's Saudi Paymasters," *The Guardian*, February 29, 1992.
31.   "The Struggle for Power in Saudi Arabia," January 5, 1964, in Jarman, *Political Diaries of the Arab World: Saudi Arabia*, Vol. 6, 465.
32.   Obaid, "Improving U.S. Intelligence Analysis on the Saudi Arabian Decision-Making Process," 13.
33.   "Saudi Arabia: Annual Review for 1969, " United Kingdom, Public Record Office, Foreign and Commonwealth Office, FCO8/1481, 1970.

34. "Jedda Despatch No. 21 to the Foreign Office, 16 April 1964, The Political Crisis in Saudi Arabia" in Jarman, *Political Diaries of the Arab World: Saudi Arabia*, Vol. 6, 508.

35. Ibid.

36. "Saudi Arabia: Annual Review for 1965," in Jarman, *Political Diaries of the Arab World: Saudi Arabia*, Vol. 5, 532.

37. Document 278, "Memorandum of Conversation: President's Second Meeting with King Faisal, June 22, 1966," U.S. Department of State, *Foreign Relations of the United States, 1964–1968*, Vol. XXI, *Near East Region: Arabian Peninsula* (Washington, D.C.: U.S. Government Printing Office, 2000), 533.

38. David Holden and Richard Johns, *The House of Saud: The Rise and Rule of the Most Powerful Dynasty in the Arab World* (New York: Holt, Rinehart, and Winston, 1981), 252.

39. Bernard Lewis, *Semites and Anti-Semites: An Inquiry into Conflict and Prejudice* (New York: W. W. Norton, 1986), 194.

40. Telegram from the Embassy in Saudi Arabia to the Department of State, July 20, 1968, *Foreign Relations of the United States, 1964–1968*, Vol. XXI, *Near East Region*. See www.state.gov/www/about_state/history/vol_xxi/zd.html.

41. Ibid.

42. Obaid, "Improving U.S. Intelligence Analysis on the Saudi Arabian Decision-Making Process," 14.

43. Said K. Aburish, *Arafat: From Defender to Dictator* (London: Bloomsbury, 1998), 58.

44. Kelly, *Arabia, the Gulf, and the West*, 16–19, 270, 271.

45. Guy Bechor, *Lexicon of the PLO* (Tel Aviv: Israel Ministry of Defense, 1991), 245.

46. Martin S. Kramer, "The Export of Islam," in Itamar Rabinovich and Haim Shaked, eds., *Middle East Contemporary Survey: 1986* (Boulder: Westview Press, 1988), 133.

47. *Foreign Relations of the United States, 1967–1968*, Vol. XX, *Arab-Israeli Dispute*.

48. Neil C. Livingstone and David Halevy, *Inside the PLO* (New York: William Morrow, 1980), 277.

49. Janet Wallach and John Wallach, *Arafat: In the Eyes of the Beholder* (Secaucus, NJ: Birch Lane Press, 1997), 296.

50. Holden and Johns, *The House of Saud*, 253.

51. Anthony Cave Brown, *Oil, God, and Gold*, 291.

52. Henry Kissinger, *Years of Upheaval* (Boston: Little, Brown, 1982), 528.

53. Aryeh Shalev, *Israel and Syria: Peace and Security on the Golan* (Tel Aviv: Tel Aviv University, 1993), 123.

54. Obaid, "Improving U.S. Intelligence Analysis on the Saudi Arabian Decision-Making Process." There has been some disagreement among observers over what triggered Faisal. In a major report on U.S.-Saudi relations in the *Washington Post* (February 11, 2002), Robert G. Kaisar and David Ottaway link Faisal's decision to President Nixon's decision to ask Congress for a $2.2 billion emergency appropriation for Israel. They still

note, however, that "Faisal yielded to the wishes of the Saudi *Ulema*, the country's Muslim elders, and wielded his oil weapon to punish the United States." In other words, Kaisar and Ottaway agree that the pressure for using the oil weapon came from Saudi Arabia's Wahhabi religious leaders. Nadav Safran discounts the idea that U.S. aid to Israel forced Faisal's hand. Faisal had not responded, several days earlier, to the beginning of the U.S. arms airlift to Israel. He believes that Faisal was responding to the changing tide of the war against Egypt and Syria. See Safran, *Saudi Arabia*, 156–58.

55. Holden and Johns, *The House of Saud*, 344.
56. "Saudi Arabia: Annual Review for 1950," United Kingdom, Public Record Office, Foreign Office, FO 371/ 91757.
57. Safran, *Saudi Arabia*, 221. His source is the Saudi Arabia Ministry of Petroleum and Natural Resources.

Chapter 6: The Hothouse for Militant Islamic Radicalism

1. L. Carl Brown, *Religion and State*, 145; Martin S. Kramer, *Arab Awakening and Islamic Revival: The Politics of Ideas in the Middle East* (New Brunswick: Transaction Publishers, 1996), 144–47.
2. Aburish, *Arafat*, 32–34.
3. Olivier Roy, *The Failure of Political Islam* (Cambridge: Harvard University Press, 1994), 110.
4. Eric Rouleau, "Trouble in the Kingdom," *Foreign Affairs*, July–August 2002, 78.
5. Abir, *Saudi Arabia*, 19.
6. Vali Nasr, *International Relations of the Islamist Movement: The Case of the Jam'at-i-Islami of Pakistan* (New York: Council on Foreign Relation, 199), 35.
7. Judith Miller, *God Has Ninety-Nine Names: Reporting from a Militant Middle East* (New York: Touchstone Books, 1996), 79.
8. *Al-Jazira*, September 7, 2001.
9. Kepel, *Jihad*, 51; David Sagiv, *Fundamentalism and Intellectuals in Egypt, 1973–1993* (London: Frank Cass, 1995), 47.
10. *As-Safir* reported that one of the apprehended leaders of the "Vanguards of the Islamic conquest" admitted that leaders of the group had visited Saudi Arabia at the invitation of Saudi intelligence; Saudi financial and military aid were provided to the group for six months beginning in September 1992. *Middle East Intelligence Report*, June 2, 1993. See menic.utexas.edu/menic/utaustin/course/oilcourse/mail/saudi/0002.html.
11. Kramer, *Islam Assembled*, 110.
12. C. W. Long, British Embassy, Jedda to P. H. C. Eyers, Arabian Department, December 6, 1966, in Burdett, *Islamic Movements in the Arab World, 1913–1966*, Vol. 4, 569.
13. L. Carl Brown, *Religion and State*, 156–57.
14. Sivan, *Radical Islam*, 68.
15. Ibid., 24.
16. Ibid., 25.

17. Bassam Tibi, *The Challenge of Fundamentalism: Political Islam and the New World Disorder* (Berkeley: University of California Press, 1998), 56.
18. Ibid., 57.
19. Roxanne L. Euben, *Enemy in the Mirror: Islamic Fundamentalism and the Limits of Modern Rationalism* (Princeton: Princeton University Press, 1999), 74.
20. Sagiv, *Fundamentalism and Intellectuals in Egypt, 1973–1993*, 38–39.
21. Doran, "Somebody Else's Civil War," 30.
22. Smith, *Islam in Modern History*, 106.
23. M. C. G. Man, British Embassy, Jedda, to T. F. Brenchley, Arabian Department, Foreign Office, February 9, 1966, in Burdett, *Islamic Movements in the Arab World 1913–1966*, Vol. 4, 545.
24. Smith, *Islam in Modern History*, 164.
25. Judith Miller, *God Has Ninety-Nine Names*, 151
26. Ami Ayalon and Bruce Maddy-Weitzman, eds., *Middle East Contemporary Survey: 1994* (Boulder: Westview Press, 1996), 128.
27. John L. Esposito, *Unholy War: Terror in the Name of Islam* (London: Oxford University Press, 2002), 18–19; Ed Blanche, "Ayman al-Zawahiri: Attention Turns to the Other Prime Suspect," *Jane's Intelligence Review*, October 3, 2001.
28. Kepel, *Jihad*, 314.
29. Fiona Symon, "The Roots of Jihad," BBC-News Analysis. See news.bbc.co.uk.hi/english/world/middle_east/newsid_1603000/1603178.stm.
30. Abdullah Azzam, *Join the Caravan* (Part One: Reasons for *Jihad*). See www.religioscope.com.
31. Kepel, *Jihad*, 146.
32. Abdullah Azzam, "Defense of the Muslim lands," Introduction. See www.religioscope.com.
33. Taken from Azzam's 1986 "Last Will and Testament of Sheikh Abdullah Yusuf Azzam," 32. See www.religioscope.com/info/doc/jihad/jihadfile.htm (or complete PDF at www.religioscope.com/pdf/islamisme/decl_war.pdf.
34. Ziad Abu Amr, *Islamic Fundamentalism in the West Bank and Gaza: Muslim Brotherhood and Islamic Jihad* (Bloomington, IN: Indiana University Press, 1994), 24.
35. *Assirat al-Mustaqeem*, No. 33, Safar 1415, August 1994. For the English translation cited here, see jihaadulkuffaarin.jeeran.com/file382.htm.
36. Basil Muhammad, *The Arab Volunteers in Afghanistan* (Jeddah: The Committee for Islamic Benevolence and the World Assembly of Muslim Youth, 1991), 143.
37. Husni Adham Jarar, *The Martyr: A Man of the Creed and the Concept of Jihad* (Amman: Dar al-Diya' lil-Nashr wa al-Tawzi, 1990), 355.
38. Peter L. Bergen, *Holy War, Inc: Inside the Secret World of Osama bin Laden* (New York: Free Press, 2001), 54–55.
39. Ibid., 135.
40. The Muslim World League was serving as a vehicle for spreading jihad internationally. Muhammad Jamal Khalifa, Osama bin Laden's brother-in-law, was a director of the Muslim World League in the Philippines

through the offices of the International Islamic Relief Organization (IIRO), which was established in 1978 as an "operating arm" of the Muslim World League. Christine Herrara, *Philippine Daily Inquirer* (Manila), August 9, 2001. On the background of the IIRO, see Steven Emerson, "Fund-raising Methods and Procedures for International Terrorist Organizations," Testimony Before the U.S. House of Representatives Committee on Financial Services, Subcommittee on Oversight and Investigations, February 12, 2002. In the early 1990s, the Abu Sayyaf group fighting the Philippines government would benefit from this source of funding. Peter Chalk, "Militant Islamic Extremism in the Southern Philippines," in Jason F. Isaacson and Colin Rubenstein, eds., *Islam in Asia* (New Brunswick: Transaction Books, 2002), 203.

41.   Ahmed Rashid, *Taliban: Militant Islam, Oil, and Fundamentalism in Central Asia* (New Haven: Yale University Press, 2000), 131.

42.   Steven Emerson, "Jihad in America," PBS documentary.

43.   Stefan Aust and Cordt Schnibben, *Inside 9-11: What Really Happened* (New York: St. Martin's Press, 2002), 170.

44.   Kepel, *Jihad*, 147. See also Abdullah Azzam, *Join the Caravan* (Part Three: Clarifications About the Issue of *Jihad* Today).

45.   Rohan Gunaratna, *Inside Al Qaeda: Global Network of Terror* (New York: Columbia University Press, 2002), 22.

46.   See www.religioscope.com/info/doc/jihad/jihadfile.htm.

47.   Emerson, "Jihad in America."

48.   Landau, *The Politics of Pan-Islam*, 284.

49.   Olivier Roy, *The Foreign Policy of the Central Asian Islamic Renaissance Party* (New York: Council on Foreign Relations, 1999), 6.

50.   Al-Yassini, *Religion and State in the Kingdom of Saudi Arabia*, 28; Alam, *Religion and State: Egypt, Iran, and Saudi Arabia*, 73.

51.   *Al-Sharq al-Awsat*, "Extracts from Al-Jihad Leader Al-Zawahiri's New Book: FBIS-NES-2002-0108," December 2, 2001.

52.   Roy, *The Failure of Political Islam*, 117.

53.   Dr. Ali Muhammad Jarishan, Assistant Lecturer in the Faculty of Shariah Studies, and Muhammad Sharif al-Zubayq, Lecturer in the Faculty of Da'wa, Islamic University in Medina, *The Methods of the Ideological Invasion of Islamic World* (Cairo: Dar al-Itissam, 1978).

54.   Ibrahim Sulaiman al-Jabhan, *The Facts That the Muslim Must Know About Christianity and Missionary Activity* (Saudi Arabia: The Directorate for Religious Research, Islamic Legal Rulings, Islamic Propagation, and Guidance, 1977).

55.   Ibid., 17.

56.   Ibid., 18.

57.   Ibid., 19.

58.   Islamic University in Medina, Number 4, Publication Year 7, 1395. See www.binbaz.org.sa/Display.asp?f=bz00232.

59.   Al-Jabhan, *The Facts That the Muslim Must Know about Christianity and Missionary Activity*, 24.

60.   "Saudis Debate the Annihilation of Christians and Jews," *MEMRI Special Dispatch Series*, No. 295, November 1, 2001.

Chapter 7: Wahhabism Reasserts Itself

1. Herb, *All in the Family*, 105.
2. Holden and Johns, *The House of Saud*, 380.
3. Anthony Cave Brown, *Oil, God, and Gold*, 284.
4. Al Rasheed, *Politics in an Arabian Oasis*, 252.
5. Holden and Johns, *The House of Saud*, 383.
6. Judith Miller, *God Has Ninety-Nine Names*, 495, note 87.
7. Joshua Teitelbaum, *Holier Than Thou: Saudi Arabia's Opposition* (Washington: Washington Institute for Near East Policy, 2000), 20.
8. Abir, *Saudi Arabia*, 81.
9. Salame, "Islam and Politics in Saudi Arabia," 314.
10. Joseph A. Kechichian, "The Role of the Ulama in the Politics of an Islamic State: The Case of Saudi Arabia," *International Journal of Middle East Studies* 18, 1986, 60.
11. Salame, "Islam and Politics in Saudi Arabia," 315.
12. Al-Azmeh, *Islams and Modernities*, 144.
13. Abir, *Saudi Arabia*, 82.
14. Ibid., 85.
15. Ibid., 88.
16. Joseph A. Kechichian, *Succession in Saudi Arabia* (New York: Palgrave, 2001), 62.
17. Sulaiman al-Hattlan, "In Saudi Arabia, an Extreme Problem," *Washington Post*, May 8, 2002.
18. Abir, *Saudi Arabia*, 88.
19. Ibid.
20. See www.fatwa-online.com.
21. Holden and Johns, *The House of Saud*, 767.
22. Sheikh Abdul Aziz bin Baz, "The Requirement to Be Hostile to the Jews and the Mushrikun." See www.binbaz.org.sa/Display.asp?f=bz00233.
23. See www.binbaz.org.sa/display.asp?f=bz00823.htm.
24. Sheikh Abdul Aziz bin Baz, "The Value of the Jihad and the Mujahidin." See www.binbaz.org.sa/Display.asp?f=bz00341.
25. See www.binbaz.org.sa/display.asp?f=bz00367.htm. An alternative view of the timing of jihad is presented by Dr. Ali Jarshia in *Foundations of Islamic Da'wa* (Jeddah: Dar al-Bashir, 1982). He writes of three distinct stages: *First stage*, creating an Islamic nation by deepening Islamic values among Muslims. *Second stage*, establishing an Islamic state that implements Islamic laws and is strong enough to carry through with the *third stage*, the spread of Islam to the entire world by means of jihad.
26. "A Note Printed by the National Guard," 1393. See www.binbaz.org.sa.
27. Safran, *Saudi Arabia*, 251.
28. Holden and Johns, *The House of Saud*, 505.
29. Ibid.
30. Alexander M. Haig Jr., *Caveat: Realism, Reagan, and Foreign Policy* (New York: Macmillan, 1984), 327.
31. Abir, *Saudi Arabia*, 127.
32. *Al-Jazira*, August 17, 1990.

33. *CIA World Factbook*, 2001. See www.cia.gov/cia/publications/factbook/index.html.
34. Piscatori, "Islamic Values and the National Interest: The Foreign Policy of Saudi Arabia," 47.
35. Nasr, *International Relations of an Islamist Movement*, 42.
36. Ibid.
37. Neamatollah Nojumi, *The Rise of the Taliban in Afghanistan: Mass Mobilizations, Civil War, and the Future of the Region* (New York: Palgrave, 2002), 119.
38. Iqbal Akhund, *Memoirs of a Bystander: A Life in Diplomacy* (Oxford: Oxford University Press, 1997), 329.
39. Ibid., 330.
40. See his willingness to work with the United States during the 1973 embargo, in Kissinger, *Years of Upheaval*, 665, 994–95.
41. This was an understanding between President Franklin D. Roosevelt and Prime Minister Winston Churchill in March 1942. See Maurice Matloff and Edwin M. Snell, *Strategic Planning for Coalition Warfare: 1941–1942* (Washington, D.C.: Office of the Chief of Military History, Department of the Army, 1953), 166–67.
42. Anthony Cordesman, *Saudi Arabia: Guarding the Desert Kingdom* (Boulder: Westview Press, 1997), 103–5.
43. "History of Defense Planning and Program Development for Persian Gulf/Southwest Asia Presence and Crisis Response," *Conduct of the Persian Gulf War: Final Report to Congress*, Table 1, Appendix D (Washington, D.C.: U.S. Government Printing Office, 1992), 367.
44. Safran, *Saudi Arabia*, 221.
45. See www.binbaz.org.sa/display.asp?f=bz01344.htm and www.binbaz.org.sa/display.asp?f=bz00795.htm.
46. Mushahid Hussain and Akmal Hussain, *Pakistan: Problems of Governance* (New Delhi: Konark Publishers, 1994), 118.
47. HRH General Khalid bin Sultan, *Desert Warrior: A Personal View of the Gulf War by the Joint Forces Commander* (New York: HarperCollins, 1995), 55.
48. Martin S. Kramer, "Islam's Enduring Feud," in Itamar Rabinovich and Haim Shaked, eds., *Middle East Contemporary Survey: 1987* (Boulder: Westview Press, 1989), 174.
49. Bergen, *Holy War, Inc.*, 55.
50. Holden and Johns, *The House of Saud*, 267.
51. Abir, *Saudi Arabia*, 111.
52. George Shultz, *Turmoil and Triumph: My Years as Secretary of State* (New York: Charles Scribners, 1993), 927.
53. Abir, *Saudi Arabia*, 110.
54. Vassiliev, *The History of Saudi Arabia*, 465.
55. Holden and Johns, *The House of Saud*, 262.
56. Anonymous correspondent with William E. Mulligan, *The Mulligan Papers*, cited in Anthony Cave Brown, *Oil, God, and Gold*, 366; Abir, *Saudi Arabia*, 110.

Chapter 8: Wahhabism's Global Reach

1. Anthony Cave Brown, *Oil, God, and Gold*, 356.
2. Holden and Johns, *The House of Saud*, 386.
3. George Church, "An Exquisite Balancing Act," *Time*, September 24, 1990.
4. Cordesman, *Saudi Arabia*, 117–18. Cordesman does not name which individuals received the commissions. Saudi opposition elements assumed that Fahd's Sudairi brothers were the beneficiaries, especially Minister of Defense Sultan bin Abdul Aziz.
5. Said Aburish, *The House of Saud* (London: Bloomsbury, 1994), 203.
6. Blaine Harden, "Saudis Seek U.S. Muslims for Their Sect," *New York Times*, October 20, 2001.
7. *Ain al-Yaqeen*, March 1, 2002.
8. *Al-Jazira*, February 16, 2002. The article notes the transfer of 6 billion Saudi riyals to the Muslim World League, but no time frame is given.
9. Roy, *The Failure of Political Islam*, 118.
10. For example, a Hamas fund-raising group in the West Bank and Gaza Strip received instructions to send letters of thanks to the executives of IIRO and WAMY for funds it had received. Richard Z. Chesnoff and Robin Knight, "A Helping Hand from Saudi Arabia: Who Funds Hamas?" *U.S. News and World Report*, July 8, 1996.
11. Judith Miller, *God Has Ninety-Nine Names*, 79.
12. Ahmed Rashid, *Taliban*, 85, 131, 197.
13. David B. Edwards, *Before Taliban: Genealogies of the Afghan Jihad* (Berkeley: University of California Press, 2002), 270.
14. Kepel, *Jihad*, 142, 395.
15. Ibid., 141.
16. Ibid., 142.
17. Bergen, *Holy War, Inc.*, 70.
18. Ahmed Rashid, *Taliban*, 131.
19. Bergen, *Holy War, Inc.*, 55.
20. Douglas Jehl, "A Nation Challenged: Saudi Arabia: Holy War Lured Saudis as Rulers Looked Away," *New York Times*, December 27, 2001.
21. Ibid.
22. Kepel, *Jihad*, 396, note 24.
23. Jamal Khashoggi, "Steven Emerson Out to Wreck Arab-U.S. Ties," *Arab News*, October 17, 2002. Khashoggi claims to have been present at a meeting between Azzam, Julaidan, and bin Laden.
24. "Inside Al-Qaeda: A Window Into the World of Militant Islam and the Afghan Alumni," *Jane's International Security*, September 28, 2001.
25. Roland Jacquard, *In the Name of Osama bin Laden: Global Terrorism and the bin Laden Brotherhood* (Durham: Duke University Press, 2002), 20. Prince Turki admitted to having met bin Laden in Saudi Arabia and at the Saudi embassy in Islamabad. He denied that bin Laden had any official status but did not rule out the possibility that he was in contact "with other Saudi officials." See Jamal Khashoggi, "Osama Offered to Form Army to Challenge Saddam's Forces," *Arab News*, August 9, 2002. Clearly, Turki wanted to pin the bin Laden connection on another Saudi official.

26. Khashoggi, "Osama Offered to Form Army to Challenge Saddam's Forces."

27. Kechichian, *Succession in Saudi Arabia*, 83.

28. Jean-Charles Brisard and Guillaume Dasquié, *Forbidden Truth: U.S.-Taliban Secret Oil Diplomacy and the Failed Hunt for bin Laden* (New York: Thunder's Mouth Press/Nation Books, 2002).

29. Ahmed Rashid, *Taliban*, 132.

30. Simon Reeve, *The New Jackals: Ramzi Yousef, Osama bin Laden, and the Future of Terrorism* (London: Andre Deutsch, 1999), 113.

31. Ahmed Rashid, *Taliban*, 198

32. Kepel, *Jihad*, 226.

33. Roy, *The Failure of Political Islam*, 119.

34. Ibid., 223.

35. Jessica Stern, "Pakistan's Jihad Culture," *Foreign Affairs*, November–December 2000.

36. Ibid.

37. Ahmed Rashid, *Taliban*, 90.

38. Thomas L. Friedman, "Foreign Affairs: In Pakistan, It's Jihad 101," *New York Times*, November 13, 2001.

39. Kepel, *Jihad*, 223; Ahmed Rashid, *Taliban*, 90.

40. Obaid, "Improving U.S. Intelligence Analysis on the Saudi Arabian Decision-Making Process," 33. See also Ahmed Rashid, *Taliban*, 201.

41. Jamal Khashoggi, "Oil Companies Might Have Funded Taleban," *Arab News*, August 9, 2002.

42. Ahmed Rashid, *Taliban*, 201.

43. Ibid., 139. See also Douglas Frantz and David Rohde, "A Nation Challenged: The Bond: How bin Laden and Taliban Forged Jihad Ties," *New York Times*, November 22, 2001.

44. Ahmed Rashid, *Taliban*, 139.

45. Ibid., 74.

46. Ibid.

47. Olivier Roy, "Afghanistan After the Taliban," *New York Times*, October 7, 2001.

48. Ahmed Rashid, *Jihad: The Rise of Militant Islam in Central Asia* (New Haven: Yale University Press, 2002), 54.

49. Ibid., 256, note 3.

50. Roy, *The Foreign Policy of the Central Asian Islamic Renaissance Party*, 5.

51. United Nations Mission of Observers in Tajikistan, "Tajikistan: Background." See www.un.org/Depts/DPKO/Missions/unmot/UnmotB.htm.

52. Robert Baer, *See No Evil: The True Story of a Ground Soldier in the CIA's War on Terrorism* (New York: Crown, 2002), 165.

53. Ibid., 166. See also James Risen, "A Nation Challenged: Qaeda Diplomacy: Bin Laden Sought Iran as an Ally, U.S. Intelligence Documents Say," *New York Times*, December 31, 2001.

54. *Muslim World News*, March 20, 1990.

55. Ahmed Rashid, 122–23.

56. Ibid., 118.

57. Bergen, *Holy War, Inc.*, 219.

58. Document 1, Untitled, in Jacquard, *In the Name of Osama bin Laden*, 168.
59. See news.findlaw.com/hdocs/docs/terrorism/usarnaout10902ind.pdf, 14.
60. Pravda: News and Analysis Online, May 2, 2002.
61. Vakhit Akaev, "Religious-Political Conflict of the Chechen Republic of Ichkeria," *Central Asia and the Caucasus, 1998–2002, Journal of Social and Political Studies.* See www.ca-c.org/dataeng/05.akaev.shtml.
62. Anatol Lieven, "Chechnya: History as Nightmare," *New York Times*, November 3, 2002.
63. "Britons Killed by bin Laden Ally," BBC News, November 28, 2001.
64. See www.fas.org/man/dod-101/ops/war/2000/01/chechyn/183.htm.
65. Ibid.
66. Bergen, *Holy War, Inc.*, 219.
67. Rajan Menon and Graham E. Fuller, "Russia's Ruinous War," *Foreign Affairs*, March–April 2000, 39.
68. Strobe Talbott, *The Russia Hand: A Memoir of Presidential Diplomacy* (New York: Random House, 2002), 356.
69. See www.lega-musulmana.it/Attualit%C3%A0/Comunicato6.htm.
70. Ibid.
71. Anna Matveeva, Royal Institute of International Affairs, "The Impact of Instability in Chechnya on Daghestan."
72. Mikhail Roshchin, "Dagestan and the War Next Door," *Perspective* XI:1 (September–October 2000), *Central Asia and Caucasus Update*, June 1998. See www.cpss.org/updates/cacu0698.txt.
73. See www.aeronautics.ru/chechenya/051900.htm. See also "Russia Targets Foreign Mercenaries," Stratfor, April 7, 2000; "Russia Security Accuses Saudi Body of Financing," Itar-Tass, May 19, 2000.
74. *Pravda*, October 22, 2001
75. "Russian Thwarts Coup Attempt in Caucasus," NewsMax.com, August 17, 2001; "The Wahhabis Reach the Volga," Vek, July 13, 2001, 3; WPS Russian Media Monitoring Agency, No. 165, July 16, 2001.
76. Charles H. Fairbanks, "U.S. Policy in the Caucasus and Caspian Region," Testimony Before the U.S. House of Representatives Committee on International Relations, October 10, 2001.
77. Gunaratna, *Inside Al Qaeda*, 68.
78. Sharon La Franiere, "Pressed by U.S., Georgia Gets Tough with Outsiders," *Washington Post*, April 28, 2002; Kavkaz-Center News Agency, May 3, 2001.
79. Gordon M. Hahn, "Putin's Muslim Challenge," *Russia Journal* 5:2, January 25–31, 2002.
80. Anthony Louis, "Sept. 11: Russia's 'Muslim Problem,'" United Press International, September 5, 2002. See www.upi.com/view.cfm?StoryID=20020905-065449-1393r.
81. Reuven Paz, "Suicide Terrorist Operations in Chechnya: An Escalation of the Islamist Struggle," June 20, 2000. See www.ict.org.il/articles/articledet.cfm?articleid=113.
82. Reuven Paz, "The Saudi Fatwah Against Suicide Terrorism," *Special Reports on the Arab-Israeli Peace Process*, Number 323, Peace Watch, Washington, D.C., May 2, 2001.

83.   Kepel, *Jihad*, 238, 249.
84.   Ibid., 407, note 20.
85.   See www.binbaz.org.sa/Display.asp?f=bz01231.
86.   Kepel, *Jihad*, 250–51.
87.   Phillip Corwin, *Dubious Mandate: A Memoir of the UN in Bosnia, Summer 1995* (Durham: Duke University Press, 1999), 203.
88.   Kepel, *Jihad*, 250–51.
89.   Press Release, Royal Embassy of Saudi Arabia, Information Office, Washington, D.C., August 14, 1995.
90.   Javid Hassan, "WAMY Calls for Muslim Forces to Defend Bosnia," *Arab News*, September 4, 1992.
91.   Chris Hedges, "Muslims from Afar Joining 'Holy War' in Bosnia," *New York Times*, December 5, 1992.
92.   See www.arab.net/iiro/finance.html. Sometimes reporters have called the IIRO the Islamic Relief Organization, leaving out the word "International." Andrew Higgins and Christopher Cooper, "CIA-Backed Team Used Brutal Means to Break Up Terrorist Cell in Albania," *Wall Street Journal*, November 20, 2001.
93.   Andrew Higgins, Robert Block, and Glenn Simpson, "Assault on Charities is Risky Front for U.S.: Crackdown on Funding for Terrorists Could Destabilize Saudi Allies," *Wall Street Journal*, October 16, 2001; John Mintz, "Saudis Crack Down on Charity Linked to Al Qaeda Network," *Washington Post*, March 12, 2002; Isabel Vincent, "Terrorist Plans Seized in Bosnia," *National Post*, March 21, 2002.
94.   Corwin, *Dubious Mandate*, 203.
95.   Kepel, *Jihad*, 251.
96.   Mone Slingerland, "Fight Over Ruins: The Struggle for the Heritage of Kosovo," *Het Parool*, December 24, 2001, translated from Dutch to English. See 194.109.221.180/domovina/html/fightoverruins.html.
97.   Brian Whitmore, "Saudi 'Charity' Troubling to Bosnian Muslims," *Boston Globe*, January 28, 2002.
98.   Michael A. Sells, "Erasing Culture: Wahhabism, Buddhism, Balkan Mosques." See www.haverford.edu/relg/sells/reports/WahhabismBuddhasBegova.htm. See also Whitmore, "Saudi 'Charity' Troubling to Bosnian Muslims."
99.   Stephen Schwartz, "Wahhabis in America: A Saudi Export We Can Do Without," *Weekly Standard*, November 5, 2001.
100. Whitmore, "Saudi 'Charity' Troubling to Bosnian Muslims." See also "Official: Targets Found in October Raid," Fox News, February 21, 2002. See foxnews.com/story/0,2933,46167,00.html.
101. Vincent, "Terrorist Plans Seized in Bosnia."
102. Gunaratna, *Inside Al Qaeda*, 112.
103. See news.findlaw.com/hdocs/docs/terrorism/burnettba81502cmp.pdf.
104. "On the Status, Method, and Fallout of the Global Spread of Wahhabism," an interview with Professor Sulayman Nyang, the Islamic Supreme Council of America. See www.islamicsupremecouncil.org/extremism/nyang_int.htm.
105. See www.isna.net/majlis/Sayyid_M_Syeed.asp.

106. Ibid.
107. Steven Emerson, *American Jihad: The Terrorists Among Us* (New York: Free Press, 2002), 217–18.
108. See www.isna.net/majlis/Sheikh_Muhammed_Nur_Abdullah.asp.
109. Michael Lewis, "Israel's American Detractors-Back Again," *Middle East Forum*, December 1997.
110. Harden, "Saudis Seek U.S. Muslims for Their Sect."
111. Ron Kampeas, "Fundamentalist Wahhabism Comes to U.S.," *Washington Post*, December 10, 2001.
112. See www.nait.net/belief.html.
113. Harden, "Saudis Seek U.S. Muslims for Their Sect."
114. Betsy Hiel and Chuck Plunkett Jr., "A Call for Holy War," *Pittsburgh Tribune-Review*, August 4, 2002.
115. The Muslim World League's New York City office dealt specifically with spreading Wahhabi Islam among America's prison population. The office coordinated its activities with each prison's chaplain. Prisoners were viewed as a "fertile" target population for proselytizing, because they usually had large amounts of spare time. *Al-Rabita al-Alami al-Islami*, Number #1553, May 1998.
116. Ibid.
117. Emerson, *American Jihad*, 128–31.
118. Steve Fainaru and Alia Ibrahim, "Mysterious Trip to Flight 77 Cockpit: Suicide Pilot's Conversion to Radical Islam Remains Obscure," *Washington Post*, September 10, 2002.
119. Khashoggi, "Steven Emerson Out to Wreck Arab-U.S. Ties."
120. Fainaru and Ibrahim, "Mysterious Trip to Flight 77 Cockpit."
121. Gunaratna, *Inside Al Qaeda*, 112.
122. Ibid., 113.
123. Matthew A. Levitt, "Charitable and Humanitarian Organizations in the Network of International Financing," Testimony Before the United States Subcommittee on International Trade and Finance, Committee on Banking, Housing, and Urban Affairs, August 1, 2002. See www.washingtoninstitute.org/media/levitt/levitt080102.htm.
124. Ibid.
125. Eric Lichtblau, "U.S. Indicts Heads of Islamic Charity in Qaeda Financing," *New York Times*, October 10, 2001.
126. See news.findlaw.com/hdocs/docs/terrorism/usarnaout10902ind.pdf, 15.
127. Emerson, "Fund-Raising Methods and Procedures for International Terrorist Organizations."
128. "Saudis Spread Hate Speech in U.S.," Saudi Institute, McLean, Virginia, September 9, 2002. See www.saudinstitute.org.
129. Carol O'Leary, "Extremists in a Moderate Land," *Washington Post*, August 11, 2002.
130. Eli Lake, "U.S. Presses Saudis on Terror-Link Charities," *Washington Times*, March 22, 2002.
131. U.S. Department of State, "Report of the Accountability Review Boards on the Embassy Bombings in Nairobi and Dar es Salaam on August 7,

1998," January 1999. See www.state.gov/www/regions/africa/
accountability_report.html.

132.   Jeff Gerth and Judith Miller, "Saudis Called Slow to Help Stem Terror Finances," *New York Times*, December 1, 2002.

Chapter 9: Countdown to September 11

1. Abir, *Saudi Arabia*, 130.
2. U.S. Department of Defense, *Conduct of the Persian Gulf War: Final Report to Congress* (Washington, D.C.: U.S. Government Printing Office, 1992), 31.
3. George Bush and Brent Scowcroft, *A World Transformed* (New York: Knopf, 1998), 334.
4. H. Norman Schwarzkopf, *It Doesn't Take a Hero: General H. Norman Schwarzkopf, the Autobiography* (New York: Bantam Books, 1992), 304.
5. Ibid., 305.
6. Ibid., 306.
7. Obaid, "Improving U.S. Intelligence Analysis on the Saudi Arabian Decision-Making Process," 20.
8. Ibid.
9. Abir, *Saudi Arabia*, 176.
10. Ibid., 178.
11. Judith Miller, *God Has Ninety-Nine Names*, 114.
12. Ibid., 74.
13. Ibid., 106.
14. Mamoun Fandy, *Saudi Arabia and the Politics of Dissent* (New York: Palgrave, 1999), 48–49.
15. Teitelbaum, *Holier Than Thou*, 31.
16. Abir, *Saudi Arabia*, 189.
17. Ibid., 33. Mamoun Fandy wrote that the Letter of Demands was addressed to both King Fahd and Sheikh bin Baz. The group of religious leaders that drafted the Letter of Demands met with bin Baz and he approved the initial draft. See Fandy, *Saudi Arabia and the Politics of Dissent*, 119.
18. Teitelbaum, *Holier Than Thou*, 52.
19. Sennott, "Saudi Schools Fuel Anti-U.S. Anger."
20. Fandy, *Saudi Arabia and the Politics of Dissent*, 64.
21. Ibid., 86.
22. Ibid., 93.
23. Teitelbaum, *Holier Than Thou*, 30.
24. See www.alsalafyoon.com/SalmanAldah/NihayetTareekh1.htm.
25. Ibid.
26. Ibid.
27. Ibid.
28. Ibid.
29. Ibid.
30. Ibid.
31. Fandy, *Saudi Arabia and the Politics of Dissent*, 101.

32. Ibid.
33. Teitelbaum, *Holier Than Thou*, 56.
34. Ibid.
35. Ibid., 42, footnote 3.
36. Joshua Teitelbaum, "Saudi Arabia," in Ayalon and Maddy-Weitzman, *Middle East Contemporary Survey: 1994*, 555.
37. Fandy, *Saudi Arabia and the Politics of Dissent*, 123.
38. Abir, *Saudi Arabia*, 198–99.
39. Ibid.
40. Judith Miller, *God Has Ninety-Nine Names*, 104.
41. Ibid.
42. Joshua Teitelbaum, "Saudi Arabia," in Bruce Maddy-Weitzman, ed., *Middle East Contemporary Survey: 1995* (Boulder: Westview Press, 1997), 543.
43. Ofra Bengio, "Iraq," in Ayalon and Maddy-Weitzman, *Middle East Contemporary Survey: 1994*, 351.
44. Ibid.
45. Teitelbaum, "Saudi Arabia," in Ayalon and Maddy-Weitzman, *Middle East Contemporary Survey: 1994*, 571.
46. Sami Al-Faraj and Laith Kubba, with Mohammad K. Shiyyab and Dov S. Zakheim, *Common Ground on Iraq-Kuwait Reconciliation* (Washington, D.C.: Search for Common Ground, 1998), 22–23.
47. Ibid., 24.
48. Kepel, *Jihad*, 184.
49. Document 4, in Jacquard, *In the Name of Osama bin Laden*, 180.
50. Shimon Shapira, *Hizballah Between Iran and Lebanon* (Tel Aviv: Hakibbutz Hameuchad, 2000), 110.
51. Fandy, *Saudi Arabia and the Politics of Dissent*, 185.
52. Bergen, *Holy War, Inc.*, 85.
53. Ibid., 78; Fandy, *Saudi Arabia and the Politics of Dissent*, 186.
54. Bergen, *Holy War, Inc.*, 82–83.
55. Joshua Sinai, "Assessing Risk: The Fire Next Time," *Middle East Insight*, November–December 2001, 21.
56. Fandy, *Saudi Arabia and the Politics of Dissent*, 186.
57. Ibid.
58. Document 2, Communiqué No. 17, August 3, 1995, in Jacquard, *In the Name of Osama bin Laden*, 172.
59. Ibid.
60. Anthony Cordesman, *Islamic Extremism in Saudi Arabia and the Attack on Al Khobar* (Washington, D.C.: Center for Strategic and International Studies, June 2001), 20. See www.csis.org/burke/saudi21/saudi_alkhobar.pdf.
61. Ibid.
62. Teitelbaum, *Holier Than Thou*, 76–77.
63. Fandy, *Saudi Arabia and the Politics of Dissent*, 177.
64. The version of the 1996 Declaration of War used here is available at www.religioscope.com/info/doc/jihad/jihadfile.htm. Kepel, who makes reference to the "Expel the Polytheists" phraseology, uses the azzam.com version, which is not always available.

65. Bernard Lewis, "License to Kill," *Foreign Affairs*, November–December 1998, 14.

66. Sermon given on September 13, 1997. See www.alminbar.cc/alkhutab/khutbaa.asp?mediaURL=1455.

67. Sermon given on September 2, 2000. See www.alminbar.cc/alkhutab/khutbaa.asp?mediaURL=2761.

68. Undated. See www.alminbar.cc/alkhutab/khutbaa.asp?mediaURL=4331.

69. Undated. See www.alminbar.cc/alkhutab/khutbaa.asp?mediaURL=4328.

70. See www.alminbar.cc/alkhutab/khutbaa.asp?mediaURL=4068.

71. Ministry of Education, Kingdom of Saudi Arabia, *Hadiths*, "Teachings of the Hadith." See www.pbs.org/wgbh/pages/frontline/shows/saudi/etc/textbooks.html.

72. Ministry of Education, Kingdom of Saudi Arabia, *Explanations*. See www.pbs.org/wgbh/pages/frontline/shows/saudi/etc/textbooks.html.

73. Sennott, "Saudi Schools Fuel Anti-U.S. Anger."

74. See Biographies: www.fatwa-online.com.

75. Ibid.

76. Joseph Kostiner, "State, Islam, and Opposition in Saudi Arabia: The Post Desert-Storm Phase," *MERIA Journal*, Vol. 1, No. 2, July 1997, 8.

77. See www.msapubli.com/affiliated/Html/categories/Jamiatul_ulama/huzaifi.html.

78. Joshua Teitelbaum, "Saudi Arabia," in Bruce Maddy-Weitzman, ed., *Middle East Contemporary Survey: 1998* (Boulder: Westview Press, 2001), 530.

79. Jim Mann and Ronald J. Ostrow, "Saudis Derailed U.S. Plan to Seize Mideast Terror Suspect," *Los Angeles Times*, April 21, 1995.

80. Elaine Sciolino, "U.S. Faults Saudi Arabia on Terrorist," *New York Times*, April 22, 1995.

81. Ibid.

82. Joshua Teitelbaum, "The Gulf States and the End of Dual Containment," *MERIA Journal*, Vol. 2, No. 3, September 1998.

83. Teitelbaum, *Holier Than Thou*, 85.

84. Elsa Walsh, "Annals of Politics: Louis Freeh's Last Case," *New Yorker*, May 14, 2001.

85. Jacquard, *In the Name of Osama bin Laden*, 130.

86. Doyle McManus and David Lauter, "Clinton Seeks Cutoff of Hamas' Mideast Funding," *Los Angeles Times*, October 28, 1994.

87. Cordesman, *Islamic Extremism in Saudi Arabia and the Attack on Al Khobar*, 28.

88. Lecture by Professor Emmanuel Sivan, Jerusalem Center for Public Affairs, August 29, 2002.

89. Jacquard, *In the Name of Osama bin Laden*, 46.

90. Barton Gellman, "U.S. Was Foiled Multiple Times in Effort to Capture bin Laden," *Washington Post*, October 3, 2001.

91. Turki described the Sudanese offer as "conditional": "President Bashir wanted guarantees regarding bin Laden's prosecution. That he would not be tried by any legal authority in the Kingdom." Khashoggi, "Oil Companies Might Have Funded Taleban: Turki."

92. Auster and Kaplan, "Saudi Royalty Gives Money to bin Laden." For an interpretation of events in the entire 1995–2001 period, see David

Wurmser, "The Saudi Connection: Osama bin Laden's a Lot Closer to the Saudi Royal Family Than You Think," *Weekly Standard*, October 29, 2001.

93.   Robinson, Cary, et al., "Princely Payments."

94.   Simon Henderson, "The Saudi Way," *Wall Street Journal*, August 12, 2002.

95.   Hersh, "Annals of National Security: King's Ransom."

96.   Ibid.

97.   Bergen, *Holy War, Inc.*, 89.

98.   Office of the Prime Minister, "Responsibility for the Terrorist Atrocities in the United States, 11 September 2001," in Appendix B, Bill Gertz, *Breakdown: How America's Intelligence Failures Led to September 11* (Washington, D.C.: Regnery Publishing, Inc., 2002), 223.

99.   John Miller and Michael Stone with Chris Mitchell, *The Cell: Inside the 9/11 Plot, and Why the FBI and CIA Failed to Stop It* (New York: Hyperion Books, 2002), 271.

100.   "Yemen President: Boat Used in Cole Attack Bought in Saudi Arabia," CNN, November 24, 2000.

101.   Charles M. Sennott, "Why bin Laden Plot Relied on Saudi Hijackers," *Boston Globe*, March 3, 2002.

102.   Gertz, *Breakdown*, 57.

103.   Sennott, "Why bin Laden Plot Relied on Saudi Hijackers."

104.   John Miller et al., *The Cell*, 226–27.

105.   Gertz, *Breakdown*, 57.

106.   Paul McGeough, "Hero of September 11 Hijackers Alive, Well, and Still Poisoning Young Minds," *Sydney Morning Herald*, October 4, 2002.

107.   Richard Bernstein, *Out of the Blue* (New York: Times Books, 2002), 54.

108.   Susan Sachs, "F.B.I. Had History of Contacts with One Terrorism Suspect," *New York Times*, September 24, 2002.

Chapter 10: The Hatred Continues

1.   *Al-Hayat*, October 23, 2001.

2.   *Arab News*, October 23, 2001.

3.   Douglas Jehl, "A Nation Challenged: The Network: Saudi Minister Asserts That bin Laden Is a 'Tool' of Al-Qaeda, Not Its Mastermind," *New York Times*, December 10, 2001.

4.   President George W. Bush, "Address to a Joint Session of Congress and the American People," September 20, 2001. See www.whitehouse.gov/news/releases/2001/09/20010920-8.html.

5.   Nicolas Pelham, "Saudi Clerics Issue Edicts Against Helping 'Infidels,'" *Christian Science Monitor*, October 12, 2001; Howard Schneider, "Saudi Arabia Wrestles with Two Views of Islam," *Washington Post*, December 15, 2001.

6.   See www.saaid.net/Warathah/hmood/h41.htm.

7.   See www.saaid.net/book/kotop.htm.

8.   Ibid.

9.   For example, he praised the Taliban for its behavior toward women, since the secularists had pushed women into driving automobiles. See www.saaid.net/Warathah/hmood/h41.htm.

10. Thomas Fuller, "Driving al-Qaeda: Religious Decrees: Terrorism Expert Lays Out Evidence."

11. See www.jihadunspun.net/BinLadensNetwork.

12. Jennifer S. Lee, "Saudi Censorship of Web Ranges Far Beyond Tenets of Islam, Study Finds," *New York Times*, August 29, 2002.

13. Douglas Jehl, "A Nation Challenged: Dissent: For Saudi Cleric, Battle Shapes Up as Infidel vs. Islam," *New York Times*, December 5, 2001.

14. Jehl, "A Nation Challenged: Saudi Arabia: Holy War Lured Saudis as Rulers Looked Away."

15. Jehl, "For Saudi Cleric, Battle Shapes Up as Infidel vs. Islam."

16. Jane Perlez, "A Nation Challenged: Shaky Ally: Saudi Cooperation on bin Laden Lags, U.S. Aides Say," *New York Times*, October 11, 2001.

17. Neil MacFarquhar, "A Nation Challenged: The Break: Saudis Criticize the Taliban and Halt Diplomatic Ties," *New York Times*, September 26, 2001.

18. See www.said.net/Warathah/hmood/2/oqala.jpg.

19. Ibid. Sheikh al-Shuaibi died January 20, 2002, after the controversy about his status was settled.

20. Algar, *Wahhabism: A Critical Essay*, 66.

21. See www.fatwa-online.com/scholarsbiographies/15thcentury/ibnjibreen.htm.

22. See www.alminbar.cc/alkhutab/khutbaa.asp?mediaURL=5387.

23. Neil MacFarquhar, "A Nation Challenged: Video: Clerics Named by bin Laden Seen as Posing Little Threat," *New York Times*, December 15, 2001.

24. Ibid.

25. "Saudi Government Official on bin Laden as a Hero: 'He Did Not Present a Distorted Picture of Islam in the West': American Jews are 'Brothers of Apes and Pigs,'" *MEMRI Special Dispatch Series*, No. 343, February 8, 2002.

26. Ibid.

27. See www.saudiembassy.net/publications/news_letter/NL_97/nl_97_10.html#WN_October.

28. Paul Martin, "Top Saudi Imam Sees Conspiracy," *Washington Times*, June 3, 2002. See also *Foreign Broadcast Information Service Report*, May 31, 2002.

29. "Saudi Efforts to Curtail Incitement in Mosques," *MEMRI Special Dispatch Series*, No. 34, November 28, 2001. See www.memri.org/bin/articles.cgi?Page=archives&Area=sd&ID=SP30401. Nawaf Obaid argued that this event, along with measures by the Ministry of Islamic Affairs, "has had a tremendous effect on toning down the extreme religious discourse in Saudi Society." But the continuation of provocative sermons like that of Sheikh al-Sudays proves that Obaid was mistaken.

30. "A Nation Challenged: In the Prince's Words: Excerpts from Talk," *New York Times*, January 29, 2002.

31. Mitch Frank, "A Wealthy Clan and Its Renegade," *Time*, October 8, 2001.

32. "Saudis Spent $2.7 M at B-M," *O'Dwyer's PR Daily*, August 2, 2002. See www.odwyerpr.com/0802saudis.htm.

33. Christopher Marquis, "Worried Saudis Try to Improve Image in the U.S.," *New York Times*, August 29, 2002.

34. "Saudis Pay Qorvis $200K A-Month," *O'Dwyer's PR Daily*, March 21, 2002. See www.odwyerpr.com/archived_stories_2002/march/0321qorvis.htm. "PB Lobbies for Saudis," *O'Dwyer's PR Daily*, January 31, 2002. See www.odwyerpr.com/archived_stories_2002/january/0131saudis_pb.htm.

35. Rudolph W. Giuliani with Ken Kurson, *Leadership* (New York: Miramax Books, 2002), 374–75.

36. Ibid.

37. Robert Satloff, "Assessing Crown Prince Abdullah's 'Normalization Plan,'" *Policywatch*, Washington Institute for Near East Policy, No. 604, February 21, 2002. See www.washingtoninstitute.org/watch/Policywatch/policywatch2002/604.htm.

38. For example, Amre Moussa, as Egypt's minister of foreign affairs, used the term "normal relations" in his address to the United Nations General Assembly on September 23, 1999.

39. James A. Baker, *The Politics of Diplomacy: Revolution, War, and Peace, 1989–1992* (New York: G. P. Putnam's Sons), 459.

40. David Makovsky, "The Arab-Israeli Peace Process," in Maddy-Weitzman, *Middle East Contemporary Survey: 1995*, 51.

41. "Concerning the Peace Treaty." See www.fatwa-online.com/fataawa/worship/jihaad/jih003/0020714.htm.

42. Teitelbaum, "Saudi Arabia," in Maddy-Weitzman, *Middle East Contemporary Survey: 1998*, 533.

43. David Sanger with Serge Schmemann, "Bush Welcomes Saudi's Proposal on Mideast Peace," *New York Times*, February 27, 2002.

44. See www.daccess-ods.un.org/doc/UNDOC/GEN/.

45. Paragraph 3 (II) of the Arab Peace Initiative. See www.al-bab.com/arab/docs/league/peace02.htm.

46. *Fox News Sunday*, April 28, 2002.

47. See www.al-bab.com/arab/docs/league/abdullah00.htm.

48. David Tell, "The Saudi-Terror Subsidy," *Weekly Standard*, May 20, 2002.

49. Joel Mowbray, "Blind Eye to the Saudis: Petro-Dollars Fuel Palestinian Terrorism, Yet State Sits Still," National Review Online, July 1, 2002.

50. "Target: Hamas—U.S. Raids Texas-Based Palestinian Charity," ABC News, December 4, 2001. See abcnews.go.com/sections/us/DailyNews/hlf011204.html.

51. Judith Miller, "U.S. Is Examining Whether Donations by Two Wealthy Saudis Indirectly Aided Terrorism," *New York Times*, March 25, 2002.

52. Douglas Farah and John Mintz, "U.S. Trails Va. Muslim Money, Ties," *Washington Post*, October 7, 2002; Glenn R. Simpson, "Report Links Charity to an al Qaeda Front," *Wall Street Journal*, September 20, 2002.

53. These last two points are raised by Judith Miller. See Judith Miller, "U.S. Is Examining Whether Donations by Two Wealthy Saudis Indirectly Aided Terrorism."

54. Minster Dani Naveh (team coordinator), *The Involvement of Arafat, PA Senior Officials and Apparatuses in Terrorism against Israel, Corruption, and Crime* (Jerusalem: Ministry of Parliamentary Affairs, 2002), 67.

55. Ben Barber, "Saudi Millions Finance Terror against Israel," *Washington Times*, May 7, 2002.

56. Robert G. Kaiser and David B. Ottaway, "Saudi Leader's Anger Revealed Shaky Ties," *Washington Post,* February 10, 2002.

57. Lawrence F. Kaplan, "How the Saudis Lobby Bush," *New Republic,* December 24, 2001.

58. Ibid.

59. Howard Schneider, "Saudi Crown Prince to Carry Warning to Visit with Bush," *Washington Post,* April 24, 2002.

60. Patrick E. Tyler, "Mideast Turmoil: Arab Politics: Saudi to Warn Bush of Rupture Over Israel Policy," *New York Times,* April 25, 2002.

61. Ibid.

62. Elisabeth Bumiller, "Mideast Turmoil: The Meeting: Saudi Tells Bush U.S. Must Temper Backing of Israel," *New York Times,* April 26, 2002.

63. The Saudi eight-point plan included: (1) Complete and immediate withdrawal of Israeli forces from recently occupied West Bank areas; (2) terminating the military siege on Ramallah; (3) deployment of an international force; (4) reconstruction of the infrastructure destroyed by the Israeli incursion; (5) condemning terrorism from all sides; (6) restart of political negotiations without prior security conditions; (7) terminating Israeli settlements; and (8) implementing UN Resolution 242, which calls for Israeli withdrawal to the June 4, 1967, borders. *MEMRI Inquiry and Analysis Series,* No. 94, May 9, 2002.

64. Ben Caspit, "'I Am Just an Official': An Interview with Efraim Halevy," *Maariv,* Shabbat Supplement, November 8, 2002.

65. Joshua Teitelbaum, "September 11 and the Saudi Arabian Connection," *Policywatch,* Washington Institute for Near East Policy, No, 573, October 12, 2001; Douglas Jehl, "Saudis Admit Restricting U.S. Warplanes in Iraq," *New York Times,* March 22, 1999.

66. Teitelbaum, "September 11 and the Saudi Arabian Connection."

67. Michael R. Gordon, "U.S. Is Preparing Base in Gulf State to Run Iraq War," *New York Times,* December 1, 2002.

68. David B. Ottaway and Robert G. Kaiser, "Saudis May See U.S. Exit," *Washington Post,* January 18, 2002.

69. Christpher Dickey and Rod Nordland, "The Fire That Won't Die Out," *Newsweek,* July 22, 2002.

70. Gause, "Be Careful What You Wish For: The Future of U.S.-Saudi Relations."

71. Jamal Ahmad Khashoggi, "Saudi Religious Establishment Has Its Wings Clipped," Daily Star Online, June 29, 2002. See www.dailystar.com.lb/opinion/29_06_02_c.htm.

72. Neil MacFarquhar, "A Nation Challenged: Islam: Bin Laden's Wildfire Threatens Might of Saudi Rulers," *New York Times,* November 6, 2001.

73. Khashoggi, "Saudi Religious Establishment Has Its Wings Clipped."

74. Ibid.

75. Dickey and Nordland, "The Fire That Won't Die Out."

76. "Saudi Arabia to Also Defy United Nations Resolution," Pakistan News Service, October 14, 2002. See www.paknews.com.

77. "No Move to Change Curricula," *Arab News,* October 27, 2002.

78. Mordechai Abir, "Saudi Arabia, Stability, and International Islamic Terror," *Jerusalem Viewpoints,* No. 481, July 1, 2002, 3.

79. Thomas L. Friedman, "War of Ideas," *New York Times*, June 2, 2001.
80. An Associated Press story reported from Kuala Lumpur, *Turkish Daily News*, May 7, 2002.
81. Donna Abu-Nasr, "Saudi Cleric Disowns Militants," *Boston Globe*, October 14, 2002.
82. McGeough, "Hero of September 11 Hijackers Alive, Well, and Still Poisoning Young Minds." See www.smh.com.au/articles/2002/10/03/1033538723198.html. A BBC reporter interviewing a Saudi religious scholar in late October 2002 reported strong pro-jihad sentiments against the United States among thousands of Saudis in "tribal areas in the north and the south of the country." Magdi Abdelhadi, "Saudi Militants 'Ready for Jihad,'" BBC News, November 1, 2002.
83. Peter Finn, "Three Saudis Seized by Morocco Outline Post-Afghanistan Strategy," *Washington Post*, June 16, 2002; "Lebanon Charges 22 People with Planning Terrorist Acts," *Wall Street Journal*, October 11, 2002; Neil MacFarquhar, "Unmanned U.S. Planes Comb Arabian Desert for Suspects," *New York Times*, October 23, 2002. On November 3, 2002, an unmanned U.S. Predator aerial vehicle shot a Hellfire missile and killed Qaed Salim Sinan al-Harethi, a key al-Qaeda operative, near the Yemeni-Saudi border. Al-Harethi was killed while driving a car with Saudi license plates; he presumably shuttled between Saudi Arabia and Yemen. Seymour M. Hersh, "Manhunt," *New Yorker*, December 23, 2002. Saudi Arabia itself, toward the end of 2002, appeared to be one of the key areas of refuge for al-Qaeda after the American campaign in Afghanistan. Omar al-Bayoumi, the Saudi national who had hosted two of the September 11 hijackers in California and had received payments from Princess Haifa, the wife of the Saudi ambassador to the United States, was known to have fled to Saudi Arabia after being detained briefly in Britain. Isikoff and Thomas, "The Saudi Money Trail." In Germany, another key figure known for his al-Qaeda connections slipped out of sight after obtaining visas for Saudi Arabia for his entire family. Desmond Butler, "Terror Suspect's Departure from Germany Raises Concern in Other Nations," *New York Times*, December 4, 2002.
84. "No 'Sleeping Cells' of al-Qaeda in Kingdom, Says Prince Naif," *Arab News*, November 24, 2002.
85. See www.alharamain.org/eng/inner.asp?order=18&num=1.
86. In September 2002, Saudi Arabia could boast of having 230 nonprofit charities that had raised $267 million in the last year. "Saudi Societies Fight Back America's Uncharitable Charges a Year On," *Arab News*, September 9, 2002. Direct private contributions by Saudi private citizens probably even elevated the amount of funds available for Saudi-supported Islamic causes.

Chapter 11: Was Saudi Arabia Finally Changing?

1. Lisa Beyer (with Scott MacLeod), "Saudi Arabia: Inside the Kingdom," *Time*, September 15, 2003
2. Ilhem Rachidi, "Morocco Struggles with Wahhabi Legacy," *Asia Times*, April 16, 2004.
3. Beyer, "Saudi Arabia: Inside the Kingdom."

4. Raymond Bonner and Carlos H. Conde, "U.S. Warns the Philippines on Terror Groups," *New York Times*, April 11, 2004.

5. Middle East Media Research Institute, Special Dispatch Series—No. 526—Saudi Arabia, June 20, 2003.

6. Ibid.

7. Jonathan D. Halevi, "Al-Qaeda's Intellectual Legacy: New Radical Islamic Thinking Justifying the Genocide of Infidels," *Jerusalem Viewpoints*, No. 508, December 1, 2003.

8. Ibid.

9. Glenn R. Simpson, "List of Early al Qaeda Donors Points to Saudi Elite," *Wall Street Journal*, March 18, 2003.

10. Steve Coll, *Ghost Wars: The Secret History of the CIA, Afghanistan, and Bin Laden, From the Soviet Invasion to September 10, 2001* (New York: The Penguin Press, 2004), 278–279.

11. Richard A. Clarke, *Against All Enemies: Inside America's War on Terror* (New York: The Free Press, 2004), 139.

12. Michael Isikoff and Mark Hosenball, "A Legal Counterattack," *Newsweek*, April 16, 2003.

13. Robert Baer, *Sleeping with the Devil* (New York: Crown Books, 2003), 167.

14. Catherine Taylor, "Taliban-Style Group Grows in Iraq," *Christian Science Monitor*, March 15, 2002.

15. Jeff Klein, "Sheikh Mohammed Mohammed Ali INC Leader Speaks on the Future of Iraq," Kurdish Media.com, February 9, 2002.

16. C. J. Chivers, "Kurds Face a Second Enemy: Islamic Fighters on Iraq Flank," *New York Times*, January 13, 2003.

17. Stephen Schwartz, "Islamists Invade Iraq," *Weekly Standard*, January 26, 2004.

18. Saeed al-Saleh and Ali al-Ahmed, "Saudi Suicide Bomber Strikes in Northern Iraq," *Saudi Information Agency*, March 26, 2003.

19. Carole O'Leary, "Extremists in a Moderate Land," *Washington Post*, August 11, 2002.

20. Jonathan Schanzer, "Saddam's Ambassador to al Qaeda," *Weekly Standard*, March 1, 2004.

21. Ibid.

22. Barton Gellman, "U.S. Suspects Al Qaeda Got Nerve Agent From Iraqis," *Washington Post*, December 12, 2002.

23. Richard Wolffe and Daniel Klaidman, "Judging the Case," *Newsweek*, February 17, 2003.

24. Chivers, "Kurds Face a Second Enemy: Islamic Fighters on Iraq Flank."

25. Schwartz, "Saudi Mischief in Fallujah," *Weekly Standard*, June 16, 2003.

26. Ibid.

27. Schwartz, "Islamists Invade Iraq."

28. Ian Mather, "Terror Alliance Targets US Force in Iraq," *Scotland on Sunday*, June 15, 2003.

29. Halevi, "Who is Taking Credit for Attacks on the U.S. Army in Western Iraq? Al-Jama'a al-Salafiya al-Mujahida," Jerusalem Issue Brief, Institute for Contemporary Affairs, founded jointly with the Wechsler Family Foundation, Vol. 3, No. 3, August 5, 2003. http://www.jcpa.org/brief/brief3-3.htm

30.   Martin Bentham, "Coalition Officials Fear Wahhabi Infiltration of Iraq," *Daily Telegraph*, July 7, 2003.
31.   *The Australian*, August 14, 2003.
32.   Bentham, "Coalition Officials Fear Wahhabi Infiltration of Iraq."
33.   http://www.saudiaffairs.net/webpage/issue07/article07r/issue07rt07.htm
34.   Neil MacFarquhar, "Saudis Support a Jihad in Iraq, Not Back Home," *New York Times*, April 23, 2004.
35.   Reuven Paz, "Qa'idat al-Jihad, Iraq, and Madrid: The First Tile in the Domino Effect?" Intelligence and Terrorism Information Center, http://www.intelligence.org.il/eng/g_j/rp-a-3-04.htm
36.   Douglas Jehl and David Sanger, "Five Requests to Saudis Went Unheeded, U.S. Says," *New York Times*, May 16, 2003.
37.   *al-Hayat* (London), February 21, 2004.
38.   *al-Watan*, December 7, 2003. http://www.alwatan.com.sa/daily/2003-12-07/index.htm
39.   Ibid., April 11, 2004. http://www.alwatan.com.sa/daily/2004-04-11/first_page/first_page02.htm
40.   *Sharq al-Awsat*, (London) February 8, 2004.
41.   "Al-Qa'ida Commander in Iraq: 'A Terror Attack Against the U.S. With 100,000 Deaths is Imminent; We Ordered the Riyadh Bombing,'" MEMRI: Special Dispatch Series No. 609, November 14, 2003.
42.   "Al-Qaida Magazine Debates Attacks in Saudi Arabia—Proposes More Attacks in the U.S. Will Boost Support," MEMRI: Special Dispatch Series No. 632, December 23, 2003.
43.   Arieh O'Sulivan, "Israeli Intelligence Officials Dismiss Abbas's Denial of Saudi Aid to Terrorists," *Jerusalem Post*, August 11, 2003.
44.   A "senior security official" was reported to have stated that the amount of Saudi aid to Hamas reached 70 percent of the organization's income. See *Ha'aretz*, July 29, 2003.
45.   *Al-Jazira* (Saudi Arabia), November 11, 2001.
46.   *Al-Hayat*, December 8, 2003.
47.   Dr. Khalil bin Abdullah al-Khalil, "The Hunt for the Riyal Designated to Charity," *al-Majallah* (London), August 30, 2003.
48.   Jane Perlez, "Saudis Quietly Promote Strict Islam in Indonesia," *New York Times*, July 5, 2003.
49.   Steve Miller, "Oregon Group Thrives Despite al-Qaeda Tie," *Washington Times*, September 15, 2003.
50.   *Al-Watan*, January 26, 2004. http://www.alwatan.com.sa/daily/2004-01-26/local/local05.htm
51.   *Al-Riyadh*, December 9, 2001. http://www.alriyadh.com.sa/Contents/2001/12/09-12-2001/page2.html
52.   http://www.al-liqa.org.sa/sa/research24.html
53.   Beyer, "Saudi Arabia: Inside the Kingdom."
54.   Michael Scott Doran, "The Saudi Paradox," *Foreign Affairs*, January/February 2004, Volume 83, No. 1, 50.
55.   Amos Harel, "Al-Qaeda Tried to Recruit Saudi Pilots for Attack on Israel," *Ha'aretz*, September 10, 2003.
56.   Gideon Alon, "Israel's Defense Minister: Al-Qaeda Trying to Infiltrate Saudi Arabia's Armed Forces," *Ha'aretz*, December 18, 2003.

Conclusion: Ending the Hatred

1. "President Bush's Address on Terrorism Before a Joint Meeting of Congress," *New York Times*, September 21, 2001.

2. *International Religious Freedom Report*, released by the Bureau of Democracy, Human Rights, and Labor (Washington, D.C.: U.S. Department of State, 2002). See www.state.gov/g/drl/rls/irf/2002/14011pf.htm; www.state.gov/g/drl/rls/irf/2002/14012pf.htm.

3. Steven Stalinsky, "Preliminary Overview—Saudi Arabia's Education System: Curriculum, Spreading Saudi Education to the World and the Official Saudi Position on Education Policy," *MEMRI Special Report*, No. 12, December 20, 2002. See www.memri.org/bin/articles.cgi?Page=archives&Area=sr&ID=SR01202. The textbook was published in 2001.

4. See the following civil action in the United States District Court in the District of Columbia (the so-called 9/11 Lawsuit): law.about.com/gi/dynamic/offsite.htm?site=http://news.findlaw.com/hdocs/docs/terrorism/burnettba81502cmp.pdf. Similar testimony was recorded at the deportation hearings of an IIRO employee nameed Mahmoud Jabara, according to Canadian court records. See Matthew Levitt, "Saudi Financial Counterterrorism Measures: Smokescreen or Substance?" *Policywatch*, Washington Institute for Near East Policy, No. 687, December 10, 2002.

5. Gunaratna, *Inside Al-Qaeda*, 22. Some Saudi sheikhs voiced the same view: Sheikh Sulaiman al-Ulwan was asked whether it was forbidden to kill innocent civilians, including women and children, in "marytrdom operations" conducted by the Palestinians. He justified the suicide bombings and permitted the murder of women and children. See www.jehad.net/download.htm. Sheikh al-Ulwan was cited in Osama bin Laden's December 2001 videotape as having issued "a beautiful fatwa" determining that the victims of the World Trade Center and the Pentagon "were not innocent people." In other words, it was permissible to kill these civilians. See www.cnn.com/2001/US/12/13/tape.transcript.

6. Michael Steinberger, "Lunch with the FT: Bernard Lewis," *Financial Times*, August 9, 2002.

7. "Leading Sunni Sheikh Yousef Al-Qaradhawi and Other Sheikhs Herald the Coming Conquest of Rome," *MEMRI Special Dispatch Series*, No. 447, December 6, 2002. See www.memri.org/bin/articles.cgi?Page=archives&Area=sd&ID=SP44702. Sheikh al-Arifi's article was posted on the Internet without a date, but it apparently was put on the newspaper *Kalemat*'s website about the same time that Sheikh Qaradhawi made similar statements, in early December 2002.

8. Karen De Young, "Saudis Detail Steps on Charities: Kingdom Seeks to Quell Criticism of Record on Terrorist Financing," *Washington Post*, December 3, 2002.

9. Royal Embassy of Saudi Arabia, "Initiatives and Actions Taken by the Kingdom of Saudi Arabia in the Financial Area to Combat Terrorism." See www.c-span.org/terrorism/Saudi.pdf.

10. Badr Almotawa, "U.S. Urged to Give Sound Proof in Julaidan Case," *Arab News*, September 9, 2002.

11. Ibid.

12.   "The Hamas Movement in an Internal Memorandum Boasts About the Positive Results from the Visit of a High-Level Delegation Led by Khaled Mashal to Saudi Arabia and Egypt," Intelligence and Terrorism Information Center at the Center for Special Studies, Israel Defense Forces. A charitable view of the Saudi-Hamas dialogue might try to argue that the Saudis wanted to influence Hamas to curtail some of its terrorism in the context of the Hamas-Fatah talks that were transpiring in Cairo during this period. But Hamas had made it clear that it planned to continue its attacks against Israeli civilians and nonetheless received assurances of continuing Saudi aid.

13.   Richard Holbrooke, *To End a War* (New York: Random House, 1998), 22–24.

14.   "Saudi Columnist: 'Our Youths Must Be Reeducated...Violence Must Be Discarded,'" *MEMRI Special Dispatch Series*, No. 448, December 11, 2002. See www.memri.org/bin/articles.cgi?Page=archives&Area=sd&ID=SP44802. The report is based on the writings of two Saudi columnists, one who wrote in *al-Sharq al-Awsat* and another who wrote in *al-Ukaz*.

Glossary

abu: *father of* (usually of eldest son)

ahl al-kitab: (literally) *people of the book*
"People of the book" are those religious groups, like Jews and Christians, who have already received revelations. Unlike infidels, they are entitled to protection and cannot be forcibly converted; nevertheless, they must pay discriminatory taxes, applied only to them, to the Islamic state.

al: *the* (the definite article)
Sometimes "al" is used to mean *son of*; for example, the Saudi foreign minister is called Prince Saud al-Faisal—meaning Saud, the son of King Faisal.

Al: *family* or *clan*

bin: *son of*

bint: *daughter of*

caliph: (literally) *successor*
The caliph was the political-religious leader of the Islamic community who succeeded the Prophet Muhammad. The caliphate was disbanded in 1924 with the dissolution of the Ottoman Empire, whose sultan had also served as the caliph of Sunni Islam.

da'wa: (literally) *the call*
The term *da'wa* refers to religious propagation or Islamic missionary activity.

emir (*or* amir): *commander, prince,* or *tribal chief*
In Saudi Arabia the term *emir* is used for a prince of the royal family, while in Kuwait and Qatar the term is used for the head of state.

fatwa (*pl.* fatawin): *formal legal opinion on Islamic law*

fitna: (literally) *sedition* or *rebellion*
The term *fitna* refers to a Muslim civil war.

hajj: *pilgrimage to Mecca*
The hajj is one of the five pillars of Islam, the others being affirming God and his messenger; prayer; charity, or *zakat;* and the Ramadan fast.

Hamas: *Islamic Resistance Movement*
Founded in 1987 in the Gaza Strip by former leaders of the Palestinian branch of the Muslim Brotherhood, Hamas is designated by the U.S. State Department as an international terrorist organization.

Hizballah: (literally) *Party of God*
Formed in late 1982, Hizballah is a pro-Iranian Lebanese Shiite militia with offshoots in the Arabian peninsula; it is designated by the U.S. State Department as an international terrorist organization.

ibn (*pl.* abna): *son of*
In more colloquial forms, *bin* is used instead of *ibn.*

imam: *prayer leader;* also, *one who leads a community by example*
Saudi leaders used the title *imam* in the past to denote that they were the religious leader of their community.

intifada: (literally) *shaking off*
The intifada was a Palestinian uprising in December 1987; a second intifada erupted in September 2000.

Islam: (literally) *submission* (that is, to the will of God)

Islamism: *movements, begun in the twentieth century, that advocate militancy in order to quash diversity in the Islamic faith and to gain political power*

jahilia: *the age of ignorance or darkness in pre-Islamic Arabia, before the Prophet Muhammad spread Islam in the seventh century*

jihad: (literally) *struggle*
The term *jihad* is often used to refer to the religious duty of holy war against the infidels, to extend the boundaries of Islam into non-Islamic territories; it is derived from the verb *jahada,* which means to strive or endeavor.

kafir (*pl.* kufar): *infidel*
One who is a *kafir* is not simply an "unbeliever," for the term implies an individual who knowingly hides the truth.

kufr: *blasphemy*
The state of being a *kafir,* or infidel; it is not just the state of unbelief, which implies passivity, for individuals in a state of *kufr* are concealing revelation.

madrasa: *a traditional school for the study of Islam*

mujahideen: *combatants on behalf of a jihad*

mufti: *a legal functionary who gives opinions on Islamic law*
The *grand mufti* is the highest religious authority. The word *mufti* is derived from the same root as *fatwa*.

mullah: (literally) *master*
The title *mullah* is used by religious leaders in Iran, Afghanistan, and Central Asia.

murtadd: (literally) *apostate*
A *murtadd* is one who converts from Islam to another religion. According to a 2002 report on Saudi Arabia issued by the U.S. State Department, under Islamic law "apostasy is a crime punishable by death if the accused does not recant."

mushrikun: *polytheists;* sometimes translated as *idolaters*

salafi: *a follower of the Prophet Muhammad's immediate successors, the pious ancestors* (al-salaf al-salihin)
Salafi movements have sought to restore Islam on the basis of its seventh-century teachings—that is, Islam as it was under the Prophet Muhammad and his immediate successors. *Salafis* usually belong to one of several groups, most notably the Muslim Brotherhood and the Wahhabis.

shahid: (literally) *witness*
A *shahid* is a martyr whose death in a jihad bears witness to his faith and who is assured a place in paradise on the day of judgment.

sharif: (literally) *noble*
The term *sharif* refers to the descendants of the Prophet Muhammad through his daughter Fatima; the Hashemites are regarded as a Sharifian family.

sheikh: *local ruler*
Sheikh is a title of respect given to a religious leader or elderly authority; it is also used to refer to the head of state in smaller Gulf states.

Shiite: (literally) *partisan*
Shiism is the minority branch in Islam; Shiites are known as the "partisans of Ali," Muhammad's son-in-law, because they attribute a special religious status to him.

shirk: *polytheism*

sufism: *Islamic mysticism*

sultan: (literally) *ruler*
The title *sultan* was used by heads of state in the Ottoman Empire and is currently used by Oman's head of state. Ibn Saud briefly used the title when he was ruler of the Najd, before his conquest of the Hijaz.

Sunni: *one who follows the traditional, or orthodox, practice of Islam*

tawhid: *belief in the oneness of God*
   Tawhid is the central Islamic tenet that Wahhabism has stressed; Wahhabi leaders have stated that those who stray from *tawhid* are guilty of *shirk*, or polytheism.

ulama (*sing.* alim): *religious leadership*
   The *ulama* in Saudi Arabia are the community of recognized Islamic scholars, including the grand mufti, judges, imams of mosques, and teachers in religious universities and schools.

Wahhabi: *one who follows Muhammad ibn Abdul Wahhab's Islamic creed*
   Ibn Abdul Wahhab established his Islamic creed in eighteenth-century Arabia; Wahhabi movements have militantly reasserted the monotheistic roots of Islam.

Acknowledgments

This book originally began as a doctoral thesis for Columbia University in the early 1980s under Professor J. C. Hurewitz. Then, the focus of my research on Saudi Arabia was the transfer of the Saudi kingdom from British hegemony to the American sphere of influence from 1933 to 1953. This interest continued when I was asked in the mid-1980s to analyze the politics of the Arab Gulf states for the Moshe Dayan Center for Middle East and African Studies at Tel Aviv University. As an Israeli envoy to some of these countries in 1996–97, I continued to follow their internal developments closely. After September 11, 2001, like many others I wanted to understand how Saudi Arabia, a country that I had once studied in depth, spawned the movement that was responsible for the attacks on the United States.

It is unlikely that I would have undertaken writing this book without the active encouragement of two individuals. First, I am deeply grateful to my friend and mentor of many years, Ronald S. Lauder, who has taught me, since we met during my United Nations service, that the struggle for ideas in the world arena is not less important than the military, political, and diplomatic battles that are in today's newspaper headlines. He immediately understood the importance of getting out of the minutiae of the

311

war on terrorism and looking at the big picture. As a former U.S. envoy
with years of experience in the Pentagon, he appreciated the need to take
a new look at one of the main players in the Middle East: Saudi Arabia.

Second, Zak Gertler, who was acquainted with my background, was
the real force who inspired this project. I would not have suspended many
other activities and returned to Middle Eastern research without his personal vision of the need to inquire into the sources of the September 11
attacks. I am indebted to him for his intellectual curiosity, nearly daily
discussions, and close friendship, all of which made this project get off
the ground.

I owe a special debt to Yigal Carmon, president of the Middle East
Media Research Institute (MEMRI), who regularly coached me through
difficult Arabic texts. His input on the development of the concept of
jihad among militant fundamentalist groups was invaluable. Lieutenant
Colonel Jonathan D. Halevi, who has acquired considerable experience
in analyzing militant Islamic *(salafi)* websites in Arabic, generously shared
his knowledge in this area. Professor Menahem Milson volunteered his
time in the translation of one particularly difficult religious text.

I have particularly appreciated the critical comments and personal
encouragement of Allen Roth, who went through earlier drafts of this
book and always made incisive suggestions. His office was ready to back
up my research, along with the special efforts of Steven Schneier. Ronni
Shalit invested considerable time to assist with detailed historical research
going back to the eighteenth and nineteenth centuries. Barbara Comeau
was always ready to locate books and materials in a timely manner and
many times took the initiative to recommend new publications that I had
not seen.

In the final stages of this work, Dr. Reuven Erlich, who heads the
Intelligence and Terrorism Information Center at the Center for Special
Studies of the Israel Defense Forces (IDF), assisted me with Arabic documents captured during the IDF's Operation Defensive Shield in March
2002. Dr. Shimon Shapira willingly shared his professional insights into
Hizballah, as well as Shiite movements in Lebanon. Steven Emerson was
also generous with the access he provided me to materials collected by
the Investigative Project in Washington, D.C. Gene Kleinhendler of
Gross, Kleinhendler, Hodak, Halevy, and Greenberg law offices, who has

considerable professional experience investigating illegal manipulation of the U.S. banking system, took out considerable time to share his knowledge. Jeffrey S. Helmreich, who used to follow the terrorism issue at the United Nations, was always ready, on short notice, to respond to my research inquiries, review my writing style, and improve the flow of the manuscript—many times at very late hours.

Completing this work would have been impossible without the patience of the entire staff of the Jerusalem Center for Public Affairs, particularly its director general, Zvi Marom, who assumed an increased burden while I was away researching in archives in London and Washington. Mark Ami-El was always prepared to make key editorial comments when I needed his input. And I owe my greatest gratitude to Rachel Elrom, who not only typed the entire manuscript but also patiently updated the text on a daily basis for half a year.

Finally, after reading an earlier draft of the book, my agent, Richard Pine, worked aggressively to get the manuscript seen by several publishers and was encouraging despite this difficult process. Vered Shatil worked on the maps with great professionalism. I owe a special debt to the team at Regnery Publishing, starting with Alfred Regnery, who made comments on the original manuscript that were right on the mark. Special thanks go to editor Jed Donahue, who served as a project director for this book, and Trish Bozell, Regnery's copy editor. Both demonstrated considerable professionalism in converting tough academic writing to readable English for the wider American public.

Index

In order to assist the English-speaking reader, the spelling of Arabic terms throughout this book has been based on common usage in the United States and the United Kingdom (e.g., spellings commonly used by major newspapers and government agencies), and not on formal transliteration of literary Arabic. Additionally, Arabic terms that have been incorporated into standard American dictionaries have not been italicized.

Abbasid caliphate, 31
Abdillah, Sulaiman bin, 57, 108
Abduh, Muhammad, 54
Abdul Aziz bin Abdul Rahman Al Saud (first king of Saudi Arabia). *See* Ibn Saud
Abdul Hamit Khan II (Ottoman sultan), 22
Abdul Wahhab, Muhammad ibn, 39, 45, 57, 73, 77, 108, 110, 141, 149; background of, 17–18; bin Laden and, 6; Christianity and, 18, 19; creed of, 52; criticism of, 8; death of, 26; history of Islam and, 17; Ibn Saud and, 20–21, 22–23; Islam and, 17–21; jihad and, 22, 25, 35; *ulama* and, 119; Wahhabism and, 3; writings of, 76, 78, 91
Abdullah bin Abdul Aziz (crown prince of Saudi Arabia), 105, 116, 171; bin Laden's attitude toward, 171; Bush summit with, 203–5; as descendant of a Rashidi mother, 46; Gulf War and, 158; Israel and, 113, 196–98; makes bedside visit to Yasin, 196; Palestinian issue and, 68, 69; takes over from King Fahd, 178; Saudi National Guard and, 107; September 11 and, 192; succession and, 209; U.S. and, 208–9
Abdullah bin Hussein (emir of Transjordan, king of Jordan), 46, 48, 53, 68–69
Abdullah, Muhammad Nur, 148
Abdul Latif, Abdullah bin, 39, 44
Abdul Rahman bin Faisal (father of Ibn Saud), 36, 38, 42
Abdul Rahman, Abdullah bin, 61
Abdul Rahman, Omar, 94, 97, 172
Abu Abdul Aziz ("Barbaros"), 96, 143–44
Abu Jihad, 89–90, 223
Abu-Nasr, Donna, 210
Aburish, Said, 49
Adham, Kamal, 113
Advice and Reform Committee, 171
afdal al-qurbat, 111

Afghanistan, 10, 12, 191; Islam in, 119; jihad and, 128–29; Saudi Arabia and, 127–32, 153; Soviet Union and, 96–98, 111, 117, 127; Taliban and, 2, 3; Wahhabism and, 127–32; war on terrorism and, 186

Aflaq, Michel, 114

ahl al-kitab, 214

al-Ahram, 13

Al al-Sheikh, Abdul Aziz bin Abdullah, 183, 208

Al al-Sheikh, Abdul Rahman ibn Hasan, 35

Al al-Sheikh, Hasan bin Abdullah, 78

Al al-Sheikh, Muhammad ibn Ibrahim, 74, 87, 110; anti-West backlash and, 165; Faisal and, 79–80; Islamic University of Medina and, 90; Muslim World League and, 76; as Wahhabi leader, 80–81

Al al-Sheikh, Saleh, 185, 210

Al al-Sheikh, Tarfa, 39, 73

Alawites, 115, 158

Albania, 144, 153

Algeria, 5, 13, 129, 171

Algiers Agreement (1975), 114

Ali (son-in-law of the Prophet Muhammad), 20, 27, 48, 115

al-Ali, Hamid bin Abdul, 142

Ali, Muhammad, 33–35

Ali, Tariq, 3

Alkifah Centers, 150

Allah, 14, 63, 95, 96, 164, 187

Alomari, Abdul Aziz, 201

amaliya istishadiya, 200

America. *See* United States

American University, 126

Anas, Abdullah, 99

Anglo-Persian Oil Company, 60

ANM. *See* Arab Nationalist Movement

al-Ansar mujahideen, 138, 154

Arabia: bin Laden and, 10; Palestinian issue and, 64; Wahhabism and, 35, 41

Arabian-American Oil Company (ARAMCO), 2, 8, 60, 66, 70, 71, 84–85, 168

Arab-Israeli War (1948–49), 53. *See also* Six-Day War (1967); Yom Kippur War (1973)

Arab Nationalist Movement (ANM), 83

Arab Peace Initiative (Beirut summit), 198

Arafat, Yasser, 113, 244; attends Islamic conference in Sudan with bin Laden, 169; Fatah movement and, 82–84; financing of suicide bombings documented, 204; Muslim Brotherhood and, 90; Oslo Agreement and, 198–99; Saudi Arabia and, 83

ARAMCO. *See* Arabian-American Oil Company

al-Arifi, Muhammad bin Abdul Rahman, 221

Arizona, University of, 150, 151

Arnaout, Enaam M., 151, 152

al-Asahi, Arafat, 218

ashura, 32, 109

al-Assad, Hafez, 90, 115, 158

Assirat al-Mustaqeem, 149–50

Associated Press, 210

Atlanta, Ga., 150

Atta, Muhammad, 14

al-Auda, Salman, 163–65, 173

awqaf, 176

Azerbaijan, 136, 139, 141, 142, 154

al-Azhar, 24, 50, 127

al-Azmeh, Aziz, 13

Azzam, Abdullah, 130; influence of, 143; jihad and, 94–99, 110, 111; radical writings of, 111; Wahhabism and, 128, 129

Azzam, Fayiz, 99

Azzam, Ibrahim, 99

Azzam, Muhammad, 99

Baath party, 84, 114–15

Badawi, Abdullah Ahmad, 210

Badía y Leblich, Domingo, 23
Baer, Robert, 135, 182
Baghdad, Iraq, 26
Bahrain, 20, 44, 58; oil revenues and, 61; Shiites in, 120; Wahhabi wars and, 26
Bahz, Abu, 63
Bakhar, Ahmed, 202, 246
al-Bakri, Mukhtar, 183
Balfour Declaration (1917), 53
Bali, Indonesia, 5
Balkans, 24, 31, 143–47, 155; charities and, 144; Ottoman Empire and, 43–44; Saudi Arabia and, 153; Saudi charities in, 144–46; Sufi Islam and, 11; Wahhabism in, 143–47
Ball, George, 82
Bamiyan Valley, Afghanistan, 12
Bandar bin Sultan (Saudi ambassador to the United States), 2, 178, 194, 203
Bangladesh, 3
al-Banna, Hasan, 55, 89, 91, 141
Barayev, Arbi, 138–39
Barayev, Movsar, 139
"Barbaros." *See* Abu Abdul Aziz
Barelwi, Said Ahmad, 35
al-Barum, Ali Muhammad, 174, 230–31
Bashir, Omar, 181
Bashkortostan, 142
Basra, Iraq, 18
Bassayev, Shamil, 138, 139
Batrafi, Khaled Muhammad, 103
Batterjee, Adel, 152
Bayazid, Muhammad, 151–52
al-Bayoumi, Omar, 2
Baz, Abdul Aziz bin, 78, 102, 126; anti-West backlash and, 161, 164–65; Baath party and, 115; Council of Senior Ulama and, 80, 132; death of, 183; Gulf War and, 158; influence of, 107; Islamic University of Medina and, 90; Israel and, 195–96; jihad and, 95,

136; Muslim World League and, 119; Palestinian terrorism and, 143; religious views of, 110–11
Benevolence International Foundation, 138, 154
Benevolentia charity, 146
Bevin, Ernest, 69
Bey, Ali, 23, 27
Bhutto, Zulfikar Ali, 116
bilad al-sham (Greater Syria), 53
bin Baz, Abdul Aziz. *See* Baz, Abdul Aziz bin
bin Laden, Muhammad. *See* Laden, Muhammad bin.
bin Laden, Osama. *See* Laden, Osama bin
Black September group, 84
Blair, Tony, 187
Book of Tawhid (ibn Abdul Wahhab), 19, 25, 147
Bosnia, 96, 143–47
Boston, Mass., 150
Boston Globe, 162
Bounouar, Boujema, 99
Brandt, Hajj Salih, 4
Britain. *See* Great Britain
British-Hijazi treaty, 64
British Isles, 33
Brooklyn, N.Y., 150
Buinaksk, 140
Bunker Hunt Oil Company, 84
Burckhardt, Jean Louis, 33
Burhanuddin Rabani, 128
Burson-Marteller, 193
Burton, Sir Richard, 37
Bush, George H. W., 9, 158
Bush, George W., 186, 187, 201; Abdullah summit with, 203–5; war on terrorism and, 213

Cairo-Amman Bank, 203
California, 147
California-Arabian Standard Oil Company (CASOC), 60
California–Santa Barbara, University of, 126

Camp David Summit (2000), 199
Cape Town, South Africa, 42
Carter, Jimmy, 9, 113, 117–18
CASOC. *See* California-Arabian
    Standard Oil Company
Castle, W. R., Jr., 61
Catholic Church, 174, 233
CDLR. *See* Committee for the
    Defense of Legitimate Rights
CENTO. *See* Central Treaty
    Organization
Central America, 121
Central Intelligence Agency (CIA), 97
Central Treaty Organization
    (CENTO), 75
Charfi, Mohamed, 3
charity organizations: in Balkans,
    144–46; Russia and, 142; in Soviet
    Union, 135; terrorism and, 126–27,
    138, 153–55, 199–203, 211–12;
    Wahhabism and, 151–52, 153–54
Chase Manhattan Bank, 201, 241
Chechnya, 10, 154; Russia's war
    against, 138–41; Wahhabism and,
    4, 5, 138–41
Cheney, Richard, 158
Chevron, 85
Chicago, Ill., 150
Childs, J. Rives, 66–67, 71
China, 24, 122
Christianity: ibn Abdul Wahhab and,
    18, 19; Islam and, 12–14, 101–3,
    177; Koran and, 66; Prophet
    Muhammad and, 63; Saudi Arabia
    and, 93–94; *ulama* and, 108; Wah-
    habism and, 25, 66, 72, 101–3, 111
Christopher, Warren, 178
Churchill, Winston, 60, 65
CIA. *See* Central Intelligence Agency
CIS. *See* Commonwealth of Inde-
    pendent States
Clinton, Bill, 168, 178, 179, 205
CNN, 10
Cold War, 71, 75, 117, 160; Saudi
    Arabia and, 2, 137
Cole, USS, 182, 220

Colorado, 106
Committee for Commanding Good
    and Forbidding Evil, 78
Committee for the Defense of Legiti-
    mate Rights (CDLR), 165–66
Commonwealth of Independent
    States (CIS), 141
Communism, 66, 122, 145
Congress of the Islamic World, 51
Constantinople, Turkey, 31
Contras, 121
Council of Senior Ulama, 80, 132,
    165, 176
Council on Foreign Relations, 11,
    196–97
Cox, Sir Percy, 44, 47
Cuba, 146
Curzon, Lord, 42, 43

Dagestan, 5, 139–42, 154
Dahlan, Ahmad bin Zayani, 38
Damascus University, 94
Dar al-Harb, 92
Dar al-Islam, 92
Dar-ul-Uloom Haqqania, 131
Davenny, Joan, 200
da'wa, 22, 111, 164, 227
al-da'wa ila al-tawhid, 21
Dayton Peace Accords, 143, 227
"Declaration of War Against Ameri-
    can Occupying the Land of the
    Two Holy Places" (bin Laden),
    172, 180
*Defending the Land of the Muslims Is
    Each Man's Most Important Duty*
    (Azzam), 95
Defense Policy Board, 2
Delta, 131
Detroit, Mich., 149
Dhahran, Saudi Arabia, 3, 158
Dickson, Harold R. P., 44
*Difference Between the Shi'ites and the
    Majority of Muslim Scholars*, 152
Diriyah, Saudi Arabia, 20, 33, 34;
    mosque in, 27
Doughty, Charles M., 39

Dual Containment policy, 168, 178
Duke University, 126

Eastern and General Syndicate, 60–61
Eddy, William A., 63
education, 11, 77–79, 122, 147, 208
Egypt, 10, 33, 42, 49; involvement of
    Egyptians in al-Qaeda, 129;
    Islamic fundamentalism in, 55;
    Israel and, 86–87, 112–14, 195;
    Muslim Brotherhood and, 55–56,
    77, 89–91; Muslim invasion of,
    12; Nasser and, 74–75; Palestinian
    issue and, 64; Sadat and, 112–13;
    Saudi Arabia and, 86–87; Wah-
    habi wars and, 33–34
Egyptian Islamic Jihad, 24, 144, 169
Eiffel Tower, 171
El Fadl, Khaled Abou, 4
"Emir of Jihad." *See* Azzam, Abdullah
End of History (al-Auda), 163
England. *See* Great Britain
Ethiopia, 181
Euphrates River, 47

*Facts That the Muslim Must Know
    About Christianity and Missionary
    Activity*, 101–2, 229
Fahd bin Abdul Aziz (fifth king of
    Saudi Arabia), 74, 77, 105, 116,
    178, 209; anti-West backlash and,
    161–62, 165; educational system
    of, 122; Egypt and Israel and,
    112–14; Gulf War and, 158–59;
    Iran and, 119, 120; reputation of,
    121, 125–26; Saudi defense policy
    and, 171; Saudi religious influ-
    ence and, 125; *ulama* and, 109,
    122–23; U.S. and, 116, 121; Wah-
    habism and, 125–26
Faisal bin Abdul Aziz (third king of
    Saudi Arabia), 8, 42, 46, 53, 73,
    79, 113, 129; assassination of,
    105–6; Israel and, 81–82; jihad
    and, 82; Muslim World League
    and, 94, 119; Nasser and, 75–76,

82, 115; oil and, 84–86; Palestin-
    ian issue and, 64, 69; pan-Islam
    and, 93; *ulama* and, 74, 77–79;
    U.S. and, 71; Wahhabism and
    Ottoman Empire and, 35–39
Faisal-Weizmann agreement, 64
"Fall of States" (al-Auda), 163
Farouk (king of Egypt), 74
Fatah movement, 82–84, 90, 223
al-Fawzan, Saleh, 176, 208
FBI. *See* Federal Bureau of Inves-
    tigation
Federal Bureau of Investigation
    (FBI), 178, 179, 192
Federal Security Service (FSB), 141,
    154
First World War, 10, 24, 45–46, 64
FIS. *See* Front Islamique du Salut;
    Islamic Salvation Front
fitna, 25, 180
Fitnatu-l-Wahhabiyyah ("The Wah-
    habi Insurrections"), 38
Fleischer, Ari, 199–200
*Foundations of the Legality of the
    Destruction That Befell America*,
    187, 236–37
Fox News Sunday, 201
France, 17, 24, 33, 121
France Soir, 130
Franks, Tommy, 117
"Free Officers" coup, 74
French Riviera, 121, 125
Friedman, Thomas, 131, 194–95,
    198, 210
Front Islamique du Salut (FIS), 169
FSB. *See* Federal Security Service
Fus Quasitum, 136

Ganon, Dick, 181
Gaza-Jericho Agreement, 168
GCC. *See* Gulf Cooperation Council
General Islamic Conference, 120
General Presidency for the Direc-
    torate of Islamic Legal Rulings,
    Islamic Propagation, and Guid-
    ance, 78, 102, 110, 190, 229

Georgia, 141
Germany, 42–43
Ghaith, Sulaiman Abu, 13
al-Ghamadi, Marzuq Salem, 175
al-Ghannush, Rashid, 169
al-Ghazawi, Wajdi Hamzeh, 190–91, 234–35
Gibb, Sir Hamilton, 24
Giuliani, Rudy, 193
Grafftey-Smith, Laurence, 54
Grand Mosque, 129; struggle over, 106–11
Great Book of Fatwas, 188
Great Britain, 6; Ibn Saud and, 57–58, 108; Ikhwan movement and, 48; India and, 33, 57; Middle East and, 42, 42–43, 45–46, 117; oil and, 59–62, 84; Ottoman Empire and, 58; Palestinian issue and, 66–70; Saudi Arabia and, 57–58, 70; Saudi-Hashemite war and, 52–53; Wahhabism and, 42, 54
Great Depression, 59
"Great Revolt" of 1936, 64
Greece, 31
Groupe Islamique Armé (GIA), 13, 171
Guantanamo Bay, Cuba, 146
Gulf Cooperation Council (GCC), 118–19, 167–68, 195
Gulf War: Iraq and, 2, 157–59; jihad and, 155, 158; Kuwait and, 157–59; Saudi Arabia and, 2, 118, 157–61; U.S. and, 157–61; Wahhabism and, 157–61
Gunaratna, Rohan, 11

Habash, George, 83
al-Haddad, Abdullah bin Matruck, 191
Haddad, Wadi, 83
hadith, 22, 99
el-Hage, Wadih, 97, 150–51, 201
Haifa bint Faisal, 2
Haig, Alexander, 113

Hail (Rashidi capital in northern Arabia), 46
hajj, 7, 32
Halevy, Efraim, 205
Hama massacres (1982), 115
Hamad, Abdel Rahman, 200, 242
Hamas (Islamic Resistance Movement): Israel and, 198–99; Saudi backing of, 126–27, 153, 169; suicide missions and, 142, 188, 196; *ulama* and, 143; Wahhabism and, 5
Hamza, Fuad, 45
Hanafi School of Islamic Law, 22, 131
Hanbali School of Islamic Law, 18, 22, 131
Hanjour, Hani, 151
Hanud, Mahmud Abu, 200
haram, 166–67
al-Haramain, 126, 141; blocking of bank accounts of, 144; Bosnia and, 144; as conduit for funding to Chechen forces, 141; as conduit for funding to al-Qaeda in Southeast Asia, 154; Saudi royal family's support for, 126; Somali office of, 144, 154; Wahhabi activism and, 153, 154
haramstan, 167
al-Harbi, Khaled, 191
al-Harkan, Muhammad Ali, 76, 77
Harvard University, 8, 109, 126
al-Hasa, Saudi Arabia, 17, 26, 43–44
Hasan bin Ali, 20
Hashemites: jihad and, 108; Palestinian issue and, 64–65, 69–70
Hatem, Sahr Muhammad, 3–4
hatred: ideology of, 3–4, 6, 7; mass murder and, 1; September 11 and, 220; teaching, 246; terrorism and, 1, 6–7, 214–28; violence and, 14–15
al-Hattlan, Sulaiman, 109
al-Hawali, Safar, 164–65, 173; anti-West backlash and, 162–63
Hawatmeh, Naif, 83

Hawley, Donald, 28
Hazaras, 133
al-Hayat, 103, 189
Hekmatyar, Gulbuddin, 128, 130, 135, 169
Helsinki Final Act (1975), 225–26
Hezb-e-Islami, 128
Hijaz, 31
hijra, 140. *See also hujar*
Hizballah: formation of, 169–70; Khobar Towers bombing and, 180; terrorism and, 178–79
Hizballah al-Khalij, 178
hizb al-shaitan (the party of Satan), 115
Hizb ut-Tahrir (HT), 136
Holbrooke, Richard, 227
Holy Land Foundation for Relief and Development, 152, 201
Hoover, Herbert, 61
Howard University, 126
HT. *See* Hizb ut-Tahrir
al-Hudaifi, Abdul Rahman, 177
hudna, 195
hujar, 44, 45. *See also hijra*
Hull, Cordell, 61
Humaid, Abdullah bin Muhammad bin, 8
Hungary, 31
al-Huquq, 172
Hussein bin Ali (grandson of the Prophet Muhammad), 20, 26, 32
Hussein bin Ali (sharif of Mecca and king of Hijaz), 46, 47, 53, 64
Hussein bin Talal (king of Jordan), 83, 109, 208
Hussein, Saddam, 114; Gulf War and, 157–58; Kuwait and, 9; Saudi support for, 130–31; Sunni Islam and, 115
al-Husseini, Hajj Amin, 64

IANA. *See* Islamic Assembly of North America
ibn Abdul Wahhab, Muhammad. *See* Abdul Wahhab, Muhammad ibn

Ibn Saud (first king of Saudi Arabia), 91; Britain and, 57–58, 108; British power and, 42; death of, 26, 27; ibn Abdul Wahhab and, 20-23; Ikhwan armies of, 13; Ikhwan movement and, 44–47, 49–50; Islam and, 58; jihad and, 48; *mutawain* and, 78; oil and money and, 59–63; Ottoman Empire and, 42–44; Palestinian issue and, 63–68; Rashidis and, 105; Saudi-Hashemite war and, 47–49, 52; *ulama* and, 62–63; U.S. and, 2, 70–72; Wahhabism and, 26, 39, 49–52
Ibn Taymiyya, 18, 76, 91, 92, 95
Ibrahim, Izzat, 198, 208
Ibrahim, Youssef M., 3
Idris (king of Libya), 40, 84
IIASA. *See* Institute of Islamic and Arabic Sciences in America
IIRO. *See* International Islamic Relief Organization
Ikhwan al-Muslimun. *See* Muslim Brotherhood
Ikhwan movement, 13, 106; Britain and, 48; Ibn Saud and, 49–50; Saudi Arabia and, 41–56; Wahhabism and, 45, 46–47, 49–50, 107–8
Illinois, University of, 147
Imam Muhammad bin Saud University, 79, 150, 152, 163
"imperial preference," 60
India, 42; Britain and, 33, 57; Islam and, 17, 24
Indonesia, 5
Institute of Islamic and Arabic Sciences in America (IIASA), 152
International Islamic Relief Organization (IIRO), 243; Balkans and, 144; as branch of Saudi government, 218, 243; employs brother of al-Zawahiri in Albania, 144; Kenyan government blacklists, 153; Pankisi Gorge and, 142;

International Islamic Relief Organization (IIRO) *(continued)*
terrorism and, 202; Wahhabism and, 126, 152, 153–54
International Islamic University, 97
International Relief Organization (IRO), 152
International Religious Freedom Report, 215
international terrorism. *See* terrorism
Inter-Service-Intelligence (ISI), 97
IPC. *See* Iraq Petroleum Company
Iran, 20; fall of shah of, 117–19; Islamic diplomacy and, 119; Kuwait and, 118; Pakistan and, 120; Saudi Arabia and, 119–21; Shiite Islam and, 109, 129; Soviet Union and, 117
Iranian revolution (1979), 9
Iran-Iraq war, 112–16
Iraq, 20, 46, 49; bin Laden and, 10; Gulf War and, 2, 157–59; Hashemite territory of, 108; ibn Abdul Wahhab and, 18; Ikhwan movement and, 50; Mongol invasions of, 91; Palestinian issue and, 64, 65; al-Qaeda in, 129; Shiite Islam in, 12; threat to Kuwait posed by, 167–68; Wahhabi wars and, 29; weapons inspections and, 167
Iraq Petroleum Company (IPC), 60, 62, 84
ISI. *See* Inter-Service-Intelligence
Islam: in Afghanistan, 119; Christianity and, 12–14, 101–3, 177; history of, 17–21; Ibn Saud and, 58; international interests of, 119; Jews and, 12–14; jihad and, 25, 92–93; mainstream, 3, 4, 22; military expansion of, 18; monotheism of, 127; Muslim World League and, 76; Ottoman Empire and, 18, 19; pillars of, 7, 22; Prophet Muhammad and, 19; al-Qaeda and, 6; radical, 3, 5; spread of, 17; terrorism and, 5; West and, 162.

See also Shiite Islam; Sunni Islam; Wahhabism
Islamic Assembly of North America (IANA), 149
Islamic Benevolence Committee, 146, 151–52
Islamic Center of Tucson, 151
Islamic Charity–Hebron, 202
Islamic Jihad: funding for, 202–3; Israel and, 198–99; suicide bombers from, 142
Islamic Renaissance Party, 135
Islamic Salvation Front (FIS), 5
Islamic Society of North America (ISNA), 148
Islamic Supreme Council of America, 4
Ismail, Muhammad Uthman, 90
ISNA. *See* Islamic Society of North America
Israel: bin Laden and, 10; Egypt and, 86–87, 112–14, 195; as "The Little Satan," 10; normalization and, 194–98; Oslo Agreement and, 148, 198–99; Palestinian issue and, 9–11, 68; PLO and, 98; Saudi Arabia and, 84, 112–14, 193–98; U.S. and, 84–85, 193–94
Istanbul, Turkey, 31

Jabal Shammar, Arabia, 46
Jabarin, Sufian, 200–201
Jacquard, Roland, 11
jahilia, 4, 92, 164
Jakarta, Indonesia, 5
Jamaat-i-Islami, 116, 120, 128, 131
Jamaat Ulama Islami (JUI), 131
Jamal, Sheikh, 38
al-Jamiya al-Islamiya (Islamic Society), 202
al-Jarbu, Abdul Aziz bin Salih, 6, 187–88, 237
al-Jazira, 188
Jeddah, Saudi Arabia, 17, 58
Jersey City, N.J., 150
Jerusalem, 10, 18, 82, 112, 173

Jews: as infidels, 184; Islam and, 12–14; Muslim Brotherhood and, 56; Palestinian issue and, 65–66, 69; Wahhabism and, 66, 103
Jibrin, Abdullah bin Abdul Rahman, 190
jihad: Afghanistan and, 128–29; financial, 111; funding of, 154–55; Gulf War and, 155, 158; Hashemites and, 108; ibn Abdul Wahhab and, 22, 35; Ibn Saud and, 48; infidels and, 13; Islam and, 25, 92–93; Islamic fundamentalism and, 95–99; Koran and, 24, 26; *kufar* and, 13; martyrdom and, 17, 26, 172–73; meaning of, 7; Ottoman Empire and, 24; relationship to *da'wa* of, 111; revival of, 17; Saudi Arabia and, 172; Shiite Islam and, 25; Sunni Islam and, 24–25, 111; Wahhabism and, 7–8, 17, 24–26, 40, 108, 110–11, 150, 215–16; West and, 155
jihad bi-l-maal, 111
jihad bi-l-sayf, 111
jizya, 24, 57
John Paul II (pope), 174, 233
Johns Hopkins University, 8, 126
Johnson, Lyndon B., 81
Jordan, 46, 49, 129
Jordan, University of, 94
Jubair, Muhammad bin, 132
al-Jubeir, Adel, 194, 200
Judaism: veneration of Jerusalem and, 18; Wahhabism and, 25, 111
JUI. *See* Jamaat Ulama Islami
Julaidan, Wael Hamza, 97, 129, 150, 224

Kabardino-Balkaria, 141
Kabbani, Hisham, 4
Kabul, Afghanistan, 130
al-Kadi, Abdul Muhsin, 174
Karachay-Cherkessia, 141
Karimov, Islam, 135
Kashmir, 96, 155

Kazakhstan, 136
Kazimi, Abdul Mutalib, 105
Kennedy, John F., 193
Kennedy, Robert F., 84
Kenya, 118, 151, 154, 182
Kerbala, Iraq, 12, 26–27
Khalid bin Abdul Aziz (fourth king of Saudi Arabia), 74, 105, 108, 109, 112, 116
Khalifa, Muhammad Abdurrahman, 97
Khalifa, Muhammad Jamal, 153
Khamenehi, Ali, 120
kharaj, 24
Kharajites, 7, 25, 190
Khatami, Muhammad, 178
al-Khattab, Umar bin, 19, 138, 142, 154, 214
al-Khattab, Zayd bin, 19
Khobar Towers bombing, 178–80
Khomeini, Ayatollah, 112, 114, 120, 162
King Abdul Aziz University, 90, 92, 94, 143
"Kingdom in the Middle: Saudi Arabia's Double Game" (Gause), 11
King Fahd Defense Academy, 221
King Fahd University, 150
King Khalid Military City, 117
King Khalid University, 162
King Saud University, 149
Kirgizia, 136
Kirienco, Sergei, 142
Kissinger, Henry, 85
Koran, 19, 22, 92, 102, 110, 136; Christianity and, 66, 111; Jews and, 111; jihad and, 24, 26; study centers of, 129
Kosovapress News Agency, 146
Kosovo, 145
Kosovo Liberation Army, 146
kufar (infidels), 13, 57, 99, 108
kufiya, 45
kufr (blasphemy), 22, 96
Ku Klux Klan, 14, 219
Kurdish revolt, 114

Kuwait, 9, 42, 49, 58; Gulf War and, 157–59; Iran and, 118; Shiites in, 120; Wahhabi wars and, 26
Kyrgyzstan, 134

Laden, Muhammad bin, 129
Laden, Osama bin, 51, 94, 96, 97, 103, 138; anti-Americanism of, 170–76; Hamas and, 196; hatred and, 3, 15; Hizballah and, 169–70; ibn Abdul Wahhab and, 6; jihad and, 110, 130; al-Qaeda and, 129, 151–52; Saudi Arabia and, 1–2, 171–72, 180–83; Saudi clerics and, 169–76; September 11 and, 185–86, 191, 192–93; Taliban and, 132–33; U.S. and, 12, 180–83, 184; Wahhabism and, 3, 5–7, 12, 128, 129, 132–33, 170. *See also* al-Qaeda
Lahidan, Salih ibn Muhammad ibn, 107
Lake, Anthony, 178
Lansdowne, Lord, 42
League of Nations, 53, 64, 220
Lebanon, 53, 112
Lewis, Bernard, 24, 219
Libya, 40, 113, 121; involvement of Libyans in al-Qaeda, 129; terrorism and, 2; U.S. and, 118
Lovett, Robert, 67

madhahib, 22
madrasa, 3, 131
Madrid Peace Conference (1981), 195
Magomedov, Bagauddin, 140–41
mahdi, 20, 106
Mahmud, Abu, 151
Mahmud II, 34
Maktab Khadamat al-Mujahideen, 97, 128, 129
Malaki School of Islamic Law, 22
al-Manar, 54
martyrdom: jihad and, 17, 26, 172–73; suicide missions and, 7

Marzouk, Mousa Abu, 172
al-Masari, Abdullah, 165–66
al-Masari, Muhammad, 165–66
Mashal, Khaled, 224, 247
Maskhadov, Aslan, 139
mass murder: hatred and, 1; Wahhabism and, 13
Massoud, Ahmed Shah, 128
Mawdudi, Mawlana Abu al-Ala, 90, 92, 100, 128, 141, 147, 149
mawlid al-nabi, 49
Mazen, Abu, 202, 244
McGhee, George, 70
McGill University, 93
McVeigh, Timothy, 192
Mecca, Saudi Arabia, 7, 17, 26, 27, 32, 106
Medina, Saudi Arabia, 17, 18, 27, 32, 106
Medina, Islamic University of, 77, 80, 90, 101, 107, 110, 147, 148, 149
Melhem, Hisham, 10
Mesopotamia, 47
Methods of the Ideological Invasion of the Islamic World, 101
Michigan, 149
Middle East: Britain and, 42–43, 45–46, 117; Ikhwan movement and, 47; Palestinian issue and, 9–11; Saudi-Hashemite war and, 52; U.S. and, 61
al-Midhar, Khaled, 182
Midhat Pasha, 37
Ministry of Islamic Affairs and Endowments, 152
Mogadishu, Somalia, 170
al-Mohsen, Mohsen, 150
Montazeri, Ayatollah, 120
Morocco, 83
Moussaoui, Zacarias, 3
MSA. *See* Muslim Student Association
Mubarak, Sheikh, 43, 181
Mughniyeh, Imad, 169–70, 177–78
Muhammad, Ibrahim bin, 77
Muhammad, Prophet, 15, 37, 106, 109; Christianity and, 63; Islam

and, 17, 19; jihad and, 25; military conquests of, 17, 31; prayer and, 22
Muhammad, Sayed Shari, 40
mujahideen, 119, 121
al-Munajjid, Muhammad Saleh, 234–35
Murphy, Caryle, 9
Musaid, Faisal ibn, 105–6
Musaid, Khaled ibn, 105
Musaid, Sharif Ghalib ibn, 26
al-Mushary, Bandar, 150
mushrikun (polytheists), 13, 19, 99, 111
Muslim Brotherhood (Ikhwan al-Muslimun), 97, 128; Assad and, 115; credo of, 55; education and, 78; Egypt and, 55–56, 77, 89–91; Saudi Arabia and, 89–92; spread of Wahhabism and, 126, 128; strategy of, 55–56; universities and, 94, 110; Wahhabism and, 91–92, 100–101, 147
Muslim Student Association (MSA), 147, 148, 150
Muslim World League, 97; as branch of Saudi government, 218, 243; Constituent Council of, 76, 92, 119; establishment of, 76; financing of, 76; influence of, 99–100; Jamaat-i-Islami and, 116; Jurisprudence Committee of, 176; Russian Federation and, 139; Shiite Islam and, 120–21; in Soviet Union, 135; Wahhabism and, 74–77, 87, 119, 126, 128, 129, 148, 149, 153
Muslim World News, 136
mutawain (religious police), 78, 122
Mutuhar, Sayyid Hassan, 135–36
muwahhidun, 8

al-Nabawi, Masjid, 177
al-Nabhani, Sheikh, 136
al-Nahda party, 169
Naif bin Abdul Aziz (Saudi minister of interior), 171, 179, 185, 209

Najaf, Iraq, 27
Najd, 17, 18, 44, 57
Namangani, Juma, 135
Napoleon, 10, 33, 42
al-Nashiri, Abdul Rahim, 182
Nasif, Abdullah Umar, 76, 99
Nasser, Gamal Abdel: Arab nationalist movement and, 74, 75; Faisal and, 75–76, 82, 115; Muslim Brotherhood and, 91; Muslim World League and, 119; PLO and, 83; rise to power of, 74–75
NATO. *See* North Atlantic Treaty Organization
Nelson, Horatio, 33
New York Times, 3, 14, 131, 149, 188, 192, 194, 196, 197
Niazi, Mullah, 133
Nimeiri, Jafar, 94
normalization, 194–98
North American Islamic Trust (NAIT), 148–49
North Atlantic Treaty Organization (NATO), 75
Northern Alliance, 133, 134
Northern Caucasus, 4, 137
Nosair, El-Sayyid, 12
Nuri, Abdullah, 135
Nuqrashi Pasha, 89
Nyang, Sulayman, 147, 148

al-Obaid, Abdullah bin Salah, 139
Obaid, Nawaf E., 8
Observer, 125
oil: Faisal and, 84–86; fall of shah of Iran and, 119; money and, 59–63; U.S. and, 118, 220–21
Oklahoma, 65, 98
Oman, 26, 29, 44, 118
Omar, Mullah, 132, 133
O'Neill, Paul H., 144
"open door," 60, 220
Operation Defensive Shield, 199
Opposite Direction, 191
Organization of the Islamic Conference, 83, 210

Oslo Agreement, 148, 168, 198
Ottoman Empire, 145; Britain and, 58; extent of, 31; fall of, 10; Hanafi Islam and, 22; Ibn Saud and, 42–44; Islam and, 18, 19; jihad and, 24; Shiite Islam and, 32; Sunni Islam and, 32; Wahhabism and, 4, 29, 31–40, 41

Padri movement, 35
Pakistan, 3, 97, 115; Iran and, 120; Saudi Arabia and, 115–16, 132; Taliban and, 133, 134; Wahhabism and, 3
Palestine Liberation Organization (PLO): Black September group of, 84; Egypt and Israel and, 113–14; Fatah movement and, 83; Israel and, 98; Oslo Agreement and, 148
Palestinian Islamic Jihad, 169, 170. *See also* Islamic Jihad
Palestinian issue: Britain and, 66–70; Hashemites and, 64–65, 69–70; Ibn Saud and, 63–68; Jews and, 65–66, 69; Saudi Arabia and, 63–70; terrorism and, 9–11; U.S. and, 10, 66
Palestinian Preventive Security, 202–3
Palgrave, William, 36
Palmerston, Lord, 35
Pankisi Gorge, 141–42, 153–54
Pasha, Ayyub Sabri, 22–23
Pasqua, Charles, 179
Peel Commission Report (1937), 65
Pentagon, 2
perestroika, 134
Persia, 18, 31
Peshawar, Pakistan, 127, 129
PFLP. *See* Popular Front for the Liberation of Palestine
Philby, H. St. John, 61
Philippines, 119, 153, 191
Philips, Bilal, 149
Pittsburgh, Pa., 150

PLO. *See* Palestine Liberation Organization
polytheism. *See shirk*
Popular Arab and Islamic Conference, 169
Popular Front for the Liberation of Palestine (PFLP), 83
Powell, Colin, 197, 201, 211
Putin, Vladimir, 142

Qabus, Sultan, 195
Qaddafi, Muammar, 40, 84
al-Qaeda: bin Laden and, 129, 151–52; evolution of, 129; hatred and violence and, 14–15; Maktab Khadamat al-Mujahideen and, 129; mass murder and, 13; Saudi Arabia and, 1–2, 181–82; September 11 and, 186; training manual for, 6; Wahhabism and, 4. *See also* Laden, Osama bin; terrorism
al-Qahtani, Muhammad ibn Abdullah, 106–7
Qaradhawi, Yusuf, 215
Qari, Abdul Aziz, 230–31
Qatar, 44, 206
Qawasim tribe, 28
al-Qazwini, Imam Hasan, 149
Qorvis Communications, 193
al-Quds al-Arabi, 173
al-Quds Intifada, 200
Quincy, USS, 65
Quraish tribe, 32
Qutb, Muhammad, 92–93, 94–95, 100
Qutb, Sayyid, 92–93, 94, 100, 141, 147, 149

Rabin, Yitzhak, 195
RAF. *See* Royal Air Force
Rafsanjani, Hashemi, 120, 177
Rahman, Mawlana Fazlur
Rahman, Omar Abdul, 12
al-Rajhi, Abdul Aziz, 201–2
al-Rajhi Banking and Investment Corporation, 201–2, 241

Ramadan, 13
RAND Corporation, 2
Rashid, Ahmed, 135
Rashid, Mohammed ibn, 39, 208
Rashidis, 43
Rashidun caliphate, 31
Razik, Ibn, 26
Reagan, Ronald, 118
Red Cross, 133
Rentz, George, 8
Revolutionary Command Council, 198
Rida, Muhammad Rashid, 54–55, 91
Riyadh, Saudi Arabia, 3
Roosevelt, Franklin D., 61, 64–65
Rousseau, J., 27
Roy, Olivier, 101
Royal Air Force (RAF), 47
Russian Federation, 5, 24; charity organizations and, 142; fragmentation of, 137; Wahhabism and, 4, 137–43. *See also* Soviet Union
Rutter, Eldon, 49

SAAR Foundation, 201, 241
Sadat, Anwar, 86, 87; assassination of, 94; Egypt and Israel and, 112–13; Muslim Brotherhood and, 91
al-Sadlan, Saleh, 188
as-Safir, 10, 91
saints, veneration of, 18, 28
al-salaf al-salihin, 19, 91
salafi, 19, 91, 131,
Saleh, Ali Abdullah, 182
salibi (crusader), 93
al-salibiyah (crusaderism), 93
Salim, Mamduh, 151
Salman bin Abdul Aziz (governor of Riyadh), 144, 146, 202
al-Sanusi, Sayyid Muhammad Ali, 40
Sanusiyyah, 40
Saud bin Abdul Aziz (second king of Saudi Arabia), 26, 27, 38, 116; ousting of, 105–6; religious reputation of, 125; *ulama* and, 73–74; Wahhabism and, 29, 33, 72

Saud al-Faisal (Saudi minister of foreign affairs), 113, 209
Saudi Arabia: Afghanistan and, 127–32, 153; Balkans and, 153; Britain and, 57–58, 70; Cold War and, 2, 137; educational system of, 11, 77–79, 122, 147, 208; Egypt and, 86–87; Gulf War and, 2, 118, 157–61; Ikhwan movement and, 41–56; Iran and, 119–21; Iran-Iraq war and, 112–16; Islam and, 107; Israel and, 84, 112–14, 193–98; jihad and, 172; Muslim Brotherhood and, 89–92; oil and money and, 59–63, 84–87; Pakistan and, 115–16, 132; Palestinian issue and, 63–70; al-Qaeda and, 129, 181–82; September 11 and, 1–6, 183, 185–93, 236–39; Taliban and, 2, 134, 153; terrorism and, 176–80, 198–203, 222–25, 229–51; U.S. and, 2, 70–72, 116–19, 121–22, 160–61, 203–6; al-Utaibi rebellion and, 106–11; Wahhabism and, 2–15, 17–21, 58, 73–87, 105–23, 125–26, 205–10, 215; West and, 183
Saudi Committee for Aid to the al-Quds Intifada, 202, 242
Saudi-Hashemite war, 47–49, 52–53
Saudi High Commission for Aid to Bosnia, 146, 154
Saudi National Guard, 107
Saudi Red Crescent Society, 150
Sayyaf, Abdul Rasul, 127, 128
Schwartz, Stephen, 11
Schwarzkopf, Norman, 117, 158
Scottsdale, Az., 151
SEATO. *See* Southeast Asia Treaty Organization
Second World War, 60, 65, 117
al-Sediry, Tawfiq, 210
al-Seif, Abu Omar Muhammad, 141
Selim I (Ottoman sultan), 32
Selim III (Ottoman sultan), 29

September 11: bin Laden and, 185–86, 191–93; hatred and, 220; hijackers of, 2, 3; al-Qaeda and, 186; roots of terrorism and, 1; Saudi Arabia and, 1–6, 183, 185–93, 236–39; Wahhabism and, 6–7

Shafii School of Islamic Law, 22

shah, fall of, 112–16

Shah, Nadir, 18

shahada, 23

shahid (martyr), 7

al-shaitan, 25

Shakespeare, William, 43

Shammar tribe, 47

Sharon, Ariel, 86

al-Sharq al-Awsat, 207

Shiite Islam, 18, 54; Alawites and, 115; in Iran, 109, 129; in Iraq, 12; jihad and, 25; *mahdi* and, 106; *mushrikun* and, 13; Ottoman Empire and, 32; polytheism and, 13; Sunni vs., 19–20, 115, 133–34; Taliban and, 133; Wahhabism and, 12, 13, 112, 119–20, 133–34, 152

al-Shikaki, Fathi, 169

shirk (polytheism), 19, 43, 96, 100, 153, 165

al-Shuaibi, Hamud bin Uqla, 142, 191, 236, 237; September 11 and, 186–90

Siami, Adnan Ahmad, 174, 232–33

Sibila, battle of, 107

Sicily, 24

Siddiqi, Muzammil H., 148

Siegman, Henry, 196–97

Sinai II Agreement (1975), 112

Singapore, 42

Sirhan, Sirhan, 84

Six-Day War (1967), 81, 82, 84, 86, 196. *See also* Arab-Israeli War (1948–49); Yom Kippur War (1973)

al-Siyasah, 185

slavery, 61, 72, 87

Smith, Wilfred Cantwell, 93–94

SOCAL. *See* Standard Oil of California

Solana, Javier, 197

Somalia, 96, 118, 144, 154, 170

South Africa, 42

Southeast Asia Treaty Organization (SEATO), 75

Southern California, University of, 147

Soviet Union: Afghanistan and, 96–98, 111, 117, 127; collapse of, 134; containment of, 160; Iran and, 117; Muslim World League in, 135; Saudi charities and, 135; Wahhabism in, 134–37. *See also* Russian Federation

Spain, 24, 98, 121

Standard Oil of California (SOCAL), 59–60, 61, 62, 220

Standard Oil of New Jersey (Esso/Exxon), 60

Standard Oil of New York (Mobil), 60

Standing Committee on Islamic Legal Rulings, 80

Stark, USS, 121

State Department (U.S.), 61

Stepashin, Sergei, 141

Stonehewer-Bird, F. H. W., 58, 65

Straw, Jack, 9

Success Foundation, 152

al-Sudairi, Husa bint Ahmad, 116

Sudan, 3, 42, 181

al-Sudays, Abdul Rahman, 191

Sufi Islam, 7, 11, 18, 54

suicide missions: fatwas supporting, 188; Hamas and, 196, 199; martyrdom and, 7; motivation for, 1; terrorism and, 6; *ulama* and, 210

Sultan bin Abdul Aziz (Saudi prince), 171, 209; bin Laden and, 171, 185; al-Qaeda funding and, 2; Supreme Council of Islamic Affairs and, 176

Sunni Islam, 18; caliph and, 10; jihad and, 24–25, 111; *mahdi* and, 106; Ottoman Empire and, 32; schools

of law of, 22; Shiite vs., 19–20, 115, 133–34; *ulama* and, 134; Wahhabism and, 13, 29
Supreme Commission for the Collection of Donations, 144
Supreme Council of Islamic Affairs, 176
Supreme Council of Mosques, 121
Switzerland, 121
Syeed, Sayyid Muhammad, 148
Sykes-Picot Agreement, 53
Symmes, Harrison M., 83
Syria, 49, 53, 113; ibn Abdul Wahhab and, 18; Palestinian issue and, 64; Sinai II Agreement and, 112; terrorism and, 2; Wahhabi wars and, 29

al-taghallub, 92
Tajikistan, 135, 136
takfir, 23
Talal bin Abdul Aziz (Saudi prince), 75
Talal, Muhammad ibn, 46
Talal, al-Waleed bin, 193
Taliban government: bin Laden and, 132–33; fall of, 3; Pakistan and, 133, 134; rise of, 131–34; Saudi Arabia and, 2, 134, 153; Shiite Islam and, 133; Trucial States and, 134; *ulama* and, 132; violence of, 12; Wahhabism and, 5
Tantawi, Mohammed Sayed, 24–25
Tanzania, 151, 182
TAPLINE. *See* Trans-Arabian Pipeline
Tartarstan, 142
tathlith (the Trinity), 102
tawhid (the oneness of God), 43, 79, 100, 102, 127, 153, 164
Tawhid Foundation, 150
terrorism: charity organizations and, 153–55, 211–12; funding of, 238–45; hatred and, 1, 6–7, 214–28; Hizballah and, 178–79; ideology of, 183–84; Palestinian

issue and, 9–11; roots of, 1–15, 5–6, 214; Saudi Arabia and, 146, 176–83, 198–203, 222–25, 229–51; suicide missions and, 6, 7, 201–2; U.S. and, 5, 176–80; Wahhabism and, 11–15, 215, 217–20; war on, 1, 186, 213–14
Texaco, 60, 85
Texas, 65
Trans-Arabian Pipeline (TAPLINE), 66, 83
Transjordan, 47, 48, 53, 86; Hashemite territory of, 108; Ikhwan movement and, 50; Palestinian issue and, 64, 65
Trott, A. C., 69
Trucial States, 28–29, 58, 70, 120, 134
True Religion, 152
Truman, Harry, 70–71
Tucson, Az., 150
Tulkarm Charity Committee, 199–201, 241–43
Tunisia, 3, 129
al-Turabi, Hassan, 94
Turkey, 64
al-Turki, Abdullah bin Abdul Muhsin, 163, 188, 207
Turki al-Faisal (head of Department of General Intelligence), 129–32, 166, 181, 207
Turkish Republic, 48
Turkmenistan, 134, 136, 137
Tyler, Patrick E., 204–5

al-Ukaz, 189–90, 206
Ukraine, 31
ulama: activities of, 169–76; authority of, 106–11, 121–23; Christianity and, 108; Faisal and, 74; foreign and security policy and, 119; Gulf War and, 158; Hamas and, 143; ibn Abdul Wahhab and, 20; Muslim World League and, 76; policy and, 86; role of, 80; Saud and, 73–74, 125; Saudi Arabia and, 106–11, 119;

ulama (continued)
    suicide missions and, 210; Sunni
    Islam and, 134; Taliban and, 132;
    Wahhabism and, 77–79
al-Ulwan, Sulaiman bin Nasr, 142,
    191
Umayyad caliphate, 31
Umayyad mosque, 174, 233
ummah, 101
Umm al-Qura, 69
Umm al-Qura University, 148, 162
United Arab Emirates. *See* Trucial
    States
United Arab Republic (UAR), 75, 81
United Nations, 67, 68, 133, 134,
    167
United Nations Resolution 181 (II),
    66
United Nations Security Council, 158
UN Security Council Resolution
    242, 196
UN Security Council Resolution
    687, 167
UN Security Council Resolution
    1373, 223, 248–51
UN Security Council Resolution
    1397, 197
United Nations Special Commission
    (UNSCOM), 167
United States: Cold War and, 2, 75;
    as "The Great Satan," 10; Gulf
    War and, 157–61; Israel and,
    84–85, 193–94; Middle East and,
    61; oil and, 2, 60–62, 65–66,
    84–85, 118, 220–21; Palestinian
    issue and, 10, 66; Saudi Arabia
    and, 2, 70–72, 116–19, 121–22,
    203–6; terrorism against, 5,
    176–80; Wahhabism in, 126,
    147–52
U.S. Central Command
    (USCENTCOM), 117
UNOCAL, 131
UNSCOM. *See* United Nations Spe-
    cial Commission

al-Uraifej, Abdullah, 190
USCENTCOM. *See* U.S. Central
    Command
USEUCOM (U.S. European Com-
    mand), 117
USPACOM (U.S. Pacific Com-
    mand), 117
Ustinov, Vladimir, 141
al-Utaibi, Juhaiman ibn Muhammad,
    106–9
al-Uthaiman, Muhammad ibn Saleh,
    95, 143, 161
Uzbekistan, 40, 135, 136, 155

Vienna, Austria, 18, 24
Vietnam, 117
violence: hatred and, 14–15; reli-
    gious-ideological underpinnings
    of, 11–15; Wahhabism and,
    11–15, 215
Volgodonsk, 140

Wahba, Hafiz, 55
Wahhabism: bin Laden and, 3, 5–7,
    12, 132–33, 170; Britain and, 42,
    54; charity organizations and,
    153–54; Christianity and, 25, 66,
    72, 101–3, 111; containment of,
    52–56; countering, 31–40; export-
    ing of, 79–84; funding of, 3;
    global reach of, 125–55; Gulf War
    and, 157–61; history of, 12,
    17–21; Ikhwan movement and,
    45–47, 49–50, 107–8; influence
    of, 3, 5, 39–40, 72; jihad and, 7–8,
    17, 24–26, 40, 108, 110–11, 150,
    215–16; Judaism and, 25, 66, 103,
    111; Muslim Brotherhood and,
    91–92, 100–101; Muslim World
    League and, 74–77, 87, 119;
    nature of, 8–9; Ottoman Empire
    and, 4, 29, 31–40, 41; patterns of
    activism of, 153–55; reactivating,
    73–87, 105–23; religious intoler-
    ance and, 12–15; Saudi Arabia

and, 2–15, 17–21, 58, 73–87,
105–23, 125–26, 205–10, 215;
Saudi-Hashemite war and, 47–49;
Shiite Islam and, 12, 112, 119–20,
133–34, 152; spread of, 34–38,
74–77; Sunni Islam and, 29; Taliban and, 131–34; terrorism and,
11–15, 215, 217–20; *ulama* and,
62–63, 106–11; universities and,
90, 94, 110; violence and, 11–15,
22–26, 215; West and, 7, 161–68,
183–84. *See also* ibn Abdul Wahhab, Muhammad
al-Wahhabiyyun (Rida), 55
WAMY. *See* World Assembly of
Muslim Youth
Washington, D.C., 2
Washington Post, 9, 192, 193, 194,
203–4
al-Watan, 192
Webster, William, 158
West: backlash against, 161–68;
Islam and, 162; jihad and, 155;
Saudi Arabia and, 183; Wahhabism and, 7, 161–68, 183–84
West Bank, 68
World Assembly of Muslim Youth
(WAMY): Balkans and, 144; as a
conduit for funding Hamas,
126–27, 224; establishment of, 79;

Islamic action and, 100; Wah-
habism and, 126, 147, 152, 153
World Islamic Front, 173
World Trade Center bombing
(1993), 12, 94, 130, 171, 172
World War I. *See* First World War
World War II. *See* Second World
War

Yasin, Ahmad, 196
Yemen, 5, 31, 59, 86, 182; involve-
ment of Yemenis in al-Qaeda,
129; Nasser and, 75; Palestinian
issue and, 64;
Yom Kippur War (1973), 85, 86, 87.
See also See also Arab-Israeli War
(1948–49); Six-Day War (1967)
Yousef, Ramzi, 130
Yugoslavia, 139, 143
Yuldeshev, Tahir, 135

al-Zahawi, Jamil, 22, 32
zakat, 7, 22, 45, 51, 131
al-Zawahiri, Ayman Muhammad
Rabi, 51, 94, 100, 137, 143–47
al-Zawahiri, Muhammad, 144, 153
al-Zawahiri, Muhammad al-Ahmad,
50–51
Zinni, Anthony, 117
Zionist movement, 64

About the Author

Ambassador Dore Gold is the president of the Jerusalem Center for Public Affairs. He was the eleventh Permanent Representative of Israel to the United Nations (1997–1999). Previously he served as foreign policy advisor to the former prime minister of Israel, Benjamin Netanyahu.

Ambassador Gold has served as an advisor to Prime Minister Ariel Sharon, who asked him to accompany his entourage to Washington and to the 2003 Aqaba Summit with President George W. Bush. He was a member of the Israeli delegation at the 1998 Wye River negotiations between Israel and the PLO, outside of Washington. He negotiated the Note for the Record, which supplemented the 1997 Hebron Protocol, and in 1996 concluded the negotiations with the U.S., Lebanon, Syria, and France for the creation of the Monitoring Group for Southern Lebanon. In 1991, he served as an advisor to the Israeli delegation to the Madrid Peace Conference. From 1985 to 1996 he was a senior research associate at the Jaffee Center for Strategic Studies, Tel Aviv University, where he was director of the U.S. Foreign and Defense Policy Project. Dr. Gold received his B.A., M.A., and Ph.D. from Columbia University. He lives in Jerusalem with his wife, Ofra, and their two children, Yael and Ariel.

Other Works by Dore Gold

Dore Gold has written numerous books and articles on the Middle East, including *U.S. Military Strategy in the Middle East*; *America, the Gulf, and Israel: Centcom and Emerging U.S. Regional Security Policies in the Middle East, Vol. 11*; and *Israel as an American Non-NATO Ally: Parameters of Defense-Industrial Cooperation*.

His articles have appeared in *Commentary*, the *New York Times*, the *Daily Telegraph*, *Die Zeit*, *Ha'aretz*, the *Jerusalem Post*, *National Review*, the *Washington Post*, the *Wall Street Journal*, and *Asahi Shinbun*.